AN INTRODUCTION TO MIDDLE ENGLISH LYRICS

New Perspectives on Medieval Literature: Authors and Traditions

UNIVERSITY PRESS OF FLORIDA

Florida A&M University, Tallahassee
Florida Atlantic University, Boca Raton
Florida Gulf Coast University, Ft. Myers
Florida International University, Miami
Florida State University, Tallahassee
New College of Florida, Sarasota
University of Central Florida, Orlando
University of Florida, Gainesville
University of North Florida, Jacksonville
University of South Florida, Tampa
University of West Florida, Pensacola

An Introduction to Middle English Lyrics

WILLIAM A. QUINN

Foreword by R. Barton Palmer and Tison Pugh

UNIVERSITY PRESS OF FLORIDA

Gainesville/Tallahassee/Tampa/Boca Raton
Pensacola/Orlando/Miami/Jacksonville/Ft. Myers/Sarasota

Cover: "Sumer is icumen in" BL MS Harley 978, f.11v. With permission of the British Library.

Copyright 2025 by William A. Quinn

All rights reserved

Published in the United States of America

30 29 28 27 26 25   6 5 4 3 2 1

DOI: HTTPS://doi.org/10.5744/9780813079431

LIBRARY OF CONGRESS CATALOGING-IN-PUBLICATION DATA

Names: Quinn, William A., 1951– author

Title: An introduction to Middle English lyrics / William A. Quinn.

Description: Gainesville : University Press of Florida, 2025. | Series: New perspectives on medieval literature : authors and traditions | Includes bibliographical references and index.

Identifiers: LCCN 2025020180 (print) | LCCN 2025020181 (ebook) | ISBN 9780813079431 hardback | ISBN 9780813074115 pdf | ISBN 9780813073958 ebook

Subjects: LCSH: English poetry—Middle English, 1100–1500—History and criticism | Lyric poetry—History and criticism | BISAC: LITERARY CRITICISM / Medieval | LITERARY CRITICISM / Poetry | LCGFT: Literary criticism | Introductory works

Classification: LCC PR351 .Q56 2025 (print) | LCC PR351 (ebook)

LC record available at https://lccn.loc.gov/2025020180

LC ebook record available at https://lccn.loc.gov/2025020181

The University Press of Florida is the scholarly publishing agency for the State University System of Florida, comprising Florida A&M University, Florida Atlantic University, Florida Gulf Coast University, Florida International University, Florida State University, New College of Florida, University of Central Florida, University of Florida, University of North Florida, University of South Florida, and University of West Florida.

University Press of Florida
2046 NE Waldo Road
Suite 2100
Gainesville, FL 32609
http://upress.ufl.edu

GPSR EU Authorized Representative: Mare Nostrum Group B.V., Mauritskade 21D, 1091 GC Amsterdam, The Netherlands, gpsr@mare-nostrum.co.uk

TO TRICIA AND THE KIDS AND THE BEER BUDDIES

CONTENTS

List of Figures
ix

List of Middle English Lyrics Discussed or Referenced
xi

Foreword
xvii

Acknowledgments
xix

ONE
Introduction
1

TWO
Bringing the Middle English Lyric into Modern Play
17

THREE
Playing Glad
38

FOUR
Playing Sad or Mad
83

FIVE
Compassioun for the Passion (and Its Perversion)
126

SIX
Contek I: Love and Longing
177

SEVEN
Contek II: Love and Loathing
211

EIGHT
The Early Modern Machining of Verse
255

APPENDIX A
Petrarch's *Rima* 132 and Chaucer's "Cantus Troili"
with Modern Translation
285

APPENDIX B
Petrarch's *Rima* 140
289

APPENDIX C
A Comparison of Petrarch's and
Wyatt's Corresponding Rhyme Schemes
291

Notes
293

Works Cited
317

Index
331

FIGURES

1

Portrait of Chaucer in Thomas Hoccleve's
The Regiment of Princes (1412)
264

2

Rima 132 "S'amor non è, che dunque è quel ch'io sento?";
Rima 140 "Amor, che nel pensier mio vive et regna"
268

3

*Le cose volgari di Messer Francesco Petrarcha.
The Rerum vulgarium fragmenta and Triumphi*,
edited by Pietro Bembo
269

4

Wyatt's "I find no peace and all my war is done," a translation
of Petrarch's *Rima* 134 "Pace non trovo e non
ho da far guerra"
270

5

Wyatt's "The Longe love, that in my thought doeth harbar"
271

6

Tottel 6 "Complaint of a Lover Rebuked" (Surrey's "Love that liveth
and reigneth in my thought"); *Tottel* 42 "The Lover for shamefastnesse
hideth his desire within his faithful heart" (Wyatt's "The longe love
that in my thought I harbar")
274

MIDDLE ENGLISH LYRICS DISCUSSED OR REFERENCED

Middle English lyrics are most commonly identified simply by their incipits [lit. "it begins"]—that is, by their first lines. The *New Index of Middle English Verse* (NIMEV) and the *Digital Index of Middle English Verse* (DIMEV) both list all extant textual witnesses for these lyrics. The DIMEV indicates the availability of each lyric in print (as of its last updating) as well as links to available facsimiles. The NIMEV specifies a "best or standard" edition as of its publication date. The item numbers of the NIMEV duplicate those of the *Index of Middle English Verse* (IMEV) unless a lyric is deemed to be composed after 1500 (or not to be verse at all). For IMEV entries that are no longer accepted by the NIMEV, the TM number provided indicates entries in W. A. Ringler Jr.'s *Bibliography and Index of English Verse in Manuscript 1501–1558* (London, 1992). Online texts of the poems in Middle English, modern translations, facsimiles, and performances are all increasingly accessible on the internet simply by searching for each lyric's incipit or by its conventional title when available.

"A blissful life a peaceable and a sweet," or Chaucer's "The Former Age" (NIMEV 28 DIMEV 14)
"Adam lay I-bounden bounden in a bond" (NIMEV 117 DIMEV 215)
"Alas alas vel evil have I sped" (NIMEV 143 DIMEV 210, see "Undo thy door my spouse dear" below)
"Alas departing is ground of woe" (IMEV 146 NIMEV TM 94 DIMEV 271)
"All this day Ich han sought," or "The Serving Maid's Holiday" (IMEV 225 DIMEV 393 cf. DIMEV 773)
"All ye that pass by this holy place" (IMEV 237 NIMEV TM 125 DIMEV 411)
"Als y me rode this endre dai," or "Now Springes the Spray" (NIMEV 360 DIMEV 614)
"A man that should of truth tell" (NIMEV 72 DIMEV 113)
"As I lay upon a night" (NIMEV 353 DIMEV 607)

"As I stood on a day me self under a tree" (NIMEV 371 DIMEV 628)
"As I went on Yule day in our procession," or "Jolly Jankyn" (NIMEV 377 DIMEV 635)
"At the time of matins Lord Thou were I-take" (NIMEV 441 DIMEV 722)
"Blodles & bonles blod had non bon" (NIMEV 542 DIMEV 881)
"By a forest as I gan fare," or "The Mourning of the Hunted Hare" (NIMEV 559 DIMEV 922)
"Bytuene Mersh and Aueril," or "Alyssoun" (NIMEV 515 DIMEV 842)
"Erthe toc of erthe," see "When earth hath earth I-won with woe" below.
"Farewell now my lady gay" (IMEV 767 NIMEV TM 404 DIMEV 1269)
"God and saint Trinity / As I believe on thee" (NIMEV 939 DIMEV 1548)
"God that all this mights may in heaven & earth thy will is oo" (NIMEV 968 DIMEV 1590)
"Go, hert, hurt with adversitee" (NIMEV 925 DIMEV 1531)
"Gracious and gay on her light all my thought" (NIMEV 1010 DIMEV 1654)
"Hail our patron and Lady of the earth" (NIMEV 1073 DIMEV 1745)
"He bore him up he bore him down," or "The Corpus Cristi Carol" (IMEV 1132 NIMEV TM 530 DIMEV 1820)
"Here I was and here I drank" (NIMEV 1201 DIMEV 1974)
"Here lieth under this marble stone" (NIMEV 1207 DIMEV 2000)
"Herod thou wicked foe whereof is thy dreading" (NIMEV 1213 DIMEV 2013)
"He that in youthe to Sensualitie" (NIMEV 1151.5 DIMEV 1868)
"Hit wes upon a screþorsday þat vre louerd aros" (NIMEV 1649 DIMEV 2768)
"Honure, joy, helthe, and pleasaunce" (NIMEV 1240 DIMEV 2055)
"Hyt semes quite and is red" (NIMEV 1640 DIMEV 2754)
"I am as I am and so I will be" (IMEV 1270.2 NIMEV TM 624 DIMEV 2105)
"I am sorry for her sake" (NIMEV 1280 DIMEV 2130)
"Icham of Irlaunde" (NIMEV 1008 DIMEV 1647)
"I conjure hem in the name of the Fader" (NIMEV 1293.5 DIMEV 2155)
"I have a gentil cok" (NIMEV 1299 DIMEV 2167)
"I haue a hole aboue my knee" (DIMEV 2168)
"I have a young sister far beyonden the sea" (NIMEV 1303 DIMEV 2174)

MIDDLE ENGLISH LYRICS DISCUSSED OR REFERENCED · *xiii*

"In a frith as I con fare fremde," or "The Meeting in the Woods" (NIMEV 1449 DIMEV 2446)
"In a tabernacle of a toure" (NIMEV 1460 DIMEV 2461)
"I ne have joy ne pleasance nor comfort" (NIMEV 1334 DIMEV 2230)
"In every place ye may well see" (NIMEV 1485 DIMEV 2497)
"I sing of a maiden that is makeles" (NIMEV 1367 DIMEV 2281)
"It was upon a Sheer Thursday that our Lord arose" (NIMEV 1649 DIMEV 2768)
"I wot a bird in a bower as beryl so bright," or "Annot and John" (NIMEV 1394 DIMEV 2324)
"Jesu that hast me dear I-bought" (NIMEV 1761 DIMEV 2915)
"Jesu that is most of might" (IMEV 1768 NIMEV TM 859 DIMEV 2922)
"Jesu sweet is the love of Thee" (IMEV 1747 NIMEV TM 859 DIMEV 2899)
"Keep well ten and flee from seven" (NIMEV 1817 DIMEV 2988)
"Lenten is come with love to toune" (NIMEV 1861 DIMEV 3050)
"Lullay lullay þu lytel chyld wy wepys þu so sore" (NIMEV 2024 DIMEV 3301)
"Love is soft, love is swet, love is good sware" (NIMEV 2009 DIMEV 3279)
"Madame for your newfangleness" (NIMEV 2029 DIMEV 3312)
"Maiden in the mor lay" (NIMEV 3891 DIMEV 3328 formerly 3891)
"Maiden mother mild / oeiz cel oreysoun" (NIMEV 2039 DIMEV 3330)
"Man, be war of thine wowing" (NIMEV 1938 DIMEV 3172)
"Men rent me on rood" (NIMEV 2150 DIMEV 3469)
"My deth I love, my lif ich hate" (NIMEV 2236 DIMEV 3592)
"My folk now answer me" (NIMEV 2240 DIMEV 3598)
"My folk what have I do thee" (NIMEV 2241 DIMEV 3599)
"My ghostly father, I me confess" (NIMEV 2243 DIMEV 3602)
"Now bairns birds bold and blithe" (NIMEV 2302 DIMEV 3717)
"Now goth sonne under wod" (NIMEV 2320 DIMEV 3742)
"Now is yole comen with gentil chere" (NIMEV 2343 DIMEV 3773)
"O excellent sovereigne, most semely to sene" (IMEV 2421 NIMEV TM 1142 DIMEV 3882)
"Off Februar the fyftene nycht," or Dunbar's "The Dance of the Sevin Deidly Synnis" (IMEV 2623.3 DIMEV 4164)
"Of all creatures women be best," see "In every place ye may well see" above.
"O mistress why" (IMEV 2518 NIMEV TM 1206 DIMEV 3997)

"Sluggy and slowe, in spetinge muiche" (NIMEV 3157 DIMEV 4926)
"Somer is comen with love to toune" (NIMEV 3222, DIMEV 5052)
"Somer is comen and winter gon" (NIMEV 3221 DIMEV 5051)
"Stond wel moder vnder rode" (NIMEV 3211 DIMEV 5030)
"Sumer is icumen in" (NIMEV 3223 DIMEV 5053)
"Swart smoked smiths smattered with smoke" (NIMEV 3227 DIMEV 5062)
"Swete Jesu, king of bliss" (NIMEV 3236 DIMEV 5075)
"Sweet Jesu now will I sing" (NIMEV 3238 DIMEV 5077)
"Tapster, fille another ale" (NIMEV 3259 DIMEV 5117)
"The law of God be to thee thy rest" (NIMEV 3410 DIMEV 5371)
"Thenc man of mi harde stundes" (IMEV 3565; initial couplet provides refrain to NIMEV 2079.5 DIMEV 3386)
"There nis so high comfort to my pleasance," or Chaucer's "Complaint of Venus" (NIMEV 3542 DIMEV 5590)
"The smiling mouth, and laughing eyen gray" (NIMEV 3465 DIMEV 5468)
"This maiden hight Mary she was full mild" (NIMEV 3628 DIMEV 5729.5)
"Thus I complain my grevous hevynesse" (IMEV 3722 NIMEV TM 1721 DIMEV 5925)
"To unpraise women it were a shame," or "I am as light as any roe" (IMEV 3782, NIMEV TM 1760 DIMEV 6033)
"To you, dere herte, variant and mutable" (IMEV 2437 NIMEV 2437.5 DIMEV 3902)
"Undo thy door my spouse dear" (NIMEV 3825 DIMEV 6108)
"Unto you most forward this letter I write" (NIMEV 3832 DIMEV 6117)
"Water and blood for thee I sweat" (IMEV 3862 DIMEV 6160)
"Weal herying and worship be to Christ that dear us bought" (IMEV 3872 DIMEV 6181)
"Weping haveth min wonges wet," or "The Poet's Repentance" (NIMEV 3874 DIMEV 6186)
"Were it undo, that is ido," see "Y louede a child of this cuntree" below.
"Whan netilles in winter bere roses rede" (NIMEV 3999, DIMEV 6384)
"When earth hath earth I-won with woe" (NIMEV 3939 DIMEV 6292)
"When Adam delved and Eve did span" (NIMEV 3922 DIMEV 6266)
"When I see blossoms spring" (NIMEV 3963 DIMEV 6334)
"When the turuf is thy tour" (NIMEV 4044 DIMEV 6456)

"Winter wakeneth all my care" (NIMEV 4177 DIMEV 6700)
"With pacience thou has us fed" (NIMEV 4197 DIMEV 6737)
"Worldes blis ne last no throwe" (NIMEV 4223 DIMEV 6791)
"Y louede a child of this cuntree" (NIMEV 1330 DIMEV 2222)

FOREWORD

Many literary studies are identified as groundbreaking, but this is a particularly apt characterization of William Quinn's study of Middle English lyrics. Quinn has produced the first critical guide to give appropriate shape and context to that heterogeneous but substantial surviving body of short poems that are known generally by a term—"lyrics"—which in its historical generality offers little in the way of what might help a contemporary reader encounter these works meaningfully. His work does much to restore these texts to the prominence they richly deserve.

Retrieved from various manuscript sources, then first edited and published during the flurry of academic interest in all things medieval during the nineteenth century, these lyrics are usually unattributed to an author, often of ambiguous provenance, and cannot for the most part be connected to any literary tradition as such. They were unacknowledged at the time as contributing substantially to the culture, playing no specific role in court life, either in London or in the provinces. They are not, at least for the most part, associated with any of the writers who have emerged in modern times as important representatives of the literary era.

Medieval poetry of all kinds gradually in the course of the twentieth century became part of literary studies programs in British and American universities, emerging from philological and historical studies that had been intended simply to offer an archaeological approach to the study of Middle English textual production. However, as medieval texts became standard elements of undergraduate programs throughout the Anglophone world, narrative works, from *Beowulf* to *The Canterbury Tales*, dominated required reading lists, just as in more modern periods, with some exceptions, story has had more appeal than song. This is as true in medieval French as Middle English studies.

Quinn's enthusiasm for the peculiar and often idiosyncratic charm of the Middle English lyric is quite infectious, and this encyclopedic introduction to the form, written with verve and style, is both accessible to the undergraduate just beginning the study of the period and sufficiently sophisticated to attract the attention of the more advanced student.

R. Barton Palmer and Tison Pugh
SERIES EDITORS

ACKNOWLEDGMENTS

First, I need to thank Tison Pugh, the anonymous readers, and the entire staff of the University Press of Florida, including most especially Carlynn Crosby, Zubin Meer, Mindy Basinger Hill, and Marthe Walters. I also need to thank Julia Boffey for her additional insights and generous admonitions. Likewise, I lack sufficient words to adequately express my gratitude to Ardis Butterfield for the extraordinary care with which she critiqued my efforts; any missteps that remain in my readings are unintended failures to follow her advice. I also wish to thank Susanna Fein, David Raybin, and John Ganim . . . just because; they have been so supportive in so many ways over so many years. It is impossible to thank all the other scholars on whose insights this *Introduction* so heavily depends.

At the University of Arkansas, I wish to thank my colleagues Joshua Byron Smith, Lora Walsh, Mary Beth Long, Freddy Cristobal Dominguez, Mohja Kahf, Daniela D'Eugenio, Annie Theresa Doucet, Lynn Jacobs, Kim Sexton, and (*prima inter pares*) Lynda Coon—all of whom contribute so much to the energy of our Medieval and Renaissance Studies Program. I want to thank all my teachers and students; almost every page of this study echoes some discussion to which they contributed. I am particularly grateful to Tiffany Elder and Emily Aguayo for contributing so diligently to the production of this text.

Last, and as always, I must thank my wife, Tricia, for her tireless love and support of this project, especially through the pandemic years.

ONE

Introduction

> Of swich matere made he manye layes,
> Songes, compleintes, roundels, virelayes.
> [Of such matter, he composed many lais,
> Songs, complaints, rondels, and virelays.]
>
> Chaucer, *The Canterbury Tales*, V, 947–948

What Are Middle English "Lyrics"?

The genre conventionally referred to as "Middle English lyrics" consists of an extremely diverse grouping of poems for which there apparently was no specific name in Middle English itself.[1] The polyglot labels used by Middle English authors to identify what we call "lyrics" were far more specific, somewhat random, and often inconsistent, naming a hodgepodge of topics and formal types, such as ballade (a seven- or eight-line stanzaic form, usually three stanzas with a last-line refrain and a concluding envoi or "sending" verse), rondel or rondeau (stanzas of thirteen or fourteen lines using only two rhymes), virelai (nine-line stanzaic pattern with alternating rhyme schemes among shorter and longer lines),[2] reverdie (celebrating the return of spring), carol (usually joyful and sung in the round), complaint, aubade (a dawn song, usually a complaint), ditty ("saying"), lullaby,[3] hymn, cantilena (a rather late term for vocal music), and so on—a substantial if somewhat uncountable subset of the more than 7,000 items indexed as Middle English verse, a remnant that represents only a small percentage of what must have been the lyric's popularity in the Middle English era because it is "generally agreed, many lyrics have failed to survive."[4] It would be lovely to assume that—by means of some Darwinian sense of survival—the best poems remain extant, but there is no real reason to think so.

As a matter of convenience, therefore, identifying any one Middle English piece of verse as a *lyric* "usually means no more than a short poem, preferably in stanzas."[5] The *Oxford English Dictionary* (OED) indicates that the first English use of the term *lyric* to specify "short poems . . . directly expressing the poet's own thoughts and sentiments" does not occur until the late sixteenth century.[6] This rather minimalist but most inclusive definition of "lyric" needs to be retooled a bit to emphasize that most Middle English lyrics are preserved as opportunities to impersonate (rather than simply witness) such a direct expression of emotion. Many modern lyrics, of course, also maintain this histrionic potential, but it becomes a diminished criterion of poetic success when the rewards of rereading are posited as the primary test of artistic excellence—that is, when the lyric is to be studied rather than listened to. So, too, any definition of the lyric as "short" is difficult to quantify in reference to the surviving Middle English lyrics. At one extreme, the mnemonic

> **Keep well ten, and flee from seven.**
> keep well x and flee from vii
> **Rule well five, and come to heaven.**
> rule well v and come to heven.

is a single couplet (recalling the 10 commandments, 7 deadly sins, and 5 senses); at the other extreme, "The Thrush and the Nightingale" (the longest lyric to be considered in this *Introduction*, in chapter 7) is 192 lines long. The "brevity" required of a Middle English lyric might be better understood as the acceptable duration of its uninterrupted performance.

Although a relatively small number of Middle English lyrics do survive with musical notation, many more should be imagined as set to music; however, few scholars insist that the word *lyric* itself, despite its etymology, should be defined exclusively as "sung verse." Rather, Julia Boffey points out that in Middle English usage *song* "may well have been a term used most readily of short (and shortish) poems."[7] One indication of the challenge of identifying Middle English shortish poems as lyrics is evidenced by the fact that the editors of the *New Index of Middle English Verse* felt obliged to expunge a number of entries in the original *Index of Middle English Verse* simply because they "do not seem to be verse" at all.[8] Furthermore, though studies dedicated to the genre of lyric normally focus on stand-alone poems, many medieval narratives include embedded lyrics meant to be read (or sung) as direct quotations. As William D. Paden has observed, "Genres are strange, and medieval lyric genres stranger still."[9] And, for Ardis Butterfield, "This quagmire of verse is a vast, nebulous, ill-defined arena which does not work well *in toto* (whatever that might be) as a means of contemplating poetic principles. The notion of medieval lyric has only worked in highly specific cases."[10]

Within this cloud of critical unknowing, it is common to consider the earlier Middle English lyrics almost sui generis: "The characteristic features of the Middle English lyric are not those of its French or Provencal predecessors. Nor do early Middle English lyrics much resemble the short poems of Lydgate, Chaucer, Charles d'Orléans, or Machaut."[11] Furthermore, any too comfortable differentiation of lyric verse from narrative verse fails to accommodate the pre-print, performative nature of both in the Middle Ages.[12] For example, "Hit wes upon a sereþorsday þat vre louerd aros" [It was upon a Blameless-Thursday that our Lord arose] is often identified as the oldest extant ballad, commonly titled "Judas" (to be considered in chapter 5).[13] However, this shortish poem is composed in couplets rather than in the conventional quatrains of ballad meter, and it can as readily be identified as a lyric. The dialogue and impersonation of "Hit wes upon a sereþorsday" requires a highly histrionic reading. Indeed, Karin Boklund-Lagopulou considers this ballad/lyric's "entire action" comparable to "the medieval drama."[14] Nevertheless, ballads, even this earliest recorded example, are typically excluded from a consideration of the Middle English lyric for two questionable reasons: (1) because they are conventionally designated narrative poems, and (2) because the earliest textual witnesses of most ballads date from the late fifteenth century (presumably, having been orally transmitted till then).

In a sense, every medieval composition that a modern reader might casually identify as "true literature" was probably initially intended for live performance. The means of presenting what we call "lyrics" could be anticipated in a variety of ways, including song, recitation, dramatic impersonation, communal or private prayer, and (perhaps now closest to our normative sense of "reading") contemplation. Furthermore, an individual composition could be appreciated in multiple ways, whether so intended by the author or not. This intuition that medieval literature in general requires rehearsed performance—which some scholars consider painfully obvious, and others, hopelessly obscure—compels the reader to approach each lyric text as both a would-be actor and as a curious literary critic. Sadly, the actual performance descriptors of most Middle English lyrics have not survived so well as those of the tradition of singing the ballads.

If the generic term *lyric* itself has proven problematic, further differentiation of subgenres within it has proven even more "resistant to logical classification."[15] Secular lyrics can be sorted from religious, romantic from political, aristocratic from folk, learned from popular, and so on—sort of. The Bannytyne Manuscript (1568 CE) offers the first anthology of Middle English lyrics gathered into topical subsets, but otherwise the preservation of Middle English lyrics seems mostly opportunistic, haphazard, or highly contingent: inserted in sermons or on flyleaves, occasionally gathered in miscellanies, or scribbled as marginalia, among other scribal interventions.

Audience and Manuscript Context

Codicological studies of the manuscripts that preserve compilations of Middle English lyrics are continuing to clarify their patronage, production, and initial ownership, and so the interpretive contexts of their original readership; these studies contribute substantially to our understanding of the history of the medieval book as well as to our appreciation of the lyrics themselves. In general terms, the major, multilingual, and multi-genre manuscripts preserving Middle English lyrics[16] suggest a literate as well as polyglot provenance, including members of the nobility, gentry, well-to-do urban commoners, and clergy. Nevertheless, it seems fallacious to assign specific subsets of Middle English lyrics to exclusive ambits of circulation (such as "secular" vs. "religious")—that is, to assume that appreciation of a particular poem was restricted to possession of its extant textual witnesses. The possibility of performance promotes the idea of granting appreciation of the poems well beyond access to these texts in hand. The religious lyrics included in the commonplace books of the Franciscan poets William Herebert and John Grimestone (many of which provide vernacular translations of Latin hymns) enhanced performance of their sermons and thereby translate the poet's own pious feelings to all the laity. So, too, the carol anthologies of John Audelay and James Ryman seem meant to popularize piety as public celebration. As readers or as listeners, friars could apparently enjoy some secular lyrics as readily as merchants could pray in verse. Each manuscript provides its own setting (which often changes over the lifespan of its contents' inclusion) for the reader's performance of each lyric in situ. The Findern Manuscript,[17] compiled during the fifteenth and sixteenth centuries for a gentry family, is thematically dedicated to Middle English love literature, including works by Geoffrey Chaucer, John Gower, John Lydgate, Thomas Hoccleve, and Richard Roos. The commonplace book of Richard Hill,[18] a sixteenth-century London merchant, preserves several lyrics ranging from drinking songs to prayers, including the sole witness of the enigmatic "Corpus Christi Carol" ("He bore him up he bore him down," considered in chapter 4).

The texts of many Middle English lyrics that survive in multiple copies display what Paul Zumthor termed *mouvance,* or exceptional variation, exceeding the changes expected solely because of dialect differences or scribal mistakes.[19] For example, the poem "In a tabernacle of a tour" (considered in chapter 5) survives in eight versions of eight or ten or eleven stanzas.[20] Such transmissions often amount to adaptations. Middle English *centos* may be considered an extreme example of such *mouvance,* producing "new" poems by freely harvesting complementary lines from other pieces. It is only near the end of the Middle English era that single-author compilations of poems appear, the products of authorial curation or scribal-editorial efforts to preserve the corpus of such poets as John Lydgate, Thomas Hoccleve, and Charles d'Orleans, as well as the shorter poems of Chaucer (who apparently had no such plan for their publication in his "Collected Works"). Shortly thereafter, the book thus becomes the primary means of both preserving and presenting Middle English lyrics for posterity—rather than performance. And it is in this transformed state of print that the modern reader is challenged to induce or imagine each lyric's emotional impact.

Divorcing the study of specifically English lyrics composed between roughly 1100 and 1500 from those composed in French or Latin for the same readers (and probably often by the same poets) has also proven not only problematic but detrimental. Many English lyrics are preserved in trilingual manuscripts, not in the poetic silo of a nationalized canon. Many "Middle English" lyrics include non-English lines and macaronic rhymes. It was only during the fourteenth and fifteenth centuries that England's post-Norman national identity first emerged, and the end of the Middle Ages does begin what became the increasing insulation of England's and France's literary canons from each other. John Gower's *Cinkante Ballades*, however, indicates an enduring preference in England for French as the language of lyric, as may be the French poems of "Ch," which could be attributable to Chaucer.[21]

What Is "Middle English"?

The concurrent enjoyment of English, French, and Latin verse in England between the Old English and the early modern eras entails another question about lyrics in a very insulated understanding of the vernacular or "native" language: when does "Middle English" composition begin and end? An absurdly precise historical bracketing of the linguistic era designated "Middle English" would be between 14 October 1066 and 22 August 1485—that is, starting with the Battle of Hastings (and the subsequent domination of French literature in England) and ending with the Battle of Bosworth Field (and the subsequent ascent of the Tudor Renaissance). The complexity of differentiating very early Middle English from Old English as well as very late Middle English from early modern English makes determining either a start or stop date for Middle English lyrics peculiarly difficult. Furthermore, the designation "English" itself does not refer to a single linguistic entity during this indeterminate era; we now conventionally recognize four main dialects of Middle English, each of which mutated substantially over five centuries. Many Middle English lyrics also incorporate mixed dialects, indicating the fluidity of a poet's own usage, transcription across time or dialect boundaries, scribal contamination, or any combination of these factors because "Popular poems tended to gain accretions," frequently challenging a modern reader's longing for a definitive version of the text itself.[22] Each transcription of a Middle English lyric may be thought, it seems, to present one stop of a poem in transit.

Overlooking the Middle English Lyric

Even in general introductions to Middle English literature, Middle English lyrics tend to be relatively neglected. In 1980, Rossell Hope Robbins lamented, "The court love poems of the fifteenth century are probably the most neglected genre in English literature."[23] Besides the surmountable challenge of linguistic change, both the formal accidents and the emotional substance of many Middle English lyrics seem (at first sight) difficult to applaud. The alterity of medieval tastes in poetic style is actually the older of these two stumbling blocks. The alterity of medieval emotions is a more recent interpretive problem, especially since "the exact term that we use, 'emotion,' was unknown to medieval people, who themselves spoke of 'passions' and 'sentiments.'"[24] The historicity of both a Middle English lyric's poetic style and its emotional content challenges the possibility of translation—that is, of continued reading. Can the modern reader acquire a response to these lyrics that approximates the experience of its original readers? John Speirs argues "we ought to try to see which of them still work... if a medieval lyric *is* there, as something experienced, it has become contemporary with the reader."[25] Mutatis mutandis, can we still enjoy the taste of carrots as served in a medieval recipe although carrots in the Middle Ages were purple or yellow? To strain this metaphor further, the color of a Middle English lyric is its textual record; its emotional content is the taste that needs to be remixed by a modern reader.

Although critical studies of the modern English lyric flourished in the 1960s and '70s, "New" or "Practical Criticism" actually came rather late to medieval studies, and exited early.[26] The recent advocacy of "surface reading" (a.k.a. "thin" or "reparative" reading) by Stephen Best and Sharon Marcus, among others, promotes (once again) a critical commitment to the affective experience of reading "the text itself." In his "Introduction to Poetry," Billy Collins voices a lyricist's desire to be so read—that is, not to "tie the poem to a chair with rope / and torture a confession out of it." Nevertheless, most medievalists, preferring New Historicism to New Criticism "as a more ethical way of reading," also remained "somewhat hesitant to embrace New Formalism as a methodology."[27] Indeed, for the last several decades, English literary scholarship in general has had diminished interest in any and all lyrics. "But," in praxis, as Seth Lerer remarks, "the most historical of literary critics read like rioters when they turn from Chaucer to the Middle English lyrics. These texts—mostly anonymous, transmitted in manuscript assemblies of hard-to-recover provenance—can transform the toughest historicist into a New Critic."[28] Many of the more frequently anthologized Middle English lyrics have thus become richly explicated and increasingly appreciated by the cumulative efforts of these "rioters."[29]

Except perhaps for the mise-en-page, "the text itself" of most Middle English lyrics is almost always devoid of interpretive prompts; even Chaucer's lyrics lack any equivalent of a *razo* ("reason," explaining the occasion of composition) or *vida* ("life," giving some biographical context) provided for much earlier troubadour poetry. John Burrow has termed the mostly anonymous Middle English lyrics "poems without contexts," which he conceded was a bit of a "dramatic exaggeration."[30] More recent textual scholarship has harvested "examination of manuscript and textual context" as "key to a thorough understanding of any Middle English lyric."[31] This reading of the lyric in situ "involves tracing a long (and perhaps always incomplete) textual journey."[32] Sometimes, the context of individual lyrics as part of a compilation has been overlooked. Susanna Fein observes, for example, that the obscurity of a sequence of moral verse circulating in the West Midlands from about 1250 to 1340 "as a group stems, in part, from how surviving specimens ... have tended to be disseminated ... via anthologies that alter and consequently blur their historical contexts."[33]

Familiarity with the cultural milieu of medieval England also provides a very general context for probable (albeit multiple) reader responses. "The tradition of the church we can easily recover.... The traditions of court and aristocratic life are a sort of liturgy, but one of which parts can be pieced together," but recovering "the imaginative life of the common folk ... is extremely doubtful."[34] In many cases, therefore, Burrow's conclusion remains valid that, without more specific contextualization, "we are in most cases condemned to conjecture and controversy."[35] Still, by and large, there is usually a strong consensus regarding the intended emotional effects of a majority of Middle English lyrics. In this *Introduction*, my efforts to suggest a true—that is, honest—appreciation of each lyric cannot pretend to be its definitive interpretation, but I shall strive to explain a plausible experience of its original reception. Nor are my readings particularly innovative except insofar as they make the lyrics' emotions renewed to me. In Elizabeth Salter's words, "We are trying to understand rather than judge. Definition is more in our minds than assessment."[36] With some sense of that original enactment, more than one actor (i.e., reader) can subsequently play the same role—movingly, if done well, even if done differently: the texts of Middle English lyrics "are meant to be used by the 'I' of the reader."[37] Cristina Maria Cervone and Nicholas Watson have described the inclusive modes of *reading* as imagined performance of the various kinds of Middle English lyrics thus:

> In these modes and others, the "pley" of poetry is a bodily activity, whether it involves singing, dancing, and joining hands in a group, or quiet, even subvocal reading, with movements of eyes, mouth, hands, and maybe feet. "Pley" is also therapeutic, arousing and releasing feeling; cognitive, aimed at reorienting the self in relation to society and perhaps the cosmos; and voluntary, involving choice both of the form of "pley" and of the game itself. Some forms of "pley" are even contemplative, serving to shape episodes of devout attentiveness Middle English texts called "meditacioun," "contemplacioun" or "eise."[38]

In my final chapter, I will consider how a change in this conception of *reading* lyrics as *play* caused a retroactive misperception of Middle English versecraft. Essentially, the "I" whom the text asks the reader to become transitions from public performer to solitary audience. In addition to a reformation of the religious content itself, Rosemary Woolf observed that the role of the lyric "I" changed fundamentally in post-medieval religious verse: "the abnegation of individuality is one of the most important differences between medieval and seventeenth-century religious lyric ... whereas the seventeenth-century poets show the poet meditating, the medieval writers provide versified meditations which others may use: in one the meditator is the poet, in the other the meditator is the reader."[39]

In short, both the style and content of Middle English lyrics have been undervalued on the basis of certain a priori criteria that, if nothing else, the well-disposed reader is compelled to question: what are the publication requirements for assessing the artistic excellence of these lyrics? And what is the enduring integrity of their impersonations of the direct expression of emotion? Rather sadly, almost all introductions to the Middle English lyric start with some sort of apology for the elusive genre's quality because "ever since Wordsworth, in the preface to *Lyrical Ballads*, defined 'all good poetry' as 'the spontaneous overflow of powerful feelings,' literary historians have been at pains to distinguish—in terms of kind—the aims and achievements of medieval lyric poets from their Romantic descendants."[40]

Stephen Manning once joked, "If we accept the catalogue of faults which some commentators level against Middle English religious lyrics, we can immediately sentence these poems to a circle in some aesthetic inferno and turn our attention to other literary matters."[41]

Old-Fashioned Poems

Middle English as a poetic language posed several peculiar challenges for lyric poets. Both the loss of Old English inflections and the introduction of loan words primarily from French and Latin often makes the accentuation of Middle English verse debatable; inconsistency of accentuation makes consonance, whether alliteration or end rhyme, all the more important for structuring audible verse forms. The transformation of English from a highly inflected to a predominantly analytic language also greatly restricted the syntactic freedom of word placement within a verse line. Although Middle English spelling is thought to be a much more reliable witness of pronunciation than is Modern English orthography, the multiple spellings of so many Middle English words (often within a single work) also indicates a good deal of acceptable variation in pronunciation. Thomas G. Duncan observes "that one can hardly doubt that there were variations in the performance of these lyrics among the Middle English readers themselves."[42]

Stylistically, Middle English poems are conventionally sorted into two seemingly competing but frequently complementary styles: an imported rhyming tradition and a "native" alliterative tradition. The alliterative style prevailed in poems composed in the Northern and Western dialects. Rhyming syllabic-accentual verse was favored in the East and South. Though some consider the alliterative style "generally unsuitable for lyric poetry,"[43] many Middle English lyrics combine formal features of both styles, and the elaborate consonance of some of these poems approximate the virtuosity of Gerard Manly Hopkins's sonnets. Paul Fussell, for example, felt that the heavily accentual meter of "I sing of a maiden" (considered in chapter 3) still appeals as it "approaches sprung rhythm" that amplifies the emphases of common speech.[44] All in all, the Middle English period was an "intense period of literary experimentation"[45]—not formally crude but richly innovative at being imitative. Ian Cornelius avoids overstating this praise: "To describe the thirteenth century as a Cambrian explosion in English verse forms would be unjust to the stylistic range and accomplishment of prior English verse. Still, the Middle English period witnessed a rapid diversification of metrical forms."[46]

The rhyming style of much Middle English lyric was an established international style long before being introduced to English verse. For later Middle English poets, France offered the most significant models for meters and rhyming. Yet, the manuscript records of Middle English lyrics preserve almost no guidance regarding their actual performance as song, and the performance of Middle English lyrics has become, at least in terms of their critical heritage, increasingly associated with recital rather than musical performance. James Wimsatt has proposed that

> these types originated as dance songs and had refrains. Because of such origins, French love poetry became even more musical than it had been in the previous centuries. By contrast, the Middle English lyrics of the time have no such musical affiliations, either in their origin or in their characteristically having musical accompaniment.[47]

This presumptive disassociation of medieval England's *lyric* from *song* may be attributed to a lack of evidence, however—that is, to a forgotten record of actual performance.

England's initial importation of regular end rhyme should be understood as within a polyglot community of poets rather than as a forced imposition across national boundaries. The earliest Middle English lyrics, those less impacted by French sophistication, are appreciated more by some readers as simpler, more direct statements of emotion. The *formes fixes* favored by French lyricists were subsequently duplicated by English poets, but this deliberate imitation also fostered original variations. As a key player in this process, Geoffrey Chaucer came to be called "the Father of English Poetry"—that is, the primary promoter of a regular rhyming tradition that prevailed in English poetry for the following five centuries.[48]

All Middle English stanzaic patterns are essentially melic, or closely tied to musical settings. However, as Ardis Butterfield indicates, there are only

> some thirty songs with Middle English texts before circa 1400 that survive with music, but again, largely sporadically; complete songbooks, where all the items have been copied with music and text together, are exceptionally rare and begin in any number only with the Tudor carol collections.[49]

Furthermore, what little musical notation survives for the Middle English lyrics provides only partial information for historically accurate reproduction. Many more lyrics that were surely meant to be sung lack any scoring at all because "melodies for many lyrics were probably carried in people's heads."[50] It remains well beyond the scope of this introduction and the skill of this reader to correct the fact that "lyric studies, and not only in the medieval period, have left music to one side to a degree that has impoverished and indeed misrepresented the object of study."[51] Nevertheless, I believe that even if the audible pleasure of most Middle English songs cannot be recovered, it can still be imagined, and I see no reason to denigrate anyone's effort to provide music for a Middle English lyric in order to achieve a modernized equivalence of what might have been its original emotional impact.

Middle English lyrics written solely in alliterative long lines were probably intended for recital rather than for singing (or for solitary reading). It has become somewhat customary to refer to the Alliterative Revival as the "so-called" Alliterative Revival, a later fourteenth- and fifteenth-century poetic movement that deployed the conspicuous repetition of initial consonants as the primary formal feature of English versification. Some think this Middle English school, as it were, to be a "Survival" of Old English prosody instead. If so, it is a substantial mutation. There is no demonstrable line of descent between the craft of Middle English alliterative poets and what came to be termed only in the nineteenth century—and for largely nationalistic reasons—the "native tradition" of the Old English scops. Furthermore, Richard H. Osberg contends "that the alliterative lyric represents an autonomous lyric tradition only peripherally related to the alliterative revival . . . but rather came to the lyric through the devotional prose."[52] Middle English alliterative poets, both narrative and lyric, essentially had to reinvent a nostalgic style. In any event, alliterative verse flourished in England only for about a century and a half, starting ca. 1350 CE. Yet, while it lasted, as much as the rhyming tradition, the Middle English alliterative versecraft accommodated a wide range of topics and tones. Considered all together, the Middle English lyrics represent a corpus of extraordinary formal variety; considered individually, these lyrics represent emotional expressions ranging from vulgar hilarity through poignant sadness to holy rapture.

Although both the alliterative and rhyming versecrafts are technically "regular"—that is, rule-following—many Middle English lyrics are presumed to be irregularly regular, or "crude"—much more so than French verse being composed at the same time. This impression of crudity of much Middle English verse became exacerbated by the (self-serving) contempt of more modern poets. Since Middle English end rhymes normatively do occur in end-stopped lines (i.e., with little enjambment to mute the rhyme), John Milton, for example, scoffed: "Rhime being no necessary Adjunct or true Ornament of Poem or good Verse, in longer Works especially, but the Invention of a barbarous Age, to set off wretched matter and lame Meeter."[53] Chaucer had himself recognized this poetic pitfall of sing-songiness and apparently coined the term "doggerel" to criticize excessive end rhyme; Chaucer likewise mocked the "rum, ram, ruf" of excessive alliteration, again as merely the noise of a barking dog.

There are a number of excuses for the apparent failure of Middle English lyrics to scan properly. The simplest, most common, and least appealing explanation is that the Middle English poets were indeed incompetent. Although there may be a special challenge to making much Middle English verse meet the formal standards of precedent French or subsequent English metrics, an alternative and more attractive explanation for the apparent irregularity of many Middle English lyrics is that the textual record does not accurately represent the pronunciation of syllables. Both dialect variation and scribal contamination can introduce what look like metrical irregularities. Ian Cornelius suggests that the often haphazardly written records of Middle English lyrics sometimes require a polydialectic (or linguistically loosey-goosey) reading: "The metrical regularity of Middle English poetry is often perceptible only through the continuous activation of and selection between the array of variant forms available in the contemporary language as possible realizations of a given manuscript spelling."[54] Chaucer too was fully aware of this "gret diversitee / In English and in writing of our tonge" (*Troilus and Criseyde*, V, 1792–1793), and he was equally aware of the "negligence and rape [hastiness]" of scribal transmission ("Adam Scriveyn," l. 7).

As John Stevens observed, "Syllabism. Clear, countable, syllable articulation is not a natural feature of English speech. We have too many indeterminate syllables—and so we had in Chaucer's day, if the extremely unpredictable orthography is anything to go by."[55] Alliterative verse especially can wander "far from 'the science of measurement,' from a perfectly numbered line and stanza."[56] And the most positive explanation of apparent irregularities in Middle English verse is that actual performance can erase these "mistakes." Both singing and recital can correct any seeming missteps in the "natural music" of a verse line as written.[57] Modern readers must consider what was heard, not what is seen, and my final chapter will return to a consideration of why English prosodists and poets later became so resistant to this concession.

To-Do List

For the sake of immediate access, this *Introduction* provides a plausible rendition in colloquial Modern English of each Middle English lyric to be considered. Brian Stone has rightly ridiculed such line-for-line prose translations of Middle English lyrics as "a work of taxidermy, not the creation of a living swan."[58] So, as must always be conceded, the fullest possible appreciation of any Middle English lyric requires its appreciation in the original language, the text of which provides only a shadow of the poem. The saying "traduttori traditori" insists rather rudely that this concession be granted; however, its translation as "translators are traitors" seems sufficiently faithful to the Italian in both sound and sense. Much is indeed lost in my prose renditions, including the original language's formal effects, nuances, puns, and equally plausible, alternative interpretations of words, phrases, and idioms. By providing readings intended to approximate the original pace of performance, my modernizations are meant to serve only as "ponies"[59]—merely a first step toward what Ardis Butterfield calls "the whole poem," be that performance song, public recital, group performance, or solitary reading. My assumption is that successful performance provided visual and audible prompts about tonal intent largely unrecorded in transcription. Explication becomes an effort at clarifying (with uncertainty) emotional signals that were once immediately evident.

For detailed scrutiny, transcriptions of the lyrics in Middle English will also be provided, but in a format not customarily provided by modern anthologies. The texts will be stripped of all interpretive prompts (punctuation, capitalization, etc.) variously provided by scribes and editors. It is easy to overlook that, fully edited in print, the punctuated text of a Middle English lyric, "like an oral performance . . . [,] is a text interpreted, or partially so."[60] This (largely paratextual) restriction of the individual reader's perception of any one version of a poem might be true of even a diplomatic edition of a single manuscript if its scribe was not the author. Nevertheless, my commentary on each poem must cite the Middle English to address original wordplay. It could be argued that excision of all scribal interventions is itself an editorial intrusion, and the reader of this *Introduction* is heartily encouraged to consult critical editions as well. Whereas my own modernizations provide very singular interpretations of each poem, the Middle English "naked text to behold"[61] is intended to free the reader "To decide for oneself... resonances of meaning, of nuance, that we can hear within, or beside, the grammatical string we decide on through our punctuation."[62]

Modern readers must also confront a more fundamental misperception of many Middle English lyrics—their apparent failure as "creative writing" intended to convey "direct expressions of [true] emotions." In chapter 2, I address a pair of issues that often motivate a priori dismissals of the integrity of Middle English lyrics as "true poetry": their apparent lack of originality and the ostensible Otherness of medieval emotions. The next seven chapters are all admittedly somewhat contrived gatherings of Middle English lyrics that enact emotionally related experiences. They are not meant to present specimens of cohesive topics from which one can induce the defining characteristics of distinct subgenres. Rather, each chapter examines a variety of texts as performable occasions for expressing a common cluster of frequently motile emotions (e.g., frustration, anger, and guilt or enthrallment, joy, and gratitude). I offer no further attempt to define the ever-elusive genre now named "the Middle English lyric." Instead, I hope to indicate the unique emotionality inherent in each lyric text. In that endeavor, chapter 3 samples Middle English lyrics that express (at least initially) joyful emotions that can range from playful ribaldry, through (some not entirely innocent) festival merrymaking, to the delight of expressing praise of an enticing woman, which can be elevated to a pure veneration of the Blessed Virgin Mary and ultimately to the consummate adoration of Christ. Chapter 4 considers a variety of lyrics expressing unpleasant feelings, mostly complaints (though not of the romantic sort considered in chapter 6); rather, these earnest lyrics whine about discomfort, or criticize social injustice, puzzle the reader with obscure yearning or dread harm, or—and most distressingly—confront the fear of death. Chapter 5 focuses on lyrics that contemplate the death of Christ as an imperative to feel compassion and so contrition; however, the emotions so aroused can also trigger anti-Semitic outrage and a profound problem of interpretation for modern readers. Chapters 6 and 7 together explore the ups and downs of what remains the most common subject of popular song, romantic love—more precisely, the *contek*, or struggle, of emotions attendant upon sexual desire and denial. Chapter 6 considers lyrics that enact the emotional turmoil before satisfaction, not only "falling in love" but also the male-female contest for consent; the effort to win a woman's "mercy" proves particularly prickly with the pastourelles, pseudo-romantic lyrics implicitly embedded in a rape narrative. Chapter 7 is full of complaints (and insults) about love gone wrong. My final chapter turns away from what I hope to have demonstrated is the true success of many Middle English lyrics as emotional scripts to a consideration of the post-medieval misreading of the texts that preserve these verses and, thereby, an enduring misevaluation of the still-elusive but falsely neglected genre.

TWO

Bringing the Middle English Lyric into Modern Play

> Poems are made by fools like me,
> But only God can make a tree.
>
> Joyce Kilmer, "Trees"

In the Middle Ages, the now commonplace celebration of creative writing as "creative" would have sounded inherently blasphemous. Only God can truly "create" ex nihilo, and "God haþ created al þing in ri3t ordre" (Chaucer, *Canterbury Tales*, X, 218). Middle English poets more humbly identify themselves as mere "makers" (which indeed preserves the etymology of *poet*). As a product of the human imagination (the *ars commemorativa*), a poem and indeed all human invention—or, discovery—can only fabricate newness by recombining precedent elements into novel combinations—that is, *make* by rejuvenating conventions. Most modern poets, many of whom could care not less about prosodic precision, do strive for complete originality or unique complexity—"one's own voice." So, the apparent commonplace themes or clichéd feelings to be performed by many Middle English lyrics can pose a substantial challenge to enjoying their affective excellence.

The Simple Integrity of Middle English Lyrics

With few and late exceptions (e.g., William Dunbar's "Hail sterne superne in eterne"),[1] most Middle English lyrics lack extravagant bravura. Simple lyric statements, however, were (and are) designed to be enjoyed concurrent to first hearing, not after recurrent scrutiny of the page and annotated decipherment. Although many Middle English lyrics were accompanied with illustrations, many were not meant to be perused by a wide readership at all. Whether heard or viewed, the normative imagery of Middle English lyrics achieves an immediate, because familiar, emotional impact: "Both medieval psychology and poetic theory stress the ability of vivid imagery to generate affective reactions. Each poetic image is in practice a memory phantasm: a combination of verbally simulated sense data and the immediate psychological reaction to it."[2] To perceive the "authenticating touch" that modern readers demand of all poems, Stephen Manning proposed quite some time ago that Middle English love lyrics be read as analogous to our own popular songs, and that "when we look at the emotion purportedly being experienced by the speaker in today's popular song, we can better appreciate the role of the cliché in the medieval love lyric."[3] Judson Boyce Allen likewise compared the Middle English lyric to popular song in order to distinguish the enjoyment of a "clear or immediately intelligible lyric" from "the difficult lyric... the normally esteemed modern form."[4]

Delight in excellent though seemingly simple versification should not be thought of as an aesthetic peculiar to the Middle Ages. As Joseph Addison famously observed, "The old song of Chevy Chase is the favourite ballad of the common people of England; and Ben Jonson used to say he would rather have been the author of it than of all his works."[5] And the melodic lyrics of the seventeenth-century Tribe of Ben remain far more singable than the *enigmatae* of their contemporary Metaphysicals. Furthermore, English popular song championed no free verse movement. Paul McCartney's "Yesterday" (1965), for example, remains a deeply moving song; yet, if only the text of its lyrics were to be discovered someday, transcribed on a scrap of paper in the middle of some random book, and the musical performance itself forgotten, "Yesterday, all my troubles seemed so far away" might seem at first a rather rudimentary bit of versifying. Sadly, the actual performance quality of Middle English "popular song is indeed the lost art of medieval England."[6]

Some of the still most appealing Middle English lyrics are exquisitely simple, such as the possibly fragmentary carol "Icham of Irlaunde" [I am of Ireland]. The carol is a "social dance... danced for the amusement and delight of the dancers themselves" as distinguished from "professional dances... danced as an exhibition before spectators."[7] This distinction may be extended to recognize all Middle English lyrics as "social," whereas modern lyrics became increasingly "professional." One can induce from the text itself of "Icham of Irlaunde" that it was sung by a woman. John Burrow suggests that a chorus could have identified the borders of "Ireland" on "the make-believe geography of the dance floor, with the area occupied by the soloist at the centre of the ring of carolers."[8]

> **I am from Ireland,**
> icham of irlaunde
>> **and of the holy land**
>> and of the holy londe
> **of Ireland.**
> of irlande
> **Good sir, I pray you,**
> gode sire pray ich thee
> 5 **For [the sake] of holy charity,**
> for of sainte charitee
>> **Come and dance with me**
>> come and daunce wit me
> **In Ireland.**
> in irlaunde

Wooed readers should allow themselves to be quasi-hypnotized by an imagined performance of the naked text.

Another formally quite simple yet greatly discussed Middle English lyric illustrates the freedom (or uncertainty) that can inform modern readings of a text without context. "Maiden in the mor lay" [Maiden in the moor lay] has provoked what seem radically opposed interpretations because, as Ardis Butterfield observes, it "has just enough notes to make the task of interpretation interesting."[9]

> **A maiden lay in the moor,**
> maiden in the mor lay
>> **In the moor [she] lay.**
>> in the mor lay
> **Seven nights full, seven nights full,**
> sevenight fulle sevenight fulle
> **In the moor [she] lay**
> maiden in the mor lay
> **In the moor [she] lay.**
> in the mor lay

5 **Seven nights full and a day.**
sevenightes fulle and a day
Good was her food.
welle was hire mete
    What was her food?
    what was hire mete
    The primrose and the . . .
    the primerole and the
    The primrose and the . . .
    the primerole and the
10 **Good was her food.**
welle was hire mete
    What was her food?
    what was hire mete
    The primrose and the violet
    the primerole and the violet
Good was her drink.
welle was hire dring
    What was her drink?
    what was hire dring
15 **The cold water of . . .**
the chelde water of the
    The cold water of . . .
    the chelde water of the
Good was her drink.
welle was hire dring
    What was her drink?
    what was hire dring
20 **The cold water of the well-spring.**
the chelde water of the wellespring
Good was her bower.
welle was hire bour
    What was her bower?
    what was hire bour
    The red rose and the . . .
    the rede rose and the

The red rose and the . . .
the rede rose and the
25 **Good was her bower.**
welle was hire bour
What was her bower?
what was hire bour
The red rose and the . . .
the rede rose and the
The red rose and the lily flower.
the rede rose and the lilie flour

Ardis Butterfield has analyzed the not-unique editorial challenge of formatting (and thereby attempting to regularize) the sketchy sole manuscript witness of this elusive lyric: "Could not this piece of writing be a set of quick notes, a rough guideline for performance where exact representation of a text is not necessary? Yes, it could."[10] Although only a minimal prompt for such a performance, the text's repetitive phrasing has little emotional impact when perceived as a maximum record for silent reading instead; so, too, the refrains of all carols are easy for the modern reader to skip over as mere redundancy. But, like many carols, "Maiden in the mor lay" was most probably a group song "evocative of a tranced mood. It has a kind of solemn gaiety."[11]

Optional and radically opposed but, I think not, mutually exclusive readings, or performances, of "Maiden in the mor lay" have been proposed largely on the basis of completely differing interpretive contexts supplied by modern critics. Focused on the lyric's number symbolism and flower imagery, for example, D. W. Robertson Jr. proposed a solution to this "poetic *aenigma*" by identifying the maiden as the Blessed Virgin Mary and the water she drinks as "God's grace."[12] Notoriously, however, E. Talbot Donaldson found this exegetical reading "disappointing if not entirely irrelevant."[13] Siegfried Wenzel, without endorsing an exclusively allegorical reading, acknowledged its legitimacy as a supplied context for decoding this lyric:

> The assumption that all medieval literature of any consequence was written in order to teach caritas has led some critics to subject even the few outwardly secular lyrics predating MS. Harley 2253 to spiritual exegesis, with the result that to their ears "Foweles in þe frith" and

"Maiden in the mor lay" no longer speak of sexual attraction to a girl and a real though mysterious woman in the woods.[14]

John Speirs, reading "Maiden in the mor" in terms of "well-wakes" promoting fertility, associated the poem with St. John's Eve (23 June, Midsummer) and identified the maiden as a faerie.[15] Speirs also notes that in a similar six-line poem, "At a sprynge wel under a thorne," the spirit of a spring maiden is more clearly adapted to be identifiable as Mary, a typical appropriation of pre-Christian customs in medieval England for an overtly Christian application. However, Richard L. Greene argues that in the fourteenth century this rondel was seen as profane by the "stern bishop" Richard de Ledrede.[16] However again, Joseph Harris questions Greene's reading and posits instead that the maiden, like an alter-Magdalene, "has fled to the sweet lily of chastity."[17] Peter Dronke maintained the lyric's folkloric, non-Christian performance be conceived as a ritualistic dance possibly enhanced by a maiden's miming.[18] Ronald Waldron specifically suggested a children's singing game playing "the enactment of a funeral, usually of a young person."[19] However, Thomas G. Duncan suggests that the scribe of an abbreviated copy of the lyric might have been its performer as well.[20] Though varied explications, such readings are complementary perceptions of the lyric's enduring tonal effect—that is, the elusive attractiveness of this maiden on the moor: "The mystery remains, but we can savour it in the curious broken lines (a rather unusual feature), the short repeated rhythms, and most of all in the succession of concretely presented, but never elucidated images."[21] The presumed dance quality of the text enriches a perception of its question-and-answer exchange; if men are imagined as repeatedly asking and women as finally answering, the incomplete lines acquire a flirtatious quality.

Scholars may loathe such speculation, but I think that the primary joy for modern readers of Middle English lyrics is the freedom to make each interpretation a personal performance. If we cannot know what a medieval lyric meant for sure, we can share our impressions and feel how medieval readers (or performers) might have felt. Peter Dronke has classified all medieval European poetry according to "three main functions: formal commemoration, entertainment, cult"[22]—with all three functions presuming some setting for an anticipated performance. The direct expressiveness of many Middle English lyrics implies some histrionic context as well. Many studies of Middle English lyrics reiterate the significance of imagining the lyric's enactment of emotions. Christiania Whitehead, for example, observes: "Sometimes the movement of identification within the lyrics is couched in distinctly performative terms."[23] Sarah McNamer reads meditations on the Passion (including lyrics) as "'intimate scripts': they are quite literally scripts for the performance of feeling—scripts that often explicitly aspire to performative efficacy."[24] Damien Boquet and Piroska Nagy likewise affirm, "Rather than being entirely defined by the words or the melody, lyrical emotion was a product of performance."[25]

Though beneficial for immediate enjoyment, the simplicity and familiarity of most Middle English lyrics may be erroneously thought to discredit their enduring emotional integrity; the repetitiveness of clichés can be especially excoriated. Late medieval courtly lyrics in particular (because of their relentless conventionality) have little modern appeal at first sight if the reader fails to recognize the social recreational function of such lyrics that "supply entertainment, and insofar as a maker makes lyrics he is functioning—whether amateur or professional—as an entertainer."[26] Indeed, the lyric "I am sorry for her sake" both records and ridicules the conventionality of the simplest declarative sentences as expressions of emotion.

> *Care away, away, away!*
> care away away away
> ***Mourning away!***
> murning away
> ***I am forsaken;***
> i am forsake
> ***Another is taken.***
> another is take
> 5 ***I can mourn no more.***
> no more murne ic may
> ***I am sorry for her sake.***
> i am sory for her sake
> ***I can eat and drink well.***
> ic may well ete and drinke
> ***When I sleep, I cannot wake***
> whanne ic slepe ic may not wake
> 10 ***So much I think about her***
> so muche on her ic thenke

Care away...
    I am brought into such a torment,
    i am brout in suche a bale
    And brought into such a torture [that]
    and brout in suche a pine
    When I rise up out of my bed
    whanne ic rise up of my bed
15   **I enjoy dining well.**
    me liste well to dine
Care away...
    I am brought into such a torture
    i am brout in suche a pine
    Brought into such a torment [that]
    ibrout in suche a bale
    When I have very good wine
    whanne ic have righte good wine
20   **I'd prefer to not drink ale.**
    me liste drinke non ale
Care away...

On the page, many elements of this lyric look simplistic. Without music, the lengths of its lines look rather random. The rhyme schemes of both the burden (aabba) and each quatrain (alternating rhyme bcbc) sound highly repetitive, as do the mirror repetitions of the first two lines of the last two stanzas. For the silent reader, full reiteration of the burden four times in a row proves boring. Each stanza reads at first like a catalogue of clichés: "I am forsaken," "I am in pain," "I am sorry"—such is the stuff of a (poorly composed) complaint. Indeed, the *Digital Index of Middle English Verse* identifies this lyric as "a lover's sad plight." But each stanza is merely providing a humorous setup. The repeated burden at the end of each of the final four stanzas is a punch line indicating that the primary singer indeed eats, drinks, and remains quite merry when in bed. The syntactic sparseness of the burden may seem artless, but if "Care away, away, away" is sung by a chorus with increasing intensity as an imperative, "No more murne ic may" at the conclusion of the burden comes to mean "I'm done with it!" rather than "Alas, I cannot mourn more so." The fun of this pseudo-complaint works well with the boys in a tavern.

If such group-dancing and singing may be considered one pole of performance possibilities for a Middle English lyric, silent prayer may be considered the other. The type of Middle English lyrics that Rosemary Woolf termed "meditative poetry" most closely approximates the modern reader's default expectation of reading as a silent, solitary savoring of the lyric.[27] So, too, Anne Klinck differentiates "three dominant aspects in which it [the Middle English lyric] presents itself: that is, in the guise of song, festivity, or personal confession," only the last of which fosters introspective reading whereas the other two require extroverted performance.[28] Julia Boffey suggests that Middle English "readers seem to have valued lyrics *as reading matter* only if they were either in French, or had strong French connections."[29]

The enduring appeal of singing of hymns requires no historicized explanation, just faith (or at least an aesthetic sympathy for such religious devotion). In a manner of speaking, chanted prose (i.e., liturgical performance of the Latin translations of the psalms) provided a lyrical experience that may be considered the medieval equivalent of free verse. Middle English lyrics that foster introspection, however audible one's reading might be, often serve a "confessional" purpose, but not simply by indulging a public disclosure of intimate information (a fashion that had its moment in the United States during the 1950s and '60s with such poets as Robert Lowell, Sylvia Plath, Anne Sexton, and W. D. Snodgrass). Rather, as the central step in the sacrament of penance, *in secreto* (or whispered) confession of the mouth verbalized contrition of the heart in order to realize satisfaction of the hand in the hope of winning forgiveness; the speech act of reciting such meditative lyrics heals while remaining private, "sealed" as in the sacrament itself.

The lyric "God that all this mights may" [God, Who all this power may] exemplifies just such an externalization of guilt and thereby a release from internal distress. Its performance requires the reader's personal investment in an emotional pose. Falling to one's knees helps.

God, You Who are Almighty,
god that all this mightes may
In Heaven and on Earth Your will is everlasting,
in hevene and erthe thy wille is o
I have been lost many a day.
iche habbe be losed mony a day

      Previously and recently, I've been your foe.
      er and late ibe thy fo
5   **I was to blame, and [although I do] know my religious rules,**
      ich wes to wite and wiste my lay
      [Yet] for a long time I have kept myself away therefrom.
      longe habbe holde me therfro
      You are full of mercy,
      ful of mercy thou art ay
      [Yet] I am entirely unready to go to You.
      all ungreithe ich am to thee to go
    To go to Him Who has purchased us,
    to go to him that hath us boght
10   **My good deeds are entirely too small.**
      my gode deden bueth fol smalle
      Of the works that I have performed,
      of the werkes that ich ha wroght
      The best is more bitter than gall.
      the beste is bittrore then the galle
      My [own] good—I knew—I did not want at all.
      my good ich wiste i nolde it noght
      I desired to fall into folly.
      in folie me wes luef to falle
15   **When I thoroughly consider myself**
      when i myself have thourghsoght
      I know that I am the worst of all.
      i knowe me for the worst of alle
    God, Who died on the cross
    god that deyedest on the rod
      All this world to profit and fulfill,
      all this world to forthren and fille
      For us You shed Your sweet blood.
      for us thou sheddest thy swete blod
20   **[All] that I have done distresses me,**
      that i ha don me liketh ille
      But ever against You I have stood stiffly.
      bote er ageyn thee stith i stod
      Formerly and recently, aloud and silently.

er and late loude and stille
Among my deeds, I find not one good.
of mine deden finde i non god
Lord, do with me as You will!
lord of me thou do thy wille
25 **In [my] heart, I could never yield**
in herte ne mighte i never bowe
Nor draw [near] to my dear Lord.
ne to my kunde louerd drawe
My worst enemy is my trust in [worldly] love.
my meste fo is my loves trowe
I never stood firm in any reverence for Christ.
crist ne stod me never hawe
I hold myself viler than a Jew,
ich holde me vilore then a giw
30 **And I want myself to be known as such.**
and i myself wolde bue knowe
Lord, mercy! Pity me now!
lord mercy rewe me now
Raise up what is fallen low!
reise up that is falle lowe
God, Whom all this world should obey,
god that all this world shall hede
Your good power, You hold in dominion.
thy gode might thou hast in wolde
35 **You came to Earth on account of our need,**
on erthe thou come for oure nede
For us sinners—[You were] bought and sold
for us sunful were boght and solde
When we are to be damned according to our deeds
when we bueth dempned after ur dede
At Doomsday, when truth be told
a domesday when rightes bueth tolde
When he [the individual sinner] shall see the blood of Thy wounds—
when he shule suen they wounde blede
40 **To speak, then we'll be afraid.**
to speke thenne we bueth unbolde

Afraid I am to ask a favor of You,
unbold ich am to bidde thee bote
   So unpleasant is my madness.
   swithe unreken is my rees
Your will I never neared on foot;
thy wille ne welk i ner afote
   I preferred to go to wicked works.
   to wickede werkes i me chees
45 **I was false from top to bottom**
   fals i wes in crop and rote
   When I said Your teaching was lies.
   when i seide thy lore wes lees
Jesus Christ, be my help,
jesu crist thou be my bote
   So prepared I am to make my peace.
   so boun ich am to make my pees
My peace is [still] all uneasy—
all unreken is my ro
50 **Lord Christ, what shall I say?**
   louerd crist whet shall i say
   I find no profit in my deeds
   of mine deden finde i non fro
Nor anything that I can think of.
ne nothing that i thenke may
   I am unworthy to come to You.
   unworth ich am to come thee to
I serve You neither night nor day.
i serve thee nouther night ne day
55 **Unto Your mercy I submit myself,**
   in thy mercy i me do
   God, You Who are Almighty!
   god that all this mightes may

As a "thourghthought" [thorough-thought] (l. 15), this lyric does not conduct a formal examination of conscience such as one would find in a *manuel des peches* (a penitential manual; cf. Chaucer's prose "Parson's Tale"). Rather, it is a lyric script for the emotional experience caused by just such a self-scrutiny if sincerely performed. The alternating rhymes (abababab, cdcd) of the lyric's seven eight-line stanzas suit well the emotional oscillation of such introspection. Stanzas 1, 3, and 5, all beginning with "God," celebrate His mercy; stanzas 2 and 4 lament the sinner's unworthiness; stanzas 6 and 7 express the sinner's abject submission and anxious trust in reconciliation. All eight stanzas sustain the emotional ambivalence of our forgiven yet still fallen humanity. From the start, God is addressed with the second-person familiar pronoun (thee/thou/thy/thine) yet acknowledged as omnipotent, eternal, righteously angry, hopefully forgiving.

This lyric articulates the "unreken" [un-ready] (ll. 42, 49) uneasiness of becoming self-aware (l. 5) of one's own foolish sinfulness. Such a meditative Middle English lyric requires and rewards reflection—that is, rereading. The first stanza contrasts God's eternal mercy to "my" persistently sinful days. More important than the doctrinal affirmation of good deeds as a means of attaining sanctifying grace is the speaker's recognition of "my" utter failure to be charitable. The analogy that the sinner's "best" deed is like "gall" (l. 12) recalls the bitter favor offered to Christ on the cross (Matthew 27:34; Mark 15:23); this regretfully ironic "best" triggers the sinner's hyperbolic self-loathing as the "worst of alle" (l. 16). Stanza 3 prolongs the stiff-necked (l. 21) sinner's painful remembrance of the Passion, which underlies (and now poisons the emotional tenor of) the poet's use of "Jew" (l. 29) to signify any stubborn non-believer—than whom, the repentant "I" confesses to be viler still. (Such casual anti-Semitism throughout medieval literature now seems all the more deplorable because it sounds so habitual; its emotional performance in Middle English lyrics will be addressed more fully in chapter 4.)

The apparent use of the present-tense verbs "come" (l. 34) and "serve" (l. 54)—when the past tense in each case seems more appropriate—may simply exemplify the vulnerability of any close reading of Middle English lyrics to both scribal and editorial transcription qua interpretation. However, reading these two present-tense verbs as received suggests that Christ still comes continuously at need despite the fact that the sinner continually fails to serve Christ even at the end of this confession. Stanza 5 leaps from the sale of Christ (i.e., Judas's betrayal) to the payback of Doomsday "when rihtes bueth tolde" [when rights will be told] (l. 38), a polysemous phrasing that probably denotes "when truth is revealed" but may connote "when religious rites are recited" or "when accounts are squared" at the Grand Assize.

The litotes "unbolde" (ll. 40, 41) seems more tonally ambiguous than "afraid" as translated; this understatement may be thought either feeble and so self-excusing or mocking and so self-ridiculing. Though this lyric does not maintain concatenation, the repetition of "unbolde" and "go" (ll. 8, 9) pairs the first two and the last two stanzas. The reiteration of this lyric's alpha-line as its omega-line completes the circle of this lyric's simultaneous experiencing of shame and hope. The enduring anxiety of "I" regarding every sinner's unworthiness (l. 53) does not indicate a lack of faith in God's mercy; instead, it provides an emotionally necessary corrective to "surquiderie" [presumption] as a false understanding of "hope." None of this lyric's "thourghthought" is new; the performative purpose of "God that all this mights may in heaven & earth thy will is oo" duplicates a communal recital of the *confiteor* in a mass or an individual's private act of contrition. The very familiarity of such prayer by rote can cause emotional numbness on occasion—a temptation strongly to be resisted. "God that all this mights may in heaven & earth thy will is oo" itself offers a rejuvenating elaboration of the contrite speech act.

The question remains, however, whether the base-line conventionality of many Middle English lyrics devalues their integrity as enduring expressions of emotion for modern, non-specialist, and especially, given so much religious verse, non-devout readers. As rehearsed performances, can Middle English lyrics still function as artificial imitations of what W. M. Reddy has termed *emotives*—that is, "emotional utterances that take the form of first-person present-tense emotion claims"?[30]

The Emotional Integrity of Middle English Lyrics

Recent scholarly interest in the history of emotions and a renewed enthusiasm for affective hermeneutics encourages treating "the content of medieval poems and romances as a poetry of emotions."[31] However, actually being moved by a Middle English lyric often poses a special challenge for the modern reader. Furthermore, the clustering of thematically and tonally similar Middle English lyrics into subsets of anthologies only exacerbates the impression of repetitive conventionality. *Centos,* or collage poems, and Middle English adaptations of French or Latin are particularly vulnerable to the criticism of being merely derivative. The seventy-seven couplets of "Jesu that hast me dear I-bought," for example, are lifted from the vernacular translation of the *Philomena*, a much, much longer meditative poem by the Franciscan John of Howden; Rosemary Woolf feels "nevertheless, the effect of the poem is not one of patchwork,"[32] and a fully invested recital performance renews sincere reiteration of its borrowed lines.

Numerous scholars have argued that the emotional redundancy of many Middle English lyrics should be better understood as expressions of common humanity. It has been often and variously remarked that "the lyric 'I' who addresses the 'you' implied in Middle English lyrics is a general, typical figure, an 'I' without ego, who may make the reader a participant in the poem."[33] Stephen Manning proposed that "in a song, the speaker is not sharply characterized; he tends to be anonymous, or Everyman."[34] Judson Boyce Allen recommended that the modern reader become the medieval lyric's "I" by "entering it ... its linear process."[35] Thomas G. Duncan likewise affirms the universal emotional integrity of Middle English lyrics as poems that "are essentially public events. . . . Neither individuality nor sincerity, whether of feeling or expression, is at issue."[36] The retrieval of "authorial intent" becomes thereby a moot point. Whereas poets today are professionally encouraged to write in an identifiably unique fashion, Anne Klinck observes that, in Middle English lyrics, "'voice,' although it implies a point of view and a perspective, does not necessarily imply a distinct persona."[37]

Comparable to rote prayers, Middle English lyrics preserve a shareable event. Indeed, "lyric" and "prayer" are often synonymous emotional experiences. Applying David Lawton's conception of "public interiority" in which a "shared first person" asks to be "inhabited" by readers,[38] Megan Murton finds that "Jesu that hast me dere iboght"

> sits precisely at the intersection of lyric, affective meditation, and prayer and shows an exceptional self-consciousness about the dynamics of inhabiting a script. . . . The premise that underlies this text and many others like it is that performing a script can change a person, as he or she internalizes the model of devotion that the script offers.[39]

So, pace William Wordsworth, Middle English lyrics need not be recollections of one individual's unique emotional overflow; the composition of medieval lyrics may have been every bit as tranquil and designed to arouse genuine affects, but most of the poems themselves are artificial impersonations of common experiences in contrast to the usually far more specifically identified "I" of modern dramatic monologues because "in many medieval first-person poems, the 'I' speaks not for an individual but for a type."[40]

Ingrid Nelson explains in more detail:

> The ethopoetic voices of medieval lyrics reflect material and social circumstances and speak from the conjunction of these factors at an imagined moment in time. They construct not a totalized psychology or subjectivity but a circumstantial utterance. Such a voice differs in important ways from the speaker of a dramatic monologue, a dominant paradigm of lyric genre as construed by many formalist readers. Dramatic monologues are spoken by characters with implied personal histories and continuous (if changeable) subjectivities and are "overheard" by a separate subject. Ethopoetic utterances, by contrast, are universally assimilable. Speaking, reading, or hearing such a voice offers an opportunity to experience intimately its difference and potentially absorb it into one's own experience.[41]

Whereas readers of modern, post-Romantic poetry may celebrate an author's individuality to the point of idiosyncrasy, the anonymity of most Middle English lyrics actually enhances their universal intimacy. The very familiarity of their recurrent tropes and themes also creates opportunities to appreciate more nuanced departures from and variations of the conventions. Emphatically, therefore, Barbara H. Rosenwein dismisses any notion that the emotions which we find expressed in medieval texts belong "to the boilerplate of particular genres and" are "therefore meaningless from the point of view of 'real feeling.'"[42]

Nevertheless, a modern reader's ability to feel again the emotional experiences performed in Middle English lyrics poses a fundamental question of translatability—can medieval emotions be truly reenacted by modern readers? New Critics generally discussed emotions as achronic expressions. Such essentialist thinking assumes that the emotions per se are a constant of human nature and that any supposed alterity of Middle English emotions needs no further consideration because it does not exist. Bemoaning the neglect of Middle English secular lyrics by literary historians, for example, George Kane affirmed with ease:

For it must turn out that once you generalize human feeling by giving it a name its quality is shown to be relatively consistent through the ages: such distinctiveness as the poem communicating it possesses lodges in what Eliot called the objective correlative, the ultimate particulars of style and form by which the poet sought to register his experience.[43]

The reader of a Middle English lyric can thus readily put on the emotion of its "I" once fluency in the language itself is achieved. Sarah Stanbury, as one such most competent reader, sees lyric in general as "the autobiographical genre above all others" because it "takes place outside of history and out of time."[44] Raymond W. Gibbs Jr. further proposes that cognitive poetics justifies reading a continuity between medieval and modern feelings insofar as

> many of the metaphorical patterns evident in Middle English lyrics ... reflect enduring embodied metaphorical concepts that are tacitly familiar to people past and present in different languages and cultures around the world. These shared cognitive, and mostly unconscious, mental structures provide one reason why Middle English lyrics can be appreciated by contemporary speakers and scholars.[45]

Historicists, however, insist that emotions be understood as expressed within differing societal contexts. Barbara H. Rosenwein, for example, observes, "Emotional communities are groups—usually but not always social groups—that have their own particular values, modes of feeling, and ways to express those feelings" like "speech communities."[46] A prevailing theory among historians of emotion today is that "neither universal nor timeless, emotions are whatever the men and women of each era, of each society, of each group make of them."[47] Glenn Burger and Holly Crocker, for example, assert "emotions are not biological ... but historically contingent ... we should not assume that medieval emotions ... even if they share the same names as modern emotions, are describing the same experience or having the same effects in the world."[48]

Throughout the Middle Ages, theoretical discussion of the etiology of emotions was the provenance of moral theologians and medical theorists. Damien Boquet and Piroska Nagy recount numerous efforts to analyze and systematize the emotions from late antiquity through the fifteenth century.

By the Middle English era, Cistercian "spiritual psychology" had differentiated emotions caused by the concupiscible faculty (e.g., "delight, rejoicing, exaltation, charity") from those produced by the irascible faculty ("compunction, heartfelt penance, boredom, fear, sadness, worry, jealousy, anger, indignation, and so on").[49] This historicized analysis of medieval emotions is quite foreign to most modern readers of lyric poetry—as it probably was to most authors of Middle English lyrics. Rita Copeland suggests an alternative and arguably far more widespread lexicon for the medieval analysis of the emotions: "rhetoric has a traceable history that can provide a kind of diachronic 'exoskeleton' of subjective experience, a way of formally apprehending emotion in time."[50] These historicized metalanguages for analyzing medieval emotion need not be considered synonymous with the emotive language of Middle English lyrics, however; as John Stevens has observed, "concern with emotional effects is a quite separate thing from concern with emotional expression."[51]

Direct expressions of emotion in the Middle English lyrics remain as comprehensible as any other textual records from the era. In other words, although the multiple Middle English meanings of such emotional labels as "passioun," "fele," and "affect" can be very false friends, lyrical declarations of loving, hating, wishing, regretting, and so on remain performable (even if, at times, only by analogy). Whereas Middle English poets had used a grab bag of often unfamiliar terms in lieu of the word *lyric*, they used a vocabulary of still quite common nouns to name the lyrical emotions being enacted. To supplement the native English lexicon, the Middle English lyricists inherited their emotional terminology essentially from Ovid and Jean de Meun and the French lyricists rather than from Galen and Avicenna.[52] Some emotions were (and still are) associated with sin, notably lust and anger. Some were considered habitual to certain temperaments, the result of a physiological imbalance of the four humors. A Middle English lyric that begins "Sluggy and slowe, in spetinge muiche" [Sluggish and slow, in spitting much] details the temperaments and behaviors associated with each humor in four easily memorized quatrains rhyming aabb.

fleumaticus
> **Sluggish and slow, excessive in spitting,**
> sluggy and slowe in spetinge muiche

Cold and moist, my nature is such,
cold and moist my natur is suche
Dull of wit, and fat, of a strange behavior,
dull of wit and fat of contenaunce strange
Phlegmatic—this complexion may not change.
fleumatike this complecion may not change
sanguineus
5   **I am generous, loving, and glad,**
deliberal i am lovinge and gladde
Laughing and playing, I am very seldom sad,
laghinge and playinge full seld i am sad
Singing, very attractive of [facial] color, bold to fight,
singinge full fair of colour bold to fight
Hot and moist, gracious, I'm called Sanguine.
hote and moist beninge sanguine i hight
colericu
I am sad and sullen with heaviness in thought.
i am sad and soleynge with heviness in thoght
10 **I covet very much; I will leave nothing.**
i covet right muiche leve will i noght
Fraudulent and subtle, very cold and dry,
fraudulent and suttill full cold and dry
Of a yellowish color, I am Choleric.
yollowe of colour colorike am i
malencolicus
Envious, deceitful, my skin is rough,
envius dissevabill my skin is roghe
Outrageous in giving, fearless enough,
outrage in exspence hardy inoghe
15 **Ingenious and slender, hot and dry,**
suttill and sklender hote and dry
Of color pale, my name is Melancholy.
of colour pale my nam is malencoly

The emotional term "complexion" (l. 4) is also false friend; its modern denotation of "facial skin-tone" is different than, though derived from, the medieval meaning of "a folding together of the humours (which determines skin tone)." As a "psychosomatic theory of the emotions,"[53] the humors emphasized the physicality of temperaments. One might translate "melancholic" as "depressed" but not think of "prolific generosity" as an attendant feature; nevertheless, on the whole, the vocabulary of this lyric still makes sense. One can even imagine that it was written by a self-approving, sanguineous poet.

Since the metalanguages of emotion have changed so over time, it is difficult to label and then gather for consideration corresponding emotional expressions among the Middle English lyrics. But there has been a rather persistent division of positive from negative categories of emotional experiences. "From antiquity," Rita Copeland observes, "we also see the beginnings of taxonomies of emotion. The Stoics divided emotion into good and bad feelings: pleasure and desire on the one hand, distress and fear on the other."[54] As noted, Cistercian anthropology also differentiated the two main categories of concupiscible and irascible passions, although each category included what we normally consider opposite emotions. The concupiscible grouping included both love and hatred, joy and sadness; irascible emotions included both hope and despair, anger and fear.[55] In performance, enactment of such emotional paradoxes (laughing in grief, crying for laughter) further frustrates a binary sorting of the emotions to be enacted, such as pleasant vs. unpleasant, *gaudium* (joy) vs. *tristia* (sorrow). The emotional dynamics of any one Middle English lyric can include both complaint and celebration, fear and hope, anger and desire, and so on—successful enactment of which depends upon the empathy of the reader. In her study of the impact of later medieval philosophical considerations of earthly "enjoyment" prompted by the rediscovery of Aristotle's *Ethics* (channeled to Middle English lyric poets primarily through Jean de Meun), Jessica Rosenfeld writes, "The experience of alikeness—of two lovers, of narrator and interlocutor, of poet and reader, of bliss and sorrow—offered by this poetry provide moments when pleasure is inextricably bound up with shared experience and a shared moral sense of the world."[56] Performance enacts this possibility of vicariously sharing the text's emotional potential.

On occasion, the text of a Middle English lyric will present a severe problem for the reader-performer wishing an enactment (or interpretation) of its sensibility with modern readers who rightly refuse to tolerate offensive expressions of vile thoughts. Blithe racism and misogyny, in particular, provide focal points for debating the historicity of (the performance) of emotions. The "pleasure" of pastourelles, for example, that are far too comfortable with the concept of "forced consent" will be especially difficult to comprehend or justify. Yet, the enactment of neither positive nor negative emotions need be either abusive or benevolent for the emotional enactment itself to be a true impersonation.

It is for each modern reader to discern in praxis rather than in theory whether each Middle English lyric remains emotionally performable. The following commentaries are offered as directorial notes for a plausible understanding of each lyric's emotional role-playing, suggestions prefatory to a reader's performance of the text with the full emotive force of speech enhancing the text's artistry for immediate and affective appreciation. Such a performance in turn initiates a collaborative and validly diverse discussion among its audience. Once so imagined by the solitary reader, the genre of Middle English "lyric" should perhaps be better approached as a subgenre of medieval drama, whereby reading becomes method acting and singing becomes musical theater.

THREE

Playing Glad

> Hise worldes joyes ben so grete,
> Him thenkth of hevene no beyete.
>
> [His worldly joys are so great that
> He does not think about the
> prosperity of heaven.]
>
> John Gower, *Confessio Amantis*, I, 2683

Middle English expressions of lyric joy range from lewd "harlotrie" to an anticipatory enjoyment of the heavenly feast. Yet, since all earthly joy was recognized as transitory, the enjoyable game to be played by a Middle English lyric proves partial or aspirational or ephemeral (like performance of the lyric itself). Exuberant carols and reverdies can descend into a closing lament. Lyrics that echo heavenly bliss are hymns of hope. Lyrics that invite romantic reward are wishful thinking. The emotion motivating most Middle English lyrics that play at joy is some sense of love, but then love is the motivation for most Middle English lyrics of misery as well.

Surprised by Joy

"Adam lay I-bounden bounden in a bond" [Adam lay bound in a bond] voices one of the more paradoxical conceptions of joy in Middle English lyric: the *felix culpa* ("happy flaw") motif that celebrates humankind's expulsion from paradise as a necessary and so fortunate prerequisite to our salvation in Heaven.[1] Despite all the negative connotations attached to the adjective "medieval" in common parlance, medieval teleology was quite optimistic; despite plague, feudal warfare, famine, poverty, and all other evils caused by the Fall, the hope for heaven offered a reason to rejoice . . .

eventually. Motivated by this common medieval trust in eternal joy, "Adam lay I-bounden" explains the "good" of Good Friday.

> **Adam lay bound,**
> adam lay ibounden
>> **Bound in a bond.**
>> bounden in a bond
>> **Four thousand winters**
>> foure thousand winter
>> **Thought He not too long.**
>> thowt he not too long
> 5 **And all was for an apple,**
> and all was for an appil
>> **An apple that he took,**
>> an appil that he took
>> **As scholars find written**
>> as clerkes finden wreten
>> **In their Book.**
>> in here book
> **Had the apple not been taken,**
> ne hadde the appil take ben
> 10 **The apple taken been,**
> the appil taken ben
>> **Never had Our Lady**
>> ne hadde never our lady
>> **The Queen of Heaven been!**
>> a ben hevene quen
>> **Blessed be the time**
>> blissed be the time
>> **That apple was taken;**
>> that appil take was
> 15 **Therefore, we may sing**
> therfore we moun singen
>> **"Deo gratias!"** [Thanks be to God!]
>> deo gracias

Learned "clerkes" [scholars] (l. 6) may debate the haunting question "How can a good and omnipotent God allow so much evil?" but this lyric provides an emotionally consoling folk-theodicy. One would not expect humankind's expulsion from Eden to provide such a happy memory; however, "the tight logic" of this lyric "establishes the basis for joy, and the meter so insists on it, that the listener shares the emotion."[2] The 4,000 (±) years between Adam's death and Christ's resurrection are dark winters when no one went to Heaven, bound by Original Sin to deserved damnation. In addition to meaning a binding cord or strap,[3] "bond" (l. 2) can mean a legal obligation and, more specifically, the Testament of Law.[4] Furthermore, in addition to "wedlock," "bond" can denote "serfdom,"[5] a completely orthodox understanding of class inequity as a postlapsarian evil. The editorial capitalization of "He" (l. 4) prompts a modern reader to think that four millennia is a mere moment on God's stopwatch. But not capitalizing "he" suggests that Adam himself accepted the duration of his deserved suffering and recognized the undeserved joy of its remittance. Stressing the triviality of Adam's sin as merely the eating of an apple emphasizes man's folly, not God's harshness. It is also a happy note in this poem that Eve's culpability as temptress is not mentioned at all; rather, Mary's coronation as Queen of Heaven is celebrated.

Revelry

If "Adam lay I-bounden" promotes a somewhat surprisingly optimistic contentment with the fundamental paradox of humanity's fallen yet redeemed state, the pleasure of performing "I have a gentil cok" [I have a noble cock] derives its naughty joy from an almost mindless celebration of sexual sensation—indeed, it indulges in verbal self-pleasuring, as it were. Its sustained double entendre could be considered a riddle, and such *aenigmata* as "Key" (44) and "Onion" (25) in the Exeter Book[6] provide Old English precedents for this playfully dirty ditty.

> **I have a noble cock**   **that crows for me daily.**
> i have a gentil cok   croweth me day
>   **He causes me to rise early,**   **my matins for to say.**
>   he doth me risen erly   my matins for to say
> **I have a noble cock**   **descended from nobility.**
> i have a gentil cok   comen he is of gret

His coxcomb is of red coral;	his tail is jet black.
his comb is of red corel	his tayel is of jet
5 I have a noble cock	who comes from excellent stock
i have a gentil cok	comen he is of kinde
His comb is of red coral.	His tail is indigo.
his comb is of red corel	his tail is of inde
His legs are azure	so noble and so small.
his legges ben of asor	so gentil and so smale
His spurs are white silver	at the base.
his spores arn of silver white	into the wortewale
His eyes are crystal	encased in amber.
his eynen arn of cristal	loken all in aumber
10 And every night he perches himself	in my lady's chamber.
and every night he percheth him	in min ladyes chaumber

A ribald recitation, or jolly musical setting, for these five long (and rather irregular) couplets would enhance the lyric's wink-wink-nudge-nudge tone. Performance of this lyric enacts the joy of simply being naughty. "Matins" (l. 2)—which of course does not literally mean morning prayers here—may suggest performing this lyric as an impersonation of some stereotypically randy friar. However, Lorrayne Y. Baird-Lange suggests that this "cock" be understood as *gallus praedictor*—that is, a priest symbolically serving as "cock-Christ" (*gallus Christus,* the Awakener): "the priest-cock who performs his matins, and the phallic cock who stirs the priest" who then (supposedly) "puts to flight all other cocks."[7] As with the Exeter Riddles, proposing the mere possibility of an innocent reading is itself part of the dirty joke. Fuller appreciation of such silliness could always be enhanced by a few pints.[8]

And there are several "pour another" drinking songs among the Middle English lyrics, such as "Tapster, fille another ale," which was to be performed as a dizzying "catch" for three voices singing in the round.

Barkeep, pour another pint!
tappster fille another ale
I've just finished.

anonne have i do
God send us a good bargain.
god send us good sale
Profit the ale stake, avail!
avale the stake avale
5   **Here is good ale found.**
here is good ale ifounde
Drink to me and I to thee,
drinke to me and i to thee
And let the goblet go round.
and lette the coppe go rounde

The Middle English "sale" [profit] (l. 3) blends the meaning of "joy" with that of "selling"[9]; if sung with a slur, "ssss ... ale" could also be just a tipsy pronunciation of "ale" or "wassail." The initial imperative "pour" makes explicit this lyric's performative intent by demanding a refill for toasting ... repeatedly.

To be performed after a last call for alcohol, "Here I was and here I drank" provides a rather tipsy adieu to the alewife. Transcribed only as an amusing trifle on the flyleaf of an Irish manuscript, it may have been played in jest as a stereotypical tippler.

Here I was and here I drank.
here i was and here i drank
Farewell, Madame, and many thanks!
farwell dam and mikill thank
Here I was and had good cheer,
here i was and had gud cheer
And here I drank quite good beer.
and here i drank well gud beer

This charming "thank-you" to be sung or recited while departing regrettably refers to "good cheer" entirely in the past tense. The "here I was" repetitions may play with the formulaic expression *hic lacet* [here lies] engraved on a tombstone. Implicit in the departing drinker's compliments to a barmaid—addressing her with rather excessive deference as a "dam"

(l. 2)—is his desire to return "here," making this lyric a valediction forbidding future sobriety.

Such Middle English lyrics that celebrate sensory joy, without any note of its transience, free the animal nature of humanity to dance in spring. Although we still feel "spring fever," it is hard to imagine the ecstasy of singing a reverdie after the depressing grief of a medieval winter, which probably intensified with the start of the "Little Ice Age" (ca. 1300 CE). "Sumer is icumen in" [Late spring has come] has become the best known example of this type of medieval lyric (not in small part because of Ezra Pound's parody, "Ancient Music").

Late spring has arrived.
sumer is icumen in
    Loudly sings [the] cuckoo.
    lhude sing cuccu
    Seed grows and meadow blooms.
    groweth sed and bloweth med
    And the woods blossom anew.
    and springth the wude nu
    Sing "Cuckoo!"
    sing cuccu
5 **Ewe bleats after lamb.**
    ewe bleteth after lomb
    Cow lows after calf.
    lhouth after calve cu
    Bull bucks; buck farts.
    bulluc sterteth bucke ferteth
    Merrily sing "Cuckoo!"
    murie sing cuccu
"Cuckoo! Cuckoo!"
cuccu cuccu
10 **Well may you sing "Cuckoo!"**
    wel singes thu cuccu
    Nor may you ever stop now.
    ne swik thu naver nu
    Sing "Cuckoo!"; now, sing "Cuckoo!"

sing cuccu nu sing cuccu
Sing "Cuckoo!" Sing "Cuckoo!" now!
sing cuccu sing cuccu nu

"Sumer is icumen in" survives from the thirteenth century in BL MS Harley 978 with its musical notation and a Latin *contrafactum*, "Perspice Christocola" (see front cover). Commonly identified as "The Cuckoo Song," this carol, meant to be "sung in canon as a part-song, is perhaps the simplest spring song in English."[10] Like the song of an actual cuckoo, performance of this lyric sounds delightful, but ambiguous, perhaps even ominous. Identifying the occasion of this particular reverdie as "summer" is itself somewhat equivocal. Cuckoos migrate to England in mid-April. Although "sumer" was "variously dated, sometimes including part of spring,"[11] the season of rebirth is by then mostly over. Nevertheless, the singers (and dancers) try to sustain a "now" that "never stops" for as long as physically possible.

Performed as a *rota* or *round* (like "Row, row, row, your boat"), "Sumer is icumen in" permits male and female voices to alternate lyrics (and thereby exchange invitations to sing). Stephen Manning has noted that their joint "exultation in spring moves" stanza by stanza "from the vegetable to the animal to the human level."[12] In stanza 2, the lamb calls for its mother, as the cow (antiphonally) calls for its calf. Meanwhile, the bull and buck are just being boys. Whether "sing cuccu" reports that the cuckoo herself is singing or that everyone is being invited to "Sing 'Cuckoo!,'" the singers impersonate the notoriously naughty bird with incremental intensity.

"Sumer is icumen in" remains a joy to hear but has become a headache to think about. There has been a good deal of relatively trivial back and forth among explicators as to whether "ferteth" (l. 8) means "farts." My country cousins inform me that deer do indeed fart a good deal from eating the fresh greenery of spring, and this lyric's "playful use of" the dominant sound "*cuccu* may be related to the sound voiced in" *farts*.[13] In general, however, most modern readers enjoyed simply playing along with the medieval merriness of this lyric until 1999, when G. H. Roscow offered a revisionist reading. Pretending to be a reverdie, the so-called Cuckoosong "is the wrong bird, the wrong season, and the wrong language for a reverdie, unless an ironic meaning is intended."[14] The prima facie pleasure that a musical performance of the poem has given modern audiences is supposedly a wrongheaded reading. The Middle English verb "swiken" (l. 11), translated as "stop," can also denote "deceive." According to Roscow, any thirteenth-century reader would surely have recognized this carol's admonitory subtext. The exultant, participatory joy of getting dizzy to the poem is utterly subverted by moralist scrutiny. Like the female cuckoo itself, this parody is a "brood parasite" laid amid the genre of the reverdie to kill all its exuberance with a warning of adultery.[15] There is thus a sad proximity between the spellings of "sing" and "sin." I suspect, however, that most medieval participants in the English carol's performance overlooked, because they wanted to ignore as long as possible, the muted warning of its ironic subtext. Roscow's reading of the carol produces, however, a performance of dramatic irony—intended by the author though unrecognized by the actors.

The Latin *contrafactum* "Perspice Christocola," though set to the same musical score as "Sumer is icumen in," hardly seems intended to be performed with the same gusto. It translates:

> Look, O Christian! Behold such magnanimity!
> The heavenly Farmer, because of the vine's defect,
> Not sparing to expose his Son to brutal death,
> Who will give [us] half-alive captives, by means of prayer,
> Life, and Who will crown us with Himself Alone in Heaven.[16]

This *contrafactum* may represent a later effort (probably by a Franciscan) to appropriate the melody for a more sanctified performance by God's *jongleurs*; "St. Francis conceived of his *ioculatores Dei* as preachers who would sing men into the kingdom of Heaven."[17] But there is no evidence that the alternative Latin lyrics are intended to supplant the vernacular song and no need to assume that Franciscans would have been offended by its (unironic) performance. Indeed, the "contra-" [against] in *contrafactum* may suggest too absolute an opposition between these conjoined secular and sacred lyrics. Rather than negating each other, the twin transcription of Latin and vernacular texts presents alternative enactments of mutually honest emotions.

Celebrating Feast Days

The celebration of Christ's nativity sanctioned a good deal of less than pious partying as well. The joy of Christmas carols "designed for group singing in settings of public celebration or conviviality"[18] defies the glumness of winter. The carol "Now is yole comen with gentil chere" [Now Yule has come with noble cheer] is quite simply an invitation to join the caroling. A note in its manuscript specifies that it was composed on 4 October 1500—that is, well ahead of time before its first performance, which allowed time for "we" to rehearse.

    Hay, ay! Hay, ay!
    hay ay hay ay
    Make we as merry as we may!
    make we merie as we may
        Now, Yule has arrived with noble cheer.
        now is yole comen with gentil chere
        Of mirth and game, he has no peer.
        of merthe and gomen he has no pere
5   **In every land where he comes near**
        in every londe where he comes nere
        [There] is mirth and game, I dare well say.
        is merthe and gomen i dar wele say
    Hay, ay! Hay, ay! . . .
        Now is come a messenger
        now is comen a messingere
10   **Of your lord, Sir New Year,**
        of yore lorde ser nu yere
        [Who] bids us all be merry here
        biddes us all be merie here
        And make as merry as we may.
        and make as merie as we may
    Hay, ay! Hay, ay! . . .
15   **Therefore, every man that is here,**
        therefore every mon that is here
        Sing a carol in his own way.

singe a carol on his manere
If he knows none, we shall teach him
if he con non we schall him lere
So that we may be merry always.
so that we be merie allway
20 *Hay, ay! Hay, ay! . . .*
Whosoever makes a serious face,
whosoever makes hevy chere
Were he never so dear to me,
were he never to me dere
I wish he would be in a ditch
in a diche i wolde he were
To dry his clothes till it were day.
to dry his clothes till it were day
25 *Hay, ay! Hay, ay! . . .*
Mend the fire and make good cheer!
mende the fire and make gud chere
Fill the cup, Sir Cupbearer!
fill the cuppe ser botelere
Let every man drink to his mate!
let every mon drinke to his fere
30 **Thus ends my carol, with care away.**
thys endes my carol with care awaye
Hay, ay! Hay, ay! . . .

All five quatrains share the same aaab rhymes, with the final b-rhymes then rhyming with the refrain as well, a sustained consonance that echoes the lyric's call to bond with one another in song. Yule, here personified as the messenger of "Sir" New Year (l. 10), has arrived "Now" with "gentil" (i.e., noble) cheer (l. 1). New Year commands us to welcome as much merriness as possible. Stanza 3 assures that all who are willing to sing shall be included in the celebration. With a rather absurd curse, stanza 4 warns any party-poopers to stay away; they should go try to dry their laundry all night in a muddy ditch. The lyric ends with a toast to merry mates who all sing the chorus once more together "with care awaye" (l. 30).

"And after wyn," as Chaucer's Wife of Bath confesses, "on Venus moste

I thynke" (*Canterbury Tales*, III, 464). Compared with the simple joy of drinking and singing together, enactments of the joy of "lust" in medieval lyrics are often more problematic. Unlike its modern derivative, the Middle English word *lust* more often than not signifies a positive feeling; the noun can signify simply "a feeling of pleasure" or "energetic happiness."[19] It must be acknowledged that chastity (both virginity and marital fidelity) was indeed idealized and that penitentials condemned in vivid detail most other options. In the eyes of the church, sexual pleasure, like all other behavior, was subject to the binary moral divide between salvific *caritas* (αγαπη "selfless love") and damnable *cupiditas* (ερος "selfish love"). Middle English lyricists, however, being more interested in artistry and emotional integrity than soteriology (the theology of salvation), often allowed themselves erotic dispensations.

David C. Fowler has described "All this day Ich han sought" [All this day I have sought] as a carol of "holiday seduction."[20] Also known as "The Serving Maid's Holiday," this lyric primarily enacts the maid's excited anticipation of tonight's carnal pleasure. Since no specific Sunday evening is named in this lyric, it could be performed enthusiastically as part of any *hoolie*—that is, any carnivalesque subversion of social and moral norms.

> *I may not clean flax, nor wind thread on a spool, nor spin,*
> ribbe ne rele ne spinne ic ne may
> *For joy that it is a holiday,*
> for joye that it is holiday
>> **All this day I have sought,**
>> all this day ic han sought
>> **[But] I have not found spindle nor whorl at all.**
>> spindel ne werve ne fond i nought
> 5 **I am brought to so much bliss**
>> to miche blisse ic am brought
>> **In anticipation of this holiday.**
>> agen this highe holiday
> *I may not ...*
>> **Our floor is all unswept,**
>> all unswope is oure fleth
> 10 **And the fire is not stoked up.**
>> and oure fire is unbeth

Our rushes are yet to be reaped
oure ruschen ben unrepe yeth
In anticipation of this holiday.
agen this highe holiday
I may not...
15 **I must fetch the vegetables in,**
ic moste feschen worten in
Gather my kerchief under my chin—
thredele my kerchef under my chin
Dear Jack, lend me a pin
leve jakke lend me a pin
To fasten myself, this holiday.
to thredele me this holiday
20 *I may not...*
Now it's nearing three o'clock,
now it draweth to the none
And all my chores remain undone.
and all my cherres ben undone
I must clean my shoes a little
i moste a lite solas mye schone
To make them soft, this holiday.
to make hem douge this holiday
25 *I may not...*
I must put milk in this pail,
i moste milken in this pail
Roll out this dough. Nuts!
outh me bred all this schail
The dough is still under my nails
yet is the dow under my nail
30 **As I knead this holiday.**
as ic knad this holiday
I may not...
Jack will bring me on my way
jakke wol bringe me onward in my wey
With me desiring to play.
with me desire for to pleye
35 **No fear of my mistress remains in me at all,**

of my dame stant me non eyghe
If [she would expect that I] never [have] a good holiday.
and never a good holiday
I may not . . .
Jack will pay for my share
jacke wol pay for my scoth
40   **On Sunday at the beer festival.**
a sonday atte the alescoth
Jack will souse well my throat
jacke wol souse well my throth
Every good holiday.
every good holiday
I may not . . .
45   **Soon he'll take me by the hand,**
sone he wolle take me be the hand
And he will lay me down upon the ground,
and he wolle leye me on the land
So that all my butt is [covered with] sand
that all my buttockes ben of sand
Upon this high holy day.
upon this hye holiday
50   *I may not . . .*
In he thrust and out he drew
in he pult and out he drow
And all the time I lay below him.
and ever ic lay on him ilow
"By God's death, you do me woe!"
by godes deth thou dest me wow
55   **Upon this high holy day.**
upon this heye holiday
I may not . . .
Soon my womb began to swell
sone my wombe began to swelle
As big as a bell.
as greth as a belle
I dare not tell my mistress

durst i nat my dame telle
What happened to me this holiday.
what me betidde this holiday

Translation erases and silent reading mutes the gleefully spin-dizzy phrasing of the refrain: "Ribbe ne rele ne spinne . . ." Most of this lyric is a checklist of chores not done (l. 22); as such, it may be considered an anti-*chanson de toile* (which were imagined as being sung while weaving linen). With the ringing of the ecclesiastical hours "nones" (l. 21) in mid-afternoon, her imagination has already fast-forwarded to a night out with Jack, her lover (perhaps clerical), whose name seems as generic and unrefined as Tom, Dick, or Harry. This maid does have time to accomplish a little self-service, however: the softening of her own shoes (a suggestive detail that Freudians can footnote).

Stanza 5 sounds frustrated and frantic as the maid struggles to be done with the milk and bread and "schail" [nut shells?] (l. 28). The declaration in stanza 6 "Of my dame stant me non eyghe" (l. 35) boldly voices her own peasant's revolt (a protest that presumably her mistress does not hear). Stanzas 7 and 8, also with blunt candor, disclose the maid's willingness to exchange sex for beer in giggly violation of all propriety. This meretricious detail may seem problematic to modern readers in various ways; it may be interpreted as a satirical jibe by the poet, a caricature of lowborn love, or, a misogynist slam at woman's appetitive nature, her own stereotypical "desire for to pleye" (l. 36). The *handfasting* of line 45 may imply that the Serving Maid presumes some sort of troth-plighting performed by Jack: "sufficiently binding for the betrothal often to be consummated before the church ceremony."[21] Even so, performance of stanza 8 should make the maid (no maiden) sound blissfully ignorant, eager, horny rather than longing, and so a caricature of singing wives in Old French *chansons de toile* who are usually portrayed sympathetically lamenting the absence of a lover, often a husband, but who then are granted a happy ending. A comical performance of this lyric could end here, but the text continues with a dramatically different emotional turn. Whereas all the preceding verbs in "The Serving Maid's Holiday" take the present or future tense, stanza 9's report of the actual *swivening* is in the past tense (l. 52), and the sex-act itself, which was over "ever" fast (l. 53), is reported with trochaic brevity. The tone of "By Godes deth, thou dest me wow" (l. 53) is entirely under the control of the performing "I." The maid's apparently last-minute recollection of the crucifixion may be expressed as a cry of guilt or as a mere nonce phrase for the wordplay of "deth" and "dest." The "wow" done to her may express some belated remorse or the welcome bother of more tipsy sex with John, with "woe" possibly sung or said as a pun on "woo."[22] This ambiguity allows a largely light-headed, so not yet truly remorseful, conclusion to be performed as the maid's final feeling about her festivities—a (now easily offensive) stereotyping of her expression of sham reluctance, the misogyny of which may only be partially mitigated by an alternative, more sympathetic performance of her sincere anxiety in the final stanza.

Similarly, "As I went on Yol day in our procession" re-enacts a merry maid's romantic ruminations—until its very last stanza, which voices a likewise surprising reversal of tone. Until this concluding performance moment, however, there is every reason to enjoy "As I went on Yol day" as a thoroughly light-hearted carol that has little to do with Christmas per se. The lyric is often titled "Jolly Jankyn" because "little John" is named in every stanza. The performing "I" of this lyric, however, is a certain Allison who has little Latin and less prudence.

Until its last stanza, this lyric may be read as "responding to ... the spiritually pressing problem of how to speak correctly (if at all) in church."[23] But it is more a comic dramatization than an admonition.

> "Kyrie!" so "Kyrie!"
> kyrie so kyrie
> **Jankyn sings merrily**
> jankin singeth merie
> **with "Aleison."**
> with aleison
>> As I walked in our Christmas procession,
>> as i went on yol day in our procession
> 5 I recognized jolly Jankyn by his merry musical tone,
>> knew i joly jankin be his mery ton
>>> "Kyrieleison."
>> kyrieleison
> "Kyrie!" so "Kyrie!" ...

10   **Jankyn began the office of the mass on a day in Yuletide**
     jankin began the offis on the yol day
     And yet it seems to me that it does me good—so merrily he did say
     and yet me thinketh it dos me good so merie gan he say
        "Kyrieleison."
        kyrieleison
15   *"Kyrie!" so "Kyrie!" ...*
     Jankyn read the epistle very pleasingly and full well
     jankin red the pistil full fair and full well
     And yet it seems to me that it does me good, as ever I have happiness.
     and yet me thinketh it dos me good as evere have i sell
        "Kyrieleison!"
        kyrieleison
20   *"Kyrie!" so "Kyrie!" ...*
     Jankyn at the "Holy, Holy, Holy" cracked a merry note
     jankin at the sanctus craked a merie note
     And yet it seems to me that it does me good. I paid for his cassock.
     and yet me thinketh it dos me good i payed for his cote
        "Kyrieleison!"
        kyrieleison
25   *"Kyrie!" so "Kyrie!" ...*
     Jankyn creaked one hundred notes all tied together
     jankin craked notes an hundred on a knot
     And yet he hacked them [up] smaller than greens for the pot.
     and yet he hakked hem smaller than wortes to the pot
        "Kyrieleison!"
30   *"Kyrie!" so "Kyrie!" ...*
        kyrieleison
     Jankyn at the "Lamb of God" carried the pax-board,
     jankin at the angnus bered the paxbrede
     He winked but said nothing, and he tread on my foot.
     he twinkeled but said nout and on min fot he trede
        "Kyrieleison"
        kyrieleison
35   *"Kyrie!" so "Kyrie!" ...*
     "Benedicamus Domino!"—**Christ shield me from shame!**

benedicamus domino crist fro schame me schilde
"*Deo gratias,*" **in response—Alas, I am pregnant.**
deo gracias therto alas i go with childe
40 **"Kyrieleison!"**
    kyrieleison
"Kyrie!" so *"Kyrie!"* ...

The seven eleven-syllable[24] couplets of this carol first provide Allison's amusing misunderstanding of Little John's performance of the Latin mass, punctuated by the burden's repetition of the liturgically reiterated Greek "Kyrie eleison" [Lord, have mercy!], which she takes to be John's audible wink to herself as "Aleison." Allison's mishearing of "Kyrie*leison*" (one word in the lyric, eliding a syllabic /e:/) indicates her fundamental misunderstanding of Jankyn's role as a celebrant of the mass. A biblical antecedent for such a misperception may be the mistake made by bystanders at the crucifixion who misinterpret Christ's cry to Eloi (Psalm 22:1) as His calling (in Aramaic) upon Elijah (Matthew 27:46–47; Mark 15:34–36). But the hilarious mishearing of one of the beatitudes from Christ's Sermon on the Mount as "Blessëd are the cheese makers" in Monty Python's *Life of Brian* seems a much closer tonal analogue. And it is easy to assume that Jankyn deliberately misled Allison's understanding of the Latin.

The "I" of this song may be played as a childlike, though not necessarily young, woman in that she is capable of purchasing the priest's "cote" (l. 22). Stanza by stanza, the poem proceeds through the "office" (l. 10) of the Latin mass. Allison clearly enjoys the "sel" [happiness] (l. 18) of Jankyn's recitation of the epistle as entertainment rather than moral instruction. After completing the Liturgy of the Word, his chanting of the *Sanctus* concludes the Preface that initiates the Liturgy of the Flesh. This Latin hymn ("Holy, Holy, Holy Lord, God of Hosts...") is supposed to be more than merely a "merie note" (l. 22); it is a reiteration of the praise of angels for Jesus on the road to the cross (Isaiah 6:3 and Matthew 21:9). Instead, Allison's memory of Jankyn's chanting still gives her a tickle.

In stanza 5, Allison compares the *prestissimo* [very quick tempo] of Jankyn's singing to her own speed at chopping vegetables for soup. Her use of "craken" (ll. 21, 26) to applaud his virtuosity may indicate someone else's (i.e., the poet's) underlying ridicule of such musical extravagance since the verb can also mean to "to fart"[25]; Jankyn's rapid singing ties all the "notes" into a "knot" (l. 25). The flirtatious toe-touching of stanza 6 occurs during the Kiss of Peace, immediately after the Agnus Dei ("Angnus" l. 31), another triple plea for Christ's mercy that Allison likewise mispronounces. The particular irony of this episode is that twinkly Jankyn is circulating the "pax-brede," or pax-board (*osculatorium* or *instrumentum pacis*), which was used specifically during the communal "Kiss of Peace" during mass to avoid the near occasion of sin caused by parishioners' actually kissing one another.

The final stanza bounces between Latin and English half-lines—antiphonally and anti-tonally. If the Gloria is performed (as it should be on Christmas Day), the versicle concluding the mass should be "Ite, missa est." Curiously, no mention of the Gloria is made in this lyric. "Benedicamus domino" [Let us bless the Lord] is a versicle that was used at the end of more penitential masses in which the Gloria has been omitted (i.e., during Advent and Lent).[26] The rote performance of the concluding liturgical exchange in Latin entails a certain role-playing by Jankyn as celebrant and his servers as respondents. But the contrasting, individual, private, lamentable English asides, "Alison herself sings as a *dramatis persona*" a personal plea in response to this formulaic closure: "Crist fro schame me schilde" (l. 37).[27] The Latin response "therto" (l. 38), "Deo grat/cias" [Thanks be to God!], resonates wrongly against the "alas" of her pregnant grief—at which performance moment a sincere cry of "Lord have mercy!" could indeed come into play. The last stanza of this carol seems such a rude surprise, perhaps meant to dramatize Allison's own initial shock at the discovery of her illicit pregnancy, and this outcome aborts all the preceding frivolity. Allison's concluding lament plays against not only the first six stanzas but the joy occasioned by Christ's birth as well. There is a cruel irony to this discord. Maureen Fries observes that "in counterpoint to the Marian *planctus* ... the emphasis lies upon the counter-type of Mary, Eve as represented in the gullibility and weakness of the secular female speaker in contrast to the clerical cleverness of her seducer."[28]

The lyric's amusing characterization of a foolish yet happy Allison seems extremely cruel in retrospect, deliberately so if its male poet anticipated that only his fellow *clerici* would enjoy such macaronic joking at the naïf woman's expense. An emotional determinant of the performance of "As I went on Yol day in our procession" is, of course, its reception context, and John F. Plummer argues that a historicized context—that is, the conventional, medieval audience's perception of such betrayed maiden's lament—need not have been at all sympathetic:

> There is every evidence that sophisticated audiences in England as in Europe enjoyed and cultivated the woman's song in *sermo humilis* [i.e., Cicero's "low" rhetorical style]. The woman who speaks in this poetry enunciates a non-courtly position which, in the case of the English examples, most often involved either a headstrong carnality or a hapless sexual carelessness. Both qualities involve medieval stereotypes and are common features in the sexual jokes of all ages.[29]

To re-enact such a cruel joke, the modern reader must in no way identify with the poem's "I" so that Allison's mistaken merriness can tickle a superior male reader's smirking condescension.

However, Allison's final, vernacular appeal to Christ may also be voiced with embryonic sincerity. J.D.W. Crowther points out this Christmas Day lyric's implicit contrast between two birthdays, "one bringing rejoicing and hope for all sinners, the other shame."[30] The "schame" (l. 38) that Allison expresses could be merely *verecundia*, "the emotion of those who feared exposure to public disapproval ... especially appropriate for women."[31] Yet, the performer of Allison's "I" can alternatively enact true hope that Mary's presumptive Bastard will indeed be forgiving—as, upon reconsideration, should the Christian reader. Meanwhile, it remains easy enough for Jankyn (or a circle of fellow carolers) to skip away singing the last refrain merrily. Once the ephemeral joy of the actual singing ends, the admonitory memory of Allison's experience endures for the carol's female audience.

Wooing Mercy

Carols to be performed by a male "I" frequently want to get a woman, whether common or noble, into trouble. Complimentary love lyrics are meant to seduce; joyful celebrations of a woman's attractiveness are intended to overcome her disdain.[32] Many such Middle English lyrics are burdened with French fashion, and numerous conventions must be played out: love is blind; love is irresistible; love ennobles; love makes you sick, and so on. Romance is redundant. But, when it comes to exuberantly youthful desire, "conventionality" may be a synonym for "reality."

As a unique composite of conventional components, "Bytuene Mersh and Aueril" [Between March and April] starts as a reverdie, becomes a *blazon*,[33] then a complaint, while voicing rhapsodic joy in every refrain. It is commonly titled "Alysoun" on account of the young woman who inspires the performing "I's" both worry and joy.

> **Between March and April,**
> bitweene merch and averil
> **When the boughs begin to spring,**
> when spray biginneth to springe
> **[When] the little birdy has her desire**
> the litel fowl hath hire wil
> **In her loud [voice] to sing,**
> on hire leod to singe
> 5   **[Then] I live in love-longing,**
> ich libbe in lovelonginge
> **For the most beautiful of all creatures.**
> for semlokest of alle thinge
> **She may bring me bliss;**
> heo may me blisse bringe
> **I am bound to her.**
> ich am in hire baundoun
> **A pleasant chance I have gotten—**
> an hendy hap ich habbe ihent
> 10 **I know it is sent to me from heaven.**
> ichot from hevene it is me sent
> **From all [other] women my love is taken,**
> from alle wimmen my love is lent,
> **And alights on Allison.**
> and light on Alisoun
> **Her hair in hue is fair enough,**
> on hew hire heer is fair ynough
> **Her brow brown, her eye black.**
> hire browe browne hire ye blake

15 **With [her] lovely face, she laughs at me,**
   with lossum cheere heo on me lough
   With [her] small and very trim waist.
   with middel smal and wel ymake
   Unless she will take me to herself,
   but heo me wolle to hire take
   To be her own *bae*,
   for to been hire owen make
   I shall forsake living long
   longe to liven ichulle forsake
20 **And, doomed to die, fall down dead.**
   and feye fallen adown
A pleasant chance I have gotten— ...
an hendy hap ...
25 **At night when I twist and turn and stay awake,**
   nightes when i wende and wake
   On account of which my cheeks grow leaden,
   forthy mine wonges waxeth wan
   Lady, all for your sake,
   levedy al for thine sake
   Frustrated desire is fixed on me.
   longinge is ylent me on
   In the world [there] is no smarter person
   in world nis noon so witer man
30 **Who can describe all her beauty:**
   that al hire bountee telle can
   Her throat is whiter than the swan,
   hire swire is whittere than the swan
   And [she is] the fairest girl in town.
   and fairest may in town
35 *A pleasant chance I have gotten— ...*
an hendy hap ...
   Because of wooing, I am entirely exhausted,
   ich am for wowing al forwake
   Weary as water in [the] surf,
   wery so water in wore
   For fear that anyone deprive me of my wife,

lest any reve me my make
40   **[For] I have longed so long.**
ich habbe yyerned yore
It is better to suffer severely for a while
bettere is tholien while sore
Than to mourn forever more.
than mournen evermore
Prettiest one in a dress,
geinest under gore
Listen to my private advice.
herkne to my roun
A pleasant chance I have gotten—...
an hendy hap...

Although the complaint of the last two stanzas of "Bytuene Mersh and Aueril" may more properly belong to chapter 5's survey of lyrics about "love-longinge" (l. 5), the unmitigated joy of its refrain permeates the entire lyric's performance. Everyone loves this early fourteenth-century lyric, by which time the name "Allison" may have already come to suggest "so gay a popelote" (*Canterbury Tales*, I, 3254). The lyric itself has been praised as pretty, simple, excellent, spontaneous, delicious, charming, exuberant, infectious, joyful, and so on—in other words, it is as attractive as Alysoun herself. Its refrain seems an uncomplicated moment of pleasure found among a "local group of secular love poems" that "depict the frenzy of love" all on the same page.[34]

It is primarily the untranslatable exuberance of the refrain's "breathless syntax"[35] that gives this lyric its predominantly jubilant effect—"An hendy hap I habbe ihente." The lyric's consonance allows the reader to feel the "blisse" (l. 7) that its "I" still only hopes to experience. In each stanza, eight lines of trimeters are followed by the bouncy iambs of the four-line refrain, the first three lines of which are tetrameter, closing with a trimeter. Since the eighth line of each of the four stanzas rhymes with the fourth line of the refrain (e.g., ababbbbc dddc)—always alighting on the name of "Alisoun"—the resulting twelve-line melic form may be considered a type of tail-rhyme stanza.

Within the all too brief reverdie of stanza 1, Alysounn appears, among the flora and fowls who sing in their own language, as a superlative creature, "the semlokest [most beautiful] of alle thinge" (l. 6), a fantasy newborn in the annual Eden of the singer's imagination—*Primavera*. The poet's I/eye is bound (l. 8) by his own creation and freely accepts his happy fate. Stanza 2 starts with a four-line, countrified *blazon* that may be considered a type of ekphrasis in which the woman is described as a work of art. Unlike most *blazons*, this poem's brief sighting of Allison avoids hyperbole. Indeed, unlike the blue-eyed blondies favored by aristocratic taste (including Petrarch's), Allison is a black-eyed brunette and "fair enogh" (l. 13). Nevertheless, the singer's complimentary enthusiasm is conventionally intense. The rest of this almost hysterically happy lyric, however, is actually dominated by his anxious groans. Stanza 2 ends with not just a typical expression of fear about dying for love should he be rejected, but with a hint of suicide ("ichulle forsake") as well.

Now recalling his nights, in stanza 3, the insomniac "all for thine sake" would serenade directly his "Levedy" (l. 27). The fourth line of this stanza reverts, however, to third-person references about her highfalutin excellence: her wisdom, her bounty or generosity, her swanlike whitest neck, and superlative beauty—at least, "in toune" [in town rather than in court]. For all this lyric's appealing directness of emotional expression, its final stanza is quite enigmatic—itself a bit of a "roun" [whisper, secret advice] (l. 44). To reiterate his worried sleeplessness, the poet alliterates "w" five times in its first two lines. He has been reduced to a rippling puddle by jealousy for an imaginary rival, it seems. Lines 41 and 42 sound like a handy bromide— "Better to suffer intensely but briefly, than grieve forever"—which seems to serve as a self-addressed bit of encouragement, before his concluding invitation to the "Geynest under gore" or "kindest in a skirt" (a common alliteration). What the "I" actually whispers to Allison alone remains private. One can hope that Allison will be as charmed by his proposal as readers have been by this lyric's refrain ending with her name and so a note of optimism regarding the yet-to-be-achieved transition from love-longing to "blisse" (l. 5). The silence at this song's ending leaves "I" and his audience in-between emotions as well as "bytuene" March and April.

For a more highborn readership, seductive lyrics must (pretend to) be motivated by more genteel feelings, expressed in a more sophisticated style, and "late medieval lyrics are more a manifestation of manners, broadly taken, than of literary inspiration."[36] Charles Duc d'Orléans was the paragon poet of this courtly conventionality and sensibility. When twenty years old, Charles was captured at the Battle of Agincourt and kept under watch for the next twenty-five years in a number of English locales that "might have proved congenial to him"[37] both socially and artistically, especially those "prisons" that provided access to books. He produced two books of lyrics, one in French, the other in English. Upon his return to France, "unfinished, the English manuscript [given the title *Fortunes Stabilnes* by Mary-Jo Arn] stayed behind in England, while the fully decorated French manuscript began a new life in France as an album."[38] The two hundred and eleven English poems in BL Harley MS 682 constitute a unique Middle English volume of collected works by a single lyric poet that A. C. Spearing would rather title "The Duke's Book" since its lyrical sequence offers "written fictions of writing."[39]

Charles's rondel "The smiling mouth, and laughing eyen gray" is a charming tour de force of fourteen pentameter lines with the remarkable rhyme scheme abbaabababab. Charles's formal achievement (albeit relying on reiteration) somewhat challenges Chaucer's notion that, compared with French, "rym in Englissh hath such skarsete."[40] No image in Charles's poem is new, but each is savored.

> **The smiling mouth and laughing grey eyes,**
> the smiling mouth and laughing eyen gray
> **The round breasts, and both long, thin arms,**
> the brestes rounde and long small armes twain
> **The smooth hands, the flanks straight and flat,**
> the hondes smothe the sides streight and plaine
> **Your small feet ... what should I say further?**
> youre fetes lite what shulde i ferther say
> 5 **It is my job, when you are far away,**
> it is my craft when ye are fer away
> **To think thereon in order to diminish my pain.**
> to muse theron in stinting of my paine
> **The smiling mouth and laughing grey eyes,**
> the smiling mouth and laughing eyen gray
> **The round breasts, and both long, thin arms,**
> the brestes rounde and long small armes twain
> **So, I would beg you, if I dare or may,**
> so wolde i pray you if i durste or may
> 10 **The sight [of you] to see as I have seen**

the sight to see as i have seene
Because that art is most delightful for me
forwhy that craft me is most faine
And will be so until the hour in which I die.
and wol ben to the houre in which i day
The smiling mouth and laughing grey eyes,
the smiling mouth and laughing eyen gray
The round breasts, and both long, thin arms.
the brestes rounde and long small armes twain

The meaning of this rondel requires no complex explication; the simplicity of this circlet's expression is immediately accessible—a joyful antidote, "a stinting of my paine" (l. 6). The art is all "craft" (ll. 5, 11). Robert R. Edwards observes that "in the conventional *effictio* [word-portrait] . . . The poet is concerned chiefly with the image as it exists in memory . . . phantasy approaches phantasm, as the vision constituted by his art displaces the figure of lived experience."[41]

The rhyme scheme, if subdivided into significant phrasal units, achieves a mirroring symmetry of the initial and final quatrains: abba ababab baab. However, the assonance of all fourteen accented final vowels in Middle English is so strong that the entire lyric sounds like a cascade of consonance. It begins with a mini-*blazon* (ll. 1–4) that particularizes the beauties of a distant beloved (a quite conventional expression of *l'amour de loin*). Charles's genteel petition to see her again sounds polite to the point of timidity "if I durste or may" (l. 9). Lines 7–8 and 13–14 reprise the recollected stimuli of her features. Curiously, this lyric never refers to the woman as a whole person; she is a sight to see (l. 14). When and since she is "fer away" (l. 5), Charles must be his own Muse (l. 6) inspiring what to say "ferther" (l. 4). His beloved is an image—that is, a memorial fabrication, and it is Charles's own verse that he is most in love with (ll. 11–12).

In "My ghostly father, I me confess," Charles converts the language of regret into a game of joy. The rondel begins with a formulaic expression used to start the sacrament of confession (cf. "Bless me, Father, for I have sinned"). "My ghostly father" may be performed, therefore, as a tongue-in-cheek whisper.

My spiritual father, I confess
my gostly fader i me confesse

    First to God and then to you
    first to god and then to you
    That at a window—do you know how?—
    that at a window wot ye how
    I stole a kiss of great sweetness
    i stale a cosse of gret sweetness
5 **Which was done without premeditation.**
    which don was out aviseness
    But it is done, not [to be] undone now.
    but it is don not undon now
    My spiritual father, I confess
    my gostly fader i me confesse
    First to God and then to you.
    first to god and then to you
    But I shall doubtless make restitution
    but i restore it shall doutless
10 **Again, if so be it that I may,**
    agein if so be that i mow
    And, God, I make a vow
    and that god i make a vow
    If otherwise I ask forgiveness.
    and elles i axe forgefness
    My spiritual father, I confess
    my gostly fader i me confesse
    First to God and then to you.
    first to god and then to you

The Duke's confession of his theft of a kiss is cleverly precise about the requirements for "verray perfit penitence" (cf. *Canterbury Tales*, X, 107–108): contrition of the heart, confession of the mouth, and satisfaction of the hand. He committed the theft "out aviseness" [without advisement] (l. 5), so he is guilty of only a venial sin. His promise to "restore" (l. 9) indicates that he intends to make satisfaction (by the mouth), though his contrition is hardly sincere. The rondel's required triple repetition of "My gostly fader . . ." (ll. 1–2, 7–8, 13–14) seems especially appropriate for this confession of a recidivist kisser.

    Another, more elegant lyric by Charles d'Orléans, "Honure, joy, helthe, and pleasuance," employs the ballade form to declare all good wishes to his beloved, then states his desire to reside in her heart, and concludes with an abject, almost masochistic (if sincere) four-line coda, hoping for his lady's happy reception of both the text and its author.

    Honor, joy, health, and happiness,
    honure joy helthe and plesaunce
        Virtue, abundant riches with good fortune,
        vertu riches abundaunt with good ure
    May the Lord grant you, Who has omnipotence,
    the lord graunt you which hath most puisshaunce
    And to live for many a cheerful year
    and many a gladsom yere for to endure
5   **With the love and praise of every creature,**
    with love and praise of every creature
        And so that my love shall win it all,
        and for my love all prevaile it shall
        I give it to you, so you may be very sure,
        i give it you as be ye very seure
        With heart, body, my little worth and everything.
        with hert body my litel good and all
  And so, not to displease you with my desire,
  and so you not displese with my desire
10   **I would ask you this: that of your grace—**
    this wolde i you biseche that of youre grace
    May it please you, indeed!—to grant me all this year
    it like you lo to graunt me all this yere
    In your heart to have a dwelling place
    as in youre hert to have a dwelling place
    Albeit never so small a space.
    all be it never of so lite a space
    For which, as rent, you shall receive
    for which as this the rente resceive ye shall
15   **My love and service in every case**
    my love and service as in every case
    With heart, body, my little worth and everything.
    with hert body my litel good and all

>   And since it is no injury to you,
>   and sin it is to you no prejudice
> > Seek some little, pretty corner for me
> > sum litel pratty corner sekes me
> > Within your heart, for—by God, indeed, the Judge—
> > within your hert for parde lo justice
> 20 If I offend, you must yourself be [the one]
>   if i offende it must yourselven be
> > To punish [me] as you see fit,
> > to punisshe like as ye the offenses see
> > Because, as for my reputation, I have nothing at all
> > for i as name nor have no thing at all
> > Except what is solely your own in every way
> > but it is soul your owen in eche degree
> > With heart, body, my little worth and everything.
> > with hert body my litel good and all
> 25 Whatsoever you decide, I will obey,
>   what so ye will i will it to obey
> > For punishment or pain, howsoever it befalls me.
> > for paine or smert how so that me bifall
> > Thus, I am yours and shall be till I die
> > so am i youre and shall to that i dey
> > With heart, body, my little worth and everything.
> > with hert body my litel good and all

This ballade retains the by-now centuries-old notion that "fin'amor" both required and revealed a lover's privileged sensibility. Despite the standard pose of humbly admitting his unworthiness—"For I as name nor have no thing" (l. 12)—the duke's initial petition that God grant "you" honor, joy, pleasure, virtue (or power), and abundant riches, all signal the customary behavior of an aristocrat.[42]

"Honure, joy, helthe, and pleasuance" also maintains the traditional *forme fixe* of three eight-line stanzas following the rhyme pattern ababacbc concluding with the hchc quatrain. All five stanzas end with the refrain "With hert, body, my litel good, and all." Rhyming "shall / all," (ll. 6/8, 14/16) may require a bit of a French accent, and "puisshaunce" (l. 3) seems new to English in the fifteenth century, so still somewhat Frenchified.[43] The rhyme-required, so somewhat floating prepositional phrase of line 3 "which hath most puissance" can have a twin antecedent. In my translation, I take it to modify Almighty God, but it can as readily acknowledge that the lady has most power over Charles. Though having "litel good" (as a POW but also as a pose of attractive modesty), Charles offers "all." The climactic (and quite Petrarchan) conceit of the poem—that is, his offer to pay rent to reside in a little corner of the beloved's heart—prompts Charles to volunteer for a happier but unbreakable enclosure "within" (l. 19). If Charles offends or disobeys, he promises to accept [corporal?] punishment by the lady herself: "it must yourselven be / To punisshe" (ll. 21–22), "For paine or smert" (l. 26). I hesitate to suggest that there may be a certain "'Spank me.' 'No, spank me'" playfulness to Charles's excessive submissiveness. In the coda, he more conventionally swears homage to his lady-lord until death. The implicit confidence informing Charles's self-degradation derives from his presumed rapport with the ballade's intended recipient. This duke knows what he's doing.

The anonymous author of "O excellent sovereigne, most semely to sene" likewise displays his verbal virtuosity in an effort to win his desire's *Bel Accueil* [Fair Welcome]. Like several (frequently misogynist) lyrics compiled in the sixteenth-century Welles Anthology, "O excellent sovereigne" exemplifies the "redeployment of fourteenth-century forms and themes in the Tudor period."[44] The extravagant alliteration of this "symple letter" (l. 40)—composed even as the Alliterative Revival is coming to its end—invites solitary appreciation of a text composed for secret seduction.

> **Oh excellent sovereign, most seemly to see,**
> o excellent sovereigne most semely to see
> **Both prudent and pure, like a pearl of [rare] price,**
> both prudent and pure like a perle of prise
> **Also fair of figure and dawning beauty,**
> also fair of figure and oreant of bewtye
> **Both comely and noble, and pleasing to observe.**
> bothe cumlye and gentil and goodly to advertise
> 5 **Your breath is sweeter than mint, sugar or licorice.**
> your brethe is sweeter then balme suger or licoresse
> **I am bold (though I be unable)**
> i am bolde on you thoughe i be not able

To write to your goodly person which is so amiable
to write to your goodly person whiche is so ameable
   By reason.
   by reason
      For you are both fair and free,
      for ye be bothe fair and free
10   **Thereto wise and womanly,**
      therto wise and womanly
      True as turtledove upon a tree
      trew as turtil on a tree
      Without any treason.
      without any treason
Your fair hair hanging down to your knee,
your fair here henging downe to your knee
With your round eyes which are as clear as glass,
with your rolling eyes whiche are as glasse clere
15 **And your strawberry lips as sweet as honey,**
and your strawbery lippes as swete as honye
With rose red in your cheeks—you have no peer.
with rose red in your chekes ye have no pere
Your face is as pleasing as a blossom on the wild rose,
your chere is as comfortable as blossome on brere
And yourself as sweet as is the carnation
and yourselfe as swete as is the gelyfloure
Or any lavender seeds strewn in a basket
or any lavender sedes strawen in a coffer
20   **To smell.**
   to smell
      Your neck like the lily;
      your necke like the lillye
      Your lips like the strawberry,
      your lippes like the strawberye
      As sweet as the honey
      as swete as any honye
      That's put on sale.
      that cumes to sell

25 **Your throat as clear as a crystal gem,**
your throte as clere as cristal stone
Nothing amiss according to my judgment,
nothing amisse after my derection
And your neck as white as ivory
and your neke as white as whales bone
I submit myself, Fair Lady, under your protection.
i submitte me fair ladye under your protection
If I do displease you, I will accept your correction,
if i do you displeise i will abide your correction
30 **Just as the teacher in the school corrects the child.**
like as the master in the scole teches the childe
To do your commandment, I will be meek and mild
to do your commandemente i will be meke and milde
    And still.
    and still
        For the sake of Jesus Who bought us dearly,
        for jesus sake that bought us dere
        And His mother, the maiden pure,
        and his moder that meiden clere
35   **Help to comfort my anxious mood,**
        helpe to comforte my careful chere
        And let me never die.
        and let me never spill
Your love, Fair Lady, I would eagerly win.
your love fair ladye i wolde feyne winne
There is nothing in this world might please me so well.
there is nothing erthely might me so well please
Wherefore I pray God before I begin
wherfore i pray god or that i beginne
40 **That my simple writing does not displease you,**
that my simple writing do you not displeise
For I am not to blame that I do praise you,
for i am not to blame that i do you prease
Oh rubicund rose, oh lily most delicious,
o rubicounde rose o lillye most deliciouse
Splendid in beauty as a diamond most precious

    splendant in bewtye as a diamond most preciouse
        In sight.
        in sight
45   **Your bright, resplendent face,**
        your bright fulgent face
        Entirely full of grace,
        replete full of grace
        And your goodly pace,
        and your goodly pace
        Makes my heart light.
        makethe my harte light
    Your love I desire without any denial;
    your love i desire without any negation
50 **If I could have it, then I would be joyful,**
    if i might it have then wolde i be feyne
    Wherefore I pray you, without changeableness,
    wherfore i pray you without vareation
    Your whole opinion, you will it write back to me.
    your whole minde ye will write to me ageine
    If it be good, then I would be happy,
    if it be good then wolde i be feine
    And, as long as I live, [I would] be obedient to you
    and ever whiles i live to you be obedient
55 **To fulfill your commandment as your humble servant**
    to fulfill your commandement as your humble servaunt
        Forever!
        forever
            And never exchange you for anyone new,
            and never to change you for no newe
            But daily sue for your grace;
            but daily for your grace to sue
        Therefore, Sweetheart, to me be true,
        therfore swetharte to me be trew
60   **For I am at your pleasure.**
        for i am at your plesure
    In this way, at this time, this bill shall be concluded,
    thus at this time this bill shall be concluded

The more briefly to make an end,
the more brefely for to make an ende
I trust truly I shall not be poorly used
i trust verely i shall not be ill usede
By you, to whom this simple letter I send.
of you to whome this simple letter i sende
65 **To continue loving, this I intend,**
with love to continue this i entende
And so I trust that you want the same.
and so i trust that ye will the same
Christ keep us both from bodily hurt and shame
criste kepe us bothe from bodely hurte and shame
    Always.
    alway
        Adieu, farewell, My Sweet,
        adeu farewell my swete
70   **Till that we meet later**
        till efte that we mete
        My heart you have in keeping,
        my harte ye have to kepe
        By God that made this day.
        by god that made this day

Explicitly identified as a "bill" (l. 61), "O excellent sovereigne, most semely to sene" actually does approximate the five-part progress of a formal letter. Stanza 1 offers a somewhat aureate salutation to the sovereign lady. Its initial "perl of prise" (l. 2) simile alludes both to the tradition of French marguerite poems and to Christ's pearl of great price parable (Matthew 13:45–46). The sensuous praise of stanza 2 and the first four lines of stanza 3 woos her favor; the rest of stanza 3 is a brief narrative of his submission to her tutelage as his would-be "maister" [*magister* or teacher] (l. 30). Stanzas 4 and 5 request first her love and then, at the very least, a letter in reply; the last stanza ends the letter with a hopeful farewell. The humility topos—that is, pretending to be "not able" to write while fearing he is "bolde" (l. 6) even to try—is itself part of the poem's conspicuous craft(iness). Formally intricate, this intimate lyric is nevertheless an emotionally uncomplicated and optimistic expression of desire.

In addition to the sustained alliteration of the lines themselves, each of the lyric's six twelve-line stanzas conjoins the seven-line ababbcc rhyme scheme of Chaucer's rhyme royal to a *deeed* "bob-and-wheel"—a type of formal closure to a verse paragraph most familiar from *Sir Gawain and the Green Knight*. Punctuated with a pause, the bob acquires special emphasis, and the sequence of words so stressed in this poem is intriguing: after "reason" (l. 9), three sensory words—"smell" (l. 20), "hearing" ("still," l. 32), and "sight" (l. 45)—precede "forever" (l. 56) and finally "alway" (l. 68). Strong stress also encourages consideration of the semantic pairing of each bob with its wheel's concluding rhyme: "reason/treason, smell/sell, sight/light, forever/pleasure, alway/day." The repetition of "feyne" [happy, eager] in stanza 5 as an exact rhyme (ll. 50 and 53) may seem a bit of a cheat but actually amplifies the parallelism of the two lines.[45]

The *blazon* of stanzas 2 and 3 reinforces the poet's conventional delight in visual details with exceptional stimuli of taste and "smell" (l. 20). The genuine pleasure of strawberry lips or the lady's breath—sweeter than mint,[46] sugar, or licorice—plays against the predominantly abstract compliments of stanza 1: "excellent sovereign, prudent, pure, fair, goodly, womanly." The metaphor comparing her lips to honey *for sale* is rhyme-required and probably innocent, with no hint of bartering; on the contrary, the lady is "free" (l. 9)—that is, noble and generous.

Nevertheless, within this wooing petition, there are several possible double entendres. "Careful chere" (l. 36) can simply mean "sorrowful face" but looks oxymoronic ("sad cheer"). "And let me never spill" (l. 36) can simply mean that "I'll die if you don't love me"—a common hyperbole. Chaucerians, however, who are inclined to find dirty puns everywhere, would note that "spillen" ("to flow") can mean "to ejaculate." The use of *you*-pronouns throughout this lyric maintains the writer's unrequited distance from his sovereign; his farewell "Till *efte* that we meet" (l. 70), however, may include a slip of the pen in that "again" implies some previous (perhaps intimate) exchange; indeed, "meet" can mean "to have sexual intercourse."[47] The elliptical phrasing of "Your love I desire without any negation / If I might it have ..." (ll. 49–50) could be quite innocent ("There's no denying I want your love") or presume that she is only a girl who can't say no. In any event, the poet's closing request for a return letter is probably a mere metonymy for the true favor he wishes in exchange for this lyric. In the conventional periphrasis of courtly love language, he desires her "mercy"—that is, her consent. Although purportedly intended to be read as a private letter, "O excellent sovereigne, most semely to sene" also serves as a display poem intended to be performed and so shared with other readers or listeners—most immediately, confidantes of the recipient, but also for posterity—as conspicuous evidence of the author's poetic talent and so erotic worthiness.[48]

Venerating Mary

Lyrics expressing joyful devotion to the Blessed Virgin Mary purify all this desire for feminine mercy, transcending heterosexual appetite. Although a precise theological distinction can be maintained between such veneration properly due to the saints and the adoration due to God alone, the emotion of passionate lyric devotion is often impossible (and undesirable) to measure. As Douglas Gray explained, "'Affective' devotion appeals to the emotions and the will rather than to the logical and speculative powers of the intellect; it is not necessarily anti-rational, though it may become so."[49]

Some lyrics of admiration for Mary, like "I-blessed be thou lady full of heaven bliss," simply amplify the praise of Gabriel (Luke 1:28) and Elizabeth (Luke 1:42)—most familiarly conjoined in the "Hail Mary"—to create a sacred serenade.[50] Some plead for intercession, like "Now shrinketh rose and lily flower." Some, like "I saw a fair maiden sitten and sing," serve as lullabies offering maternal consolation—often by instructing the child to sympathize with Mary's own grief as in "As I lay upon a nilit." Many seem exquisitely simple, like "I sing of a maiden that is makeles," which Stephen Manning considers "the supreme achievement of the Middle English religious lyric."[51] Rosemary Woolf thought "I sing of a maiden" an early example of the English lyric exploiting imagery for emotional impact, a poem that should be appreciated for "its exquisite imagination, whereby an originally logical image has been transformed into one conveying the mystery, simplicity, and beauty of the manner of Mary's conception."[52] This poem seems a straightforward love song; yet "for all its delicacy of touch and deep personal feeling, that poem was firmly rooted in the worship and the teaching of the Church about Mary."[53]

> **I sing of a maiden**
> i sing of a maiden
>   **Who is matchless.**

that is makeles
   The King of all Kings
   king of alle kinges
   She chose to be her Son.
   to here sone she ches
5 **He came as silently**
   he cam also stille
   Where His mother was
   ther his moder was
   As dew in April
   as dew in aprille
   That falls on the grass.
   that falleth on the gras
   He came as silently
   he cam also stille
10 **To His mother's bower**
   to his moderes bowr
   As dew in April
   as dew in aprille
   That falls on the flower.
   that falleth on the flour
   He came as silently
   he cam also stille
   Where His mother lay
   ther his moder lay
15 **As dew in April**
   as dew in aprille
   That falls on the branches.
   that falleth on the spray
   Mother and maiden,
   moder and maiden
   There was never any other than she.
   was never non but she
   Well may such a lady
   well may swich a lady
20 **God's mother be.**
   godes moder be

To acknowledge the obvious, it should be noted that "I sing of a maiden" is a eulogy *about* Mary, not—as is more common among the Middle English lyrics—a hymn of praise or a prayer of petition addressed *to* her (e.g., "Hail our patron and Lady of the earth," which offers a loose vernacular adaptation of the "Salve Regina").[54]

An early fifteenth-century transcription of "I sing of a maiden" formats the poem as five decasyllabic couplets, but it is commonly printed as pentasyllabic quatrains rhyming abab with the first and third lines of stanzas 2, 3, and 4 sharing the same rhyme because of phrasal repetition. This apparent simplicity cloaks—or allows emotional access to—the doctrinal suggestiveness of this song. Stephen Manning perceived a tripartite structure to the lyric progressing from stanza 1, through stanzas 2 to 4, then stanza 5.[55] The lyric begins and ends with "I" singing solo praise for the uniqueness of "she"; the three stanzas in between, focus on "He." Although the immediate antecedent of "He" (l. 5) is Jesus, the dew of April is "commonly used in the liturgy as a symbol of the Incarnation" based upon biblical passages such as Judges 6: 36–37.[56] Specifically, the Hebrew Bible's references to "dew" were often read as prefiguring the Holy Spirit (e.g., Hosea 14:5–7; cf. the Nicene Creed's "Et incarnatus est de Spiritu Sancto ex Maria Virgine"). So less literally, more spiritually—that is, in terms of medieval exegesis rather than pronominal agreement—the triple referencing of "He" rather than "They" invites recognition of Christ's birth as the result of Mary's wooing by the Triune God; so, too, "the threefold occurrence of the dew image ... has doctrinal significance ... the operation of the Trinity."[57]

The twin significance of the epithet "makeles" [without a match / without a mate] (l. 2) in the first stanza is commonplace: the Blessed Virgin Mary is both "without a peer" and "virginal." John Speirs has suggested an association of the word "makeles" with "maskelles" (cf. *Pearl*, l. 780) that would recognize Mary as Immaculate.[58] Yet, there is also a serenade-like, so quasi-erotic allure to this lyric. Analogously, visual representations of the Annunciation frequently pose Gabriel as a wooer at Mary's window. Like every lady-love in the *fin'amor* tradition, Mary is *sans pareil*, beautiful without equal in the eye of the Divine Beholder. Sarah Stanbury finds that "the shock of the poem lies in its eroticizing of incest as a trope for the holy."[59] Indeed, the repetitions of "stille" (ll. 5, 9, 13) can suggest the stealth of a lover's approach. Here, the amorous idiom seems a deliberate misdirection meant to revive what should be the greater shock of too familiar doctrinal paradoxes, such as the Trinity, the God-Man, and the Virgin-Mother. As song, "I sing of a maiden" can be thoroughly appreciated as a passionate performance, and that is a sufficient emotional experience. However, its metonymically erotic representation of the relationship between Jesus and Mary also offers a whispered hint of more profound, indeed incomprehensible, love affairs between God and Mankind, including the divine carnality of the Incarnation, as well as consumption of the body of Christ in the Eucharist. The primary artistic shock of "I sing of a maiden" is the paradox of its simultaneous simplicity and complexity—like that of the Virgin Mother herself.

The most startling statement of the first stanza is that Mary chose Jesus to be her Son rather than the other way around—that is, the normative notion that God chose Mary to be Christ's mother. The free consent of Mary to being impregnated is here conceived to be a salvific necessity and the basis for Mary being praised (rather too enthusiastically for many post-Reformation readers) as Co-Redemptrix.[60] This simple yet highly nuanced iteration of Mary's uniqueness as Virgin Mother heralds acknowledgment of her singular worthiness to be the *Theotokos* (l. 20, "Godes moder") and Queen of Queens, the "lady" (l. 19) beside the "King of alle kinges" (l. 3).[61] Her alpha and omega stanzas of praise thus embrace the central three stanzas that catalogue three salvific arrivals by her Son: the Annunciation, the Nativity, and the Transubstantiation—a reading of the lyric's subtext that requires substantive glossing but may be unnecessary to appreciate its immediate emotional impact.

Each of the three central stanzas repeat the same "dew in Aprille" simile to suggest the stillness of Christ's arrival and require only the slightest phrasal variation to accommodate differing rhymes for the dew's differing manifestations: ("was/gras"; "bowr/flour"; "lay/spray"): "Images of grass, flower, and spray. Each is a simile for the Virgin."[62] It is sufficiently moving to recognize, as Raymond Oliver has, that the "imperceptible, refreshing" arrival of dew provides a natural detail that "we still find lovely" as well "a flawlessly apt metaphor" for Christ's virgin birth.[63] The dew being sighted on grass, then flower, then treetop may seem so straightforward as to be insignificant. In the simplest sense, it is an ascending catalogue from ground to leafy branch, which connotes "a symbol of victory" (MED s.v. "sprai" def. 1a).

So, too, the slight variation of the places to which "He" comes may signify more than appears at first sight. Sarah Appleton Weber has observed that the locales change (almost imperceptibly): the first is unspecified;

the bower provides a setting for Christ to approach "as lover," yet "Mary's enclosure came to symbolize the necessary intactness of her womb, her unassailable virginity";[64] and the third locale reflects frequent thirteenth- and fourteenth-century depictions of "Mary reclining at the birth of Christ."[65] The stillness of all three stanzas preserves the silence of the Holy Spirit's coming and the painlessness of Mary's giving birth, "appropriate to . . . the silent night of Christmas eve."[66]

The dew was also interpreted as a prefiguration of the Annunciation, celebrated on 25 March (i.e., nine months before Christmas); Michael Steves explains "Since 25 March was commonly referred to as eight days from the Kalends of April in the Middle Ages, repeated references to April in the poem would seem to be appropriate."[67] The image of dewfall as a foreshadowing of the Incarnation was familiar throughout the Middle Ages as the versicle and response performance of "Rorate coeli" [Drop down dew, ye heavens, from above] (Isaiah 45:8), retrospectively interpreted as the prophet's longing for Christ's First Coming. Liturgical use of this biblical verse is associated with both Advent and the Annunciation as well. So, in a number of senses, the dew "refers to the coming of the Holy Spirit."[68]

The simile also alludes to the dew that leaves behind the life-saving manna for God's Chosen People in the desert (Exodus 16:13–15). Whereas the burning bush foreshadows the Virgin Birth of Christ,[69] the dew and manna prefigure the Eucharist as "panis quem dedit Dominus vobis ad vescendum" [bread that the Lord gave you to eat]. Indeed, repetition of the phrase "like the dewfall" occurs as early as the third century in the Anaphora of Hippolytus (incorporated into the Anaphora of the Apostolic Tradition) and remains in the *epiclesis* (the pre-consecration invocation of the descent of the Holy Spirit) of the Second Eucharistic Prayer: "Make holy, therefore, these gifts, we pray, by sending down your Spirit upon them like the dewfall." This invocation invites the Holy Spirit to transubstantiate the bread and wine into the Real Presence of Christ.

All these rather elusive allusions implied by the simple surface of this lyric affirm that a priest, Mary-like, gives birth to Christ's flesh and blood in the sacrifice of the Mass—the Real Presence. Nevertheless, despite all this implicit complexity, Stephen Manning, though providing two more annotations showing that this simple lyric also includes a learned pun on the Aramaic *maria* ("lady") and that the number of its five stanzas itself also symbolizes Mary, perceived that the true "greatness" and enduring emotional appeal of "I sing of a maiden that is makeles" derives from its immediate "freshness and simplicity."[70]

Adoring Jesus

For the medieval heart, the joy of loving Mary can be excelled only by the bliss of receiving Jesus's love. Multiple versions of the lyric "Swete Jesu, king of bliss," ranging from three to fifty stanzas, testify to the immediate appeal of this adaptable hymn. These Middle English adaptations are based upon a twelfth-century Latin hymn "Iesu dulcis memoria" [Jesus the Sweet Memory of You], authorship of which was attributed to St. Bernard of Clairvaux, though it may have been composed by a Benedictine nun. Versions of the Latin hymn range from forty-two to fifty-three stanzas. Sections of this hymn are chanted on the Feast of the Holy Name of Jesus (usually 1 January): "Iesu dulcis memoria" (Vespers), "Iesu rex admirabilis" (Matins), "Iesu decus angelicum" (Lauds).

Siegfried Wenzel identifies "Swete Jesu, king of bliss" as an "expandable" lyric:

> What these expandable lyrics have in common besides their formlessness is their concentration on the speaking persona. They are not concerned with events of salvation history, whether it is Christ's Passion or Mary's joys or her intercession, but instead focus on a penitent 'I' who—it is not unfair to say—wallows in generalities.[71]

All versions of the Middle English lyric are composed in mono-rhymed quatrains with trimeter odd lines and tetrameter even lines. This "common meter" closely approximates the octosyllabic mono-rhymed quatrains of the original Latin (and so can be sung to much the same musical settings). "Swete Jesu, king of bliss" is thus a remarkable exercise in form-to-form translation:

[The memory of sweet Jesus (or, the sweet memory of Jesus)]
Iesu dulcis memoria   swete jhesu king of blisse
[giving the heart true joy]
dans vera cordis gaudia   min herte love min herte lisse
[but beyond honey and all things]

sed super mel et omnia   thou art swete mid iwisse
[His sweet presence (or, the presence of sweet Him).]
eius dulcis praesentia.   wo is him that thee shall misse

The early fourteenth-century BL Harley MS 2253 version of "Swete Jesu, king of bliss" begins with the same first three stanzas that comprise the entire thirteenth-century Oxford MS Bodleian 1687 version, and so both start with an expression of childlike delight. The Harley version then adds twelve more stanzas, all passionately reiterating the initial vocative to "Sweet Jesus."

    Sweet Jesus, King of Bliss,
    swete jesu king of blisse
        My heart's love, my heart's joy,
        min herte love min herte lisse
    You are sweet for sure.
    thou art swete mid iwisse
    Woe is he who loses You.
    wo is him that thee shall misse
5   **Sweet Jesus, my heart's light,**
    swete jesu min herte light
    You are day without night.
    thou art day withoute night
    You gave me strength and also might
    thou geve me streinthe and eke might
    To love You properly.
    for to lovien thee aright
    Sweet Jesus, my heart's salvation,
    swete jesu min herte bote
10 **Plant in my heart a root**
    in min herte thou sete a rote
    Of Your love that is so sweet
    of thy love that is so swote
    And grant that it may bloom.
    and leve that it springe mote
    Sweet Jesus, my heart's radiance,
    swete jesu min herte gleem
        Brighter than the sunbeam,

brightore then the sonnebeem
15 **You Who were born in Bethlehem**
ibore thou were in bedleheem
Make me here Your sweet song.
thou make me here thy swete dreem
Sweet Jesus, Your love is sweet.
swete jesu thy love is swete
Woe is he who will depart from You.
wo is him that thee shall lete
Grant me grace to welcome
gif me grace for to grete
20 **Wet tears for my sins.**
for my sinnes teres wete
Sweet Jesus, King of the world,
swete jesu king of londe
Make me understand
thou make me fer understonde
So that my heart can discover
that min herte mote fonde
How sweet Your love-yoke is.
how swete beth thy lovebonde
25 **Sweet Jesus, my lord,**
swete jesu louerd min
My life, my heart, everything is Yours.
my lif min herte all is thin
Undo my heart and enter in
undo min herte and light therin
And protect me from the Devil's trickery.
and wite me from fendes engin
Sweet Jesus, my soul's food,
swete jesu my soule fode
30 **Your deeds are both sweet and good,**
thin werkes beth bo swete and gode
You redeemed me upon the cross.
thou boghtest me upon the rode
For me, You shed Your blood.
for me thou sheddest thy blode

Sweet Jesus, I am heartily sorry [for]
swete jesu me reoweth sore
    The sins that I have formerly committed;
    gultes that i ha wroght yore
35   **Therefore, I beg your pardon and forgiveness.**
    tharefore i bidde thin milse and ore
    Mercy, Lord! I want nothing else.
    mercy lord i nul namore
Sweet Jesus, Lord God,
swete jesu louerd god
    You ransomed me with Your blood—
    thou me boghtest with thy blod
    Out of your heart rushed the flood.
    out of thin herte orn the flod
40   **Your mother, who stood by You, saw it.**
    thy moder it segh that thee by stod
Sweet Jesus, bright and glorious,
swete jesu bright and shene
    I pray that You hear my petition
    i preye thee thou here my bene
    Through the intercession of the Queen of Heaven,
    thourgh ernding of the hevene quene
    So that Your love may be seen within me.
    that thy love on me be sene
45 **Sweet Jesus, best human being,**
swete jesu berne best
    With You I hope to have rest;
    with thee ich hope habbe rest
    Whether I be in the south or the west,
    whether i be south other west
    May Your help be nearest to me.
    the help of thee be me nest
Sweet Jesus, well may he be
swete jesu well may him be
Who may see You in bliss.
    that thee may in blisse see
With ropes of love draw me

>   with lovecordes drawe thou me
> **So that I may come and live with You.**
>   that i may comen and wone with thee
> **Sweet Jesus, King of Heaven,**
>   swete jesu hevene king
> **Fairest and best of everything,**
>   feir and best of alle thing
> **Bring me out of this longing**
>   thou bring me of this longing
> **To come to You at my death.**
>   to come to thee at min ending
> **Sweet Jesus, everyone's wisdom,**
>   swete jesu all folkes reed
> 50 **Grant before we die**
>   graunte us er we buen ded
> **To receive You in the form of bread**
>   thee underfonge in fourme of bred
> **So that then You may lead us to heaven.**
>   and sethe to heovene thou us led

The speaker's self-references all use the first-person singular pronoun ("I/me/my") until the final stanza's prayer for "us" with the antecedent "all folkes" (l. 57). However, as with recital of the Creed, even "I" can be voiced by many voices in concord. Christ is addressed exclusively by means of the second-person singular or familiar pronoun, "Thou," which seems especially appropriate as an indication of this lyric's intimacy with God.

There is a childlike innocence—the kind that Jesus welcomed (Matthew 18:3, Mark 10:15, Luke 18:17)—to the lyric's opening. The first three stanzas sound almost like a nursery rhyme—a bedtime song, perhaps a mother's solo. Stanzas 4 to 8 sustain a focus on the sweetness of Jesus adored as all light and loving and joyful and healing and hopeful. But, following the Latin, there are shifts in tonal register as the poem moves from the "swete dreem" (l. 16) of the Nativity—the "song" and "dream" and "vision" and "joy"[72] of Christ's birth—through regret and petition to a joyful-again hope for salvation after death. Baffled by the cursed "wo" (l. 18) of anyone who would turn from the joy of Jesus, the "I" happily welcomes that redemptive "teres wete" (l. 20) of recognizing one's own sinfulness.

Before explicitly pleading for "Mercy" (l. 36), stanzas 6–8 affirm Christ's unfathomable "swete love-bonde" (l. 24) that guarantees the soul's escape "from fendes engin" (l. 28). The sweetness of this love-bond recalls "iugum enim meum suave est et onus meum leve est" [For my yoke is sweet and my burden light] (Matthew 11:30). An emotional pivot to compassionate grief occurs in the lyric, however, with the mention of Christ's Crucifixion that "boghtest" [purchased] (ll. 32, 38) all this forgiveness. Stanza 9 juxtaposes the sinner-I's own former "guiltes" to Christ's constant "milse and ore" [mercy and forgiveness] (ll. 34–35). Stanza 10 briefly visualizes the sight of Mary at the foot of the cross, which should be mirrored by the emotional pose that the "I" aspires to achieve "That Thy love on me be sese" (l. 44). So moved, stanza 11 attributes the conventional praise of a lady "bright and shene" (l. 41) to crucified Jesus. The promise of Mary's intercession in stanza 11 assures hope everywhere on earth in anticipation of Christ's heavenly "blisse" (l. 50). "At my ending" (l. 56)—of life, as well as of the poem—the lyric "I" reprises delighting in superlative praise of sweet Jesus. This final stanza transubstantiates the figural sense of Christ as "my soule fode" (l. 29; i.e., "inspiration," "grace," etc.) into His Real Presence "in fourme of bred" (l. 59), the literal Eucharist, more specifically, the *viaticum* of the Last Rites "er we buen ded" (l. 58). Sincere performance of this lyric makes the emotional experience of reading itself a "swete dreem."

The lyric enactment of joy should produce the audience's resonant (yet temporary) achievement of actual joy insofar as performance occupies moments of reality. And, solely in terms of experiencing concurrent joy on first hearing, I would again defend the immediate accessibility of many Middle English lyrics as a performance strategy. However, an emotionally much richer appreciation of the devotional simplicity of Middle English lyrics like "I sing of a maiden" or "Sweet Jesu king of bliss" has been provided by St. Theresa of Avila, who felt "The closer one approaches to God, the simpler one becomes." Sadly, for some reason—perhaps inevitable suffering or philosophical skepticism or the Fall—it has become difficult to sound content with current happiness and sophisticated at the same time. This intellectualized distrust of simple joy is hardly new: "cor sapientium ubi tristitia est et cor stultorum ubi laetitia" [The heart of the wise is where there is mourning, and the heart of fools where there is mirth] (Ecclesiastes 7:5). The emotional confrontation with sorrow, to be considered next, is only intensified when set in relief to these medieval moments of performed joy.

FOUR

Playing Sad or Mad

> Turne all thy mirth and musik in murning
> [Turn all your joy and music into mourning]
>
> Robert Henryson, *Orpheus and Eurydice* (l. 135)

Untroubled by the complexities of Aristotle's *Poetics*, the medieval understanding of "tragedy" was simply an emotional fall from *gaudium* into *tristia*, joy into sadness. For Middle English lyricists, there was no critical imperative to analyze the plot causality of "true tragedy" as the ineluctable result of a protagonist's *hamartia* [tragic flaw]. As an emotional occasion for poetic performance, it is sufficient to accept that sadness simply happens. The pleasure of sharing an expression of such sadness is too complicated to explain, yet common to experience. Perhaps, it is sufficient to recognize that the lyric performance of unpleasant feelings is fictional and, in terms of medieval theorizing, such "fictions bring delight, alleviate tedium and anxiety, and induce joy."[1] The enactment of negative feelings by Middle English lyrics, though representing unpleasant experiences as such, teaches or heals—providing both harsh thematic lessons and hard emotional medicine, the earnest means to some therapeutic (i.e., cathartic) or didactic (e.g., admonitory) end. Unlike lyrics expressing compassion for another person's sorrow (to be considered in the next chapter), the following lyrics either vent an "I's" distress or admonish the reader as "you."

Grumblings

A harangue posing as a farewell-lyric (actually more of a good-riddance carol) is "With pacience thou has us fed." In it, a reluctant (so normal) layman, forced to abstain and fast throughout Advent, rages against this unnecessarily redundant distress because "It is enough to faste in Lente"

(l. 41). All but the last stanza of these fifteen mono-rhymed tercets shout resentment—the first word of each refrain, "Farewele," could be translated "Get out!" The lyric's mock outrage offers a release of real aggravation.

Farewell, Advent! Christmas has come.
farewele advent cristemas is cum
Farewell from us, both one and all.
farewele fro us both alle and sume
    With patience you have fed us,
    with paciens thou hast us fedde
    And made us go hungry to bed.
    and made us go hungrie to bedde
5 **For lack of meat we were nearly dead.**
   for lak of mete we were nighe dedde
Farewell from us, both one and all.
farewele fro us both alle and sume
    While you have been within our house,
    while thou haste be within oure house
    We ate no desserts nor any sauce,
    we ete no puddinges ne no souce
    But stinking fish not worth a louse.
    but stinking fisshe not worthe a louce
10 **Farewell from us, both one and all.**
   farewele fro us both alle and sume
    There was no fresh fish, neither far nor near;
    there was no fresshe fisshe ferre ne nere
    Salted fish and salmon were too expensive,
    salt fisshe and samon was too dere
    And thus we have had heavy cheer.
    and thus we have had hevy chere
Farewell from us, both one and all.
farewele fro us both alle and sume
15   **You have fed us with thin flatfish—**
    thou hast us fedde with plaices thinne
    Nothing on them but skin and bone.
    nothing on them but bone and skinne

> **Therefore, you will not win our love.**
> therfore oure love thou shalt not winne
> **Farewell from us, both one and all.**
> farewele fro us both alle and sume
> **With mussels, gaping at the moon,**
> with muskilles gaping afture the mone
20 **You have fed us at night and noon**
> thou hast us fedde at night and none
> **Only once a week—and that too soon.**
> but ones a wyke and that too sone
> **Farewell from us, both one and all.**
> farewele fro us both alle and sume
> **Our bread was brown; our ale was thin.**
> oure brede was browne oure ale was thinne
> **Our bread was musty in the bin.**
> oure brede was musty in the binne
25 **Our ale sour before we did begin.**
> oure ale soure or we did beginne
> **Farewell from us, both one and all.**
> farewele fro us both alle and sume
> **You are completely thankless,**
> thou art of grete ingratitude
> **To exclude us from good meat.**
> good mete fro us for to exclude
> **You are not kind but very rude.**
> thou art not kinde but verey rude
30 **Farewell from us, both one and all.**
> farewele fro us both alle and sume
> **You live with us against our will,**
> thou dwellest with us agenst oure wille
> **And yet you did not give us our fill.**
> and yet thou gevest us not oure fille
> **For lack of food you would kill us.**
> for lak of mete thou woldest us spille
> **Farewell from us, both one and all.**
> farewele fro us both alle and sume

35   **Above everything, you are a means**
     above alle thinge thou art a meane
    To make our cheeks both bare and lean.
     to make oure chekes bothe bare and leane
    I would you were [away] at Boughten-Under-Blean!
     i wolde thou were at boughton bleane
Farewell from us, both one and all
farewele fro us both alle and sume
    Come no more here to Kent
     come thou no more here nor in kent
40   **For, if you do, you shall be hurt**
     for if thou do thou shalt be shent
    It is enough to fast for Lent!
     it is enough to faste in lent
Farewell from us, both one and all.
farewele fro us bothe alle and sume
    You may not stay with any estate.
     thou maist not dwelle with none eastate
    Because you played "Checkmate!" with us [all],
     therfore with us thou playest chekmate
45   **Go away or we will break your skull.**
     go hens or we will breke thy pate
Farewell from us, both one and all.
farewele fro us both alle and sume
You may not dwell with knight or squire—
     thou maist not dwell with knight nor squier
As for them, you can [go] lie in the swamp.
     for them thou maiste lie in the mire
They don't love you nor Lent, your lord.
     they loe not thee nor lent thy sire
Farewell from us, both one and all.
farewele fro us both alle and sume
    You may not dwell with laborers,
     thou maist not dwell with labouring man
    For, on your diet, he can do no craft
     for on thy fare no skille he can
    Because he must eat both now and then.

  for he must ete bothe now and than
50 **Farewell from us, both one and all.**
  farewele fro us both alle and sume
   Although you shall dwell with monk and friar,
   though thou shalt dwell with monke and frere
   Canon and nun once every year,
   chanon and nonne ones every yere
   Nevertheless you should make us better cheer.
   yet thou shuldest make us better chere
  Farewell from us, both one and all.
  farewele fro us both alle and sume
55 **At this time of Christ's birthday,**
   this time of cristes feest natall
   We will be merry, great and small,
   we will be mery grete and small
   And you must go out of this hall.
   and thou shalt go oute of this halle
  Farewell from us, both one and all.
  farewele fro us both alle and sume
   Advent is gone. Christmas is come.
   advent is gone cristemas is cume
60 **Be we merry now, one and all.**
   be we mery now alle and sume
   He is not wise who will remain silent
   he is not wise that wille be dume
   "In ortu Regis omnium." ["At the dawn of the King of all."[2]]
   in ortu regis omnium

Although this carol ends on a merry Christmas note, its performance should otherwise be a prolonged grumble. Advent is addressed as "thou" throughout, suggesting the speaker's somewhat condescending distaste for an unwelcome houseguest; perhaps, some effigy of Advent would be defenestrated during the performance.

  If this carol were an anonymous piece, the reader might think it a sincere complaint about imposed penitence—what they, the clergy, "made us" (l. 4) do. This institutionally enforced "paciens" has left only a bitter taste in the singer's mouth. But "With pacience thou has us fed" is one of two playful carols (from among the 119 carols preserved in a single manuscript) attributed to a late fifteenth-century Franciscan of Canterbury, James Ryman.[3] Little is known about Friar Ryman except what can be deduced from his manuscript. Like all Franciscans, he loved Jesus and Mary and Christmas, recurrently celebrated in song by such poems as "A maiden mild hath born a child" (NIMEV 67 DIMEV 106) or "Auctor of health Christ have in mind" (NIMEV 449 DIMEV 730). As a pastoral impersonation of the recalcitrant laity, "With pacience thou has us fed" seems an affectionate parody, but its performance also permits the lay reader a carnivalesque moment of rebellious release from ecclesiastical constraint (as from the restricted winter diet).

"With pacience thou has us fed" was presumably intended to be sung at a party on Christmas Day, though the Solemnity of the Nativity itself is hardly being celebrated. The first eight stanzas are all belly-driven: stinky fish, musty brown bread, and thin beer have reduced the hardly penitent grumbler to skin and bone. In stanza 10, the singer wishes Lent would go to Boughton [under] Blean (to rhyme with "lean")—that is, about six miles west of Canterbury (for a very localized joke).[4] Since Ryman himself lived in the cathedral city, perhaps the phrase simply means "get out of town." In the next stanza, however, the speaker would banish Advent from all of Kent.

Stanza 11 expels Advent from every "eastate" because it is life-threatening— that is, it "playest chekmate"—and so deserves a broken "pate" (ll. 44–5). The following three stanzas acknowledge *bellatores* [those who fight], then *laborores* [those who work], and lastly *oratores* [those who pray]—the three traditional classes not so easily differentiated as nobles, serfs, and clergy by the late fifteenth century. Knights and squires would bed Advent in mud along with his "sire" (perhaps "father") Lent. Commoners have no use for Advent's "skille" and need more nourishment to work. Only religious folk should endure the liturgical calendar's double seasons of deprivation.

In the next to last stanza, with the arrival of Christmas day, Advent must exit. The four *-um* rhymes of the final stanza (and apparent omission of a "Farewell" refrain) set this last stanza formally apart from the preceding stanzas (each with its own three end rhymes and *-um* refrain), making the last four lines serve as a sort of coda. The grumbler's complaint now ended, Friar James can celebrate the holy day itself (not just the termination of Advent) in propria persona. This last stanza's end rhyme links its words; its use of macaronic rhyme links languages, and Christ, as "Rex omnium," unites laity and clergy and all. The carnival now over, time has come for the friar-author to assert the reason for the season and a truer cause for celebration than the end of abstinence.

In a likewise amusingly angry fashion, "Swart smoked smiths smattered with smoke" bemoans the nocturnal noise of blacksmiths. Its banging alliteration (largely lost in my translation) achieves an "onomatopoeic masterpiece."[5] This very loud lyric may also be considered an example of the "imitative fallacy" in that it mimics what it loathes but for comic effect in what amounts to "almost a parody of the alliterative style."[6]

Dark sooty smiths, grimy with smoke,
swarte smeked smethes smattered with smoke
Drive me to death with the din of their strokes.
drive me to deth with den of here dintes
Men never heard such noise at night,
swech nois on nightes ne herd men never
With the shouting of knaves and the clattering of hammering.
what knavene cry and clattering of knockes
5 **The pug-nosed oafs cry one after another "Coal! Coal!"**
the cammede kongons crien after col col
And they blow their bellows [so] that their brain bursts.
and blowen here bellewes that all here brain brestes
"Huff, puff!" says that one. "Haff, paff!" that other.
huff puff seith that one haff paff that other
They spit and writhe and tell many tales.
they spitten and sprawlen and spellen many spelles
They gnaw and gnash. They [all] groan together
they gnawen and gnacchen they grones togedere
10 **And overheat themselves with their hard hammers.**
and holden hem hote with here hard hammers
Their aprons are [made out] of bull's hide.
of a bole hide ben here barmfelles
Their legs have greaves on account of the sparks.
here schankes ben schakeled for the fereflunderes
They have heavy hammers that are hard to handle.
hevy hammers they han that hard ben handled
Stiff strokes they strike on an anvil:
stark strokes they striken on a steled stokke

15 **"Luss! Buss! Lass! Dass!" they grunt in turn.**
luss buss lass dass routen be rowe
Such a sad sound—the Devil be rid of it!
sweche dolful a dreme the devil it todrive
The master stretches [the metal] a little and shrinks [it] smaller;
the maister longeth a litel and lascheth a lesse
He intertwines those two, and strikes a high note.
twineth hem twein and toucheth a treble
"Tik! Tak! Hic! Hak! Tiket! Taket! Tik! Tak!
tik tak hic hac tiket taket tik tak
20 **Luss! Buss! Lass! Dass!"—such a life they lead!**
luss buss luss dass swich lif they leden
All Farriers! Christ give them sorrow!
alle clothemeres crist hem give sorwe
No man may have his rest at night on account of the Water-Burners.
may no man for brenwateres on night han his rest

These hammering alliterative long lines convey the performer's intense (because sleep-deprived) aggravation. The formal demands of such sustained alliteration often force the poet to introduce less familiar words. "Kongons" [oafs?] (l. 5), for example, is a strange word and a deliberately offensive insult.[7] Andrew Breeze interprets "cammede kongons" to mean bowlegged changelings, deformed or imbecilic "offspring of fairies ... substituted for a normal child" with a strong connotation that they are hellish demons.[8] "Steled stokke" maintains both the "s" and "k" noise of "Stark strokes they striken" (l. 14) and satisfies the need for a synonym for "anvil" (a word unrecorded in English till the later fourteenth century). A reference to "Alle clothemeres" (lit. "mare-dressers") in the exclamatory curse of line 21 is the only recorded example of this word in the *MED* and seems a coined synecdoche for blacksmith or horseshoer. The reference to blacksmiths as "brenwateres" (l. 22) recalls their process of tempering iron; "Brenwatere" is also recorded as a surname, though hardly so common as "Smith."

This lyric should be performed as a headlong, almost random, rant. Yet, several details seem quite studied and subtle. The alliteration of "They spitten and spawlen and spellen many spelles" (l. 8), for example, causes the reciter to spit as well, and the rhythm achieved by this line's "and/and" polysyndeton (the emphatic use of superfluous conjunctions) suggests the excessive chattiness of the shouting "knaves" (i.e., apprentices). So, too, the alliteration of "they gnawen and gnacchen they grones togedere" (l. 9) grinds the reader's own teeth, and such gnashing of teeth enhances the lyric's ever increasingly hellish portrayal of the smithy at night (cf. Matthew 8:12: "ibi erit fletus et stridor dentium" [there shall be weeping and gnashing of teeth]).

Political Protest

Less amusing, more sincere, and more significant expressions of outrage address social injustice. Much of the satiric verse in Middle English, being descriptive or even narrative, must "stretch the definition of lyric."[9] Many Middle English political complaints are occasional (and, now burdened by footnotes, more informative than enjoyable): "Some of the pieces are merely narratives studded with unintegrated commentary."[10] Others lament universal evils which still persist in our fallen state. Performance of these more cosmic complaints may be emotionally cathartic but need not be thought *performative* in J. L. Austin's sense of the term, which, as distinguished from a *constative* utterance that describes reality, enacts what it says. It is unlikely that the poets anticipated their laments would actually change sad reality. These more general complaints about an unchanging human condition acknowledge that all injustice results from Original Sin and shall endure till the Second Coming, but do so bitterly without a bemused, Horatian indulgence of mere human folly. Sadly as well, more bitter, Juvenalian complaints against social ills—outbursts of sarcasm and invective intended to renounce vice—often carry an awareness that such lyrics spoke to a power who would not listen; the mere copying of such protest lyrics, however, enacts an enduring resistance by the disenfranchised audience.

The most familiar Middle English lyric of political protest is both occasional and general: John Ball's ditty "When Adam delved and Eve did span, / Who was then a gentleman?" This couplet helped ignite the "Peasants Revolt," the fourteenth-century violent uprising in England against reinforced exploitation of laborers and extravagant taxation—now often more appropriately referred to as the "Rising of 1381" (because not confined to peasants).

This small yet powerful verse can still serve as a placard in a protest march. In retrospect, this battle cry may seem surprisingly progressive—an anticipation of "Proletarier aller Länder, vereinigt Euch!" [Karl Marx's "Workers of the world, unite!"]. Its implicit challenge of social hierarchy did not at all succeed in the Middle Ages.

In "The Former Age," Chaucer pictures a (prelapsarian) utopia when "Yit nas the ground nat wounded with the plough" (l. 9). However, Adam's digging (Genesis 3:17) and Eve's distaff indicate their postlapsarian status in John Ball's couplet, a political order immediately after their expulsion from paradise. "When Adam delved and Eve did span," therefore, implies that the Fall itself did not initiate class distinctions. Social equality should, therefore, remain an extra-Edenic and recoverable status. Ball's originally embedded lyric thus crystallizes "the oral and social 'event' of preaching, that is, its performance . . . preachers recruited poetry within their sermons for its immediate generative power, not just to reinforce moral lessons but to cue passionate responses and change minds."[11] Of course, the very conciseness of Ball's excerpted lyric foreshadowed the brevity of his fantasy of an egalitarian society; the primary participants in the Rising of 1381 would be promptly forced to suffer the brutal retaliation of their social reality.

As an exercise in sarcasm, "A man that should of truth tell" vents a more universal and perennial frustration of searching for honesty in this world.

God be with Truth! (Wherever He may be,
god by wyth trewthe qwer he be
I wish he were in this country.)
i wolde he were in this cuntre
    A person who would speak about Truth,
    a man tha xuld of trewthe telle
    He may not dwell with great lords.
    wyth grete lordys he may not dwelle
5   **In true account—as clerks tell—**
    in trewe story as klerkes telle
    Truth is placed in low degree.
    trewthe is put in low degre
    In ladies' chambers He does not come;
    in laydyis chaumberes comethe he not
    there, He dares not set foot.

ther dar trewthe settyn non fot
Though He may want to, He may not
thow he wolde he may not
Come among the high society.
comyn among the heye mene
God be with Truth! ...
With lawyers, He has no space;
with men of lawe he hanon spas
10 **They love Truth in no place.**
they lovyn trewthe in non plas
It seems to me they have a miserable grace
me thinkit they han a rewly grace
That Truth is debarred so.
that trewthe is put at swyche degree
God be with Truth! ...
15 **In Holy Church he may not sit,**
in holy cherche he may not sythe
They toss him from man to man.
fro man to man they xuln hym flythe
It seriously saddens my thought—
it rewit me sore in myn wytte
I have great grief on account of Truth.
of trewthe i have gret pete
20 *God be with Truth!* ...
Clergy, who should be good ...
relygius that xulde be good
If Truth should come there [among], I'd hold Him crazy.
if trewthe cum ther i holde hum wood
They would probably tear His tunic and hood
they xuldyn hum rynde cote and hood
And make Him flee naked.
and make hum bare for to flye
25 *God be with Truth!* ...
Anyone who would uncover Truth,
a man that xulde of trewthe aspye
He ought to search easily
he must sekyn esylye

> **In the bosom of Mary**
> in the bosum of marye
> 30 **For there Truth is truly.**
> for there his is for sothe

The refrain of this carol should be voiced with irritated despair. The personification of Truth as "He" to be found only in Mary's bosom uncovers the true identity of *truth* (i.e., fidelity) as Christ alone Who is no longer welcome in either court or church. His constancy may be found only within Mary's true-blue cloak. The need for such a reformist critique of fraud, lambasting those who would again strip Jesus (l. 23), is both immediate and constant. Yet, it is the promise of this lyric's final stanza that saves it from descending into the cynicism of a Diogenes futilely searching for one other honest man.

Distressing Puzzles

In terms of the lyric as an emotional experience, most Middle English proverbs, charms, and recipes in verse, which are generally instructional, seem void of emotional intensity. Proverbs imprint ready-made wisdom on the memory. Likewise, recipes often simply versify data.[12] And many riddles may merely provoke an initial puzzlement followed by the delight of a clever solution. Some riddles, however, can disturb the reader and, thereby, evoke a far more emotional aftermath—*enigmatae* for the wise to discern (Proverbs 1:5–6).

The DIMEV identifies a mono-rhyming quatrain "Blodles & bonles blod had none bon" [Bloodless and boneless, blood had no bone] as a meditation on the Eucharist. But as Stephen Manning contends, "This poem has been misread as 'lines on the host'; the subject is instead the Incarnation."[13] Perhaps, both interpretations are valid solutions to the same, seemingly grim riddle.

> **Bloodless and boneless, blood had no bone.**
> blodles & bonles blod had non bon
> **Father had father that father had none.**
> ffadur had fadur þat ffadur had non
> **The work and the workman, they be all one.**
> Þe werk & werkmon hoe ben alon

He that never went, first has gone.
he þat neuer ne ede ffyrryst had ygon

The most incomprehensible mysteries of Jesus as the Son of God made man are here reduced to a mono-rhymed puzzling quatrain. Line 1 requires recognition that Christ existed before taking human form, as affirmed by the Nicene Creed "ex Patre natum ante omnia saecula" [born of the Father before all ages]. Line 2 requires recognition of Christ's virgin birth. Line 3 may refer to transubstantiation, the "work" of making bread and wine into Himself.[14] And line 4, recognizing Christ as firstborn of the dead, recalls His Resurrection. Michael P. Kuczynski has observed that

> It is as if the poet has set himself the task to be as banal as possible in pursuing a rarefied spiritual problem... Each line... underscores the collision... between what our senses tell us is true and what belief insists on, in a way that could enhance rather than allay doubt.[15]

There is no emotion expressed in the riddle, no joy at the Nativity nor any compassion for the Crucifixion—just statements of the mysteries of doctrine. As such, this little lyric poses a major emotional challenge: either accept a humble, indeed humiliated, submission of reason to revelation, or lose your faith.

There is something far more emotionally engaging about the enigmatic and still-popular song "He bore him up he bore him down," better known as "The Corpus Christi Carol."

> *Lully, lulley, lully, lulley,*
> lully lulley lully lulley
> *The falcon has born away my mate.*
> the faucon hath born my mak away
>   **He bore him up, he bore him down,**
>   he bare him up he bare him down
>   **He bore him into a brown orchard.**
>   he bare him into an orchard brown
> 5 *Lully, lulley...*
>   **In that orchard, there was a hall**
>   in that orchard ther was an hall
>   **That was draped with purple and fine cloth.**
>   that was hanged with purpil and pall

10 *Lully, lulley ...*
    And in that hall there was a bed.
    and in that hall ther was a bede
    It was draped with gold so red.
    it was hanged with gold so rede
    Lully, lulley ...
15   **And in that bed there lies a knight,**
    and in that bed ther lithe a knight
    His wounds bleeding day and night.
    his woundes bleding day and night
    Lully, lulley ...
    By that bedside there kneels a maiden,
    by that bedes side ther kneleth a may
20   **And she weeps both night and day.**
    and she wepeth both night and day
    Lully, lulley ...
    And by that bed's head there stands a stone,
    and by that beddes side ther stondeth a ston
    "Corpus Christi" [Body of Christ] written thereon.
    corpus christi wreten theron

This lullaby lament is so mysterious, emotionally simple yet indecipherable, that it has tempted many precise decodings. Richard L. Greene, for example, has read the poem as a masked occasional complaint that "refers specifically to the displacement of Queen Catherine of Aragon by Anne Boleyn"[16]—despite the specificity of this context, any abandoned or widowed woman can identify with the grief of Henry VIII's first queen. Eamon Duffy is certain, however, that "there can be no question whatever" that the carol's "strange cluster of images" is derived "directly from the cult of the Easter sepulchre."[17] Both readings seem very pro-Catholic, so reason for camouflaging the lyric's intended meaning during Henry's later reign. Stephen Manning has suggested that it be read within a setting of the Forty Hours' Devotion, the annual prayer vigil in remembrance of Christ's forty hours in the tomb, proposing "If Mary speaks the refrain, the emotional intensity of the poem increases; if Ecclesia, the poet shows a greater insight into the significance of the Crucifixion. I prefer the latter."[18]

    The general consensus (or intuition) is that "he" refers to Christ who is "my mak" (l. 2)—that is, the singer's lost love. The bird of prey, "faucon" (l. 2), may be the devil or simply death or some other agent who carried Him away—that is, who "bare him up" [onto the cross] and bore him down "into an orchard brown" [or grave] (ll. 3–4)—the price He paid for our withered apple of Eden. "Bore" simply means "carried" but with a possible wordplay on "To bore a hole, make a perforation,"[19] a denotation that graphically recalls Christ's nail-wounds. The bed "hanged" (ll. 8, 12) with gold so blood-like [as on a cross] images the burial slab but also an altar draped with "A fine covering for an altar."[20]

Whereas the first half of the lyric (and the refrain) are all in the past tense, the carol's conclusion is in the present tense. The knight-Christ still "lithe . . . bleeding" [lies bleeding] (ll. 15–16) night and day,[21] and so the weeping maiden still kneels "both night and day" (l. 20) keeping vigil like Mary Magdalene or any devout "I." "Corpus Christi" inscribed on a "ston" (l. 23), beside the living corpse, may signify the dogma of Christ's Real Presence in the Eucharist as indelibly maintained by St. Peter's successors. The Latin tag "Corpus Christi" refers not only to the feast day,[22] but also to the priest's repeated affirmation that what had once been a wafer of bread is now the body of Christ at each distribution of communion. Harmonizing with that moment, a reader's emotional response to the specific unknowns of "The Corpus Christi Carol" should resurrect both the wonder and grateful grief due Christ's singular sacrifice re-enacted in every celebration of the Eucharist.

The lyric "I have a young sister far beyonden the sea" remains a likewise still popular song, perhaps too much so. The opening phrasing "I have a . . ." provides a formulaic start to numerous riddles, and the seven ballad quatrains (rhyming xbxb) seem to appeal for relief from sexual frustration, but do so in an emotionally most enigmatic fashion.[23]

> **I have a young sister**
> i have a yong suster
> **Far beyond the sea.**
> fer beyonden the see
> **Many are the keepsakes**
> many be the drowries
> **That she has sent to me.**
> that she sente me

5 **She sends me the cherry**
she sente me the cherye
    Without any pit,
    withouten ony ston
And so she did the dove
and so she ded the dove
Without any bone.
withouten ony bon
She sent me the briar
sche sente me the brer
10 **Without any bark.**
withouten ony rinde
    She asked me to love my beloved
    sche bad me love my lemman
Without any longing.
withoute longing
How should any cherry
how shuld ony cherye
    Be without a pit?
    be withoute ston
15 **And how should any dove**
and how shuld ony dove
Be without a bone?
ben withoute bon
How should any briar
how shuld ony brer
    Be without bark?
    ben withoute rinde
How should I love my beloved
how shuld i love min lemman
20 **Without longing?**
without longing
When the cherry was a flower,
whan the cherye was a flour
    Then it had no pit.
    than hadde it non ston
When the dove was an egg,

whan the dove was an ey
Then it had no bone.
than hadde it non bon
25 **When the briar was a seed,**
whan the brer was onbred
Then it had no bark.
than hadde it non rind
When the maiden has what she desires
whan the maiden hath that she loveth
She is without longing.
she is without longing

This song sounds simply alluring, but there is a teasing play of innuendo throughout. "Cherye" (l. 5), "dove" (l. 7) and "brere" [wild rose] (l. 9) all suggest feminine sexuality. The missing items of the three redundant puzzles—"ston" (l. 6), "bon" (l. 8), and "rinde" (l. 10)—all have a phallic suggestiveness.[24] The answering images—"flour" [flower] (l. 21), "ey" [egg] (l. 23), and "onbred" [unborn, undeveloped, a seed] (l. 24)—all suggest the maiden's immaturity (that is, her virginity).

Finally in this earnestly romantic riddle, the word that needs to be reconceived is "suster" (l. 1). In Middle English, the primary meaning of *sister* was, as it remains, "female sibling,"[25] but this sister has sent "drowries" (l. 3)[26] to her *amor de loin* from "Fer biyonde the see" (l. 2). "Suster" could also be used to refer to a fellow female or "as a term of endearment for a lover, wife, etc."[27]—but, in this case, the lovers' relationship has remained chaste and presumably heterosexual. The poem's most pressing question, then, the one that informs its other three (relatively trivial) *impossibilia*, is posed in lines 19–20: How should the maiden love her "lemman / Without longinge?" His blunt answer is provided in lines 27–28: "Whan the maiden hath that she loveth / She is without longinge." His final answer is when their physical love matures, then the conundrum of their physical (not necessarily geographical) distance from each other will be solved.

Dread of Harm

Whereas Middle English riddles pose interrogatives, the texts of charms are intended to be enacted as performatives that can be invested with intensely troubled emotion. "I conjure hem in the name of the Fader," for example, would dispel the fear of being robbed. In the sole manuscript that preserves this charm, it follows without a line break after a very similar lyric, "God and saint Trinity / As I believe on thee." Both poems perform the same speech act, and both, indeed, may have been read as one continuous prayer. However, the four trimeter couplets of "God and saint Trinity" pray quite conventionally for safety. The irregular nine couplets of "I conjure hem in the name of the Fader" have the threatened energy of an incantation. It is immediately followed in its manuscript by a slightly garbled Latin spell apparently intended to ward off evil: "Versus disperibus (disparibus?) meritis / pendent tria corpora ramis" [Although what they deserve be unequal / three bodies hang on a branch].[28]

The sequence of verse lines in "I conjure hem" approximates the driving cadences of a litany, and the MED does recognize the prayerful senses of "urge" or "implore" as the first denotations of "conjure"; however, the verb can also mean "To invoke or conjure up (a devil, a spirit), as by incantation or magic."[29]

> *I conjure them in the name of the Father and Son and Holy Ghost*
> i conjour hem in the name of the fader and sone and holy gost
> **In Them is power above all** ✠
> in hem is vertu althermost ✠
> **In the beginning and in the ending**
> in the beginning and in the ending
> **And in the *power* of every thing**
> and in the vertu of all thing
> **Is and was and ever shall be**
> is and was and ever schal be
> **In the *power* of the Holy Trinity**
> in the vertu of the holy trinitee
> 5   **By the *power* of every mass**
> by the vertu of every masse
> **That ever was said, more or less** [i.e., as a "high" or "low" mass],
> that ever was seyde more and lasse
> **In the *power* of herb, grass, stone, and tree**
> in the vertu of herbe grass ston and tree
> **And in the *power* that ever may be**

and in the vertu that ever may be
If here come any enemies
if here come eny fon
10 **To rob me or to kill me**
me to robbe other me to sclon
They [must] stand as still as any stone.
they stond as stille as eny ston
They have no ability to go
they have no *powere* away to gon
By the *power* of the Holy Trinity
by the vertu of the holy trinitee
Till they have life from me.
tille they have life of me
15 **Lord Jesus grant me this**
lord jesu graunte me this
As You are in the bliss of heaven.
as ye ben in heven bliss

This modernization's use of the noun "power" is italicized whenever it translates the lyric's incessant repetition of a "vertu" being invoked; the lyric's sole use of "powere" (l. 13) means only the robber's physical mobility. "Vertu" instead calls upon some preternatural assistance. Recital should be driven by a conviction (or desperate hope) that this charm's "vertu" cripples the robbers' mere "powere."

In theory, there is a fundamental difference between spell-casting and prayer; yet, according to Rossell Hope Robbins, "the distinction between a charm and a prayer was subtle."[30] Magic (based on animism) manipulates reality directly by means of conjuration properly performed as commands. Prayer, however, (based on theism) petitions divine intervention in the subjunctive ("oremus" [Let us pray]). Yet, popular piety has little emotional grasp of such a semantic distinction, especially in times of stress. It is when fear arises as an irresistible reflex—say, at the stroke of midnight on a moonless Friday the 13th while walking through some decrepit cemetery (as one does)—that recollected lyric-antidotes to panic may percolate in the imagination.

If performed as a prayer, the insistent phrasing of "I conjure hem in the name of the Fader" may be thought somewhat similar to that of the thoroughly orthodox "Lorica [breastplate] of St Patrick," also known as "The Cry of the Deer." Whereas recital of such a true sacramental appeals to God's will, magic ritual would compel the forces of nature by means of a false sacrament. The references in "I conjure hem" to the sign of the cross ("In the name of"), to Christ as Alpha and Omega, and to the doxology ("is, was, ever shall be"), all sound orthodox enough. It is the invocation of the everlasting "vertu of al thing" including herbs, grass, stone and tree (ll. 5, 9–10) that seems a bit druidy. The conjurer claims the power to petrify enemies (l. 14) until a reviving counter-charm is spoken (l. 16).

"I conjure hem in the name of the Fader" should be performed as an apotropaic (lit. "turns away") gesture that repels evil. The cross transcribed after line 2 is a directive to make the sign of the cross (as commonly indicated in sacramentaries). Though theologically vulgar, apotropaic prayers and amulets were popular in the late Middle Ages, and, in this poem, the body language of making a sign of the cross seems more a prophylactic gesture than a self-blessing, comparable to the familiar idea that a crucifix or garlic can ward off vampires.

The closing invocation of the Trinity in "I conjure hem" circles back to the poem's beginning to complete the conjuration. Similarly, a *caim* ("circle" or "sanctuary") poem attributed to St. Columba is traditionally said while drawing a circle around oneself or simply pointing to the ground while turning clockwise for self-protection. Whether prayer or incantation, it is the emotional investment of the performing "I"—not the plausibility of the text's "vertu"—that empowers "I conjure hem" to dispel real fear.

Performance of "By a forest as I gan fare," or "The Mourning of the Hunted Hare," requires an even more remarkable impersonation of fear—that of a terrified bunny named "Watte."[31] The lyric's nineteen quatrains of alternating rhyme suit well the reported complaint of such an innocent and vulnerable voice.

> **By a forest as I was going,**
> by a forest as i gan fare
>   **Walking by myself all alone,**
>   walking all myselven alone
> **I heard a lament of a hare.**
> i hard a morning of an hare
> **Sadly she made her moan.**

roufully schew mad here mone
5 **"Dearest God, how shall I live**
dereworth god how schal i leve
 And lead my life in the land?
 and leid my life in lond
 From valley to hill I am driven.
 frow dale to doune i am idreve
 I don't know where I can sit or stand.
 i not where i may site or stond
"**I may neither rest nor sleep**
i may nother rest nor slepe
10 **Beside any valley that is so hidden**
 by no vallay that is so derne
 Nor any shelter can protect me,
 nor no covert may me kepe
 But always I run from hiding place to hiding place.
 but ever i rene fro herne to herne
"**Hunters will not hear their Mass**
honteres will not heire ther masse
 Hoping to go hunting.
 in hope of hunting for to wend
15 **They leash their hounds, bigger and smaller, in pairs**
 they coupelleth ther houndes more and lasse
 And bring them to the edge of the field.
 and bringeth them to the feldes ende
"**Scent dogs run on every side**
roches rennen on every side
 That hope to find me in furrows.
 in forrows that hope me to find
 Hunters take [to] their horses and ride
 honteres taketh ther horse and ride
20 **And cast their grounds to the wind.**
 and cast the contray to the wind
"**As soon as they come behind me,**
anon as they cometh me behinde
 I sit completely silent and meek.
 i loke and sit full stille and lowe

The first man that does find me
the furst man that me doth finde
Immediately he cries 'Hey, here!'[32]
anon he crit so howe so howe
25 **"'Look,' he says, 'where a hare sits!**
lo he saith where sitteth an hare
'Get up, Watte, and run away fast!'
arise up watte and go forth blive
With sorrow and with great grief.
with sorrowe and with mich care
I escape away with my life.
i schape away with my life
"During winter, in the deep snow,
at winter in the depe snowe
30 **Men will seek to track me**
men will me seche for to trace
And by my footprints I am discovered
and by my steppes i am iknowe
And followed from place to place.
and followeth me fro place to place
"And if I come or return to the town—
and if i to the toune come or torne
Be it for greens or for leeks—
be it in wortes or in leike
35 **Then will the women also gladly**
then will the wives also yeorne
Chase me with their dogs as well.
flece me with here dogges eke
"And if I sit and chomp the kale
and if i sit and crope the koule
And the woman is in the way,
and the wife be in the waye
At once she will curse 'by Cock's soul,
anon schowe will swere by cokkes soule
40 **There's a hare in my hay!'**
there is an hare in my haye

"Quickly she will scream 'Get the rascal, [you] mongrel watchdog!'
anon sche wille clepe forth cure knave
    And look right well at where I'm sitting.
    and loke right weel where i sitte
Following behind with a stick,
behind sche will with a stave
    She full well intends to hit me.
    full well porpos me to hitte
45 "'Scram, Watte! With Christ's curse,
go forthe watte with cristes curse
    And if I live, you shall be taken.
    and if i leve thou schalt be take
I have a rabbit trap in my purse;
i have an harepipe in my purce
    It shall be set entirely for your sake.'
    it schal be set all for thy sauke
"Next, this wife has two great dogs, [and]
then hath this wyf two dogges grete
50   **She orders them to go after me,**
    on me sche biddeth heme goe
And like a shrew she continues to threaten me,
and as a scrowe sche will me thret
    And constantly she shouts, 'Go, doggies, go!'
    and ever sche crieth go doggee goe
"But always I must wander thus:
but all way this most i go
    By no riverbank can I stay—
    by no banke i may abide
55   **Lord God, woe is me that**
    lord god that me is wo
Many a misfortune has happened to me.
many a happe hath me betide
    "There is no beast in the world, I suspect,
    there is no beest in the world i wene
Hart, hind, buck, nor dove,
hert hind buke ne dove

> **That suffers half as much harm**
> that sufferes halfe so miche tene
60 **As does the simple Watte—go wherever he goes.**
> as doth the silly wat go where he go
> "**If a nobleman will have any game**
> if a gentilmane will have any game
>> **And finds me in a burrow where I'm sitting,**
>> and find me in forme where i sitte
>> **For dread of losing his name,**
>> for dred of losinge of his name
>> **He will not strike me.**
>> i wot welle he wille not me hitte
65 "**Rather, he will leave me [to run] for the width of an acre**
> for an acures bred he will me leve
>> **Before he will let his hounds run.**
>> or he will let his hondes rene
>> **Of all the men that are alive,**
>> of all the men that beth alive
>> **I am most beholden to noblemen.**
>> i am most behold to gentilmen
> "**As soon as I can run to the open ground,**
> as sone as i can ren to the laye
70 **At once the greyhounds will have me.**
> anon the greyhondes will me have
>> **My bowels will be thrown away,**
>> my bowels beth ithrowe awaye
>> **And I am carried home on a stick.**
>> and i am bore home on a stave
> "**As soon as I've arrived home,**
> als soon as i am come home
>> **I'm hanged high upon a pine tree,**
>> i am ihonge hie upon a pine
75 **With leek plants I am eaten soon**
> with leekwortes i am eete anone
>> **And puppies play with my skin."**
>> and whelpes play with my skine

Given that this lyric starts with the conventional phrasing of a *chanson d'aventure* [song of a chance encounter], one might expect to overhear an amorous complaint. Instead, one must attend the fatalistic groan of a hare. Several small details intensify its pathos. Despite being called "Watte" twice, the hare is identified as "schew" (l. 4) from the start.[33] This pronoun, if not a mere inconsistency, introduces some resonance of a rape narrative to the "hunting." Her gratitude for "a gentilmane . . . For drede of losinge his name . . . I am most behold to gentilmen" for letting her run is ironic or misplaced; the hunter flushes her for sport, not clemency (ll. 61–68). She will be eaten with garnish that had been her own diet (ll. 34, 75).

Within her almost Hamletian soliloquy, the hare must in turn briefly impersonate those who terrify her (ll. 25–26, 39–48), whereby she gets to show the vulgarity of the hostile housewife "by cokkes soule" (l. 39) and obsessiveness of the "Hunteres" who "will not heire ther masse / in hope of hunting for to wend" (ll. 13–14). The last detail of "whelps" playing with her hide is especially gruesome (cf. rolling dice for Christ's *vestimenta*, Matthew 27:35). Of course, it is possible for hard-hearted hunters and housewives to perceive all this "morning" [mourning] (l. 3) as comically absurd. But the hare, it/him/herself as "I," dreads being crucified: "I am bore home on a stave . . . ihonge upon a pine" (ll. 72–74). And the rude inevitability of death impels the emotional earnestness of many of the most disturbing Middle English lyrics.

Timor Mortis

Justified by a healthy but nonetheless unwelcome acknowledgment of death, many Middle English lyrics posit as a compelling corollary that the only reasonable emotional stance toward the ephemerality of idolatrous pleasures is *contemptus mundi* [scorn of this world].[34] The three great temptations were conventionally identified as the World, the Flesh, and the Devil (cf. Luke 4:1–13 and Matthew 4:1–11). The didactic purpose of death-focused lyrics is to motivate the reader's penance for succumbing to prior temptation and to inspire prudence regarding the (ever so brief) future. This rhetorical strategy is foundational to the corrective imperatives of many Middle English lyrics and, indeed, to Christianity: "quae enim secundum Deum tristitia est paenitentiam in salutem stabilem operatur saeculi autem tristitia mortem operatur" [For the sorrow that is according to God worketh penance, steadfast unto salvation; but the sorrow of the world worketh death] (2 Corinthians 7:10). The sincere sorrow of earnest self-awareness, or "secundum Deum tristitia," sows salvation.

In this didactic context, another very riddle-like lyric, "Erthe took of erthe," offers an exceptionally enigmatic invitation to be sad about the post-lapsarian human state. It may also be voiced as a sarcastic reminder of just who earned the wages of sin.

> **Earth took of earth, earth with woe.**
> erthe tok of erthe erthe with woh
> **Earth other earth to earth drew.**
> erthe other erthe to erthe droh
> **Earth laid earth in an earthen tomb.**
> erthe leide erthe in erthene throh
> **Then earth had of earth earth enough.**
> tho hevede erthe of erthe erthe inoh

This is the briefest and most riddle-like version of this lyric.[35] A particularly intriguing explication of this deliberately obscure lyric requires that its insistent repetitions of "erthe" be translated as multiple metonymies:

> *Man* took *Eve* out of *his body* with woe,
> *Eve* drew *Adam* to *evil.*
> *Man* laid *mankind* in the *ground.*
> Then had *man* of this *world dirt* enough . . .

and to dust we did return. Underlying these verbal conceits for "erthe" may be a (clerically macaronic) pun of "human" with Latin "humus" (soil). So conceived, the second line of the poem in particular can be stained with misogynist disdain. But the initial and probably most valid response to this poem should probably remain our disturbed confusion about the logic of sinning: what is the attraction of sin-soil?

As a *memento mori* [remember to die] poem, the brevity of "When the turuf is thy tour" sounds similarly stark.

> **When the turf is your tower**
> when the turuf is thy tour

> **And the pit, your bower,**
> and thy put is thy bour
> **Your skin and your white throat**
> thy wel and thy white throte
> **Worms will enjoy.**
> shulen wormes to note
> 5 **What help then to you is**
> what helpet thee thenne
> **All the world's delight?**
> all the worilde wenne

This lyric probably rebukes noble women in particular. However, "bour" (l. 2) need not indicate only a woman's "boudoir"; it can also connote any (white-necked) person's false sense of security. Edmund Reiss suggests that "*note* should be read as *uote*" (l. 5) in the sense of "guard" representing "an ironic continuation of the emphasis on safety … found in *tuur* and *bour*."[36]

Read without the context of being an admonitory lyric, performance of "When the turuf is thy tour" could be deployed to encourage a young woman to gather her rosebuds, which was Horace's response to the brevity of "invida aetas" [the hostile or envious age].[37] But, as an English rendition of the original "Cum sit gleba tibi turris" (under which the English version was directly transcribed and which was "evidently copied for the use of preachers"[38]), "When the turuf is thy tour" was clearly meant to renounce privileged self-indulgence. The entire lyric is one dismissive rhetorical question hardly hiding intense contempt for "all the worilde wenne" [all worldly winnings] (l. 6). The English translation preserves the Latin's trochaic couplets, adding alliteration to emphasize the cruel contrasts imposed by death: those between "turuf/tour"; "put/bour"; "wel, white/wormes"—all "achieving a concentration" that the Latin original does not have.[39]

Another *contemptus mundi* lyric, "The law of God be to thee thy rest," may now be read as a critique of nascent capitalism. It actually goes much further in its renunciation of "all" worldly "winning" (l. 12) and asks the reader to adopt an anchorite's contempt for the entire "fest" (l. 11) of this life.

> **May the law of God be to you, your comfort;**
> the law of god be to thee thy rest
> **The flesh, your sacrifice; the world, [your] exile;**

the flesh thy sacrifice the world exile
[May] God [be] your love and your best treasure;
god thy love and thy tresour best
Heaven, your country forever.
heven thy contre thorogh every while
5 **Take repentance into your breast**
repentaunce thou take into thy brest
For your unkindness and vile wickedness
for think unkinnesse and wikkidness vile
And be patient alone at home—
and abide at thyself withinne thy nest
Lest you be trapped by trickery under [the name of] "pity"—
lest under pite thou be trapped with gile
Except sometimes, as an impromptu guest,
except at somwhile as a hasty gest
10 **You hasten to do good, but at no great distance.**
thu stert to do good but thorogh no long mile
Stop, Glutton! Flee to this feast,
have do glutoun flee to this fest
For herein lies the heads and tails of all wealth.
for herein of all winning lyth crosse and pile

The purpose of this contempt for "flesh" (l. 2)—both for carnal desire and for meat—is to buttress an invitation to maintain as holy and as solitary a life as possible "withinne thy nest" (l. 7). Alternating "-ile" and "-est" rhymes throughout its twelve lines, this lyric poses several inversions of mundane perspectives: poverty is treasure; our worldly home—ever since the expulsion from Eden (Genesis 3:23–24)—is, in fact, our "exile"; isolation, except briefly to do good deeds nearby, keeps the best company with God. Playing on the twin meanings of "kinde" (l. 6), this call to repent condemns our all-too-common lack of "kindness" (charity) as "unnatural." The word "pity" (l. 8) may be misused to mask the temptation to dwell with bad company. And, as gluttony is a sin of excess, so, too, St. Augustine thought, the desire to have an unnaturally prolonged life should be recognized as a sin of avarice. Instead, as a hungry (i.e., fasting) exile, one should "flee" to the feast of the Eucharist and, in due time, to the Heavenly Feast (Matthew 22:1–14). This (hard-to-swallow) asceticism is here declared to be the required currency for salvation—the "cros and pil" (l. 12), or obverse and reverse of a coin—an emotional entrance fee that cannot be paid from the hedge fund of Pascal's wager.

Performance of the song "Worldes bliss ne last no throwe" should make our inherently reluctant consent to *contemptus mundi* ultimately, perhaps surprisingly, attractive. The emotion informing this lyric's enactment should be a deep care, and, as Stephen Manning has observed, "When we approach these songs we must remember that they concern themselves more with eliciting emotional response (for spiritual purposes) than with describing and analyzing emotional experience on the assumption that the experience is valuable in and of itself."[40]

    The bliss of this world lasts but a moment.
    worldes bliss ne last no throwe
        It parts and goes away at once.
        it wit and wend awey anon
        The longer I know it,
        the lenger that ich it iknowe
        The less I value it.
        the lasse ic finde pris theron
5   **For it is entirely mixed up with care,**
    for all it is imeind wid care
    With sorrow and with evil doings.
    mid sorewe and wid evel fare
    And, in the end, poor and naked
    and at the laste pouere and bare
    It leaves man when it starts to go.
    it let mon when it ginnet gon
    All the bliss there is here and there
    all the blisse this here and there
10 **Finally holds weeping and moaning.**
    bilouketh at ende wop and mon
    Everything shall go that man owns here,
    all shall gon that here mon owet
    All of it shall go to nothing.
    all it shall wenden to nout
    The man who sows no good here,

the mon that here no good ne sowet
When others reap, he'll catch his recompense.
when other repen he worth bikakt

15 **Think, Man, therefore, while you have strength,**
thenk mon forthy whil thu havest mikte
That you correct your misdeeds here,
that thu thine gultes here arikte
And do good works by day and night
and worche good by day and nikte
Before you are seized from comfort.
ar then thu be of lisse ilakt
You do not know when Christ Our Lord
thu nost wanne crist ure drikte

20 **Will ask you for what He has granted.**
thee asket that he havet bitakt
All the bliss of this life—
all the blisse of thisse life
You shall, Man, end in weeping.
thu shalt mon enden in wep
Of house and home and child and wife,
of huse and home and child and wife
Simple Man, take keep thereof,
sely mon tak therof kep

25 **For you shall leave here all**
for thu shalt all beleven here
The wealth of which you were lord.
the eykte whereof louerd thu were
When you are lying, Man, upon a bier
when thu list mon upon bere
And sleeping a very sad sleep,
and slepest a swithe druye slep
You'll have no companion with you
ne shaltu haben wit thee no fere

30 **Except [good] works in a heap.**
butte thine werkes on an hep
Man, why do you set your love and heart
mon why seestu love and herte

On the bliss of this world that lasts not at all?
on worldes blisse that nout ne last
Why do you endure what so often hurts you
why tholestu that thee so ofte smerte
For desire that is so unstable?
for love that is so unstedefast
35 **You are surely licking honey from a thorn**
thu lickest huny of thorn iwis
When you set your love on the world's bliss
that seest thy love on worldes bliss
For it is full of bitterness.
for full of bitternis it is
Sorely you may be frightened,
sore thu mikt ben ofgast
[You] who spend wealth here badly,
that despendes here eykte amiss
40 **On account of which, to be taken into hell.**
werthurgh ben into helle itakt
Think, Man, what Christ created you for,
thenk mon wharof crist thee wroukte
And put away your pride and filthy desire.
and do wey prude and fulthe mood
Think how dearly He ransomed you
thenk how dere he thee bokte
On the cross with His sweet blood.
on rode mit his swete blood
45 **He gave Himself for you as the price**
himself he gaf for thee in pris
To buy bliss for you if you are wise.
to buye thee bliss if thu be wis
Ponder, Man, and get up
bithenk thee mon and up aris
Out of sloth, and start to do good works
of slouthe and gin to worche good
While there is [still] time to work,
whil time to worchen is
50 **Or else you are stupid and crazy.**

for elles thu art witless and wood
All day you can understand
all day thu mikt understonde
    And see your mirror before yourself
    and thy mirour bifor thee sen
    What there is to do and [what] to refrain from,
    what is to don and to wonden
    And what to hold and what to flee.
    and what to holden and to flen
55   **For all day you see with your [own] eyes**
    for all day thu siyst wid thin eyen
    How this world passes and men die.
    how this world went and how men deiet
    Know this well: that you will endure
    that wite well that thu shalt dreyen
    Death ... and also another death.
    det also another det
    It helps not at all to lie about it—
    ne helpet nout ther non to lien
60   **No one may oppose death.**
    ne may no mon bu det ageyn
Neither shall there [after death] be any good unrewarded
ne wort ne good ther unforgulde
    Nor shall any evil be unpaid for.
    ne non evel ne worth unboukt
    When it pleases you, Man, underground
    whanne thu list mon under molde
    You shall receive as you wrought.
    thu shalt haven as thu havest wrokt
65   **Consider well, therefore, I advise,**
    bithenk thee well forthy ic rede
    And cleanse yourself of your sin
    and clanse thee of thine misdede
    So that He will help thee at need
    that he thee helpe at thine nede
    Who so dearly has purchased us
    that so dure us havet iboukt

And leads [us] to heaven's bliss
and to hevene blisse lede
70 That is everlasting and fails not a bit.
that evere lest and failet nout

The text of "Worldes blis ne last no throwe" survives in three manuscripts, indicating its popularity—that is, its promulgation.[41] The didactic message of this lyric seems at first antithetical to bliss; yet it is not a depressing *cri de cœur*. The tone of its recital (if stripped of music) should seem initially indignant, righteously so, motivated by a parental or pastoral concern to overcome the listener's ignorant arrogance (l. 52) and spiritual indigence (l. 58). As a father to his child—or as priest to his flock—the lyric begs its audience to "do wey prude" (l. 42).

When set to its surviving music, the full acoustical appeal of this poem assuages its didactic sting, making this admonition itself a "blissful" experience because "the fundamental emotive effect of music is pleasure."[42] The intent is to win consent that "worldes blisse" (l. 1) be disowned in anticipation of "hevene blisse" (l. 69). Paradoxically, the poem thereby simultaneously provides and rejects sublunary pleasure. The sung performance delights; its message berates. And that paradox enacts in miniature the experience promised of renouncing fleeting pleasure for the bliss of eternal reward. The poem's last line promises that heavenly bliss will never end in contrast to the ephemeral pleasure of this song that immediately ends on that note.

Whether "Worldes blis" be sung by a choir, read in silence, or recited (possibly from a pulpit), it enacts a call to confession. The lyric's "I" invites a singular "thee," one "sely man" (l. 24), to repent for being pleasantly numb, asleep (l. 28) to the proximity of death. The MED's definitions of "seli" include: "blessed; holy, virtuous . . . worthy, noble; fine, excellent; fortunate, lucky, prosperous; happy . . . wealthy; innocent, harmless; good; simple, guileless" on the one hand, and "foolish, gullible; doting; ignorant; weak, helpless, defenseless, hapless; wretched, unfortunate, miserable; pitiable; humble, lowly; poor; worthless, trifling, insignificant" on the other. Its use in the third stanza, therefore, is a caring insult—this "sely man" is pitiably unfortunate because of foolish confidence in fragile happiness.

The use of melic verse to deliver such a verbal spanking may now seem a questionable stylistic choice, though quite common in Middle English verse. Each line is not robotically octosyllabic, but each does contain four strongly accented syllables, and singing can easily adjust pronunciation to fit the musical measure. There is little or no enjambment, so each of the predominantly masculine end rhymes can emphasize its line's didactic punch. This rhetorical consonance is further enhanced by some intra- and interlinear alliteration, such as the breezy opening "Worldes/wit and wend" (ll. 1–2), the insultingly redundant "witless and wod" (l. 50), and the closing "lede/lest" (ll. 69–70).

Each of the poem's seven stanzas rhymes ababcccbcb; the medial c-couplet of each stanza's central triplet is, thus, bracketed by harmonious quatrains of alternating end rhyme abab . . . cbcb. Perhaps only coincidentally, the ten lines of each stanza recall the number of Commandments or the count of beads in each decade of the rosary. Each stanza is not devoted to a single deadly sin; nevertheless, the seven-step structure is suggestive of the conventional order of a manual of sins for the review of conscience before confession. In addition to pride and sloth, the poem explicitly renounces any definition of "love" that reduces its "worldly bliss" (l. 46) to a "filthy mood" (l. 52)—that is, to the appetitive sins of lust and gluttony (sins against both self and others). The text thus offers the reader a "mirror" (l. 61) or *speculum conscientiae.*

The first three stanzas and the last three are primarily indicative statements sprinkled with a few imperatives, especially the command to "Think!" (ll. 15, 65, and three times within the fifth stanza, 51, 53, 57). These three calls to think follow the poem's only interrogative in its central stanza: "Why" (l. 43)—that is, why, silly man, are you addicted to worldly "bliss" that only causes pain? The focus is on folly while alive rather than on the fear of hell after death, a warning that is not explicitly deployed until the conclusion of stanza 4. Having devalued the fading "pris" (l. 4) of worldly goods, the poem focuses instead on the debt owed to the Redeemer (ll. 19–20) Who gave Himself "in pris / To buye thee bliss" (ll. 51–56). Christ, the Giver and Taker (l. 19) and Best Worker (l. 51), demands as recompense not worldly goods but good works. This call to do good works (l. 17) is likewise an affirmation that such acts of charity make satisfaction of the hand—the third necessary step of true penance after contrition of the heart and confession of the mouth—a sacramental necessity to escape the second, worse death of damnation (l. 68). Any possible ambivalence to calling Everyman "seli" anticipates the alternative responses that a listener or reader may have at the poem's conclusion. The choice posed is either to enter a confessional or to walk away. Not an internal debate, "Worldes bliss" must now be read as a soliloquy of self-criticism.

Having accepted that all earthly joy ends, a less didactic, more minstrel-like "I" performs "Now bairns birds bold and blithe" as an extended metaphor that likens his departure from court to Everyman's exit from life.

>   **Now, ladies and gentlemen, brave and happy,**
>   now bernes buirdes bolde and blithe
>   **Now I am obliged to bless you here.**
>   to blessen you her now am i bounde
>   **I thank you all a thousand times,**
>   i thonke you alle a thousand sithe
>   **And pray that God keep you sound and healthy.**
>   and prey god save you hol and sounde
> 5 **Wherever you go, on dirt or grass,**
>   wherever ye go on gras or grounde
>   **May He rule you without distress.**
>   he you governe withouten greve
>   **On account of the friendship that I have found here,**
>   for frendschipe that i here have founde
>   **[It is] against my will [that] I take my leave.**
>   ageyn my wille i take my leve
>   **For the friendship and for good gifts,**
>   for frendschipe and for giftes goode
> 10 **For meat and drink such great plenty,**
>   for mete and drinke so gret plente
>   **[May] that Lord Who was stretched on the cross—**
>   that lord that raught was on the roode
>   **May He take care of your lovely company**
>   he kepe thy comely cumpayne
>   **On sea, on land, or wherever you are,**
>   on see or lond wher that ye be
>   **May He rule you without distress.**
>   he governe you withouten greve
> 15 **Such good merry-making you have made for me,**
>   so good disport ye han mad me

Against my will, I take my leave.
ageyn my wille i take my leve
Against my will although I go,
ageyn my wille althaugh i wende
    I may not always dwell here
    i may not alwey dwellen here
    For everything shall have an end
    for every thing schal have an ende
20 **And friends are not together always.**
    and frendes are not ay ifere
    [Though we'll] never be as beloved and dear [as we are here]
    be we never so lef and dere
    Out of this world we all shall depart,
    out of this world all schul we meve
    And when we prepare [to go] onto our bier,
    and whon we buske unto ur bere
    Against our will we take our leave.
    ageyn ur wille we take ur leve
25 **And go we shall, I never know when**
   and wende we schulle i wot never whenne
    Nor whereto we shall travel.
    ne whoderward that we schul fare
    But [either] endless bliss or forever to burn
    but endeles blisse or ay to brenne
    Is already ready for everyone.
    to every mon is yarked yare
    Therefore I advise each person to beware,
    forthy i rede uch mon beware
30   **And let our deeds confirm our actions**
    and lete ur werk ur wordes preve
    So that no sin ruins our soul
    so that no sunne ur soule forfare
    When our life has taken its leave.
    whon that ur lif hath taken his leve
When our life has taken its leave,
whon that ur lif his leve hath laught
    Our body lies ensnared by woe.

      ur body lith bounden by the wowe
35   **Our riches are all taken from us.**
      ur richesses alle from us ben raft
      Into cold clots [of dirt] our corpse is thrown.
      in clottes colde ur cors is throwe
      Where are your friends who will know you?
      wher are thy frendes who wol thee knowe
      Let's see who will relieve your soul.
      let see who wol thy soule releve
      I advise you, Man, before you are laid low,
      i rede thee mon ar thou ly lowe
40   **Be ever ready to take your leave.**
      be redy ay to take thy leve
  Be ready always, whatever happens,
  be redy ay whatever bifalle
      Lest you be caught all suddenly.
      all sodeynly lest thou be kight
      You never know when the Lord will call.
      thou wost never whonne thy lord wol calle
      Look that your lamp is burning bright,
      loke that thy laumpe be brenninge bright
45   **For—believe me well—unless you have [your] light [ready],**
      for leve me well but thou have light
      Your Lord will condemn you very foully
      right foule thy lord wol thee repreve
      And banish you far out of His sight
      and fleme thee fer out of his sight
      Because all too late you took your leave.
      for all too late thou toke thy leve
  Now God that was born in Bethlehem,
  now god that was in bethleem bore
50   **May He give us grace to serve Him so**
      he give us grace to serve him so
      That we may come before His face
      that we may come his face tofore
      When, out of this world, we shall go.
      out of this world whon we schul go

And [may He give us grace] in order to amend what we do amiss,
and for to amende that we misdo
Before we congeal into clay and become gooey,
in cley or that we clinge and cleve
55 And [may He] make us fair and square with friend and foe,
and mak us evene with frend and fo
And [ready] to take our leave in good time.
and in good time to take ur leve
Now, have good day, all good men!
now haveth good day gode men alle
Have good day, young and old!
haveth good day yonge and olde
Have good day, both great and small!
haveth good day bothe grete and smalle
60 And thank you, a thousand times!
and grauntmercy a thousand folde
If ever I could, most happily I would
if evere i mighte full fain i wolde
Do anything that would be pleasing for you.
don out that were unto you leve
May Christ keep you from cold cares,
crist kepe you out of cares colde
For now it is time to take my leave.
for now is time to take my leve

"Now bairns birds bold and blithe" is a borrowed French ballade form rhyming ababbcbc, called "double croisée" because its b-rhymes crisscross; having no specific name in English, it is commonly termed "the Monk's tale stanza" because of Chaucer's (largely unsuccessful or parodic) use of it.[43] Catherine Addison thinks the form "a rather unsatisfactory stanza, being anticlimactic because everything seems leading up to and away from the middle couplet."[44] Yet formal disappointment seems particularly appropriate to this admonitory lyric sung by an "I" departing from worldly joy. Each line is also strongly alliterated, and the very musicality of this lyric seems at first tonally misleading: "I've had such a good time, I wish I could stay." Blessing a happy, mixed audience (l. 1), thanking them for their "comely cumpayne" (l. 12) and "good disport" (l. 15), this "I" sounds about ready to perform a *quête* (the minstrel's request for payment). The only troubling note in the first two stanzas is an explicit recollection of Christ "that raught was on the roode" (l. 11); within a blessing, this sad note may be considered a nonce phrase, but almost immediately the pleasantry of this lyric's opening stanzas changes direction; "everything schal have an ende" (l. 19) because whatever goes up on Fortune's wheel must come down.

Since the "Now . . . now" of the first two lines cannot endure "alwey" (l. 20), the formerly merry minstrel is "bounde" (l. 2) to leave; the compulsory nature of his departure is emphatically reiterated in the last line of the first two stanzas and the first line of stanza 3. About to join the dearly departed, the minstrel starts to sound somewhat magisterial; his audience shall likewise perforce share the emotional experience of his own sad departure for so must "we" all against "ur" will (ll. 21–24). Anxiety regarding the uncertainty of both the "whenne" of dying and the "whoderward" of life after death (ll. 25–26) promotes prudence. There is no agnosticism being expressed about the alternatives waiting after death: either "endeles blisse or ay to brenne" (l. 27), so we must "beware" that our "werk ur werdes preve" (ll. 34–35)—phrasing recollective of the Confiteor's "verbo et opere" [in my words and in my deeds] once more affirming the notion that only satisfaction of the hand truly proves the integrity of confession of the mouth.

The renunciation of "riches" in stanza 5 adds a slight echo of Jesus's Sermon on the Mount (Matthew 6:19–21) to its memento mori imaging of a corpse's decay. The rhetorical question, "Wher are thy frends and who wol thee knowe?" (l. 37), introduces the poem's first use of the second-person singular pronoun. Everyone departs alone, and this asking of the individual dead soul "ubi sunt?" inverts the conventional trope; the departed dead must wonder where are the living who remain behind. Stanza 6 far more directly recalls the "laumpe" (l. 44) of the wise and foolish virgins (Matthew 25:1–13). And the warning of stanzas 5 and 6 should approximate the tone of Jesus's parable: Be ever vigilant!

Whereas stanza 2 had recalled Christ crucified, stanza 7 begins with an appeal to the newborn Jesus. This penultimate stanza sounds both optimistic about our once again communal repentance and optative regarding the reception of God's grace. Nevertheless, there will be no reprieve: all will leave against their will "in good time" (l. 56). The triple anaphora of "haveth good day" (ll. 49–51) in the final stanza might be thought to imply a "seize the day" response to the inevitability of death, but it should be performed as a farewell with gratitude, wishing that Christ shall keep "gode men alle" (l. 49) from "cares colde" (l. 57). Resentment has been released; well-disposed, the departing "I" lives in the "now" (l. 56) again, having effectively performed the sadness of departing to achieve a good ending. In that ending, "Now bairns birds bold and blithe" serves as a sort of lyric *ars moriendi* [treatise on the art of dying well].

More commonly, Middle English lyrics wail and beg when their "I" is compelled to recognize the imminence of death. "Dies Irae," the Latin sequence sung at requiem masses and on All Souls' Day, provides an emotional template for lyrics that voice a sinner's salutary groan ("ingemisco," st. 12): fear hell, flee sin, find mercy, be loved. Its sixteenth stanza hits all these notes:

> Confutatis maledictis,
> Flammis acribus addictis,
> Voca me cum benedictis.
> [After the damned have been confounded, sentenced to bitter flames, call me to be with the Blessed.]

The first line's matter-of-fact statement of a terrifying fait accompli ("confutatis maledictis" [the cursed having been proven wrong]) anticipates the Day of Doom, the fear of which is ultimately identical to a dying individual's fear of immediate personal judgment. Chanted, the lyric's accentual trochaic rhyming triplets can sound terrifying, but it does not enact fear simply for the vicarious experience of horror; this anguish is an opportunity for the individual "I" to repent, and for the Church Militant (i.e., struggling on earth) to pray "Pie Jesu Domine, / Dona eis requiem" [Merciful Lord Jesus, / Give them rest] (st. 19) for the Church Penitent (in Purgatory).

"Winter wakeneth all my care" exemplifies this dread seeking hope by means of very straightforward declarative sentences.

> **Winter awakens all my worries.**
> winter wakeneth all my care
> > **Now, these leaves grow bare.**
> > now this leves waxeth bare
> > **Often I sigh and sorely mourn**
> > ofte i sike and mourne sare

When it comes into my thought
when it cometh in my thoght
5 **Of this world's joy ... how it all goes for nothing!**
of this worldes joye how it geth all to noght
Now it is, and now it isn't,
now it is and now it nis
As if it surely never was.
also it ner nere iwis
What many men say, it is the truth:
that mony mon seith soth it is
"Everything passes except God's will.
all goth bote godes wille
10 **We all shall die though we like it ill."**
alle we shule deye thagh us like ille
All the grain that I planted green,
all that grein me graveth grene
Now it yellows completely.
now it faleweth all bidene
Jesus, help!—so that it be plain to see!
jesu help that it be sene
and shield us from hell,
and shild us from helle
For I do not know whither I shall go nor how long I will remain here.
for i not whider i shall ne how longe her dwelle

The syntactic simplicity of this lyric suits the sensibility of a plowman, as does the straightforwardness of his "thought," but his anxiety is universal. As in Shakespeare's "That time of year thou mayst in me behold" (Sonnet 73), the macrocosm (winter in the Middle English lyric rather than autumn) reflects the microcosm (the "I's" own advanced age). But "Winter wakeneth all my care" sounds far more down to earth, especially in lines 11 and 12. Unlike Shakespeare's affirmation of a "love more strong," the fear of death's proximity in "Winter wakeneth all my care" never relieves a greater fear of what happens next. If the exclamation "Jesus, help!" (l. 13) should be cried with desperate dread, the elongated last line of the final "helle/dwelle" rhyme finally fails to find any rest in peace.

Two Middle English epitaphs most succinctly exemplify the pleasure of impersonating morbid emotion: "All ye that pass by this holy place" and "Here lieth under this marble stone." Each addresses a passerby viewing the inscribed tomb.[45] "All ye that pass by this holy place" presents a conventionally pious admonition and petition.

All you who pass by this holy place,
all ye that passe be this holy place
Both clergy and lay folk of every rank,
both spiritual and temporal of every degree
Give heed to yourself while you have time and space.
remember yourselfe well during time and space
I was as you are now. And like me you shall be.
i was as ye are nowe and as i ye shall be
5 **Wherefore I beseech you of your mercy—**
wherfor i beseche you of your benignitee
For the love of Jesus and his mother Mary—
for the love of jhesu and his mother marye
To say for my soul a "Pater Noster" and an "Ave [Maria]."
for my soule to say a pater noster and an ave

The text should be seen as inscribed on a cadaver monument, gruesomely displaying postmortem decay. The "I" of this rhyme-royal stanza is to be imagined as the corpse speaking directly to everyone, irrespective of class or vocation because death levels all. Performed by a *transi* (rotting corpse < transire "to pass"), the central warning "I was as ye are nowe, and as I, ye shall be" (l. 4) is a commonplace scare tactic. Revived by the act of being read, the "I" asks a very small favor: the recital of one Our Father and one Hail Mary to help release his soul from Purgatory.

Very simple, very sincere, "All ye that pass by this holy place" is the norm from which "Here lieth under this marble stone" departs so surprisingly as an epitaph, first etched in Latin verse, the lyric is then rendered "Anglice."

Alanus calvus [bald Alan]
iacet hic sub marmore duro [lies here under hard marble]
utrum sit salvus [whether he be saved]
non curavit neque curo [he didn't care, nor do I.]

Here lies under this marble stone
here lieth under this marbill ston
Rich Alan, the bald man.
riche alane the ballid man
Whether he be saved or not,
whether he be safe or noght
I'll never care for neither did he.
i recke never for he ne roght

The tombstone provides a script for passersby to voice as the "I" of its author who is explicitly indifferent about the current state of Alan's soul and who is implicitly still angry about the dead man's stinginess while alive.

As a witty double-decker epigram (as well as epitaph), "All ye that pass" lyric mirrors the sort of marble tomb on which it could be etched: a Latin inscription for the splendid effigy above, English for the corrupt corpse below. The Latin quatrain with alternating rhyme (4a8b4a8b, more or less) sounds like a mockery of the elegiac couplet, still used in the Middle Ages for fancier gravestone inscriptions. The English translation into roughly tetrameter couplets is quite accurate, merely inverting the phrasal order of the final (punch) line. The tit-for-tat sarcasm of "Non curavit, neque curo / I recke never for he ne roght!" delivers a final judgment on Alan, one that accords with the *lex talionis* [the law of the scales, or "an eye for an eye"] and reveals that the lyric's "I" could not care less about the careless miser. The Latin phrasing in particular mocks the emotionless *tranquillitas* of the so-called Epicurean epitaph NFFNSNC (Non fui; fui, non sum; non curo [I was not; I was; I am not; I don't care]). However, it is the earnest disdain with which "All ye that pass by this holy place" should be performed that makes reading this lyric so emotionally pleasurable as a sort of medieval Schadenfreude.

More generally, the *gaudium* of performing another's person's *tristia* requires the reader's ability (so predisposition) to identify with another "I's" aggravation, frustration, fear, shame, gloom, regret, contempt, and so on. The vicarious experience of earnestly performing such unwelcome emotions dispels—like true tragedy—the fear of and the pity for such emotional experiences in reality. The compassionate lyrics to be considered in the next chapter, however, fuse joy and sorrow into a single expression, and the successful performance of such lyrics produces the "I's" actual experience of pity.

FIVE

Compassioun for the Passion (and Its Perversion)

"Lo, pitee renneth soone in gentil herte"
[Behold, pity flows quickly in a noble heart]
Chaucer (*Canterbury Tales*, IV, 1986)

"Compassion" and "pity" are loan words, first introduced into Middle English with religious denotations. Subsequently, synonyms for this emotion were appropriated to apply to a far wider range of feeling, including an inamorata's willingness to grant "mercy" to her lover—that is, to have sex. But the compassionate poems to be considered in this chapter are impersonations of directly sharing another's pain. The twin foci of most Middle English lyrics that enact such a "virtuous sadness"[1] are the passion of Christ and the com-passion of Mary—that is, her psychological suffering at the sight of her Son's physical torture. Sarah McNamer views expressions of such "medieval Christian compassion as a historically contingent, ideologically charged, and performatively constituted emotion—and one that was, in the broad period considered here (ca. 1050–1530), insistently gendered as feminine."[2]

An exceptionally brief yet poignant lyric, "Now goth sonne under wod" [Now the sun goes beneath the woods], makes Mary's pain immediate, "Now," but does so by inference rather than by means of vivid detail. Variations among this lyric's forty-one textual witnesses, as well as the fact that it was frequently transcribed as prose, suggest its widespread memorial transmission and popular appeal. It is not hard to imagine that "Now goth sonne under wod"—sometimes identified as "Speculum Ecclesi[a]e" [Mirror of the Church] because it was embedded in a devotional manuscript, St. Edmund of Canterbury's *Speculum Ecclesiae*—would be whispered from memory while contemplating some visual representation of Mary at the foot of the cross. Rosemary Woolf proposed the "possibility that" this brief lyric "was originally part of an early poem on the Hours of the Cross or that it was part of a longer Passion poem"[3] The Mother of Mercy is here the focus of the reader's required pity.

> **Now the sun sets beneath the woods.**
> now goth sonne under wod
> > **Your fair face grieves me, Mary.**
> > me reweth marye thy faire rode
> **Now the sun sets beneath the trees.**
> now goth sonne under tree
> > **It grieves me, Mary, your Son and you.**
> > me reweth marye thy sone and thee

This lyric addresses Mary by name twice (just as in the *Ave Maria*); for a believer, these vocatives are not apostrophes—they are direct addresses truly heard. Like the "Hail Mary," this mini-prayer should be uttered with guileless affection—an emotional enactment that devotion to Mother Mary deliberately encourages.

A fairly commonplace wordplay informs "Now goth sonne under wod." The death of Mary's Son is mirrored in "The darkness which covers the earth . . . the symbolic parallel to the setting of the true Sun."[4] Instead of directly viewing the cross or *rood*, itself identifiable as a "tree" (l. 3) harvested from the "wod" (l. 1), we envision Mary's "faire rode" (i.e., rosy complexion). Within the *Speculum*'s reading for a "Contemplacion bifor mydday"—that is, in anticipation of the hour when Christ was first raised on the cross—this lyric draws contextual resonance from a citation of the Song of Songs: "As Seynt Barnard seiþ in a songe of love 'Ne merveile ȝe þat þouȝe I be broune & pale, for þe sunne haþ miscoloured me.' And þerfore men sey in English seye." [As St. Bernard says in the Song of Songs: "Do not marvel that I am brown and bloodless, for the sun has discolored me." And therefore men say in English:].[5] In situ, the image of Mary's shadowed face "draws its essential power from the lines quoted immediately before it . . . [based] upon *Canticles* I. 15. The 'sun' which has stained the Virgin's face is also her 'son': she is suffused with fading sunlight, grief and reflected divinity."[6] If read within a church setting, itself an *Alma Mater,* stained-glass light could project Mary's discolored grief onto the reader's face during a prolonged contemplative moment.

Simple repetition produces medial rhymes of "sonne" (ll. 3 and 4) embraced by "Marie" (ll. 2 and 5). However, as Edmund Reiss remarked, "We should not be deceived into thinking that its wordplay and ambiguities are present merely to give intellectual pleasure. Rather . . . they lead to an awareness" of compassion.[7] The lyric's melancholy image of sunset recalls that Christ died at "nones," the ninth hour (3:00 p.m., rather than modern "noon") when darkness fell, an unnatural sunset.

The default expectation of male readers is that the lyric's "I" who gazes upon Mary is likewise masculine; if so, "Now goth sonne under wod" plays as a sad serenade expressing the painful attractiveness of Mary's suffering beauty. In a woman's voice at vespers, however, especially if remembered by a mother who has herself lost a child, the sheer anguish of "Me reweth" (l. 4) can still be heard. Liturgically, the most frequent occasion for such a compassionate contemplation of Mary's grief would be performance of the thirteenth-century "Stabat Mater" attributed to Pope Innocent III or, more probably, Friar Jacopone da Todi.[8] Individual verses of "The Mother Stands" are still sung to accompany movement from one Station of the Cross to another.

Performance of the Stations of the Cross recalls fourteen scenes of Christ's Passion, a contemplative devotion and a sort of imaginary pilgrimage. The twelfth Station focuses on Christ's death on the cross, the isolated scene of "Now goth sonne under wod." But then the thirteenth Station pictures the *Depositio*—that is, Jesus being taken from the cross and laid in Mary's lap—as at birth, so "fusing the nativity with the crucifixion."[9] Recited in such a contemplative context, "Now goth sonne under wod" requires the reader to feel fully Mary's pain as the *Pieta* (Pity Personified), to endure the labor she was exempted from suffering at Christ's birth.

A quite different strategy for arousing comparable compassion for Mary is enacted by "This maiden hight Mary she was full mild," commonly identified as a lullaby because of its introductory stanza (xaxa), which, however, need not be repeated as a burden after each stanza of what becomes a dialogue poem (aabbcddc). This lyric begins by overhearing a less than silent night, Mary's distraught efforts to soothe a colicky Jesus.

This other night I saw a sight,
this ynder night i sawe a sighte
A star as bright as any day
a sterre as bright as ony daye
And all the while a maiden sang:
and ever amonge a maidene songe
"By, by, lully, lullay."
by by lully lullaye

5   **This maiden was named Mary. She was very mild.**
    this maiden hight mary she was full milde
    She kneeled before her own dear child.
    she knelede bifore here owne dere childe
       She lulled, she clasped,
       she lullede she lappede
       She turned, she swaddled,
       she rullede she wrapped
       She cried—there is no denial—
       she wepped withoutene nay
10 **She rolled Him over, she dressed Him,**
    she rullede him she dressede him
    She comforted Him, she blessed Him,
    she lissed him she blessed him
       She sang "Dear Son, lullay."
       she sange dere sone lullay
    She said, "Dear Son, lie still and sleep.
    she saide dere sone ly still and slepe
    What cause have You so sore to weep
    what cause hast thu so sore to wepe
15   **With sighing, with sobbing,**
       with sighing with snobbinge
       With crying and with screeching
       with crying and with scrycchinge
       All day long
       all this londeday
       And thus awake weeping sorely
       and thus wakinge with sore wepinge

        Dropping many salty tears?
        with many salt teres droppinge
20   **Lie still, Dear Son, I pray You."**
        ly stille dere sone i thee pray
   "Mother," He said, "for mankind I weep so sorely
   moder he saide for man i wepe so sore
   And because of [My] love of him I shall be sorely torn
   and for his love i shall be tore
        With scourging, with menacing,
        with scorging with thretning
        With buffeting, with beating—
        with bobbing with beting
25   **Truly, mother, I'm saying—**
        for sothe moder i saye
        And on a cross hanging very high
        and on a crosse full hy hanging
        And into my heart sticking all painfully
        and to my herte foll sore sticking
   A spear on Good Friday."
   a spere on good fridaye
   This maiden answered with a sad face,
   this maidene aunswerde with hevy chere
30   **"Will You suffer so, my sweet dear Son?**
   shalt thu thus sofere my swete sone dere
        Now I mourn, now I worry,
        now i morne now i muse
        I deny all gladness
        i all gladness refuse
        Forever [from] this day [forth].
        i ever for this day
        My dear Son, I pray You
        my dere sone i thee pray
35   **[That] this pain You put away**
        this paine thu put away
   If it may be [at all] possible.
   and if it possibil by may

This portrayal of a mother struggling to calm her crying child is far easier for parents to identify with than the idealized tranquility of conventional Nativity scenes. The second stanza should likewise be played as Mary talking to her baby as mothers typically do when trying to make them "ly stille." There is a touching nasal quality to Middle English "snobbynge" (l. 15) lost in translation. There is also a didactic reason for Mary's suffering caused by Christ's weeping prophecy: the anticipated pain of the crucifixion here imposes itself (with identical syntax) on Mary's otherwise having a painless delivery.

The lyric's premise that an infant Jesus could miraculously reply to His mother's presumably rhetorical question "What cause?" (l. 14) provides a stumbling block only for those readers who doubt He can foreknow His crucifixion in vivid detail. The phrase "for his love" (l. 21), explaining why Christ will suffer and die, can mean both "on account of My love for mankind" and "to win his love." Intense compassion then informs the Mother of Sorrow's even more poignant expression of grief in the final stanza: "I all gladness refuse" (l. 30). With an anticipatory echo of Christ's own request in the garden of Gethsemane (Matthew 26:39), Mary prays "This paine thu put away, / And if it possibil be may" (ll. 35–36). Knowing that neither Christ nor Mary is spared the pain, the reader, in turn, weeps regretfully.

Another cradle song, "Lullay, lullay, litel child, why wepest thu so sore," requires no impersonation of Mary. Performed before a crèche by any sinner, John Grimestone's sad lyric thanks the baby Jesus for His *Great Condescension* (i.e., the willingness of the Son of God to become mortal man).[10]

> **Lullaby, lullaby, little child,**
> lullay lullay litel child
> **Why do you weep so sorely?**
> why wepest thu so sore
>   **Lullaby, lullaby, little child,**
>   lullay lullay litel child
>   **You Who were so strong and free**
>   thu that were so sterne and wild
> 5   **Now are made meek and mild**
>   now art become meke and mild
>   **To save what was lost.**
>   to saven that was forlore

But for my sin I know it is
but for my senne i wot it is
That God's son suffered this.
that godes sone suffret this
Mercy, Lord! I have done amiss.
mercy lord i have do mis
10 **Surely, I shall [sin] no more.**
iwis i wile no more
Against my Father's will I chose
agenis my fadres wille i ches
An apple with lamentable haste;
an appel with a reuful res
Therefore, I lost my heritage,
wherfore min heritage i les
And now You weep . . . therefore.
and now thu wepest therfore
15 **I took an apple off a tree**
an appel i tok of a tree
That God had forbidden me,
god it hadde forboden me
Wherefore I should be damned
wherfore i shulde dampned be
If it were not for Your weeping.
if thy weping ne wore
Lullaby for sorrow, You little thing,
lullay for wo thu litel thing
20 **You little baron, You little king.**
thu litel barun thu litel king
Mankind is the cause of Your mourning
mankinde is cause of thy murning
Whom you have loved for so long.
that thu hast loved so yore
For You have always loved man so,
for man that thu hast ay loved so
Yet You will suffer more pains
yet shaltu suffren peines mo
25 **In head, in feet, in two hands**

>   in heved in feet in hondes two
>   **And will weep yet more.**
>   and yet wepen well more
>   **That pain makes us free of sin!**
>   that peine us make of senne free
>   **That pain bring us, Jesus, to You!**
>   that peine us bringe jhesu to thee
>   **That pain help us always to flee**
>   that peine us helpe ay to flee
> 30 **The [alluring] lore of the wicked fiend.**
>   the wikkede fendes lore

Stanzas 2 through 5 obliterate the time gaps between Adam's original sin, the birth of a formerly "wild" [unrestrained] (l. 4) Christ, His future death, and this current act of contrition—all expressions of present emotion. The anaphora of "That peine" in the final stanza (ll. 27–28) recognizes the ongoing suffering of compassionate Christ for sinful humankind; this perception translates penance for the past into a petition for the future. To achieve this trust in Christ's compassion, one must first share the emotional experience of singing Mary's sad lullaby.

A protracted Marian complaint, "In a tabernacle of a toure," again requires compassionate readers to impersonate Mary in order to reproach themselves for the lunacy of lacking compassion for Christ on the cross. Like a *chanson d'aventure*, this lyric begins with the poet reporting his eavesdropping, allowing the reader to hear (and speak) Mary's candid reproach of Everyman.

>   **In a turret of a tower,**
>   in a tabernacle of a toure
>   **As I stood musing on the moon,**
>   as i stode musing on the mone
>   **A beautiful queen of highest honor**
>   a comly quene most of honoure
>   **Appeared in spiritual view. Very quickly,**
>   apered in gostly sight full sone
> 5 **She complained thus alone.**
>   she made compleynt thus by hir one

On account of man's soul, [she] was wrapped in woe.
for mannes soule was wrapped in wo
"I may not leave mankind alone,
i may nat leve mankinde allone
'Quia amore langueo' [*Because I languish for love*].
quia amore langueo
"I long for the love of man, my brother,
i longe for love of man my brother

10 I am his advocate to annul his vice;
i am his vokete to voide his vice
I am his mother; I cannot do otherwise.
i am his moder i can none other
Why should I despise my dear child
why shuld i my dere childe dispise
If he angers me in various ways?
if he me wrathe in diverse wise
Because of the weakness of the flesh, he falls away from me;
through flesshes freelte fall me fro

15 Nevertheless, I must pity him till he arises
yet must me rewe him till he rise
Because I languish for love.
quia amore langueo
"I plead [while] I wait in great longing.
i bid i bide in grete longing
I love. I watch for when man will pray.
i love i loke when man woll crave
I complain out of pity for [his] pain.
i pleyne for pite of peyning

20 If he would [only] ask for mercy, he would have it.
wolde he aske mercy he shuld it have
Speak to me, Soul, and I shall save.
say to me soule and i shall save
Call me, my child, and I shall come
bid me my childe and i shall go
You never prayed to me but that my Son then forgave
thou prayde me never but my son forgave
Because I languish for love.

quia amore langueo

25 "**O wretch in this world, I look on you,**
o wreche in the worlde i loke on thee
    I see your trespasses everyday:
    i see thy trespas day by day
    With lechery, against my chastity;
    with lechery ageyns my chastite
    With pride, against my poor array.
    with pride agene my pore aray
    My love endures; yours departs.
    my love abideth thine is away
30 **My love calls you; you sneak away from me.**
my love thee calleth thou stelest me fro
    Appeal to me, Sinner, I pray you
    sewe to me sinner i thee pray
    Because I languish for love.
    quia amore langueo
"**As the Mother of Mercy I was made for you—**
moder of mercy i was for thee made
    Who needs it except only you?
    who nedeth it but thou alone
35 **I am happier to get grace for you**
to gete thee grace i am more glade
    Than you are to ask for it. Why don't you want any?
    than thou to aske it why wilt thou noon
    When did I ever say 'no,' tell me, to anyone?
    when seid i nay tell me till oon
    Truly never yet, neither to friend nor foe.
    forsoth never yet to frende ne foo
    [It's] when you ask not at all, then I make [my] moan
    when thou askest nought than make i moone
40 **Because I languish for love.**
    quia amore langueo
"**I seek you in prosperity and wretchedness.**
i seke thee in wele and wrechednesse
    I seek you in riches and poverty.
    i seke thee in riches and poverte

You, Man, behold where your mother is!
thou man beholde where thy moder is
Why don't you love me since I love you?
why lovest thou me nat sith i love thee
45   **However sinful and sorry you may be,**
sinful or sory how evere thou be
You are so welcome to me—there are none more so—
so welcome to me there ar no mo
I am your sister, truly trust in me
i am thy suster right trust on me
Because I languish for love.
quia amore langueo
"My child is condemned on account of your sin.
my childe is outlawed for thy sinne
50   **My child is beaten because of your trespasses.**
my childe is bete for they trespasse
It still pierces my heart that [He] so close to me
yet prikketh mine hert that so ny my kinne
Should suffer. O Son, alas,
shuld be disseased o sone allasse
You are his brother; I was His mother.
thou art his brother his moder i was
You sucked my breast; You loved man so [much that]
thou soked my pappe thou loved man so
55   **You died for him. He has my heart**
thou died for him mine hert he has
Because I languish for love.
quia amore langueo
"Man, leave your sinning then, for my sake.
man leve thy sinne than for my sake
Why should I give you what you don't want?
why shulde i gif thee that thou nat wolde
Nevertheless, [even] if you sin [again], say a prayer
and yet if thou sinne som prayere take
60   **Or trust in me as I have said—**
or trust in me as i have tolde
Am I not called your mother?

am nat i thy moder called
Why should you flee? Behold, I love you!
why shuldest thou flee i love thee lo
I am your friend. Behold your help!
i am thy frende thy helpe beholde
Because I languish for love.
quia amore langueo

65 "Now, Son," she said "will You say 'no'
now sone she saide wilt thou sey nay
When a person would make amends for his sin
whan man wolde mende him of his mis
You caused me never yet pray in vain.
thou lete me never in veine yet pray
Then, Sinful Man, see you to this:
than sinfull man see thou to this
Whatever day you come, you are welcome.
what day thou comest welcome thou is

70 **If you were away for this, the hundredth year**
this hundreth yere if thou were me fro
I'd take you [in] full eagerly. I'd hug. I'd kiss
i take thee full faine i clippe i kisse
Because I languish for love.
quia amore langueo
"Now, I will sit and say no more, [but]
now wol i sit and sey nomore
Depart and watch with great longing.
leve and loke with grete longing

75 **When man will call, I will make restitution.**
when man woll calle i wol restore
I love to save him. He is my offspring.
i love to save him he is mine ofspringe
No wonder if my heart hangs on Him—
no wonder if mine hert on him hinge
He was my dear one. What [else] may I do?
he was my neighbore what may i do
On account of Him, I had this devotion,
for him had i this worshipping

   80   *And therefore I languish for love.*
              and therefore amore langueo
          "**Why was I crowned and made a queen?**
             why was i crouned and made a quene
              Why was I called 'the well of mercy'?
             why was i called of mercy the welle
              Why should a mortal woman be
             why shuld an erthly woman bene
              So high in heaven, above angels?
             so high in heven above aungelle
   85   **For you, Mankind—I'm telling the truth!**
             for thee mankinde the truthe i telle
              You, ask my help and I shall do
             thou aske my helpe and i shall do
              What I was ordained to do: keep you from hell
             that i was ordained kepe thee fro helle
              Because I languish for love.
             quia amore langueo
          "**Now, Man, be mindful of me forever.**
             nowe man have minde on me forever
   90   **Look on [me], your love, languishing so.**
             loke on thy love thus languisshing
              Let us never separate from one another.
             late us never fro other dissevere
              My help is your own. Crawl under my wing.
             mine helpe is thine owne crepe under my winge
              Your sister is queen, Your Brother is King.
             thy sister is a quene thy brother a kinge
              Your inheritance is reserved, Son. Come get it.
             this heritage is tayled sone come therto
   95   **Take me for your wife and learn to sing**
             take me for they wife and lerne to singe
              Because I languish for love."
             quia amore langueo

The twelve eight-line stanzas of this ballade (rhyming ababbcbc) share a macaronic refrain that is an excerpt from the Song of Songs 2.5 "Fulcite me floribus, stipate me malis, quia amore langueo" [Prop me up with flowers, stuff me with apples: because I languish from love]. Spent by love-longing, the *Song*'s "sponsa" (wife), who commonly came to personify *Ecclesia* (as heir to *Synagoga*),[11] is sighing her reciprocal love for God the Groom. The use of this erotic versicle as the lyric's refrain emphasizes the passion of Mary's compassion for unworthy man. Despite their patent guilt, made clear in stanza 2, Mary longs to serve as humanity's attorney, a role that informs her occasionally lawyerlike vocabulary: "vokete to void" (l. 10), "bid" (l. 17), "trespas" (ll. 26, 50), "sewe" (l. 31), "outlawed" (l. 49), "restore" (l. 75), "tayled" (l. 94). Mary's appeal for a commuted sentence is ensured because of Christ's clemency—once Mary brings each of her sinful sons to confess that her Son "is bete for thy trespasse" (l. 50).

Casting herself first as sister, then mother, and finally as wife and friend, Mary embodies the perfection of feminine compassion for fallen humankind. The phrase "tabernacle of a toure" (l. 1) could modify where the eavesdropper stood musing, but it would be a very rare use of "tabernacle" for the more commonplace and equally alliterative "touret" [turret].[12] This tabernacle should probably be imagined instead as a grotto-like niche from which a "gostly" (l. 4) apparition of the Virgin (an animated statue?) is perceived to speak. In Middle English, *tabernacle* retained its sense of a "portable sanctuary of the Hebrews."[13] As "Moder of Mercy" (l. 33) borrows a familiar epithet from the Marian litanies, so, too, identifications of Mary as "Turris Davidica" [Tower of David] and "Turris eburnea" [Ivory Tower] inspire the incipit. Mary herself, as a tabernacle of virginity and pure vessel of grace, provided Christ's only acceptable abode; "this image of the virginal Mother of God as a sealed chamber is a patent evocation of the Incarnation."[14]

Rosemary Woolf felt that "the language of love-longing in this lyric is not fitting to a loving mother."[15] However, a "gostly" (l. 3) or non-literal perception of Mary as Mother Church—the *sponsa* to whom brother Christ is married—seems to inform this lyric's compound conceit of loving her as mother-sister-wife. Adopted under Mary's wing, man returns to the womb of his Alma Mater. Although "In a tabernacle of a toure" is quite precise about Mary's role as intercessor, its idealization of her as Total Forgiveness came to be perceived as *mariolatry*: "One must be struck by the way medieval English religious poems, with rare exceptions, were forgotten after the Reformation."[16]

Whereas Mary languishes like a spurned lover of humankind in "In a tabernacle of a toure," she argues with her Son in "Stond wel moder vnder rode," objecting vehemently that He is allowing Himself to suffer so for unworthy humanity. Within this lyrical dialogue, as it "transforms from command to instruction to pleading, Christ's speech moves from Mary's individual sorrow over his passion to the greater spiritual benefit his passion will gain for the entire Christian community."[17] Formally, this lyric consists of eleven six-line stanzas (rhyming aabccb). The first nine stanzas present alternating tercets of Jesus first telling his mother not to mourn, and then her responding with unreconciled anguish. They are thus both united and opposed with competing statements of compassion.[18] There is an easily recognized emotional intensity to this dialogue that is "exceptionally responsive to literary analysis because of the tense psychology of the mother-son relationship."[19]

    "Stand well, Mother, beneath the cross.
    stond well moder under rode
        Behold your son with a glad heart.
        bihold thy sone with glade mode
        Happy, Mother, you can be."
        blithe moder might thou be
    "Son, how should I stand by happily?
    sone how shulde i blithe stonde
5   I see your feet; I see your hands
        i see thin fet i see thin honde
        Nailed to the hard tree."
        nailed to the harde tree
    "Mother, stop your weeping.
    moder do wey thy wepinge
        I suffer death for mankind;
        i thole deth for monkinde
        I suffer not at all for My own guilt."
        for my gult thole i non
10   "I feel the death wound,
    sone i fele the dedestounde
        The sword is at my heart's root—
        the swert is at min herte grounde
        What Simeon promised me."

        that me bihet simeon
"Mother, have mercy! Let Me die
        moder mercy let me deye
            In order to buy Adam out of hell
            for adam out of helle beye
15   **And his kin that are lost."**
            and his kun that is forlore
"Son, what will [You] advise me?
        sone what shall me to rede
            My pain tortures me to death.
            my peine pineth me to dede
            Let me die before you!"
            lat me deye thee bifore
"Mother, instead, pity all your children.
        moder thou rewe all of thy bern
20   **Wash away all your bloody tears**
            thou woshe away the blody tern
            Which hurts Me more than My own death."
            it doth me worse then my ded
"Son, how can I dry up my tears?
        sone how may i teres werne
            I see the streams of blood run
            i see the blody stremes erne
            From Your heart to my feet."
            from thin herte to my fet
25   **"Mother, now I can tell you—**
        moder now i may thee seye
            It is better that I alone die
            betere is that ich one deye
            Than [that] all mankind go to hell."
            then all monkunde to helle go
"Son, I see Your body all flogged,
        sone i see thy body biswongen
            [Your] feet and hands thoroughly pierced,
            fet and honden thourghout stongen
30   **No wonder that I am in agony."**
            no wonder thagh me be wo

"Mother, now I shall tell you
moder now i shall thee telle
    If I do not die, you [yourself] will go to hell.
    if i ne deye thou gost to helle
    I suffer death for your own sake."
    i thole ded for thine sake
"Son, You are so meek and considerate,
sone thou art so meke and minde

35   Don't reproach me at all—it is [because of] my kind nature
    ne wit me naught it is my kinde
    That I sorrow for you."
    that i for thee this sorewe make
"Now [at last], you may well understand
moder now thou might well leren
    What sorrow they have who bear children,
    whet sorewe haveth that children beren
    What pain [there is] in giving birth."
    whet sorewe it is with childe gon

40 "Sorrow, certainly, I can tell You,
sorewe iwis i con thee telle
    But it is the pain of hell,
    bote it be the pine of helle
    More sorrow is unknowable."
    more serewe wot i non
"Mother, have pity on mothers' grief
moder rew of moder kare
    For now you know how motherhood goes
    for now thou wost of moder fare

45   Although you yourself are a pure virgin."
    thou thou be clene maidenmon
"Son, [I shall] help at every need
sone help at alle nede
    All those who implore me,
    alle tho that to me grede
    Maiden, wife, and foolish woman."
    maiden wif and fol wimmon

"Mother, I may no longer abide.
moder may i no lengore dwelle
50   The time has come [that] I must go to hell.
the time is come i shall to helle
I shall rise on the third day."
the thridde day i rise upon
"Son, I will fall with you.
sone i will with thee founden
I surely will die because of your wounds."
i deye iwis for thine wounden
Such a sad death, there never was none other!
so soreweful ded nes never non
55   When he arose, then ended her sorrow.
when he ros tho fell hire sorewe
Her bliss [as well] sprung up on the third morning.
hire blisse sprong the thridde morewe
Happiness itself, Mother, you were then.
blithe moder were thou tho
Lady, on account of that same joy,
levedy for that ilke blisse
Beseech your Son for relief of [our] sin.
bisech thy sone of sunnes lisse
60   Be our shield against our foe.
thou be oure sheld ageyn our fo
Blessed are you, full of grace!
blessed be thou full of blisse
Let us never fail [to attain] heaven
let us never hevene misse
Through your sweet Son's power.
thourgh thy swete sones might
Lord, by means of that same blood
louerd for that ilke blod
65   That You shed on the cross,
that thou sheddest on the rod
Bring us to the light of Heaven.
thou bring us into hevene light

Conventionally, Mary suffers in silence at the foot of the cross. Her intense protests here require Jesus to explain the inexplicable goodness of Good Friday, the reasoning for His invitation to have a "glade mode" (l. 2), which makes no emotional sense until the retrospective "blisse" (ll. 56, 57) of Easter. Jesus explains (with what sounds almost like a footnote) that "For my gult thole I non" (l. 9); utterly innocent, His Mercy overrules Justice and, from Mary's perspective, defies logic. In stanza 4, Mary recognizes the torture of her own compassion as the fulfillment of Simeon's prophecy: "et tuam ipsius animam pertransiet gladius" [And thy own soul a sword shall pierce] (Luke 2:35).

The bluntness of Christ's remark "Moder, mercy, let my deye" (l. 13) is deeply disturbing, but Mary's reply hurts more to perform—"Lat me deye thee bifore" (l. 18)—because it is difficult to imagine a greater anguish than outliving your child. The intensity of Mary's com-passion is imaged by her "blody tern" [bloody tears] (l. 20), equivalent to her Son's anguish on the Mount of Olives (Luke 22:44 "et factus est sudor eius sicut guttae sanguinis" [And his sweat became like drops of blood]). In turn, Christ's compassion for Mary's psychological suffering hurts more than His physical torture: "it doth me worse than my ded" (l. 21). That His blood flows directly "From thin herte to my fet" (l. 24) indicates their proximity of their suffering together.

Christ has tried to convince Mary that His death will free humankind (ll. 14–15, 27) from the due debt of going to Hell, including Adam's offspring born before the Incarnation as Mary's children too—"all thy bern" (l. 19).[20] A somewhat startling (though quite orthodox) declaration by Christ is that even Mary, born without the stain of Original Sin, would be duly damned—"thou gost to helle" (l. 32)—without His redemptive sacrifice. And Mary apologizes for her feminine "kinde" (l. 35), so compassionately kind by gender.

In lines 37–39, Jesus reminds Mary that the Nativity was painless and explains that she is now enduring the equivalent (and equivalently undue) pain of being His Co-Redemptrix. Since "leren" can mean both "teach" and "learn," Mary, having so suffered, can henceforth "wel leren" (l. 37) the pain of women who "with childe gon" (l. 39) and personify maternal compassion: "Moder, rewe of moder fare" (l. 44). Though herself a "clene maidenmon" [pure virgin] (l. 45), Mary's compassion extends even to a "fol wimmon" (l. 48).

Ingrid Nelson rightly remarks that "the dialogue between Christ and Mary both describes and legitimates two very different affective responses to the same event . . . It concludes in a stalemate."[21] The dialogue so ends, but the text then resurrects Mary's bliss, and this lyric finally transforms into a straightforward prayer. As in the "Ave Maria," the poem's "we" ("us," "oure") ask Mary "fulle of blisse" (l. 61) to intercede that we may share "that ilke blisse" [that same bliss] (l. 58). The last tercet appeals directly to the "Louerd" (l. 64) for the saving bliss of "that ilke blod" (l. 64) that He shed on a Friday that now can be called "Good."

"When I see blosmes springe" starts blissfully with birds singing and the lyric's "I" voicing a harmonious "swete love-longinge" (l. 3) for a "love newe" (l.5) who is identified simply as "him" (l. 10). It is initially easy to assume that this lyric is to be performed by a young woman. But the second stanza reveals that "I miselve stonde" (l. 11) at the foot of the cross (as did Mary), and the first stanza's reverdie evolves into a compassionate lament: "Wel, wel oghte min herte / For His love to smerte / And sike and sory beo" (ll. 18–20). As Megan Murton observes, the "I" of such a lyric need "not, then, refer to an individual with a particular gender identity but serves as a place holder for anyone who wishes to use the prayer"—especially during Lent.[22]

When I see the blossoms bloom
when i see blosmes springe
    And hear the birds sing,
    and here foules song
A sweet love-longing
a swete lovelonginge
Stabs right through my heart—
min herte thourghout stong
5   **All because of a fresh love**
    all for a love newe
Which is so sweet and true
that is so swete and trewe
That it cheers my entire song.
that gladieth all my song
I know certainly all
ich wot all mid iwisse
My joy and also my bliss

> my joye and eke my blisse
10 > **Are entirely dependent on Him.**
> on him is all ilong
> **When I myself stand**
> when i miselve stonde
>> **And see with my own eyes**
>> and with min eyen seo
>> **[His] hands and feet pierced**
>> thurled fot and honde
>> **With three huge nails.**
>> with grete nailes threo
15 >> **His head was blood-soaked.**
>> blody wes his heved
>> **There was no belief at all in Him**
>> on him nes nout bileved
>> **Who was free of sin.**
>> that wes of peines freo
>> **Very well should my heart**
>> well well oghte min herte
>> **Hurt for His love,**
>> for his love to smerte
20 >> **And sigh and be sorry.**
>> and sike and sory beo
> **Jesus, mild and merciful,**
> jesu milde and softe
>> **Give me the strength and power**
>> gef me streinthe and might
>> **To yearn intensely and frequently**
>> longen sore and ofte
>> **To love You properly,**
>> to lovie thee aright
25 >> **To be patient and endure pain**
>> pine to tholie and dreye
>> **For you, Sweet Mary.**
>> for thee swete marye
>> **You are so free and bright,**
>> thou art so free and bright

Maiden and gentle mother.
maiden and moder milde
For the love of your Child,
for love of thine childe
30 **Earn for us Heaven's light.**
ernde us hevene light
Alas that I cannot
alas that i ne con
Turn my thoughts to Him
turne to him my thoght
And choose Him for my lover
and cheosen him to lemmon
So dearly He has paid for us
so duere he us hath iboght
35 **With deep and heavy wounds,**
with woundes deope and stronge
With pains severe and lasting.
with peines sore and longe
We know nothing of [such] love.
of love ne conne we noght
His blood that fell to the ground
his blod that feol to grounde
Out of his sweet wounds
of his swete wounde
40 **Has saved us from hellfire.**
of peine us hath iboght
Jesus, Sweet and Mild,
jesu milde and swete
I sing my song to You.
i singe thee my song
I cry to You frequently
ofte i thee grete
And pray to You constantly.
and preye thee among
45 **Let me give up [my] sins**
let me sunnes lete
And repent in this life

and in this live bete
What I have done wrong.
that ich have do wrong
At our life's end,
at oure lives ende
When we shall depart,
when we shule wende
50 **Jesus, receive us!**
jesu us undefong

Despite the joyful expectations of its reverdie-like opening and its jaunty ababccbddb stanzaic pattern, "When I see blossoms spring" compels the reader to suffer visualizing Christ's suffering directly "with min eyen" (l. 12). There is something ambiguous about the phrasing that Christ is "of peines freo" [free of penalties/pains] (l. 17). He was truly not deserving "punishment for a fault," though He is not at all free of "physical torture."[23] But there is something far more emotionally paradoxical about the lyric's expression of "A swete love-longing" (l. 3) that "gladieth all my song" (l. 7); sinners are saved from the "peine" of Hell by Christ's "swete wounde" (ll. 39–40).[24]

The third and final stanzas address "Jesu, milde and softe" directly, turning heartache into a hopeful prayer. But the fourth stanza interposes a moment of doubt "Alas" (l. 31). "I" shall ever again fail to "cheosen" [choose] Christ as "lemmon" [beloved] (l. 33) despite recognizing His incomprehensible love for us "ne conne we noght" (l. 37). At its completion—as, it is hoped, "At oure lives ende" (l. 47)—performance of "When I see blosmes springe" regains its initial joy: "I singe Thee my song" (l. 42) with grateful prayers after contrite compassion.

Differing versions of a lyric that casts Christ as an *amans exclusus* [locked-out lover] articulate the pathos of failing to feel sufficiently contrite compassion for Christ's suffering in due time. The conceit of Christ as neglected lover derives from Revelation 3:20: a loving Christ knocking to enter a penitent heart ("Ecce sto ad [h]ostium et pulso" [Behold I stand at the door and I knock]),[25] which has been "creatively blended with the Christ-as-lover-knight theme, drawing upon the Song of Songs verse *Aperi mihi* ("Open to me, my sister and beloved," Cant. 5:2)."[26] Rosemary Woolf thought "Alas alas evel have I sped" to be not only the earliest but also the best version because it performs as "more than a sermon verse, being in itself a complete and exceptionally moving complaint."[27]

> **Allas, allas, full evilly have I done.**
> allas allas vel yuel y sped
> **Because of sin, Jesus has fled from me,**
> for synne jesu fro me ys fled
> > **That faithful friend.**
> > þat lyuely fere
> **At my door, He stands alone**
> at my dore he standes al one
> 5 **And calls "Undo yet, Sinful Man!"**
> and kallys vndo yit senful mone
> > **In this manner**
> > on þis manere
> **"Undo [the door], My Beloved, My Dear Dove!**
> vndo my lef my dowue dere
> **Why do I stand beseeching [you] out here**
> vndo wy stond sekyn out here
> > **As [I] am your spouse.**
> > Iyk am þi make
> 10 **"Behold my head and my locks of hair**
> lo my heued and myne lockys
> **Are entirely covered with bloody drops**
> ar al by wevyd wyt blody dropys
> > **For your sake."**
> > for þine sake

There is a certain bitter irony to the opening use of the verb "sped" (l. 1) to rhyme with "fled" since "spedden" so strongly connotes success. So, too, Christ's slightly pleonastic reference to the "lockys" (l. 10) of His hair may be heard as a rebuking pun since it also means "a lock for securing a door"[28] that has been closed unto Him. The primary modern appeal of this brief lyric is its unadulterated expression of emotion.

"Undo thy dore, my spuse dere" preserves a substantial adaptation of the lyric in John of Grimestone's *Commonplace Book,* "where it appears as a lyric intended for use during a Good Friday."[29] Grimestone's rendition "inverts the stanzas of the earlier poem, and adds a responding stanza that has received a less positive critical response."[30] However, this version too can be quite successfully played as a rejected call and dejected response.

[Jesus]   **Undo your door, my dear spouse!**
                            undo thy dore my spuse dere
                Alas, why do I stand here locked out?
                  alas why stond i loken out here
                For I am your spouse.
                  for am i thy make
                Look at my hair and my head
                  loke my lokkes and eek min heved
5   **And my entire body covered in blood**
                  and all my body with blod bewewed
                For your sake.
                for thy sake

[Reader aside]   **Alas, alas, I have done poorly**
                          alas alas evel have i sped
                Because of my sin Jesus has fled from me
                for senne jesu is fro me fled
                My true companion.
                my trewe lere
10   **Outside my gate He stands alone**
                withouten my gate he stant alone
                Sorrowfully He makes his moan
                sorfuliche he maket his mone
                In His manner.
                on his manere

[Reader aloud]   *Lord, on account of sin, I sigh sorely.*
                          lord for senne i sike sore
                Forgive, and I will [sin] no more.
                forgef and i ne will no more
                With all my might I will forsake sin
                with all my might senne i forsake
                And open my heart to take You in,
                and opne min herte thee inne to take

For Your heart is split to catch our love.
for thin herte is cloven oure love to kecchen
   Your love has chosen to fetch us all.
   thy love is chosen us alle to fecchen
It would pierce my heart if I were kindly disposed
min herte it therlede if i wer kende
   To have Your sweet love in mind.
   thy swete love to haven in mende
Pierce my heart with Your loving
perce min herte with thy lovinge
That I may have my dwelling in You.
that in thee i have my dwellinge

Andrew Galloway reads this lyric as initially establishing "an erotic dialogue, verging on drama... How this might have been exploited as a performance that is many-sided (metaphorically or literally...), and whether in a church or private chapel or merely a matter of private reading, is unclear."[31] The first two six-line stanzas voice, first, Christ's passionate serenade (aabccb) and then the corresponding remorse (ddeffe) of the enclosed "I" after Christ's departure. This is followed by a "Responsio peccatoris" [Response of the sinner] as indicated in the margin of the manuscript at line 7.

The marital diction of stanza 1 remains intimate, indeed a bit more erotic—"my spuse dere" (l. 1), "thy make" (l. 3) as well as "My trewe fere" (l. 9).[32] Still, the horrific wounds of Christ-the-would-be-Groom cause shame "Alas, alas evel..." (l. 7). Sarah Stanbury has felt this version's domestic familiarity in Christ's lines eludes standard exegesis: "Since the speaker is covered in blood, the voice could be that of a battered wife... [or] might as well be that of a husband who has just defended his wife's honour."[33]

In the last four couplets, the left-behind "I" speaks to a distanced but not unhearing Christ. The still beloved sinner fears that excluded Jesus will have "fled" (l. 8). Christiania Whitehead explains that such lyric expressions of unworthiness frequently produce "a poetics of anxiety, characterized by declarations of pronounced inadequacy."[34] However, here, the optative verb "forgef" (l. 14) offers an emotional pivot away from despair to confidence that a renunciation of sin, sincerely performed, assures forgiveness (echoing John 8:11). The last four stanzas all focus on opening one's heart (st. 6) to the opened Sacred Heart of Jesus with a conceit bordering on the metaphysical. The piercing of Christ's heart on the cross opened an entrance or a snare "to keechen" [catch] (l. 17) human love. The final two stanzas embrace the sweet piercing of the "I's" own heart, moving from the conditional "if I wer kende" [if I were compassionate] (l. 19) to the closing anticipation of a mutual indwelling.

The very familiarity of medieval conventions repeatedly used to teach God's salvific plan allows a lyric like "Somer is comen and winter gon" to reference with stunning rapidity the Expulsion, Nativity, Crucifixion, Stabat Mater, Harrowing of Hell, Resurrection, and Judgment Day, all as emotionally intertwined scenes.

Summer has arrived, and winter departed.
somer is a comen and winter gon
 This daytime starts [to get] too long,
 this day biginneth to longe
and these birds—every one of them—
and this foules everichon
 enjoy themselves with song.
 joye hem wit songe
5 **[Yet] so strong a care constrains me,**
 so stronge care me bint
Utterly opposite to the joy that is found
all wit joye that is funde
 throughout the land.
 in londe
All for a Child
all for a child
Who is so forgiving
that is so milde
10 **To deal with.**
 of honde
That Child Who was so mild and noble
that child that is so milde and wlonk
 And also of great strength,
 and eke of grete munde
Both in the woods and hills,
bothe in boskes and in bank

[He] **tracked me for a while.**
isout me havet astunde

15 **He found me**
ifunde he hevede me
For an apple of a tree
for an appel of a tree
    Bound.
    ibunde
He broke the bond
he brake the bond
That was so strong
that was so strong

20   **With [His own] wounds.**
    wit wunde
That Child, Who was so mild and beautiful,
that child that was so wilde and wlonk
    Bowed low to me.
    to me alute lowe
From me to Jews, He was sold.
fram me to jewes he was sold
They could not recognize Him at all.
ne cuthen hey him nout knowe

25 **They said, "Let's**
do we saiden he
"Nail Him upon a tree
naile we him opon a tree
    Shamefully,
    a lowe
But first we shall
ac arst we shullen
mock him
scumi him
    For a while."
    a throwe

30 **Jesus is the child's name,**
jhesu is the childes name
    King of all the land.

king of all londe
They made fun of the King
of the king he meden game
And struck Him with [their] hands
and smiten him wit honde
To test Him upon a tree.
to fonden him opon a tree
35 **They gave Him wounds two and three**
he geven him wundes two and three
   With [their] hands.
   mid honden
Of bitter drink,
of bitter drinck
They sent Him
he senden him
   A serving.
   a sonde
40 **[The] debt He undertook upon the cross-tree**
det he nom o rodetree
   [For] the life of us all,
   the lif of us alle
Nor might it otherwise be.
ne mighte it nout other be
Otherwise, we would have to fall
bote we sholden falle
And fall into deep hell.
and fallen in helle dep
(Were it never so sweet.)
nere nevere so swet
45   **Furthermore,**
   wit alle
[Nothing else] could save us,
ne mighte us save
Not castle, tower,
castel tur
   Or hall.

    ne halle
Virgin and mother stood there,
maide and moder thar astod

50   **Mary full of grace,**
    marye full of grace
    And she shed blood from her eyes
    and of here eyen heo let blod
    Dropping on the spot.
    fallen in the place
    The streaks of her blood ran [down]
    the trace ran of here blod
    [And] changed her skin and blood
    changed here fles and blod

55   **And face.**
        and face
    He was torn apart
    he was todrawe
    So harshly killed
    so dur islawe
        In the hunt.
        in chace
    He took death, the Sweet Man,
    det he nam the swete man

60   **Very high upon the cross.**
    well heye opon the rode
    He washed away every one of our sins
    he wes ure sunnes everichon
    With His sweet blood.
    mid his swete blode
    On account of [its] flowing, He bowed down
    mid flode he lute adun
    And broke the gates of that prison
    and brac the gates of that prisun

65   **That stood**
        that stode
    And chose [a] host,

and ches here
[To go] out of there, [of] those who
out that there
   Were good.
   were gode
He Himself rose on the third day
he ros him ene the thridde day
   And seated Himself upon His throne.
   and sette him on his trone
70 **He will come [again] on doomsday**
   he wule come a domesday
To judge us everyone.
to dem us everich one
He may groan and weep forever
grone he may and wepen ay
That man who dies without faith
the man that deiet withoute lay
   Alone.
   alone
75 **Grant us, Christ,**
   grante us crist
With Your rising
with thin uprist
To go.
to gone

This lyric begins as a very melancholic *reverdie* precisely because its performer is bound by a "stronge care" (l. 4), the *compunctio* or prick of conscience that precedes repentance and compassion. Though Christ is "Milde / of honde" (ll. 10–11), "I" must be "isout" [sought, pursued] (l. 14) far and wide to be freed of Original Sin. To do so, Christ will allow Himself to be caught on the Cross and killed "in chace" [in the hunt] (l. 58).

The first four stanzas all refer to Christ as a child (ll. 8, 11, 21, 30). "Child" can mean a "young man," but its primary denotation in Middle English is "a young child; a baby."[35] Line 50 recalls Gabriel's greeting to Mary "gratiae plena," but now she stands at the foot of the cross, and, as Cristina Maria Cervone observes:

Considering the Annunciation and the Passion together was common. In the Roman rite the feast of the Annunciation was celebrated on March 25, the same date thought to be the day of Christ's Crucifixion and death (the Passion). The liturgical association of the two moments—at Mass and in the liturgical hours—is important because they mark the beginning and ending of Jesus's earthly life. Both crucial events for salvation history are witnessed and experienced by Mary.[36]

It is particularly disturbing to think of Christ crucified as an infant, a conceit that tacitly hints at the slanderous blood libel against Jews as baby-killers.

Christ was stretched on the cross, but the use of "todrawe" (l. 56)—as in "drawn and quartered"—rather than "honged" may suggest a more Middle English than Roman means of torture and execution, making the crime more contemporary. Among the many reiterations in this poem (e.g., "wlonk" [splendid] ll. 11 and 21), the reiteration of "Det he nom o' rode-tree" (l. 41) and "Det he nam" (l. 59) has a special duality; "det" can be translated both as "death" and as "debt," both of which Christ took upon himself. So, too, the phrasing "The lif of us alle" (l. 42) can recognize that Christ is Himself the "lif" (as well as the way and the truth, John 14:6) and that He accepted death "for the life of us all."

It is primarily in stanzas 3 and 4, however, that, for the sake of a vivid memory of the crucifixion, this lyric introduces an all too conventional statement of anti-Semitism; the lyric "I" confesses "Fram me to Jewes he was sold" (l. 23). "I" must assume the role of a repentant Judas. But the abuse of ignorant Jews who "Ne cuthen hey him nout knowe" [who could know nothing about Him] (l. 24) is then briefly dramatized (and so made current again). "Somer is comen and winter gon," thus, offers an inkling of how intense compassion can provoke an equally intense though completely contrary emotion—racial hatred.

Though intended to arouse shame, Middle English lyrics that impersonate Jesus Himself reprimanding humankind for our cruel ingratitude often sound far more irate than compassionate. The most distressing lyrics of this sort imitate (or replicate) the *Improperia* [the *Reproaches*], antiphons that were performed annually as part of *Tenebrae* [shadows] services, which enacted a funereal extinguishing of candles in commemoration of Christ's execution.[37] Dating from at least the ninth century, each reproach voiced by Christ on the cross is meant to be answered by a communal response of praise and a prayer for mercy. When only Christ's reproaches are recited, stripped of this liturgical setting's emotionally corrective replies, lyric adaptations of the *Improperia* become dramatic monologues in which Christ reminds His ungrateful fellow Jews of His role in their own salvific history. Indeed, several verses of the *Improperia* are drawn directly from the Tanakh (Psalm lxvi, Micah, vi, 3, Jeremiah, ii, 21, and Isaiah, v, 2, 40). The emotional impact of hearing Christ's reprimands so performed should, by analogy, provoke the sinful Christian's shame on every Good Friday, then repentance, and then hope for forgiveness. The emotional "should" of this liturgical/lyrical progress can be grossly misdirected, however.

Both Friar John of Grimestone and the somewhat-earlier Franciscan William Herebert (ca. 1270–1333)[38] composed vernacular adaptations of the *Improperia*. Herebert's "My folk what habbe I do thee" and Grimestone's "My folk now answer me" are both quite faithful renditions. Indeed, they are identified as such in their respective manuscripts and differ mainly in alternative paraphrasing required to accommodate two different rhyme schemes.

Rosemary Woolf did not approve of either lyric: "the earlier is stilted and the second diffuse."[39] Line-for-line comparison discloses the close correspondence of equivalent statements in both adaptations of what now becomes Christ's monologue. The fundamental complaint is the same: "Quid feci tibi? Aut in quo contristavi te?" [What have I done to You? Or in what have I offended you?]. Yet, Herebert's verbs tend to make this complaint against His killers more immediate, and so less a recollection of a former crime, and so potentially more volatile upon performance.

HEREBERT

My people, what have I done to you
my folk what habbe i do thee
Or in what thing harmed you?
other in what thing tened thee
Start now and answer me!
gin nouthe and onswere thou me

Because I led you out of Egypt,
for from egypte ich ladde thee

GRIMESTONE

My people, now answer me
my folk now answere me
And say what is my guilt.
and sey what is my gilt
What more might I have done for you
what might i mor ha don for thee
That I have not fulfilled.
that i ne have fulfilt

5 **You led me to the cross.**
  thou me ledest to rode tree
  My people, what have I done to you? ...
  my folk what habbe i do thee

  I led you through the wilderness
  thorou wildernesse ich ladde thee
  And took care of you for forty years
  and fourty yer bihedde thee
  And I gave you angels' bread
  and aungeles bred ich gaf to thee
10 **And I brought you to rest.**
  and into reste ich broughte thee
  My people, what have I done to you? ...
  my folk what habbe i do thee

  What more should I have done
  what more shulde ich haven idon
  That you have not already received?
  that thou ne havest nouth underfon
  My people, what have I done to you? ...
  my folk what habbe i do thee
15

  I fed you and clothed you

  I brought you out of Egypt
  out of egipte i broughte thee
  Where you were in your woe
  ther thu wer in thy wo
  And wickedly you took me
  and wikkedliche thu nome me
  As if I had been your foe.
  as i hadde ben thy fo

  I led you over all around,
  over all abouten i ledde thee
  And I walked before you
  and oforn thee i yede
  And I found no friendship in you
  and no frenchipe fond i in thee
  When I had need.
  whan that i hadde nede

  [For] forty winters I sent you
  fourty wenter i sente thee

  Angel's food from heaven
  angeles mete fro hevene
  And you hanged me on the cross
  and thu heng me on rode tree
  And you reviled [me] with a loud voice.

ich thee fedde and shrudde thee
And you toast me with vinegar
and thou with eysel drinkest
   to me
And stab me with a spear.
and with spere stingest
**My people, what have I done
   to you?** ...
my folk what habbe i do thee

20 **I beat Egypt for you**
ich egypte bet for thee
**And I slew their children
   for you.**
and here tem i shlou for thee
**My people, what have I done to
   you?** ...
my folk what habbe i do thee

I divided the sea for you
ich delede the see for thee
And drowned Pharaoh for you.
and pharaon dreynte for thee
**My people, what have I done
   to you?** ...
my folk what habbe i do thee
25

In a pillar of cloud I led you

in bem of cloude ich ladde thee
And to Pilate you led me.
and to pilate thou ledest me

and greddest with loud stevene

Wholesome water I sent you
heilsum water i sente thee
Out of the hard stone,

out of the harde ston
And you sent me vinegar and gall
and eysil and galle thu sentest me
Or gave me nothing.
other gef thu me non

I parted asunder the sea for you
the see i parted osunder for thee
And led you through, far and wide.
and ledde thee thoru wol wide
And to see the heart-blood of me
and the herte blod to sen of me
You struck me through the side.
thu smettest me thoru the side

I slew all your foes for you
alle thy fon i slou for thee
**And made well-known by
   [your] name,**
and made thee cout of name
And you hanged me on a cross
and thu henge me on rode tree

My people, what have I done to you? ...
my folk what habbe i do thee
With angels' food I fed you,
with aungeles mete ich fedde thee

30 **And you beat and scourged Me.**
and thou buffetest and scourgest me
My people, what have I done to you? ...
my folk what habbe i do thee

Out of a stone I drank to you,
of the ston ich dronk to thee
And you drink to me with gall.
and thou with galle drinkst to me
My people, what have I done to you? ...
my folk what habbe i do thee

35

I defeated the Kings of Canaan for you,
kinges of canaan ich for thee bet
And you beat My head with reeds.
and thou betest min heved with red
My people, what have I done to you? ...
my folk what habbe i do thee
I gave you the crown of a kingdom,
ich gaf thee crowne of kinedom

And did me much shame.
and dedest me michil schame
I bestowed a king's rod to you
a kinges yerde i thee betok

Until you were over all [others],
til thu wer all beforn

And you hanged me on a cross
and thu heng me on rode tree
And crowned me with a thorn
and corounedest me with a thorn
I made you and your enemies
i made thin enemies and thee

To be recognized apart
for to ben knowen osunder
And on a high hill you hanged me
and on an hey hill thu henge me
[For] all the world to wonder at me.
all the werld on me to wonder

40   **And you gave Me a crown
       of thorns.**
   and thou me givst a crowne
       of thorn
   **My people, what have I done
       to you? . . .**
   my folk what habbe i do thee
   I did you much honor,
   ich muchel worshipe dede
       to thee
   And you hang me on the cross.
   and thou me hongest on rode
       tree

            **And you gave Me a crown
       of thorns.**

            **My people, what have I done
       to you? . . .**

            I did you much honor,

            And you hang me on the cross.

    In Middle English, both of these renditions of the *Improperia* use the singular, familiar pronoun "thee" to address "my people," as does the Latin ("Popule meus, quid feci *tibi*?"). Neither lyric adaptation explicitly condemns all Jews per se, and indeed the necessity of translating all second-person pronouns as "you" distorts their seemingly anti-Semitic implications—somewhat. Both adaptations of the *Improperia* describe the crucifixion far more vividly. Both call for a response *now* ("Responde me" [Answer me]; cf. Herebert l. 3, Grimestone, ll. 1) though there is a certain temporal ambiguity to the Latin syntax "parasti crucem salvatori tuo," which may be translated either "you have prepared a cross for your Savior" [on which I now hang] or "you have crucified your Savior." Herebert's poem imagines far more clearly Christ speaking while still on the cross ("hongest" l. 43), whereas Grimestone recurrently recalls the crucifixion as a past event (ll. 15, 27, 31, 35). Herebert's three-line refrain also sounds far more relentlessly accusatory. Its humiliating reproof of "thee" should shame a Christian listener/reader into compassion and repentance; yet emotional transference far too readily tempts the reader to transfer all guilt to "the Jew." Although these dramatic impersonations of Christ's anguish were intended to excite compassion, their performance can become incitements to riot.

    Like so many seemingly blithe expressions of a medieval rape culture to be considered in the next chapter, such casual insults of the Jew in Middle English lyrics pose an emotional crisis for the modern reader. Whether or not these contemptible emotions can themselves be historicized, surely our reader responses should be. When impersonating Christ's reproaches of "my people,"[40] the only positive interpretive assumption to be made is that the lyric's "I" is addressing a Christian congregation/readership, who far too often—based upon an especially hateful reading of Matthew 27:25—habitually charged Jews with taking the guilt of the crucifixion upon themselves and their children.

The inherent risk to English renditions of the *Improperia* is that a Christian reader can so easily transfer God's anger to contemporary Jews; indeed, in Middle English, only "Jeu" rather than "Ebreu" can indicate followers of Mosaic law in post-biblical times. Regrettably, "the 'persecuting society' of post-Gregorian Western Christendom," though motivated by an "ideal of inclusive Christian love to build cohesion," simultaneously "engendered exclusion, violence, and hatred of others."[41] Though Jews had been expelled from England since 1290, virulent anti-Semitism remained all too frequent in Middle English narrative and dramatic literature as well.

Grimestone and Herebert both composed passionate lyrics with what now seem gratuitously anti-Semitic slurs. In Grimestone's "Water and blood for thee I sweat," Christ reports his immediate suffering, including being spat upon by Jews (l. 5).

Water and blood I sweat for you
water and blod for thee i swete
    And I am taken as a thief.
    and as a thef i am itake
I am bound. I am beaten.
i am ibounden i am ibete
    And all this, Man, is for you.
    and all it is man for thy sake
5   **I suffer Jews to spit on me,**
    i suffre jewes on me to spete
    And all night long I stay awake with them
    and all night with hem i wake
To see when you would give up
to loken whan thu woldest lete
    Your sin for love of your Spouse.
    thy senne for love of thy make
10   **My body is as red as a roe deer.**

  my body is as red as ro
> Thorns very painfully prick my head.

  thornes prikken min hed fol sore
> My face grows black and blue.

  my visage waxeth wan and blo
> I have bled so much that I can no more.

  i have so bled i may no more
> My heart is cut in two,

  min herte is forsmite ato

15 > All [of this], Man, for love of you!

  all mankinde for love of thee
> To see when you would

  to loken whan thu woldest go
> Leave your sin for love of Me.

  fro thy senne for love of me
> Though you will [still] not love Me at all—

  thou thu will nought loven me
> Even after I show you My love—

  sithen i thee my love schewe

20 > Of necessity, I must love you

  nedes i mot loven thee
> Whether or not you are forever unfaithful...

  ne be thu nevere so untrewe
> The nails, the scourges and the spear,

  the nailes the scourges and the spere
> The gall, and the sharp thorns,

  the galle and the thornes sharpe
> All these may bear witness

  alle these moun witnesse bere

25 > That I have won you with My [hurt] heart.

  that i thee have wonnen with min harte

This lyric's third-person references to Jews disassociates "them" (ll. 5–6) from "you" who must be loved (l. 20). The last stanza recalls the *Arma Christi* ("The Arms of Christ"; i.e., contemplation of the instruments of His torture and execution) often associated with "The Man of Sorrows" in the visual arts. A compassionate reading should induce suffering what Christ suffers:

"the lyric speaker is formulating the stages of this exemplary response in such a way as to give them [listeners or readers] a metaphorical *equivalence* to Christ's passion experience."[42] Simple omission of the second stanza could purge this poem of its anti-Semitism. However, too often Christian compassion for Christ's passion provokes hatred and violence, a reader response that totally ignores Christ's appeal "Pater, dimitte illis" [Father, forgive them] (Luke 23:34).

"At the time of matines Lord thu were I-take," another crucifixion lyric preserved in Grimestone's commonplace book, encapsulates "The Hours of the Cross," a contemplative exercise that was commonly part of the *Book of Hours*, a devotional text popular among the laity. This lyric can be prayed in solitary silence, or its couplet refrain "We honouren thee, Crist, and blessen thee with vois / For thou boutest this werld with this holy croys" can be repeated communally.[43]

>   **At the time of matins, Lord, You were arrested,**
>   at the time of matines lord thu were itake
>   **And You quickly were forsaken by Your disciples.**
>   and of thine disciples sone were forsake
>   **The false Jews took you in that same moment,**
>   the felle jewes thee token in that iche stounde
>   **And led you to Caiaphas, Your hands tightly bound.**
>   and ledden thee to caiphas thin handes harde ibounde
> 5 *We honor You, Christ, and bless You with [our] voice*
>   we honuren thee crist and blissen thee with vois
>   *For You redeemed this world with your holy cross.*
>   for thu boutest this werld with thin holy croys
>   **At prime, Lord, You were led before Pilate**
>   at prime lord thu were ilad pilat beforn
>   **And there very false testimony was brought against You.**
>   and there wol fals witnesse on thee was iborn
>   **They smacked Your ears and said, "Who was that?"**
>   he smiten thee under the ere and seiden who was that
> 10 **Your beautiful face was spat upon foully by them.**
>   of hem thy faire face foule was bespat
>   *We honor You . . .*
>   **At 9:00 a.m., they started to crucify You**

at underne lord they gunnen thee to crucifiye
And draped you in purple in scorn and in envy.
and clotheden thee in pourpre in scoren and in envye
With very sharp thorns You were crowned,
with wol kene thornes icorouned thu were
And You carried Your holy cross on your shoulder to [further] your suffering.
and on thy shulder to thy peines thin holy croys thu bere
We honor You . . .

15   **At midday, Lord, You were nailed to the cross,**
    at midday lord thu were nailed to the rode
Between two thieves, all bloodily.
betwixen tweye theves ihanged all on blode
Because of your torment, You were overcome with thirst and said "Sicio"
for thy pine thu wexe athirst and seidest sicio
Gall and vinegar they gave You then to drink.
galle and eysil they geven thee to drinken tho
We honor You . . .

    At 3:00 p.m., Lord, You took Your leave,
at the heye noon lorde thu toke thy leve
20   **And into Your Father's hand, You gave Your holy soul.**
and into thy fader hond the holigost thu geve
Longinus the knight thrust a sharp spear deep into Your heart.
longis the knight a sharp spere all to thin herte pighte
The Earth shook and trembled. The sun lost its light.
the erthe quakede and tremlede the sunne les hire lighte
We honor You . . .

    Down off the cross He was taken at the time of evensong.
    of the rode he was idon at the time of evesong
Mildly and silent He suffered all their wrongs.
mildeliche and stille he suffrede all here wrong
25   **Such a death He undertook to be able to help us.**
suich a deth he underfeng that us helpen may
Alas that the Crown of Joy [should] lie under thorns!
allas the crune of joye under thornes lay
We honor You . . .

>   At compline, he was buried and placed in a stone [sepulchre],
>   at cumplin time he was ibiriyed and in a ston ipith
>   **Jesus Christ's sweet body, and—as Holy Scripture says—**
>   jhesu cristes swete body and so seith holy writh
>   **Anointed with an ointment, and then all was fulfilled**
>   enoint with an oniment and than was cumpliyed
> 30 **What had been prophesied before about Jesus Christ.**
>   that beforn of jhesu crist was ipropheciyed
>   *We honor You ...*
>   **This same holy prayer about Your Passion,**
>   this iche holy orisoun of thy passioun
>   **I focus on You, Jesus Christ, with devotion,**
>   i thenke to thee jhesu crist with devocioun
>   **So that You, Who suffered severe torture for me,**
>   that thu that suffredest for me harde pininge
>   **May be my solace and my comfort at my final ending.**
>   be my solas and my confort at my last endinge

There are several nice turns of phrase in this lyric. For example, the verb "boutest" [you bought] (l. 6) revives the etymology of *redeem* [< Latin redimer "to purchase back" or "to ransom"]. The macaronic rhyming of "Sicio" [I thirst, John 19:28,] with "tho" (ll. 17–18) amplifies the contrast between what Christ wants and what his tormentors offer. And the conceit that "The crune of joye under thornes lay" (l. 26; cf. l. 13) conjoins the twin meanings of "crune": both "the top of the head" and "crown."[44] Polite phrasing also emphasizes that Christ, before being stabbed by blind "Longi[nu]s" (l. 21), died voluntarily: "thu toke thy leve" (l. 19) and "thu geve" (l. 20). Devout modern readers could read this lyric as an individual's splendidly abbreviated contemplative exercise—a prayer that "I thenke" (l. 32)—were it not for its gratuitous slur of "felle Jewes" (l. 3), the "they" who so brutalize Christ.

In a properly informed performance context—that is, as a call to confession—such lyrics can supposedly be played as non-racist efforts to arouse only a Christian's sympathy, shame, remorse, and then penance. To do so, some Middle English crucifixion-focused lyrics, like "Men rent me on rood" and "Thenc man of mi harde stundes," omit any specific reference to the Jews, past or present. Instead, the six emphatically mono-rhymed stanzas of "Men rent me on rood" have Christ recall the crucifixion as a historical event (l. 1) that becomes present again, asking "man" to recognize it was for "your" sake now (l. 4).

      Men tore Me apart on the cross
      men rent me on rode
          With wounds perversely mad.
          with woundes woliche wode
      My blood drained entirely.
      all blet my blode
      Think man! All of it is for your good"
      thenk man all it is ye to gode
5   **Think Who first created you;**
      thenk who ye first wroghte
          On account of what deeds, you [then] sought hell;
          for what werk helle you soughte
      Think Who redeemed you again.
      thenk who ye agein boughte
      [So,] behave carefully! Do not fail Me.
      werk warly faile me noughte
    Behold My side,
    biheld my side
10   **My wounds spread so wide.**
      my woundes sprede so wide
      Restless I ride.
      restless i ride
      Look upon Me [and] put aside your pride.
      lok upon me put fro ye pride
    My palfrey is [made] of a tree,
    my palefrey is of tree
      With nails nailed through me.
      with nailes nailede thurgh me
15   **There is no greater sorrow to see;**
      ne is more sorwe to see
      Surely, there can no greater be.
      certes non more no may be
    Under my clotted blood,

under my gore[45]
    Are wounds incredibly sore.
  ben woundes selcouthe sore
    Learn, Man, My teaching.
  ler man my lore
20   **For the sake of My love, sin no more!**
  for my love sinne no more
    Fall not because of temptation!
  fall nought for fonding
    [So] that you must return to goodness,
  that schal ye most turne to goode
    Make a strong resistance.
  mak stif withstonding
    Think well who tore me on the cross!
  thenk well who me rent on the rode

"Thenc man of mi harde stundes" similarly shames "man" by having Christ recall His suffering ("I tholede") without any explicit mention of the Jews. The accusatory mono-rhymes of this lyric amplify the imperatives of its insistent refrain.

  Think, Man, about My harsh hours!
  thenk man of min harde stundes
    Think, Man, about My harsh wounds!
    thenk of mine harde wundes
      Man, you [should] have your thoughts [only] on Me.
      man thu have thine thout one me
5   **Think how dearly I bought you [back]:**
      thenk how dere i bouthe thee
      I allowed Myself to be nailed to a tree—
      i let me nailen to the tree
      A harder death, none can be—
      hardere deth ne may non be
      Think man! It was all for thee.
      thenk man all it was for thee
10   **Think, Man, ...**
    I gave my flesh; I gave my blood.

> i gaf my fles i gaf my blod
> **For you, [I] allowed it to be done to me on the cross,**
> for thee me let idon on rod
> **Out of my side ran the flood.**
> out of my side ern the flod
> **I suffered it all with a forgiving heart and mind.**
> i tholed it all wid milde mod
> 15 **Man, it was all for your good.**
> man it was all for thy god
> *Think, Man, ...*
> **My pains were harsh and great.**
> mine peines weren harde and stronge
> **My mother thought it very long.**
> my moder thouth es swithe longe
> 20 **Think, Man, before you do your sin,**
> thenk man er thu do thy sinne
> **What I endured for mankind.**
> what i tholede for mankinne
> **My hard death shall cause you to stop.**
> min harde deth thee shall don blinne
> *Think, Man, ...*

The rhetorical strength of this lyric is its pounding simplicity, repeating Christ's imperative to "Think!" as many as eleven times. The rhyme-required use of "stundes" (l. 1) can mean simply Christ's time on the cross as "a time of trial or suffering,"[46] but it also suggests "a relatively short space or length of time."[47] Christ was on the cross for "only" three hours. He lived for only thirty-three years (annually mirrored by the mere thirty-three weeks of Ordinary Time in the liturgical calendar). Performance of this lyric can seem somewhat abbreviated as well, with its final stanza stopping on the word "blinne" [cease, desist] (l. 22)—a short duration, as seem all our lives.

Performance of accusatory lyrics like "Men rent me on rood" and "Thenc man of mi harde stundes" should shame Everyman for a prior lack of compassion; the guilt is universal. When the guilt of Jews is explicitly referenced in Middle English passion lyrics, however, the targeted contempt now sounds utterly repulsive, even if not so intended. Friar Herebert's "Weal herying and worship be to Christ that dear us bought," for example, is based upon "Gloria, laus et honor" by Theodulph of Orleans (d. 821), commonly sung as a processional hymn on Palm Sunday. This lyric may not be overtly hostile to Hebrews. Jesus Himself is recognized as "of David's kunne" (l. 3), but couplets 4, 5, and 6 provide significant contrasts between the Jews' behavior during Christ's entry into Jerusalem and the annual Christian commemoration of that event during Holy Week.

    Happiness, praise, and worship be to Christ Who redeemed us dearly,
    wele herying and worshipe be to crist that dere us boughte
    To Whom cry out "Hosanna!" [we] Children of Clean Thought.
    to wham gladden hosanna children clene of thoughte
        You are King of Israel and kin of David,
        thou art king of israel and of davides kunne
        Blessed King Who comes to us without stain of sin.
        blessed king that comest till us withoute wem of sunne
5   **All who are in Heaven as one praise You,**
    all that is in hevene thee herieth under on
        And all Your own creation and each mortal man.
        and all thin owen hondewerk and euch dedlich mon
    The folk of Jews came before You with palm fronds,
    the folk of jewes with bowes comen ageinst thee
        And we with prayers and song humble ourselves to You.
        and we with bedes and with song meketh us to thee
    They cared for You with honor . . . before You had to die.
    heo kepten thee with worshiping ageinst thou shuldest deye
10   **And we sing to Your worship Who sits enthroned on high.**
        and we singeth to thy worshipe in trone that sittest heye
    [As] their wish and their praise You took then with favor,
    here will and here mekinge thou nome tho to thonk
        May it please You then, Merciful King, our offering of this song.
        queme thee thenne milsful king oure offringe of this song
    Happiness, praise, and worship be to Christ Who redeemed us dearly,
    wele herying and worshipe be to crist that dere us boughte
    To Whom cry out "Hosanna!" Children of Clean Thought.
    to wham gradden hosanna children clene of thoughte

At least two of the lyric's "and" conjunctions (ll. 8 and 9) should be read as contrastive "but" conjunctions. The fundamental contrast being proposed is between the worldly, fleshly, literalist "them" and spiritual "us," between God's first (but formerly) Chosen People and Christians as younger (so now more biblically favored) "children clene of thoughte" (ll. 2 and 14).

Hetta Elizabeth Howes has argued in good faith that Herebert's "Quis est iste qui uenit de Edom?" [Who is that man who comes from Edom?] (Isaiah 63:1)—which also references the Jews—elides anti-Semitism.

> Through an emphasis on the performance of these feelings and emotions, a performance that is modeled in the lyric itself by the penitential Jews . . . [the lyric] teaches readers and listeners how to appropriately convert these emotional responses into something more productive: contrition and penitence.[48]

Even if so, several such allegedly well-intended lyrics can present near occasions for misreading. For example, although there is no mention of Jews whatsoever in "Now goth sonne under wod," St. Edmund's *Speculum Ecclesiae*, in which it was included, makes repeated references to "þe fals Iewis" [the false Jews]. It is impossible to ignore that so many Middle English lyrics recalling Christ's betrayal, trial, and death include even more vehement anti-Semitic remarks, almost exclamations, about Jews as Christ-killers.

Many other, seemingly less explicitly virulent Middle English lyrics can frequently lapse into casual anti-Semitism with nonce expressions. For example, Herebert's "Herod thou wicked foe whereof is thy dreading," which celebrates the Epiphany and the Baptism of Jesus, starts with an angry apostrophe to the Jewish king who slaughtered the Innocents—a hint of the blood libel. The third stanza of the bilingual "Maiden mother mild / oeiz cel oreysoun [hear this prayer]" renounces Judas's betrayal and identifies "the Jew" collectively as Christ's actual torturers. In "Behold me I pray thee with all thy whole reason," Jesus, the bloody lamb, appeals to the reader as "dear brother" (st. 4); the imperative "behold" emphasized His betrayal by the dissembler Judas and then His abuse by spitting spiteful Jews. The usurers ("ockeraris") who accompany Covetousness to hell in William Dunbar's "Off Februar the fyftene nycht" were probably imagined to be Jews.[49] And so on. And so on. So much anti-Semitism so frequently expressed in Middle English lyrics can still have dangerous affective success; if so, they should be remembered as historical testimony, but no longer performed as emotive impersonations.

Happily, one dialogue lyric (or mini-play), set on Holy Thursday rather than Good Friday, offers a curious anomaly to the alternatively explicit or implicit, intense or nonchalant insults of Jews found in so many passion poems. "It wes upon a shere thorsday that our louerd arose" (somewhat misleadingly known as "The Bargain of Judas") enacts a familiar narrative backstory, the "selling" of Christ for thirty pieces of silver (Matthew 26:15; Matthew 26: 25, John 13:26–30). J. D. W. Crowther has shown this particular enactment to be "a masterpiece of ironies."[50] In this lyric's portrayal, Judas seems more a buffoon than a satanic plotter; his lines may even be played to win some sympathy for the lost apostle.

> **It was on a Maundy Thursday that our Lord arose.**
> it wes upon a shere thorsday that ure louerd aros
> **Very gentle were the words He spoke to Judas,**
> full milde were the wordes he spec to judas
> **"Judas, you must go to Jerusalem to buy our food.**
> judas thou most to jurselem oure mete for the bugge
> **Thirty silver coins you will carry upon your back.**
> thritty platen of selver thou bere upon thy rugge
> 5 **You will arrive far into Broad Street, far into Broad Street.**
> thou comest fer i the brode stret fer i the brode strete
> **Some of your kinsmen you may meet there."**
> summe of thine cunesmen ther thou meist imete
> **[And he] did meet with his sister, that sneaky woman.**
> imette wid his soster the swikele wimon
> **"Judas, you yourself deserve to be stoned by me with stones;**
> judas thou were wurthe me stende thee wid ston
> **Judas, you deserve that I [too] should be stoned with stones**
> judas thou were wurthe me stende thee wid ston
> 10 **Because of the false prophet that you believe in."**
> for the false prophete that thou bilevest upon
> **"Shut up! dear sister, [I wish] you had a heart-attack—**
> be stille leve soster thine herte thee tobreke
> **If the Lord Christ knew [about it], He'd avenge it full well."**

wiste min louerd crist full well he wolde be wreke
"Judas, go onto the rock high upon the stony hill.
judas go thou on the roc heye upon the ston
Lay your head in my lap [and] quickly go to sleep."
ley thine heved i my barm slep thou thee anon
15   As soon as Judas woke from sleep,
sone so judas of slepe was awake
[He realized] thirty pieces of silver were taken from him.
thritty platen of selver from him weren itake
He pulled his own hair out [so much so] that his scalp flowed
      with blood.
he drow him selve by the top that all it lavede ablode
The Jews of Jerusalem thought he had gone mad.
the jewes out of jurselem awenden he were wode
To face him came the rich Jew that was named Pilate.
foret him com the riche jew that heiste pilatus
20   "Are you willing to sell your Lord who is called Jesus
wolte sulle thy louerd that heite jesus
"I will not sell my Lord for any [other] kind of wealth
i nul sulle my louerd for nones cunnes eiste
Except it be for the thirty coins that he gave to me."
bote it be for the thritty platen that he me bitaiste
"Would you sell your Lord for any type of gold?
wolte sulle thy lord crist for enes cunnes golde
"No, only if it be for the coins that He wanted to have."
nay bote it be for the platen that he habben wolde
25   In went our Lord to him as His apostles were sitting at [their] meal.
in him com ur lord gon as his postles setten at mete
"How [is it that] you are sitting, Apostles, and why won't you eat?
how sitte ye postles and why nule ye ete
How [is it that] you are sitting, Apostles, and why won't you eat?
how sitte ye postles and why nule ye ete
I am bought and sold today for our food."
ic am aboust and isold today for oure mete
Judas stood up before Him, "Lord, am I that man?
up stod him judas lord am i that frec
30   I was never in the place where [anyone] spoke evil about You to me."

i nas never o the stude ther me thee evel spec
Peter stood up and spoke with all his might,
up him stod peter and spec wid all his miste
"Though Pilate should come with ten hundred knights,
thau pilatus him come wid ten hundred cnistes
Yet I would, Lord, fight for Your love."
yet ic wolde louerd for thy love fiste
"Shut up, Peter! I know you well—
stille thou be peter well i hee iknowe
You will forsake me three times before the cock crows.
thou wolt fursake me thrien ar the cok him crowe

The plot of this ballad-lyric makes sense only to those who already know the biblical narrative. Early on Holy or Maundy Thursday, so named for the *mandatum* [command], "Do this in memory of me" (1 Corinthians 11:24, Luke 22:19), Jesus "aros" (l. 1)—that is, He simply awoke, but this verb surely anticipates the Resurrection. With "milde wordes" (l. 2), He entrusts [thirty pieces of] silver to Judas in order to buy "mete" [meat] (l. 3) for the Last Supper. Jesus also foretells that Judas will meet some "cunesmen" [kin] (l. 6) in Jerusalem ("kin" not otherwise identified as being Jewish). Apparently still sleepy, Judas is intercepted indeed by his "swikele" [deceitful, treacherous] (l. 8) sister—an epithet that may be as misogynist as it is anti-Semitic. Mary-Ann Stouck casts her as an "unredeemed daughter of Eve" (as opposed to the redeemed Mary Magdalene).[51] She threatens her brother with stoning for following a false prophet (i.e., the equivalent punishment for a woman taken in adultery). Judas, in reply, warns her to keep quiet because Jesus is a vengeful wizard—a remark that makes Judas seem more absurd than evil. Judas's sister, somewhat incestuously, then persuades him to take a quick nap in her lap on a hilltop (Golgotha itself perhaps) and robs him. When he awakes, Judas panics, so much so that the Jews of Jerusalem think him insane (l. 18). The wretched sight of Judas when "He drow him selve by the top that all it lavede ablode" [He pulled himself by the top that it all streamed bloodily] (l. 17) provides a parodic anticipation of the crown of thorns. Judas then sells Christ to a "riche Jew" named Pilate (ll. 19–20), a conspicuous gaffe.[52] Judas will take only the lost "thritty platten" of silver, not gold (l. 23), again suggesting his foolish fear of Christ's wrath and a stereotypically Jewish "letter of the law" mentality. As soon as Judas returns, Christ announces to the apostles "Ic am aboust and isold today" [I am bought and sold today] (l. 28) to pay for their "mete"—that is, for the food on the table, but (well beyond Judas's or, for that matter, the other apostles' comprehension at the time) the Eucharist as well. Judas has one couplet to deny his betrayal, or lie, and then is forgotten.

The somewhat puzzling issue is not so much the omission of any mention of Judas's subsequent despair and suicide, but that the poem then turns so abruptly to Christ's reprimand of mighty Peter who wants to fight against Pilate-the-Jew's thousand knights (ll. 31–34). The extravagance of this boast exaggerates Peter's violent reflex at the arrest of Jesus (John 18:10). Christ's command—"Stille thou be" (l. 35)—echoes what had been Judas's warning to his sister, but Christ's call for constraint is motivated by forgiveness, not fear. As at the poem's beginning so at its ending, Christ predicts the proximate future. Peter, too, will betray Christ—a crucial difference being that Peter will then repent and be forgiven as Judas did not. Donald G. Schueler has remarked that this lyric has "less to do with Judas" or—by association—Jewish culpability than with "the universality of human guilt."[53] The salubrious moral of this lyrical ballad is that compassion in the name of Christ's "love" (l. 34) does not justify violence.

Middle English lyrics that enact sympathy for the sufferings of Christ or of Mary or of anyone pose no special problem for the modern reader to perform. Their expressions of immaculate compassion ennoble the reader. However, the innocence of Middle English lyrics intended to provoke the reader's compassion by means of arousing guilt proves far more problematic to maintain. Any reader's "emotional" response to such lyrics that indulges ensuing anger or hatred instead of compassion and contrition should be stifled as an "irrational" if not "damnable" response.

SIX

Contek I

Love and Longing

> Love is mine songe iliche, / For hit nis bute a lutel breþ/
> Đat sone kumeþ and sone geþ.
>
> [Love is like my song, / for it is only a little breath/
> that quickly comes and quickly goes.]
>
> *The Owl and the Nightingale* (ll. 1460–62)

The emotional interplay performed by Middle English love lyrics generally seems as heteronormative as the couples "male and female of every living thing" boarding Noah's ark (Genesis 7:16). It must be acknowledged that such a binary conception of sexuality was the prevailing medieval conviction. Leah DeVun explains that medieval theorizing in natural philosophy, jurisprudence, medicine, and alchemy, though varied and complex, all "assimilated intersex individuals to a male or female sex and, for the most part, they made nonbinary sex disappear as a social problem and a biological category"—hence Chaucer's confusion about the Pardoner.[1] But the frequent opposition of male and female voices in the following lyrics is more rhetorical than biophysical or socio-psychological; collectively, these lyrics voice a never-ending "contek" [discord]—each sex's emotional tension with the other, often expressed in complaints or debates. As in Renaissance drama, the performance of several such Middle English lyrics also creates the opportunity for readers to assume alternative gender roles.[2] And medieval readers may have occasionally shared this opportunity as, for example, Sarah McNamer observes, when "male readers had the option of imagining themselves as the women whom the Virgin addresses in 'An Appeal to All Mothers,' of entering into the maternal role for the duration of the reading process."[3]

The gendered roles of Middle English lyrics, whether addressed to the opposite sex or addressed to homosocial readers about the opposite sex, range tonally from pathetic to outraged. Poems expressing either male or female feelings of cupidinous desire, oscillating between *gaudium* and *tristia*, often end in regret, especially when such love is retroactively understood as having been compelled by the God of Love whom Chaucer nicknamed blind "Seynt Idiot" (*Troilus and Criseyde*, I, 910). Numerous single-stanza lyrics offer simple, brief verse statements of a lover's sad longing (which itself, it is usually hoped, will likewise be only short term). Three such single-stanza statements—"Thus I complain my grevous hevynesse," "Go, heart, hurt with adversitee," and "Alas departing is ground of woe"—follow one another in the same manuscript separated as reading experiences only by blank spaces.[4] Read in order as a sort of mini-sequence, these three lyrics first complain that the woman is "merseless" [merciless] (l. 3); this criticism of her disdain is couched in a compliment, but the poet's use of "ye" pronouns admits her initial aloofness.

> **Thus I complain my severe heaviness**
> thus i complain my grevous hevynesse
>   **To you who knows the truth of my intention.**
>   to you that knoweth the treuth of min entent
> **Alas, why should you be unrelenting**
> alas why shuld ye be merseless
> **Since God has sent you so much beauty.**
> so moch beutee as god hath you sent
> 5 **You may release my pain.**
>   ye may my pein relees
> **Do as you please; I hold myself content.**
> do as ye list i hold me content

In "Go, heart, hurt with adversitee," the poet then addresses his own heart (with a conventional pun on "hurt") as "thee" and provides a message to be delivered verbatim to "hir" with a petition that they unite "againe."

Go, Heart, hurt by adversity,
go hert hurt with adversitee
  And let my lady see your wounds,
  and let my lady thy wondes see
  And tell her this, as I'm saying to you:
  and sey hir this as i say thee
  "Farewell my joy and welcome pain
  farwell my joy and welcom peine
  Till I see my lady again."
  till i see my lady againe

If this lyric's conceit of displaying the heart's wounds presumes some analogy to viewing Christ on the cross, then the intensity of this poet-lover's passion approximates quasi-blasphemous hyperbole.

The DIMEV identifies "Alas departing is ground of woe" as a "love song for two voices"—two singers harmonizing, I presume, rather than solos singing antiphonally. If in dialogue, performance of the first two lines can be assigned to a woman and the last six to her despairing lover.

"'Alas, departing is the basement of woe.'
alas departing is ground of wo
I can sing no other song."
other songe can i not singe
"But why [must] I part from my lady,
but why part i my lady fro
Since love was the cause of our meeting.
sith love was cause of our meeting
5 **The bitter tears of her weeping**
the bitter teres of hir weeping
Have pierced my heart so fatally
min hert hath pershed so mortally
That it will bring me unto death
that to the deth it will me bring
Unless I see her quickly."
but if i see hir hastily

It is possible, though not necessary, to read this lyric's first line as a reference to yet another song to be performed.[5] The first line's image of the "ground"

(l. 1) refers to "the lowest part of something."⁶ The remaining lines are simple and simply emotive. Enforced separation causes her amorous grief, which causes his fatal longing. Insofar as performance (be it the singing, or transcribing, or reading) of such a lyric externalizes such frustration, it offers a curative release.

"I ne have joy ne pleasance nor comfort" is just a simply sad, love-longing song.

I have no joy, nor pleasure, nor comfort,
i ne have joy plesauns nor comfort
In your absence, True Queen of my heart.
in youre absens my verrey hertes quene
What other men consider joy or entertainment,
what other men think joy or disport
To me it is nothing but anguish or pain.
to me it nis but anger or tene
5 **If that I laugh, it is only for show.**
if that i laugh it is but on the splene
Thus I make a happy-sorry face
thus make i a gladful sorry chere
[Because] the absence of my true dear lady so distresses me.
so noyth me the absens of my verrey lady dere

This rhyme-royal stanza unmasks the "I's" (no longer) apparent cheerfulness. The use of the word "pleasure" in my translation of line 1 provides a somewhat inadequate sense of "plesaunce," which can mean "the satisfaction, gratification, or propitiation of a deity"⁷ as well as "a wish, will, or desire; sexual desire; love."⁸ The vocative "my verrey hertes quene" (l. 2) can also be taken to mean "queen of my true heart." The idiom "But on the splene" (l. 5) to qualify forced laughter is enigmatic; the MED suggests "(on) the ~, in jest; ?cheerfully," but the spleen can also be identified as the emotional seat of melancholy (not to mention courage).⁹ The closing oxymoron describing the frustrated lover's good show of "Gladful sorry chere" (l. 6) does not entail an inexplicable emotional paradox comparable to Catullus's "odi et amo" [I love and I hate at once], or Petrarch's bitter-sweetness; rather, the contradiction confesses an absolute discrepancy between the lover's private feeling and the public perception of his "chere"—that is, "the face as expressing emotion."[10]

Longing need not always be expressed as semi-suicidal in Middle English lyrics. Although "Gracious and gay / on her light all my thought" starts with this gambit, it then enacts a simply hopeful happiness.

> **Gracious and gay—**
> gracius and gay
>   **On her [alone] rest all my thoughts.**
>   on her lieth all my thoght
>   **Unless she takes pity on me today,**
>   but sche rew on me today
>   **She'll bring me to [my] death.**
>   to deth sche hath me broght
> 5 **Her fingers are both long and slim.**
>   her feingeres bith long and small
>   **Her arms are both curvy and firm-bodied.**
>   her armes bith rown and toght
>   **Her mouth [is] as sweet as licorice—**
>   her mouth as sweet as licory
>   **On her [alone] rest all my thoughts.**
>   on her lieth all my thoght
>   **Her eyes are fair and [shining] grey.**
>   her eyne bith feir and gray
> 10 **Her brows are well-arched.**
>   her brues bith well ibent
>   **Her face is as rosy as roses in May.**
>   her rode as rede as rose in may
>   **Her waist is small and graceful.**
>   her medill is small and gent
>   **She is sweet under the sheets.**
>   sche is sweet under schete
>   **I love her and no other.**
>   i love her and no mo
> 15 **She has my heart for keeps**
>   sche hath mine hart to kepe

> **In [whatever] lands wherever she goes.**
> in londes wher sche go
> **Quickly tell [me], I pray,**
> sodenly tell i pray
> **"To you, my love is fixed!"**
> to thee my love is lend
> **Kiss me on my way**
> kisse me in my way
> 20 **Once before I go.**
> ones ar i wend

The dominant emotion of this lyric is an almost skipping happiness, and its bouncy alternating rhymes suit well the lover's conventional compliments. The central three stanzas simply celebrate a woman's sex appeal. She sounds so merrily carnal, "sweet under schete" (l. 13), that the phrasing "On her lieth all my thought" (l. 2) may be a double entendre.[11] The final stanza, however, makes his parting request directly to her with some slight anxiety. The singer prays "sodeynly" (l. 17) that her love remain "lend" [granted] (l. 18)[12] to him as he bows out. His "gracious and gay" performance of this song all but guarantees that he shall be comforted.

Alternatively, a quite common type of emotional "dis-ease," the frustration of unsatisfied longing, is voiced in the sixteenth-century lyric "Jesu that is most of might." It initially poses as a man's prayer that Jesus "Save my true-love" (l. 3), then enfolds his billet-doux about her *sans pareil* attractiveness (l. 11), and concludes as a complaint about his "wo" (l. 33).

> **Jesus, who is mightiest,**
> jesu that is most of might
> **And made man above all thing,**
> and made man above all thing
> **Protect my true love both night and day**
> save my truelove bothe day and night
> **Keep her well and in happiness.**
> and kepe her well and in good liking
> 5 **For she is always completely courteous,**
> for she is alwey full curteisse
> **True and steadfast in every degree,**

true and stedfast in every degree
Sweet as the rose that grows on the bough,
swete as the rose that groeth on the risse
As faithful [as a] turtledove [who] sits upon a tree.
as true turtill that sittes on a tree
She is the most demure that I can see
she is the demurest that i can see

10 **Wherever I walk by east or west.**
wheras i walke by est and weste
She has no equal in my eye
no peere she hase in my eye
For, of all women, I love her best.
for of all women i love her beste
Her lips are like unto [the] cherry,
her lippes are like unto cherye
With teeth as white as ivory;
with teethe as white as whales bone

15 **Her eyebrows curvy as any can be,**
her borwes bente as any can be
With eyes as clear as crystal gems.
with eyes clere as cristal stoune
Her fingers are both plump and long,
her fingers be bothe large and longe
With breasts round as any ball.
with pappes rounde as any ball
It seems to me nothing on her is wrong.
nothing methinke on her is wronge

20 **Her waist is both thin and small.**
her medill is bothe gaunte and small
She has my heart and ever shall,
she hathe my harte and ever shall
And [I vow] never to change her for anyone new
and never to change her for no newe
But to love her while on [this] earth
but for to love her terrestreall
And while I am alive to be true to her.
and whiles i live to her be true

25 **For I have gone through England on every side,**
   for i have gone throughe englond on every side
      Brittany, Flanders, with many another place,
      brettin flanders with many an oder place
      Yet I have never found in these wide travels
      yet founde i never non in these ways wide
      Such a one as she is to my purpose.
      suche one as she is to my purpasse
   Wherefore I love her without ceasing,
   wherfore i love her without let
30 **And for no thing can I stop;**
   and for no thing i can cease
      So fervently on her my heart is set,
      so ferventlye on her my harte is set
      But I dare not force the issue.
      but i dare not put me in preace
   Woe be the time [it takes] for my compensation,
   wo be the while for my redress
      Since I am born to live in pain
      sithen i am borne to live in peine
35   **And thus to be left all comfortless,**
      and thus to be lafte all comfortless
      To love and not be loved in turn.
      to love and be not loved ageine
   Yet, through self-discipline grace grows.
   yet throughe governance growethe grace
      I have heard men say in town and street
      i have harde men say in towne and strete
      How Fortune comes into many a place,
      how fortune cumethe into many a place
40   **And with good fortune I trust to meet.**
      and with good fortune i trust to mete
   Adieu, Dear Heart, who is so sweet!
   adeu dere harte that is so swete
      God grant you grace to do well.
      god grante you grace well for to do

> **I must walk forth to seek true love**
> i most walke forthe true love to seke
> **Into some place where it grows.**
> into some place where it dothe growe
> 45 **But one branch I will leave with you.**
> but one branche i will leve with you
> **I pray [to] Jesus [that] you may keep it well,**
> i pray jesu ye may it well kepe
> **For hereafter you shall know:**
> for hereafter ye shall knowe
> **"Where nature cannot walk, it will crawl!"**
> where kinde cannot go it will crepe
> **Wherefore I greet you as many times**
> wherfore as many times i grete you
> 50 **As clerks are able to [write] with pen and paper,**
> as clarkes can write with paper and inke
> **And as many more [greetings] as grasses grow,**
> and as monye mo as gresses grewe
> **Or tongue can tell, or heart can think . . .**
> or tonge can tell or harte can thinke
> **I'll write no more to you at this time,**
> no more i write to you at this time
> **But wherever you be, on land or water,**
> but wherever ye be on lande or water
> 55 **Christ's dear blessing and my own,**
> cristes dere blessing and mine
> **I send you in greeting of this letter.**
> i sende you in greeting of this letter

As a metrical letter, "Jesu that is most of might" largely follows a five-part template taught by the *ars dictaminis* (or *dictandi*) "As clarkes can write with paper and inke" (l. 50). The blessing of this lyric's first stanza serves as a *salutatio*, although it refers to "my true love" in the third person. Stanzas 2 to 5 offer the *captatio benevolentiae* attempting to win the woman's goodwill by means of its charmingly simple details (which once again are stylistically appropriate to the poem's common meter). This happy interlude dwells in a recollected space of imagined proximity. Within this happy memory, stanzas 3 and 4 offer a standard *blazon* of the beloved's physical attractiveness, compliments *prêt-à-porter* for any idealized woman. Her fingers are "large" (l. 17) probably in the literal sense of well-shaped (and well-fed) but also "generous" (as in "largesse"). Stanzas 6 to 8 recount the *narratio* of their relationship, which should preface his *petitio*. But, instead, the poem ends anticipating the woman's continuing refusal to requite his love and so his own hesitancy to force her choice: "I dare not put me in preace" (l. 32)—"in press" here meaning "in crisis."[13]

In lieu of a petition, stanzas 9 and 10 foretell what will be his resulting reaction to rejection. His woe will last only a while; loving and not being loved in return seems a legal, contractual failure on her part.[14] Other clerical expressions in the poem include identification of humanity as the crown of creation (l. 2), the designation of this love as "terrestreall" (l. 23), the affirmation of "governance" (l. 37), and the odd use of "branche" (l. 45) to signify a theological lesson or "one of the species or subspecies into which a generic moral concept is divided."[15] His schoolboy love-logic, "Wherefore," compels him to love her "without let" (l. 29)—an implicit vow to which he adds a codicil, a "Yet" (l. 37) that allows some escape from the prospect of relentless "wo" (l. 33). Stanza 10 seems a rather skewed appeal to the reasoning of Boethius's *Consolation of Philosophy* as understood "in towne and strete" (l. 38): since "fortune cumethe into many a place," he will seek "good fortune" elsewhere as "I trust to mete" (ll. 43–44).

The last four stanzas, all directly addressed to his [former] "dere herte," provide a *conclusio* starting with the farewell "Adieu." Unless she changes her mind (as Lady Fortune always does), this lyric-epistle ends as a "Dear Jane" kiss-off. But there remains one more "But" (l. 45)—a sort of *sed contra* postscript [a Thomistic "on the contrary"] to his adieu. Should there be any chance that she will relent, he leaves her a twig of his truncated love for possible future grafting, since, sooner or later, Nature gains entrance everywhere. Then, he extravagantly claims himself able to write lawns of lyric greetings (ll. 49–51) rather than farewells, a quantity so great it rivals (absurdly) the countless joys of heaven "Or tonge can tell, or harte can thinke" (l. 52). The text closes with a repetition, its *salutatio* (l. 56), and its author awaits the return post. I myself suspect she'll probably ghost him.

"O mestress why" again expresses a dismissed lover's frustration, and its bouncy versification (four eight-line stanzas of very brief lines, rhyming aaabcccb) builds to a dismissive sarcasm.

    O Mistress, why
    o mestres why
        Outcast am I
        outecast am i
    Entirely
    all utterly
    From your loving
    from your pleasaunce
5   **Since you and I**
    sithe ye and i
    Before now, truly,
    or this truly
    Familiarly
    familiarly
    Have had *recreation*,
    have had pastaunce
    And lovingly
    and lovingly
        You would apply
        ye wolde apply
10 **Your company**
    thy company
    To my comfort?
    to my comforte
    But now, truly,
    but now truly
    Unlovingly,
    unlovingly
    You do deny
    ye do deny
15 **Me to come again**
    me to resorte
    And to see me.
    and me to see

      As aloof you are
      as strange ye be
      As though you
      as thowe that ye
      Should now deny [me]—
      shuld nowe deny
20   **Or else [pretend to] possess**
      or else possess
      The nobility
      that nobilness
      To be Duchess
      to be dochess
      of great Savoy.
      of grete savoy
      But, since you
      but sithe that ye
25   **Will remain so sour**
      so strange will be
      Towards me
      as toward me
      And will not mingle,
      and will no medill
      I trust, perhaps,
      i truste percase
      To find some blessing [for myself],
      to finde some grace
30   **To go hunt game freely**
      to have free chaise
      And succeed as well.
      and spede as welle

This lyric may be suspected of sexual periphrasis throughout. In addition to the erotic connotations of "pleasaunce" (l. 4), "familiarly" (l. 7) can suggest "playing house." "Pastaunce" (l. 8) seems almost a nonce word playfully dropped to rhyme with "pleasaunce"; the MED cites only one other instance of it as an equivalent for "pastime." "Medill" (l. 27) is especially provocative; it can mean: "to blend, mix"; or "to busy oneself"; or even "to join sexually, have sexual intercourse."[16] Perhaps, a more idiomatic understanding of "medill," therefore, might be "mix it up" or "get busy with it." Except for line 10, "I" addresses the would-be duchess as "you," suggesting a denial of continued familiarity. His single use of "thy" refers to the time when she used to keep him "company" (l. 10), which itself can mean "intimacy between the sexes; sexual union, intercourse."[17] With line 20, frustration turns into aggravation. He mocks her for now putting on airs; perhaps she has traded up. He therefore asks her ladyship leave so that he may henceforth "chaise" [hunt] (l. 30) others.

"I wot a bird in a bower as beryl so bright," also known as "Annot and John," is particularly difficult to modernize. The precise sense of every phrase in its five, ten-line stanzas rhyming aaaaaaaabb enhanced by extraordinary, perhaps excessive alliteration, is often inexplicable, but it seems clear that this "I" is "deliriously lovestruck."[18]

> **I know a girl as shiny as beryl in [her] bower,**
> ichot a burde in a bowr as beryl so bright
>   **As lovely to see as sapphire set in silver,**
>   ase saphyr in silver seemly on sight
>   **As noble as jasper that gleams with light,**
>   as jaspe the gentil that lemeth with light
>   **As garnet in gold and ruby, just right.**
>   as gernet in golde and ruby wel right
> 5   **As an onyx, she is the one most valued.**
>   ase onycle he is on iholden on hight
>   **As the precious diamond, whenever she is dressed.**
>   as diamaund the dere in day when he is dight
>   **She is coral, well-known to emperor and to knight.**
>   heo is coral ycud with cayser and knight
>   **As the emerald in the morning, this maiden has might;**
>   as emeraude amorewen this may haveth might
>   **The might of the pearl, this maiden has more.**
>   the might of the margarite haveth this may mere
> 10   **Instead of the red gemstone, I choose her by chin and by face.**
>   for charbocle ich hire ches by chin and by chere
> **Her face is like a rose that is red on its stem.**
> hire rode is as rose that red is on ris

With lily-white cheeks, she is lovely.
with lilye white leres lofsum he is
She surpasses the primrose [and] the prized periwinkle
the primerole he passeth the perwenke of pris
As well as the golden alisander, the flowering celery and anis.
with alisaundre thereto ache and anis
15 **Elegant as columbine—such is her nature.**
cointe as columbine such hire cunde is
Happily dressed in grey fur,
glad under gore in gro and in gris
She is a blossom in complexion, brightest under precious linen,
he is blosme upon blee brightest under bis
With the celandine poppy and sage, as you yourself see,
with celydoyne and sauge as thou thyself sis
[Whoever has] that sight of that beauty, he is brought to bliss.
that sight upon that semly to blis he is broght
20 **She is the marigold that is sought for a cure.**
he is solsecle to sauve is forsoght
She is a parrot [whose wings] beat away my torment [when I am] in pain.
he is papejay in pyn that beteth me my bale
To a true dove in a tower, to you I tell my tale.
to trewe tortle in a towr i telle thee my tale
She is a thriving song-thrush, that excellent one who sings in the great hall,
he is thrustle thriven in thro that singeth in sale
The wild skylark and hawk and the oriole.
the wilde laueroc and wole and the wodewale
25 **She is a falcon in a park, most secret in the valley,**
he is faucoun in frith dernest in dale
And with every man she delights in singing.
and with everuch a gome gladest in gale
From coast to coast, she is most discreet.
from weye heo is wisest into wyrhale
Her name is in a note of the nightingale—
hire nome is in a note of the nightegale

> In *Annote* is her name—don't say it [out loud]!
> in annote is hire nome nempneth it non
30 **Whoever reads it rightly, whisper to John.**
> whose right redeth roune to johon
> **She is musk and mandrake [plucked] with the might of the moon.**
> muge he is and mandrake thourgh might of the mone
>> **True treacle told by tongues enthroned,**
>> trewe triacle itold with tonges introne
>> **Such licorice can heal from north to south,**
>> such licoris may leche from lyne to lone
>> **Such sugar one seeks that saves men straightaway.**
>> such sucre mon secheth that seneth sone
35 **Happily blessed by Christ, the one who grants my prayer**
> blithe iblessed of crist that baytheth me my bone
> **When private deeds are done secretly in daylight.**
> when derne dedes in day derne are done
> **As the gromwell wildflower in a grove, the grain of which is green,**
> ase gromil in greve grene is the grone
> **As peppercorn and cumin (famous for the crown of its flower)**
> ase quibibe and comyn cud is in crone
> **Cumin known in court, cinnamon in a case,**
> cud comyn in court canel in cofre
40 **With ginger and white turmeric and the clove.**
> with gingiure and sedewale and the gilofre
> **She is powerful medicine, reward of mercy,**
> he is medicine of might mercie of mede
>> **Ready as Regnas reason to advise.**
>> rekene ase regnas resoun to rede
>> **True as Tegeu in tower, as Wyrwein in clothing,**
>> trewe ase tegeu in tour ase wyrwein in wede
>> **More bold than Byrne who often sought the boar,**
>> baldore then byrne that oft the bor bede
45 **As Wylcadoun she is wise, doughty of deeds,**
> ase wylcadoun he is wis doghtyof dede
> **Fairer than Floyres folks to feed,**

feyrore the floyres folkes to fede
Renowned as Cradoc in court for carving the bread,
cud ase cradoc in court carf the brede
Nobler than Hilde, who has taken notice of me,
hendore then hilde that haveth me to hede
She has taken heed of me at once, this noble one,
he haveth me to hede this hendy anon
50 **Gentle as Jonas, she's enjoying John.**
Gentil ase Jonas heo joyeth with jon

On the surface of it, this lyric seems an extended and increasingly elated expression of infatuation. Drunk on consonance, this lyric's "I" seems to play at least three games at once: the performance of a formal tour de force; the presentation of a complimentary, so-wooing poem; and yet, by virtue of its very extravagance, a burlesque of both the alliterative style and of lyrics that so hyperbolically catalogue a woman's qualities.[19] Each stanza is a cluster of similes: gems, flora, birds, medicines, and finally several (weirdly obscure) heroes. The poem's sustained series of similes often requires very strained semantics to maintain each line's alliteration. For example, the common marigold must be identified as "solsecle" (l. 20) [sun-seeking, i.e., heliotropic] in order to echo "sauve" and "forsoght."[20] The poet's selection principles also become increasingly shaky, so his rather frenzied praise becomes "a bundle of contradictions—delightfully so."[21]

Stanza 1 seems obsessed with a medieval lapidary. One could footnote each of the named gemstone's virtues, but that scholarly effort adds little to the immediate emotional celebration of Annot's attractiveness. Within the floral imagery of stanza 2, Daniel J. Ransom has discovered a surprising subtext; having conventionally praised her face, the poem focuses on Annot's "coynte" (l. 15) which "we might translate . . . *Queinte* pretty as / like a columbine, such is her cunt (beautiful under her skirt) in its grey fur."[22] Such a pun calls into question the sincerity of the entire lyric. If *queinte* is the second stanza's focal point, its call for affirmation that "þou þiself" (l. 18) see Annot's beauty then becomes most (amusingly) awkward. The obvious pun of "a [musical] note" with the name *Annot* (ll. 28–29) supposedly discloses a rather common girl's name to the confidante reader; this disclosure only poses as her *senhal,* or pseudonym, conventionally protecting some noble woman's secret identity.

The sudden pronominal shift from "he" [she, i.e., Annot] (l. 21) to "thee" (l. 22) is puzzling. It is easy to assume that "tortle in a tour" is another compliment for Annot herself—perhaps too easy, if performance does not indicate otherwise. The "true dove" whom the poet is now directly addressing could be some other female confidante, the recipient of this lyric, not Annot whose own bird-similes are attractive but may not be so virtuous. As a "laueroc," Annot herself is "wilde" (l. 24); as a "faucon in frith," she is "dernest" (l. 27), which need not but can suggest "Stealthy, insidious, crafty; dishonest, deceptive; immoral, evil"[23]; "frith" can be given a somewhat wilder translation than "park," meaning "a royal forest, a game preserve."[24] Annot's singing delights every "gome" (l. 26), which I translate as "every man"; there is a temptation to read it as "everyone" but in Middle English the noun "gome" has specifically masculine denotations,[25] unlike "man," which retained its sense of a "person, a man or woman."[26] This diction, therefore, suggests that rather flighty Annot is also rather flirty.

The tone and intent of the final stanza is most enigmatic, and so most adaptable to remarkably different performances. No small part of the interpretive problem (or performance potential) are the lyric's two third-person references to John. A modern reader, prompted by the conventional title, finds it easy to infer that this lyric's "I" is "Johon," the self-identified "Jon" in the last line, and that Annot "joyeth with" him (l. 50). Either Annot or Jon may here be praised as "Gentil as Jonas"—a rather meaningless analogy in itself, so "Jonas" may simply be intended to sound like "John is." If the performing "I" makes clear that he himself is not "dear John," then the poem plays as a sort of "I wish I had Johon's girl" performed as a parody of a lovelorn alliterating lad.

Whoever "right redeth" Annot's obvious name should "roune [it] to Johon" (l. 30). Susanna Fein translates the phrase "nempneþ hit non" (l. 29) as a question "Can anyone name it?"[27] Alternatively, "nempneþ hit non" (l. 29) can be taken as an imperative in apposition to "roune" [whisper]. This fictional sharing of a secret note pretends that the lyric is not meant for public recital despite its extravagant consonance. Susanna Fein, again most plausibly, reads "me" in lines 48 and 49 as an indefinite pronoun that "means 'one, mankind in general.' See MED, *me* pron (1)."[28] But if "me" means simply "I," Annot has noticed the performer (despite currently being in a relationship with John)—it's complicated.

Eager for his turn to come, "I" becomes wildly Welshy in his last stanza.

In addition to the pointlessly obscure, perhaps deliberately absurd Celtic and Norse names being dropped, the geographic references of this stanza point to Brythonic regions: line 27 specifies "From Weye (the River Wye in south Wales)... into Wyrhale (the forest north of Chester)," and line 32 names two rivers "from Lyne (Devon) to Lone (Cumbria, Lancashire)," one step over the border. Therefore, "Ichot a burde in boure bright" may be a parody not only of versified shopping lists and of romantic hyperbole but of *cynghanedd* (bardic harmony) as well.

For modern readers, the least problematic Middle English expressions of male desire and frustration respect, at least implicitly, a woman's freedom to consent or to refuse—that is, her right to grant "mercy" or not. However, the performance of lyrics composed in the tradition of the pastourelle (so named for a shepherdess to be seduced) has become especially difficult to enjoy. The pastourelle usually enacts clever banter between a wayward knight and some lowborn woman whose (not always sham) resistance is presumed to be only part of "the olde daunce" (*Canterbury Tales*, I, 476).[29] Unlike habitual, so often uncalculated though now inexcusable, moments of offensive anti-Semitism in the Middle English lyrics, the underlying reprehensibility of many pastourelles seems deliberate—allegedly intended to transgress in "jest, the civilized veneer for sex antagonism."[30] However, any pastourelle's apparent indifference regarding rape, implied or explicit, has proven emotionally impossible for the modern reader to re-enact innocently: "To insist that one can laugh at rape without considering it rape is to refuse to account for the ways that the object informs the humor, to refuse to separate laughter from its source."[31]

The proposition that pastourelle should be played with carnivalesque license—that is, inherently disturbing but "just kidding"—is facing a reckoning. The nonchalant amusement of many former readings are now themselves offensive. For example, although the DIMEV describes "As I stood on a day me self under a tree" as "a love song" and "ribaldry," Carissa Harris points out that this lyric in fact "portrays the female speaker's fear of assault and fierce resistance in spite of her fear."[32] Harris proposes a more "capacious" definition of pastourelle as "a debate poem between a man and a woman on the topic of sex and consent."[33] In truth, a modern reader's aversion to the emotionally indifferent pose of the pastourelle's performer regarding rape is not a peculiarly "presentist" or "woke" anxiety, though in the Middle Ages some might term it "sinful" rather than merely offensive.

Chaucer's Parson, for example, renounces "double tonge," in which "they maken semblant as though they speke of good entencious, or eles in game and pley, and yet they speke of wikked entente" (*Canterbury Tales*, X, 644). Finding any intended humor in a pastourelle requires a reader's a priori consent (or a rapport between performer and audience) that accepts its transgressiveness as venial fun. Whether tolerating such a licensing of the pastourelle's performance then promotes or exorcises our culture's rapist mentality must then be debated. This *contek* about the pastourelle as a subgenre seems comparable, as such, to the current debate regarding the social and psychological impact of violence in video games.

Rosemary Woolf considered "In a frith as I con fare fremde," or "The Meeting in the Wood," to be "the earliest and also the best of the English pastourelles."[34] This lyric seems to start innocently enough as a man's happy recollection.

>**In a strange park, as I made my way,**
>in a frith as I con fare fremede
>   **I discovered a very fair catch to accompany.**
>   i founde a well feir fenge to fere
>   **She glistened like gold when it gleams.**
>   heo glistnede ase gold when it glemede
>   **There was never a creature so beautiful in a dress.**
>   nes ner gome so gladly on gere
>5 **I wanted to know who in the world gave birth to her.**
>   i wolde wite in world who hire kenede
>   **This bright lady—if it were her wish—**
>   this burde bright if hire will were
>   **She asked me to take a hike or else it would anger her.**
>   heo me bed go my gates lest hire gremede
>   **She wanted to hear no little rascal.**
>   ne kepte heo non hening here
>   [He] **"Listen to me now, you most noble in grace,**
>   ihere thou me now hendest in helde
>10 **I have no slanders to mock you [with].**
>   nav i thee none harmes to hethe
>   **I will rescue you from cares and the [winter] cold.**
>   casten i wol thee from cares and kelde

> **I will clothe you now splendidly."**
> comeliche i wol thee now clethe
> [She] **"I already have clothes to put on,**
> clothes i have on for to caste
> **The type that I may wear by working for [my own] money.**
> such as i may weore with winne
15 **[It is] better to wear thin [clothing] without guilt**
> betere is were thunne boute laste
> **Than long robes and sink into sin.**
> then side robes and sinke into sinne
> **Were you to have your will, you would grow wicked;**
> have ye yor will ye waxeth unwraste
> **Afterwards, your thanks would be 'thin.'**
> afterward yor thonk be thinne
> **It's better to make firm pledges [first]**
> betre is make forewardes faste
20 **Than later to complain and have second thoughts."**
> then afterward to mene and minne
> [He] **"About 'thinking,' don't think anymore.**
> of munning ne munte thou namore
> **You deserve high status by my might;**
> of menske thou were wurthe by my might
> **I pledge to keep, until I grow grey,**
> i take an hond to holde that i hore
> **Everything that I have promised you.**
> of all that i thee have bihight
25 **Why are you so disinclined to trust my story then**
> why is thee loth to leven on my lore
> **[That] longer [ago than just now] my love alighted on you?**
> lengore then my love were on thee light
> **Another might have desired you so before**
> another mighte yerne thee so yore
> **Who didn't at all inform you so properly."**
> that nolde thee noght rede so right
> [She] **"Such advice I may especially regret**
> such reed me mighte spacliche reowe

CONTEK I: LOVE AND LONGING · 197

30   When all my peace and quiet is dragged from me.
      when all my ro were me atraght
      Quickly you will fetch a new one
      sone thou woldest vachen an newe
      And take [yet] another within nine nights.
      and take another withinne nye naght
      Then, I might go hungry in appearance,
      thenne might i hongren on heowe
      In every household to be hated and regretted,
      in uch an hyrd ben hated and forhaght
35   **And to be separated from all I know**
      and ben icaired from all that i kneowe
      And to be told to stick to what I had been stuck.
      and bede clevien ther i hade claght
   "[Nevertheless it's] better to take a handsome man of the cloth
   betere is taken a comeliche i clothe
      In [one's] arms to kiss and to hug
      in armes to cusse and to cluppe
      Than to be a wretched woman married [to a man] so angry
      then a wrecche iwedded so wrothe
40   **[That though] he [try to] kill me, I may not slip away from him.**
      thagh he me slowe ne might i him asluppe
      The best advice that I know for both of us
      the beste red that I con to us bothe
      Is that you take me and that I hop to you
      that thou me take and i thee toward huppe
      Even if I were to have sworn in truth and by oath
      thagh i swore by treuthe and othe
      'What God has ordained,' [which] no one can escape.
      that god hath shaped mey non atluppe
45   **With [an accusation of] shape-shifting, no one can scare me.**
      mid shupping ne mey it me ashunche
      I was never a witch or a sorcerer.
      nes i never wicche ne wile
      I am [only] a girl—[and] that grieves me.
      ich am a maide that me ofhunche

Would there were a love for me, a man free of fraud!"
luef me were gome boute gile

This lyric clusters its highly alliterative lines into speeches of alternating rhymes: abababab cdcd efefefef ghghghgh ijijijij klkl; these rhyme segments are themselves then linked by concatenation: "here/Ihere" (ll. 8–9), "clethe/Clothes" (ll. 12–13), "minne/Of munning" (ll. 20–21), "rede so right/Such rede" (ll. 28–29), "clagh t/clothe" (ll. 36–37), and "shaped...atluppe/shupping" (ll. 42–43).

As a first example of the Middle English pastourelle, there is a strangeness about "In a frith as I con fare fremde." *Fremed* might as readily modify the "I" (as a stranger or foreigner) rather than the place as a "frith." The man is not a knight; his "fair fenge" [pleasant taking] (l. 1) occurs in a royal forest for hunting game, not a meadow; the glistening "burde bright" [shining young woman] (l. 6) of unknown birth appears fey at first, though she feels compelled in the end to deny being a witch (l. 46). After his initial scene-setting, the poet-"I" recollects their conversation verbatim. He offers to keep her safe and comfortably clothed. She answers that she can dress herself; she is self-sufficient (l. 14). She hears his proposition as "sinne" (l. 16), a bribe and not a "foreward" [pledge] (l. 19). In reply, he vows to keep all his promises and asks "Why is the loth to leven on my lore?" [Why is it hateful to believe my teaching] (l. 25). "Lore" and "rede" [advice] (l. 20) may indicate the mansplaining of any "he," but the phrasing especially suits a cleric.

Her answer does indeed seem at first to loathe his pretentious advice. She anticipates his infidelity to herself (as well as to his vow of celibacy), and she vividly expresses her dread of being abandoned and despised. Rosemary Woolf reads lines 37–44 as if spoken by the "narrator."[35] Alternatively, the remainder of the poem may be acted as spoken by the woman (i.e., l. 40). As is not uncommon in a pastourelle, she rethinks her rejection of the initial proposition, a bribe of mere clothing. She concedes it is better to enjoy the kisses of a handsome seminarian "in clothe" (l. 37)[36] than to be married to an abusive wretch. This is now her "beste red" (l. 41), that they hop on each other though she violate marital "truethe and othe" (l. 43)—that is, "What God has joined together, let no man put asunder" (Mark 10:9).

Carissa Harris observes that in BL MS Harley 2253 this lyric is "sandwiched between . . . two male-voiced secular love lyrics that feature a sustained focus on women's sexualized bodies," and this mise-en-page guides "readers to view women as corporeal objects, as perpetually available for men to look at, touch, and proposition at will."[37] In situ, this pastourelle becomes a how-to exemplum teaching "higher-status young men how to use their privilege to exploit structural inequalities for their own sexual gratification" thus normalizing eroticized "aggression in the pastourelle."[38] In the last four lines of "In a frith," the mere "maide" (l. 47) concludes her reconsideration of the privileged man's proposition and is "seemingly on the verge of capitulation, decrying her lack of options to her status."[39] Or, she may simply regret still being a virgin, marriageable only to a churl. The fact that the lyric's clerical "I" is reporting all this discourse as a past event implies that her consent, if any, was only to a come-and-go affair; in the end, she still seeks a "gome boute gile" [a man without guile] (l. 48).

"Als y me rode this endre dai" [As I was riding this other day] enacts how another chance encounter revealed a spurned woman's inclination to have revenge sex.[40] This carol is commonly known by the first line of its burden, "Now Springes the Spray." The refrain explains little other than that the lyric's insomniac "I" should be played as lovelorn yet opportunistic.

> **Now the stems are sprouting.**
> now springes the spray
> **Entirely because of love, I am so sick**
> all for love ich am so seeke
> **That I may not sleep.**
> that slepen i ne may
> > **As I was riding this other day**
> > als i me rode this endre day
> > **For my sport,**
> 5 o my pleyinge
> > **I saw where a little maiden**
> > seih i whar a litel may
> > **Began to sing:**
> > bigan to singe
> > **"May he drop dead!**
> > the clot him clinge
> > **Sad is anyone [who] in love-longing**
> > wai is him I louve longinge

10	**Shall live forever."**
	shall libben ay
   Now the stems are sprouting . . .
	As soon as I heard that merry note,
	son ich herde that mirie note
15	**I drew [my reins] towards [her].**
	thider i drogh
	I found her in a sweet arbor
	i fonde hire in an herber swot
	Under a bough
	under a bogh
	With joy enough.
	with joye inogh
	Promptly I asked "You merry maiden,
	son i asked thou mirie may
20	**Why do you constantly sing?"**
	why singes thou ay
   Now the stems are sprouting . . .
	Then the sweet maiden answered
	than answerde that maiden swote
25	**With few words:**
	midde wordes fewe
	"My lover made promises
	my lemman me haves bihot
	Of true love,
	of louve trewe
	[But] he exchanges me for a new.
	he chaunges anewe
	If ever I can—he'll regret it
	if i may it shall him rewe
	By this day!"
30	by this day
   Now the shoots are springing . . .

Like "In a frith," this carol may also be termed a *chanson d'aventure* with its quasi-formulaic "As I . . ." opening.[41] As a carol, "Now Springes the Spray" sounds festive. The number of accented syllables per line in each stanza is varied: 4/2/4/2/3/2, while the accentuation of the refrain is 3/4/3. Stanza 1 with its refrain rhymes ababbba axa. The second and third stanzas share c-rhymes and the concluding [ai:] rhyme links all three stanzas together with each iteration of the refrain to produce a sort of tail-rhymed nine-line stanza, three of which approximate a conventional ballade: cdcddaa ceceeea. All very musical and dance like. Yet, the woman's emotional circumstances call for a spiteful tone. The recurrent, unrhymed so-discordant non-rhyme of the middle line of the three refrains emphasizes that "I am sick." There is a discord within the refrain between the season and the "I's" nocturnal disease, as there is between the recurring so static lament of the refrain and the implicit emotional transitions from stanza to stanza. The lyric's perception of time oscillates between the "Now" (beginning each iteration of the refrain as well as the "By this day" concluding stanza 3) and the "ay" [always] (concluding stanzas 1 and 2).

In stanza 1, the singing "I" overhears a maiden singing three lines of a complaint: "The clot him clinge!" [may the soil cling to him] (l. 8). In stanza 2, the eavesdropping "I" perceives her cursing as the "mirie note" (l. 14) of this "mirie may" (l. 19)—because they promise gratification of his happy availability. Within the *locus amoenus* of "an herber swot" [sweet arbor] (l. 16) as well as at the center of the poem, he asks why she is singing. Her answer harmonizes with his intentions. "Mid wordes fewe" (l. 25) and with an enticing subtext, she answers that her lover has been untrue and that "it shall him rewe" (l. 29); her use of the verb "rewe" [regret] here plays against the conventional application of the noun "rue" in courtly love lyrics as a synonym for "mercy" (i.e., the woman's eventual willingness to grant a would-be lover's romantic desires). An "I" for an "I," the end of the adventure suggests the wandering poet will serve well enough as a rebound lover; she will welcome the springing of his spray.[42]

Whereas the woman's anger in "Als y me rode this endre dai," prompts her desire for revenge sex, the prolonged expression of a man's intensely sad longing in "My deth I love, my lif ich hate" is meant to transform a woman's pity into "mercy"—a frequently futile ploy, but not in this case. All by itself, the incipit of this lyric suggests (misleadingly) that its "I" will sustain a morbidly sad complaint, and the first two stanzas do sound like an isolated "moan" (l. 8)—performed as a means to his own happy ending.

The manuscript provides a title "*De clerico et puella*," which itself is a bit of a joke, since the Latin preposition "De" [Regarding] normally introduces philosophical treatises rather than such a dialogue between the medieval equivalents of a frat boy and a townie.[43]

[Cleric] "**My death I love; my life I hate,**
my deth i love my lif ich hate
Because of a bright and beautiful lady.
for a levedy shene
She is as shining as daylight
heo is bright so dayes light
That is well seen [reflected] on me.
that is on me well sene
5   **I totally fade as the leaf does**
all i falewe so doth the lef
In summer when it is [initially] green.
in somer when it is grene
Nothing helps [me] in my reflections;
if my thoght helpeth me noght
To whom shall I make my moan?
to wham shall i me mene
Sorrow and sighing and a dreary spirit
sorewe and sike and drery mod
10 **Bind me so tightly**
bindeth me so faste
That I expect to go mad
that i wene to walke wod
If it lasts any longer for me.
if it me lengore laste
My sorrow, my care—all with one word
my serewe my care all with a word
She could cast away.
he mighte awey caste
15 **What good does it do you, my sweet lover,**
whet helpeth thee my swete lemmon
To torment my life so much?"
my lif thus for to gaste
[Girl] "**Stop, you priest, you are a fool!**
do wey thou clerk thou art a fol

  I've asked to debate nothing with you.
  with thee bidde i noght chide
  You shall never live [to see] that day
  shalt thou never live that day
20 **[On which] you will hope to get my love.**
  my love that thou shalt bide
  If you were ever arrested in my bedroom,
  if thou in my boure art take
  Shame would happen to you.
  shame thee may bitide
  'It's better for you to walk on foot
  thee is bettere on fote gon
  Than to ride a bad horse!'"
  then wicked hors to ride
25 [Cleric] **"Woe is me! Why do you say so?**
  weylawey why seist thou so
  Have pity on me, your servant!
  thou rewe on me thy man
  You are always in my thought
  thou art ever in my thoght
  In any place I am.
  in londe wher ich am
  If I should die for your love,
  if i deye for thy love
30 **It would be a great shame to you.**
  it is thee mikel sham
  Allow me to live and be your love,
  thou lete me live and be thy lef
  And you [will be] my sweet lover."
  and thou my swete lemman
  [Girl] **"Shut up, you fool—I call you [this] correctly.**
  be stille thou fol i calle thee right
  Can you never stop!
  cost thou never blinne
35 **You are watched day and night**
  thou art waited day and night
  By [my] father and all my family.

      with fader and all my kinne
   Were you caught in my bedroom,
      be thou in my bour itake
   They wouldn't stop [for fear of committing] any sin,
      lete they for no sinne
   To imprison me and to execute you—
      me to holde and thee to slon
40 **You might 'win' your death thus."**
      the deth so thou maght winne
  [Cleric] **"Sweet lady, change your attitude,**
      swete ledy thou wend thy mod
   Or you will make me know sorrow.
      sorewe thou wolt me kithe
   I am as sorry a man
      ich am all so sory mon
   As I was happy before.
      so ich was whilen blithe
45 **At a window where we stood,**
      in a window ther we stod
   We kissed each other fifty times
      we custe us fifty sithe
   Many a man makes [a] fair pledge
      feir biheste maketh mony mon
   [While he] hides all his sorrows."
      all his serewes mithe
  [Girl] **"Alas, Why say you so?**
      weylaway why seist thou so
50 **You renew my sorrow.**
      my serewe thou makest newe
   I loved a cleric all out of wedlock.
      i lovede a clerk all paramours
   In loving he was entirely faithful.
      of love he wes full trewe
   He was never happy any day at all,
      he nes nout blithe never a day
   Unless he saw me at once.
      bote he me sone seye

55   I loved him better than my [own] life.
      ich lovede him betere then my lif
     What good is it to lie?"
      whet bote is it to leye
   [Cleric] **"While I was seminarian in school,**
      whil i wes a clerk in scole
     I knew very much about learning.
      well muchel i couthe of lore
     [Yet] I have suffered for loving you
      ich have tholed for thy love
60   **Many painful wounds,**
      woundes fele sore
     Far from home and also from mankind
      fer from hom and eke from emn
     Within the forest.
      under the wode gore
     Sweet lady, have pity on me!
      swete ledy thou rewe of me
     Now may I [say] no more."
      now may i no more
65 [Girl] **"You seem well-[made] to be a cleric**
      thou semest well to ben a clerk
     Because you speak so humbly.
      for thou spekest so stille
     You shall never [more], because of my love,
      shalt thou never for my love
     Endure fierce wounds.
      woundes thole grille
     Father, mother, and all my relatives
      fader moder and all my kun
70   **Shall not restrain me**
      ne shall me holde so stille
     So that I am not yours, and you are mine
      that i nam thin and thou art min
     To do all your will."
      to don all thy wille

The idiom of the first two stanzas is entirely conventional, indeed book-learned—a scripted performance of a serenade set to the tone of the doublets of ballad meter.[44] *Puella* is the daylight; *Clericus*, a leaf withering in summer heat. About to expire on account of unrequited love, he asks "thee, my swete lemmon" [paramour, which as yet is only wishful thinking] (l. 15)—how she would profit by his death—which may be played as a transparent sham to extort sex.[45] The rest of the poem is a tribute to his clerical persistence. Her initial annoyance, like that of Allison toward Absalon in Chaucer's "Miller's Tale," sounds like a sort of down-home *Daunger* [reluctance]: "Do wey, thou clerk, thou art a fol!" (l. 17). Although her reference to "boure" [room] (l. 21) has a whiff of pretentiousness about it—as the *bower* of the clerk's "Swete lady" (l. 41)[46]—*Puella*'s idiom remains rather more folksy than fancy: "is betere on fote gon / Then wicked hors to ride" (ll. 23–24).[47]

Stanza 4 simply reiterates the clerk's fatal frustration; the shame of his death would be hers (l. 30). But in the next stanza, she again calls him "fol" (l. 33) because proverbially such a fool "never blinne" [never stops] (l. 34).[48] More worried about the shame (l. 22) of getting caught than his suicide, she points out that his murder is a more likely cause of death (l. 40). The debate could end at this impasse. But, in stanza 6, the still "sory" (l. 43) clerk first uses the pronoun "we" (l. 45) to remind *Puella* that they once exchanged fifty kisses at her window sill (ll. 45–46)—a sexual boundary yet to be fully crossed, it seems. He then also concedes that many a man will make "fair biheste" [pleasant promise] (l. 47) to conceal (the frustrated reason for) his sorrow. Now it is *Puella*'s turn to cry "Welaway" (l. 49, cf. l. 25), recalling a paramour-cleric whom she loved "betere than my lif" (l. 55) once upon a time. One would like to believe that *Clericus*, having departed for school where he "tholed [suffered] for thy love" (l. 59o), has now returned. But *Puella*'s far more ambiguous phrasing implies that he as "a [one such] clerk" (l. 65) will be as good as any other "a [one such] clerk" (l. 51)—all cassocks look black in the night. In any event, she is one step closer to consent. The clerk finally obeys her imperative to be silent, "Now may I no more" (l. 64), and yields the final word to *Puella*.

She finally grants that this clerk's manner of speaking so "stille" (l. 66) makes him an attractive option. Not meaning "silent" as in her earlier imperative to "Be stille!" (l. 32), *Puella*'s use of "stille" here to describe the clerk's preceding complaint-petition means "quietly" or "meekly" or "secretly" or "continually."[49] So wooed, she herself will no longer be kept "stille" (l. 78) by familial constraints. In the end, she claims joint possession of their desire: "thou art min / To don all thy will" (l. 72). This *contek* ends in consent.

The *contek* of "Love is soft, love is swet, love is good sware" may be read either as a debate between a thirsty man and a reluctant woman or as an internal dialogue voiced by only one "I." I prefer imagining its performance as a rhetorical duel between the sexes, a tit-for-tat exchange of their opposing perceptions of love. It ends, however, as a duet of mutual regret. The lyric's manuscript provides an Anglo-Norman notation "Ci commence la manere quele amour est pur assaier" [Here begins the way to test what sort of love is pure]. This lyric's attempt to define "pure love" hardly rises, however, to St. Paul's understanding of true caritas (1 Corinthians 13:4–8).

Love is soft, love is sweet, love is [a] good reply.
love is soft love is swet love is goed sware
    Love is much harm, love is much care.
    love is muche tene love is muchel care
Love is most rejoicing, love is eager reward.
love is blissene mest love is bot yare
Love is misery and woe to deal with.
love is wondred and wo with for to fare
5 **Love is luck for those who have it, love is good health.**
love is hap who it haveth love is good hele
    Love is lechery and lies, and eager to mock.
    love is lecher and les and lef for to tele
Love is brave to have dealings with in the world.
love is douty in the world with for to dele
Love makes many traitorous in the land.
love maketh in the lond mony unlele
Love is robust and strong to straddle like a steed;
love is stalewarde and strong to striden on stede
10   **Love is a lovely thing for women's need.**
    love is loveliche a thing to wommone nede
Love is vigorous and hot as a glowing coal.
love is hardy and hot as glowinde glede

> **Love makes many a maiden go mad with tears.**
> love maketh mony may with teres to wede
> **Love has his steward nearby [on] road and street.**
> love had his stiwart by sty and by strete
> **Love makes many a maiden wet her cheeks.**
> love maketh mony may hiere wonges to wete
> 15   **Love is a chance—whoever has it—to heat oneself.**
> love is hap who it haveth on for the hete
> **Love is wise. Love is wary and willful and fitting.**
> love is wis love is war and wilful and sete
> **Love is the softest thing that may sleep in [one's] heart.**
> love is the softeste thing in herte may slepe
> **Love is skill. Love is good at keeping [you] full of cares.**
> love is craft love is goed with cares to kepe
> **Love is false. Love is dear. Love is longing.**
> love is les love is lef love is longinge
> 20   **Love is a fool. Love is steadfast. Love is frowning.**
> love is fol love is fast love is frowringe
> **Love is a wonderful thing—whoever shall sing the truth!**
> love is sellich an thing whose shall soth singe
> **Love is riches. Love is woe. Love is gladness.**
> love is wele love is wo love is gleddede
> **Love is life. Love is death. Love can feed us.**
> love is lif love is deth love may us fede
> **If Love were as long-suffering as it is passionate at first,**
> were love also londrey as he is furst kene
> 25   **It would be the worthiest thing in the world, I suppose.**
> it were the wordlokste thing in werlde were ich wene
> **It is said in a song—[the] truth [of which] is seen—**
> it is isaid in an song soth is isene
> **Love starts with anxiety and ends with pain:**
> love cometh with care and endeth with tene
> **With lady, with wife, with maiden, with queen.**
> mid lavedy mid wive mid maide mid quene

The twenty-eight lines of the received text are a bit of a formalist nightmare consisting of the first four mono-rhyming quatrains, two couplets (ll. 17–

18, 22–23), one triplet (ll. 19–21), and a five-line mono-rhymed concluding stanza. It could be a compiled poem of discrete aphorisms—"Love is [predicate adjective]"—but the juxtaposition of statements produces a dramatic entity, a sort of lyrical quodlibet, turning a medley of familiar statements into a *sic et non* exchange. If performed as a lyric dialogue, like the pastourelle, "Love is soft" calls into question the notion that everyone is subject to erotic imperatives, that consent to seduction is mandatory, or, as damned Francesca claims "Amor, ch'a nullo amato amar pardona" [Love, that pardons no one loved from loving back] (Dante's *Inferno*, V, 103).

The first two quatrains sound almost antiphonal: each of the positive statements in the odd numbered lines is countered by a negative statement in the (nevertheless rhyming) even lines. Conventional casting would assign the praise of love to a "douty" [bold] (l. 7) male wooer, and the answering objections to a woman (ll. 10, 12) disinclined to be so wooed. If "wede" may be taken as "wedde," an alternative, more poignant interpretation of line 12 could be "love makes many a young girl marry with tears." But then the sequence of alternating assertions becomes more complicated—gradually joining, then reversing perspectives. "Love is hap" [chance] (l. 15) simply repeats line 5, but with less confidence in achieving happiness. Subject to Fortune, the "having" of love, which is at best optative, causes "hete"—the flame of desire, or a fever, or—for cynics—"hate." The debate then seems to become more concessive or, at least, more ambivalent. After four mono-rhymed quatrains, the pace of back-and-forth statements accelerates within the following couplet and triplet (or cinquain ffggg), making it difficult to determine who is singing what truth (l. 21)—unless, of course, an audience were to witness two voices sing these lines in harmony, uniting as "us" (l. 23) for a moment.

If the final stanza's initial fantasy—that long-suffering (because long-lasting) love might remain as passionately fresh as when new—were not an impossibility, then (for the sake of ornamental alliteration rather than actual hope) such love would indeed be "wordlokste" (l. 24), a rather weird word: "-lokste" is a variant of "-ly," but Middle English "word" is recorded only as an error of "wonder."[50] Alternative readings as "werd-ly" (destined) or "world-ly" are less likely, but—as homophones—both suit this admission that first love has a very limited shelf life. Concluding in hostile harmony, the performers of this lyric, having been former lovers, can now be imagined exiting in opposite directions, free to loathe each other.

Extended medieval narratives of romance may meander at leisure through a myriad of emotions attendant on vegetable love: after resistance, infatuation, anxiety, obsession, frustration, ecstasy, jealousy, despair, renewed hope, and so on. Middle English lyrics of longing provide only brief scenes of this entire play. And, after complete denial, loathing rules. The Middle English lyrics to be considered next no longer hope to win mercy at last. Rather, dead desire gives birth to remorse or spite or ridicule. Performance of the following lyrics heals the "I" insofar as they successfully hurt the objects of now-renounced desire.

SEVEN

Contek II

Love and Loathing

> What sholde I seyen? I hate, ywis, Cryseyde;
> And, God woot, I wol hate hire evermore!
> [What should I say? I surely hate Criseyde,
> And, God knows, I will hate her evermore!]
>
> Chaucer, *Troilus and Criseyde*, V, 1732–1734

Middle English laments to be voiced by a male "I" who has been rejected or not yet accepted as a lover can sound like simple pity parties. By singing his sorrow, such a lyricist hopes to present himself as pathetically attractive. But numerous complaints that impersonate a man whose ego has been bruised by one woman's rejection often degenerate into categorically misogynist invective. This is not a peculiarly medieval failing of the male imagination; for example, Boccaccio has Troilo complain after Criseida's betrayal, "Chi crederà ornai a nessun giuro, / chi ad amor, chi a femmina ornai" [Who will now believe in any vow, who in Love, who now in womankind?] (*il Filostrato*, VIII, st. 13).[1] Middle English lyrics that enact female retaliation for such contempt or for male infidelity are relatively rare but scathing. The exchange of such single-voiced lyrics constitutes a megatext of a more virulent strife between the sexes than that of as-yet unfulfilled desire. With equivalent intensity, dialogue poems allow both voices to debate which sex behaves more despicably toward the other; the woman often wins, but her rhetorical victory is usually Pyrrhic.

A rhyme-royal ballade, "Madame for your newfangleness," for example, berates one "Madame" for her (supposedly stereotypical) "unstedfastnesse" [inconstancy] (l. 3); she, like the favors of Lady Fortuna, forever changes.[2]

Madame, [given] that through your newfangledness
madame for your newefangelnesse
    Many a servant has [been] put out of grace
    many a servaunt have ye put out of grace
    I take my leave of your faithlessness,
    i take my leve of your unstedfastnesse
    For I know well that while you have the space of life
    for wel I wot whyl ye have lyves space,
5   **You cannot love for an entire six months in one place.**
    ye can not love ful yeer in a place
    For some new thing your pleasure is always so keen—
    to newe thing your lust is ay so kene
    Instead of blue, you should therefore wear all green.
    in stede of blew thus may ye were al grene
Just as in a mirror, nothing can make an impression,
right as a mirour nothing may impresse
    But [as] lightly as it comes, so must it go,
    but lightly it cometh so mot it pace
10 **So wanders your love—[to which] your deeds bear witness.**
    so fareth your love your werkes beren witnesse
    There is no faithfulness that can embrace your heart,
    ther is no feith that may your herte enbrace
    But, like a weathervane that turns its face
    but as a wedercok that turneth his face
    With every wind, [so] you go—and that is well seen.
    with every wind ye fare and that is sene
    Instead of blue, you should therefore wear all green.
    in stede of blew thus may ye were al grene
15 **You might [as well] be enshrined for your fickleness**
ye might be shryned for your brotelnesse
    Better than Delilah, Criseyde or Candace.
    bet than dalyda creseyde or candace
    Forever in changing is your [only] certainty—
    for ever in chaunging stant your sikernesse
    That habit no one can pluck from your heart.
    that tache may no wight from your herte arace
    If you lose one, you can easily buy two.

if ye lese oon ye can wel tweyn purchace
20   **All afloat for summer (you know well what I mean).**
al light for somer ye woot wel what I mene
Instead of blue, you should therefore wear all green.
in stede of blew thus may ye were al grene

The contempt of this complaint is arguably aimed at only one "Madame." However, stanza 3 would place her idol in a temple of wicked women: a Philistine seductress, an Ethiopian queen who frightened Alexander the Great, and an unfaithful Trojan widow (with whom Chaucer sympathized more than most). The vanity [emptiness] of the mirror image (l. 8) is likewise particularly misogynist; indeed, the alchemical/astrological/medical symbol for "female" ♀ itself is a stylized image of the *speculum* [mirror] of Venus. The color blue, which only Mary blessed among women seems entitled to wear, still symbolizes constancy or fidelity (as in "true blue"). The refrain's repeated assignment of green instead symbolizes the "color of unfaithfulness."[3] In truth, green (ironically the color of hope liturgically) might as readily clothe the jealousy of the leave-taking "I."

An even more disturbed and disturbing lyric, "Lenten is come with love to toune" (frequently identified simply as "Spring"), starts as an exultant reverdie but ends as an incel's insult. Because of its exceptional musicality (even though no musical setting survives), this lyric can be enjoyed simply for its vitality—at first.

Spring is come with love to town,
lenten is come with love to toune
   With blossoms and with the secret songs of birds
   with blosmen and with briddes roune
   That bring all this joy.
   that all this blisse bringeth
   Daisies in the broad valleys,
   dayeseyes in this dales
5 **The sweet music of birds,**
   notes swete of nightegales
   Each bird sings [its] song.
   uch foul song singeth
   The male thrush wrangles constantly.

the threstelcok him threteth o
Gone from here is winter-woe
away is here winter wo
When the sweet-scented bedstraw blooms.
when woderove springeth
10 **These birds sing wondrously well**
this foules singeth ferly fele
And warble about their joyful well-being,
and wliteth on here winne wele
So that all the forest rings.
that all the wode ringeth
The rose dresses herself in red;
the rose raileth hire rode
The leaves on the vivid trees
the leves on the lighte wode
15 **All grow eagerly.**
waxen all with wille
The moon emits her light;
the mone mandeth hire bleo
The lily is lovely to see
the lilie is lossom to seo
[As is] the fennel and the French parsley.
the fenil and the fille
The wild drakes woo;
wowes this wilde drakes
20 **Beasts please their mates.**
miles murgeth here makes
[Yet] as a stream that flows silently
ase strem that striketh stille
The proud man complains, as do [many] more;
mody meneth so doth mo
I know I am one of those
ichot ich am one of tho
Because of a love who pleases [me] poorly.
for love that likes ille
25 **The moon emits her light;**
the mone mandeth hire light

So does the beautiful bright sun
so doth the semly sonne bright
When the birds sing gaily.
when briddes singeth breme
Dew dampens the hills;
deawes donketh the dounes
Deer, with their secret whispers,
deores with here derne rounes
30 **Pass strict judgement.**
domes for to deme
Worms woo underground.
wormes woweth under cloude
Women grow incredibly arrogant—
wimmen waxeth wounder proude
So proper it would seem to them.
so well it wol hem seme
If I shall lack the consent of one [of them],
if me shall wonte wille of on
35 **I shall forgo this toil**
this wunne weole i wole forgon
And become an exiled creature in the forest.
and wight in wode be fleme

"Lenten is come with love to toune" is a formal tour de force. Each of its three twelve-line stanzas sustains a tail-rhyme pattern aabccbddbeeb, the b-lines being trimeters and the couplets tetrameters. Further enhancing the acoustics of "Lenten is come with love to toune" is its pronounced ornamental consonance, using both proximate and exact, often interlinear consonance. Yet, mid-song, this lyric hits a sour note.

The imagery of the first two stanzas seems entirely conventional and joyful: winter is away, the birds sing, flowers bloom, trees regreen, animals pair, streams flow. Deidre Kessel-Brown perceives this forest setting as an escape "from the exposure of the city to woodland privacy" for the sake of this soliloquy's candid expression of emotion.[4] Yet, despite these "lossom" [lovely] (l. 17) stimuli of spring, the "mody" [proud, stubborn, passionate] "I" moans as one (ll. 22–44) who dislikes the joy of others. The emotional *volta* at the end of stanza 2 might not seem so surprising, as it does on first reading, if all the preceding lines were performed with a sigh or grumble. Susanna Fein remarks, "Conflicted emotions gradually introduced give the lyric a taut tension," a quality that she concedes A. K. Moore found to be "the poem's 'most obvious flaw' because the 'intrusive love motif... seriously disturbs the unity of the nature study.'"[5] Performance, however, could clarify from the start that the moody speaker is out of tune with the "Notes swete" (l. 5) of spring's arrival in "toune."

The third stanza's alliteration is heaviest; the tenor of its imagery increasingly enigmatic. The *m*'s of its first line merely repeat, it appears, the sense of line 16 (substituting the rhyme word "light" for "bleo"). In both lines, the moon "mandeth" its light; the only instances of the verb "mandeth" meaning "send forth" cited in the MED are these two lines.[6] The alternative significance of the verb is as a variant for "commaunden," and the commands of the moon are notoriously fickle, often causing moans. *S*-sounds in the second line acknowledge the usually more comforting sunlight, but plosive *b*-sounds in the third line report that "briddes" (a common spelling for "brides" as well as "birds") sing "breme" [gaily but also fiercely].[7] *D*-sounds then dominate the next three lines. That the dew "dampens"[8] the hills seems normal enough, but the worry of deer whispering secret judgments sounds suspicious; perhaps "I" worries what the "dears" are saying.

W-sounds permeate all the last six lines of the poem (which can be excerpted as a stand-alone complaint). The juxtaposition of worms and proud women seems especially angry, and the concluding lines of "Lenten is come with love to toune" can be voiced as spiteful despair. If evermore rejected by "on," the moody man will renounce all women and then flee: "in wode be fleme" (l. 26). This statement can be taken to mean that he will henceforth live as a chaste hermit. Or, perhaps, he anticipates going mad.[9] In either case, the "I" is now enacting a misery with which some readers may sympathize. Alternatively, such pathos may be performed as the impersonation of a contemptuous and contemptible persona non grata.

Stephen Manning, however, proposes an entirely different conception of the tone for performing this lyric. He thinks it "treats the usual reverdie with a deft touch of humor."[10] For Manning,

> a strong wave of pent-up feeling thus finally breaks, revealing what we might well call a typical adolescent petulance. Consequently, a sharply-etched personality emerges as a result of the presentation

of the emotion, and the modern reader appreciates this 'dramatic' quality.[11]

Stephen Manning's response to the text can indeed inform a thoroughly viable performance of its sharply-etched petulance. As always, *interpretation as a histrionic performance* is much less restrictive than any effort to achieve some definitive reading of the text itself. For me, a major appeal of many Middle English lyrics is that they can be "covered" in many plausible ways.

The ambiguous carol "I am as light as any roe" can also accommodate alternative emotional enactments—concurrently. It seems to celebrate womankind at first, invoking the two unimpeachable exemplars of feminine goodness: anyone's own mother and the Blessed Virgin Mary. But the refrain's joyful praise of women collides with the lyric's rude recognition of their exploitation in its last two stanzas.

I am as light as any roebuck deer
i am as light as any roe
   To praise women wherever I go.
   to preise wemen wher that i go
To un-praise women, it would be a shame,
to onpreise wemen it were a shame
   For a woman was your mother.
   for a woman was thy dame
5   **Our Blessed Lady bears the name**
   our blessed lady bereth the name
Of all women wherever they go.
of all women wher that they go
I am as light . . .
   A woman is a worthy thing.
   a woman is a worthy thing
10 **They do the wash and do the wringing [dry].**
   they do the washe and do the wringe
The lullaby she does sing,
lullay lullay she dothe thee singe
   And yet she hath but care and woe.
   and yet she hath but care and wo
I am as light . . .

15   **A woman is a worthy being:**
       a woman is a worthy wight
       She serves a man both day and night;
       she serveth a man both daye and night
       For that she puts all her effort,
       therto she putteth all her might
       And yet she hath but care and woe.
       and yet she hathe but care and wo
20   **I am as light ...**

    The *contek* of this carol can be greatly intensified if the burden is sung by a happy group of men and the intervening stanzas by an exhausted woman. As she performs the hard work of solo-singing, they skip about like roebucks who are notorious herd-breeders and largely indistinguishable from one another. Her litotes "onpreise" [disparage] (l. 3) undercuts their obtuse admiration. Mary's consent to serve as handmaiden of the Lord (Luke 1:38) should not provide a paradigm for such an overworked and undervalued hausfrau. Though "Dame" (l. 4), "Lady" (l. 3), and "worthy" (l. 9) are honorifics, the woman's role is that of a functional "wight" [being, thing] (l. 15) who does the wash, cares for the kids, and "serveth a man both daye and night" (l. 16). The primary singer thus laments the "care and wo" (l. 19) of all housebound womankind as the male chorus happily roams about. The most positive result of this carol's conjoined performance would be some recognition by the circle of young bucks that their joyfully complimentary burden has been a parody of such male hypocrisy.

    Conversely, "Man, be war of thine wowing" satirizes exploitive women.

   Man beware of whom you woo
   man bewar of thine wowing
   For marriage is the long woe.
   for wedding is the longe wo
      Look before your heart becomes set.
      loke er thine herte be set
      Watch whom you woo before you tie the knot,
      loke thou wowe er thou be knet
5   **And if you see you can do better**
      and if thou see thou mow do bet

Loosen the halter and let her go.
knet up the heltre and let her go
Man beware...
Wives are both stout and bold,
wives be bothe stoute and bolde
10 **Their husbands dare not oppose them,**
her husbondes agens hem durn not holde
And if he does, his heart is cold
and if he do his herte is colde
However the game goes.
howsoevere the game go
Man beware...
15 **Widows are surely very false**
wedowes be wol fals iwis
For they can both hug and kiss
for they cun bothe halse and kis
Until one's purse is picked
till ones purs piked is,
And [then] they say "Go, boy, go!"
and they seyn go boy go
20 *Man beware...*
Of maidens, I will say only a little
of madenes i will seyn but litil
For they are both false and fickle,
for they be bothe fals and fekil
And under the tail they are very ticklish
and under the tail they ben full tekil
By the names of twenty devils! Let them go!
a twenty devel name let hem go
25 *Man beware...*

Medieval anti-matrimonial literature, both sincere and satiric, when addressed to voluntary celibates, may have been primarily intended to promote a count-your-blessings contentment with virginity. When weaponized by men to ridicule women, however—as most familiarly by the "Book of Jenkyn" in Chaucer's "Wife of Bath's Tale"—the incessant repetition of commonplace misogynist witticisms amounts to verbal abuse. "Man, be war of thine wowing," addressed as it is to bachelors, fails to offend if read only by jaundiced men.

This admonitory carol consists of four roughly tetrameter quatrains rhyming aaab plus a two-line burden rhyming xb. The ornamental *w*-alliteration of the burden conjoins wooing to wedding and, so, inevitably to woe. To rhyme with the refrain's "woe," each of the four stanzas ends with a quite differing iteration of "go." The first quatrain warns twice "loke" [look out] (ll. 3, 4) before being ensnared by a woman, punning "knet up" [conclude] (l. 6) with "knet" [tied as by a knot] (l. 4).[12] So, too, the young man's "herte" (l. 3) must be set free from the "heltre" [halter] (l. 6) of marriage if a better opportunity presents itself.

Each of the next three stanzas is dedicated to condemning one of the three standard categories of women in medieval society: wives, widows, maidens. However the "game" goes, the stout wife wins—or, if a husband resists her sovereignty, he loses any desire for her (l. 11).[13] Widows scam younger men out of all their money and then discard them once impoverished. Maidens are false and fickle and horny—everyone "full tekil" [very ticklish, lecherous, changeable] (l. 23).[14]

Misogyny often masks frustrated fantasy, and "Whan netilles in winter bere roses rede" presents an extended exercise of sardonic *adynaton* (hyperbolic absurdity).[15] Once its series of *impossibilia* come true, then you can find a true woman.

> **When stinging nettles bear red roses in the winter,**
> whan netilles in winter bere roses rede
>   **And thorns bear figs naturally,**
>   and thornes bere figges naturally
>   **And the broom-shrubs bear apples in every meadow,**
>   and bromes bere appilles in every mede
>   **And laurels bear cherries on the sprigs so high,**
>   and lorelles bere cheris in the croppes so hie
> 5   **And oaks bear dates so abundantly,**
>   and okes bere dates so plentuosly
>   **And leeks give overflowing honey,**
>   and lekes geve hony in ther superfluens
>   **Then put your trust and confidence in a woman.**
>   than put in a woman your trust and confidence

When cod walk in forests in order to chase deer,
whan whiting walk in forestes hartes for to chase
   And herring boldly blow horns in parks,
   and heringes in parkes hornes boldly blowe
   And flounder embrace marsh hens in swamps,
   and flounders morehennes in fennes enbrace
10   And soldier fish shoot shoes out of crossbows,
   and gornardes shote rolions out of a crosse bowe
   And young geese ride hunting to overthrow the wolf,
   and grengese ride in hunting the wolf to overthrowe
   And smelt run to the defense with spears in harness,
   and sperlinges rone with speres in harness to defence
   Then put your trust and confidence in a woman.
   than put in a woman your trust and confidence
When sparrows build churches and high steeples,
whan sparrowes bild chirches and stepulles hie
15   And [when] wrens carry sacks to the mill,
   and wrennes carry sakkes to the mille
   And curlews carry rags in order to dry horses,
   and curlews carry clothes horses for to drye
   And gulls bring butter to sell at the market,
   and semewes bring butter to the market to sell
   And pigeons wear hunting knives to kill thieves,
   and wood doves were woodknives theves to kill
   And griffons do homage to goslings,
   and griffons to goslings don obedience
20   Then put your trust and confidence in a woman.
   than put in a woman your trust and confidence
When crabs capture woodcocks in forests and parks,
whan crabbes tak woodcokes in forestes and parkes
   And hares with the sweetness of snails are caught,
   and hares ben taken with sweetness of snailes
   And camels grab swallows and perch with their hair-nets,
   and camelles with ther here tak swallowes and perches
   And mice mow the grain by waving their tails,
   and mise mowe corn with waveing of ther tailes

>   And ducks [get] off the dunghill [to] seek [Christ's] blood at
>   Hailes [Abbey],
>   whan dukkes of the dunghill seek the blood of hailes
> 26 **When shrewd wives do no offence to their husbands,**
>   whan shrewd wives to ther husbondes do non offens
>   **Then put your trust and confidence in a woman.**
>   than put in a woman your trust and confidence

This lyric consists of four rhyme-royal stanzas conjoined by a refrain that also provides its relentlessly repeated punch line: only if and when the impossible happens ... "then you can trust a woman." The use of elegant rhyme royal might sound formally inappropriate and so tonally just right. The easy anaphora of repeating "and" at the start of every line beats like a drum. The emotion informing this lyric's catalogue of freakish conceits may indicate a pervasive medieval unease regarding women as monsters. Or, it may be performed as simply blowing off steam.

The first stanza confines itself to plant imagery: winter roses, oak trees producing dates, leeks flowing with honey, and so on. The middle two stanzas extend the conceits to include fish and fowl: herring who play horns, geese who hunt wolves, and so on. The idea of "gornardes" (red gurnards, a spiny headed fish) shooting "rolions" (l. 11) as bolts (or quarrels, darts) from a crossbow is deliberately baffling.[16] The focus on food in the first stanza suggests the diet of the peasant estate. The chase, hunting, spears, and crossbows of stanza 2, suggest the pastime of nobles. Stanza 3 includes quick allusions to both the clerical and the bourgeois estates. In sum, no one has met a trustworthy woman. The image of a griffon (l. 20)—which symbolizes Christ's two natures as God and man—doing homage to goslings suggests that women have likewise usurped the status due men and thereby disrupted the entire *ordo tranquilitatis* [order of social peace] of the two sexes.

There is a historical irony to the grotesque image of shit-stained ducks going on pilgrimage to see a vial of Christ's blood because Henry VIII indeed denounced this relic as merely a vile duck's blood. The final stanza of this ascending (or descending) catalogue of absurdities is a mishmash climaxing in the most unimaginable monster of all: a "shrewd" (l. 27) but not shrewish wife. That three transcriptions of this poem survive indicates the popularity of such scabrous wit.

Another wickedly provocative lyric, "Of all creatures women be best," repeats every clichéd compliment and denies every clichéd insult about womankind—in English. It then subverts its feminist posturing with a Latin contradiction.

> *Of all creatures women are the best,*
> of all creatures women be best
> ***Cuius contrarium verum est.*** [Of which the opposite is true.]
> cuius contrarium verum est
>   **Everywhere, you may well see**
>   in every place ye may well see
>   **That women are faithful as doves in a tree,**
>   that women be trewe as tirtil on tree
> 5   **Not loose-lipped, but ever discreet,**
>   not liberal in langage but ever in secree
>   **And a great joy it is to be among them.**
>   and gret joye amonge them is for to be
> *Of all creatures . . .*
> cuius contrarium verum est
>   **The unwavering loyalty of women will never end,**
>   the stedfastnes of women will never be don
> 10 **So noble, so courteous, they are—everyone,**
>   so jentil so curtes they be everychon
>   **Meek as a lamb, quiet as a rock!**
>   meke as a lambe still as a stone
>   **A wicked or spiteful one you'll not find.**
>   croked nor crabbed find ye none
> *Of all creatures . . .*
> cuius contrarium verum est
> 15 **Men are a thousand times more trouble,**
>   men be more cumbers a thousand fold
>   **And I'm amazed how they dare be so bold**
>   and i mervail how they dare be so bold
>   **To hold against women,**
>   gainst women for to hold
>   **Seeing that they are so patient, soft, and cold.**
>   seeing them so pacient softe and cold
> 20 *Of all creatures . . .*

cuius contrarium verum est
> **For if you tell a woman all your counsel,**
> for tell a woman all your counsaile
> **She can keep it [secret] wonderfully well;**
> and she can kepe it wonderly well
> **She'd rather go living to hell,**
> she had lever go quik to hell
> **Than tell it to her neighbor.**
> than to her neighbour she wold it tell

25 *Of all creatures...*

cuius contrarium verum est
> **For, by women, men are reconciled,**
> for by women men be reconsiled
> **For, by women, no man was ever beguiled.**
> for by women was never man begiled
> **For they are of courteous Griselda's disposition,**
> for they be of the condicion of curtes grisell
30 **For they be so meek and mild.**
> for they be so meke and milde

Of all creatures...

cuius contrarium verum est
> **Now speak well of women or else be silent,**
> now say well by women or elles be still
> **Because they never displeased man by their willfulness.**
> for they never displesed man by ther will
35 **How to be angry or mad, they have no knowledge,**
> to be angry or wroth they can no skill
> **For—I dare say—they think no evil.**
> for i dare say they think non ill

Of all creatures...

cuius contrarium verum est
> **Do you believe that women like to talk foolishly**
> trow ye that women list to smater
40 **Or to chatter against their husbands?**
> or against ther husbondes for to clater
> **No, they'd rather fast on bread and water**
> nay they had lever fast bred and water

Than deal in such a matter.
then for to dele in suche a mater
Of all creatures...
cuius contrarium verum est
45 **Though all the patience in the world were drowned**
though all the paciens in the world were drownd
And none was left here on the ground,
and non were lefte here on the ground
It again could be found in a woman,
again in a woman it might be found
So much virtue in them does abound!
suche vertu in them dothe abound
50 *Of all creatures...*
cuius contrarium verum est
To the tavern they will not go,
to the tavern they will no go
Nor to the alehouse evermore,
nor to the alehous never the mo
Because—God knows!—their hearts would grieve
for god wot ther hartes wold be wo
To spend their husbands' money so.
to spende ther husbondes money so
55 *Of all creatures...*
cuius contrarium verum est
If there were a woman or a girl here
if here were a woman or a maid
Who liked to go freshly dressed
that list for to go freshely arrayed
Or to go adorned with fine kerchiefs,
or with fine kirchers to go displayed
65 **[If] you would say, "They are proud!" it is evilly spoken.**
ye wold say they be proude it is ill said
Of all creatures...
cuius contrarium verum est

"What is immediately striking here for the reader of Middle English is the Chaucer resonances"[17]—notably Chaunticlere's cockish translation of

"Mulier est hominis confusio" [Woman is man's confusion] as "womman is mannes joye and al his blis" (*Canterbury Tales,* VII, 3164–6). Aloud, "Of all creatures" applauds all women as true, steadfast, patient, confidential, peaceful, never deceptive, never deceived, meek, mild, quiet, silent, secret, sober, modest, and humble—NOT! The safety of playing this lyric game depends—either upon women in the audience not comprehending the Latin, or, more probably, upon women being inured to male whining.

There are a number of hide-and-go seek details in the English stanzas that subvert the surface enthusiasm. Calling women "cold" (l. 18) is not so much an insult as a biological statement. In terms of the "complexion" or "folding together" of bodily humors, "males tended to be hot and dry in complexion, while females were cold and wet."[18] But, emotionally, the adjective "cold" also indicates "lacking warmth of feeling."[19] The lyric's recollection of "curtes" Griselda's legendary patience (l. 29) alludes to Chaucer's "Clerk's Tale" (if not to precedent versions by Petrarch and Boccaccio), but this female-Job's proper name is comically mispronounced "Grissel" for the sake of rhyme; the noun "grisle," unfortunately, denotes horror or dread.[20] Griselda's perfect sufferance of her abusive husband, whether perceived as miraculous or monstrous, was clearly unique, not women's common "condicion" (l. 29). So, too, the hyperbolic claim (ll. 45–48) that, if a flood were to drown all human patience, it would somehow resurface in a woman (contra "Uxor," Noah's belligerent wife, an allusion not irrelevant to Chaucer's "Miller's Tale") is very hard to swallow.

Though women's equivalent mockery of men is relatively rare among the extant Middle English lyrics, it is loud. Two rhyme-royal epistles, exchanged by former lovers—to be read one after the other, as prompted by their manuscript sequence—exemplify how readily a failed love affair falls into mutual contempt. Each lyric presents an ever-intensifying catalogue of insults, and the two read together might be considered a flyting (i.e., an acerbically contentious verse exchange).[21] Each ex-lover takes for granted that the other has been unfaithful, justifying the verbal abuse and giving an acid flavor to their use of the formulaic phrase "dear heart." Both now address each other as "you" rather than affectionately as "thou." As a *billet acide* that the lady sends first, "Unto you most forward this letter I write" delivers a shriveling slap to the face.

Unto my true and able love,
to my trew love and able

(He is constant as a weather-vane.)
as the weder cok he is stable
This letter be delivered to him.
this letter to him be delivered
    Unto you, Most Hateful, I write this letter
    unto you most froward this lettre i write
5   **Which has caused me so long [to be] in despair.**
    which hath caused me so longe in dispaire
    It is easy to write about your appearance,
    the goodlinesse of your persone is esye to endite
    For no one is alive who can make your appearance worse:
    for he leveth nat that can youre persone appaire
    So handsome, best shaped, most fair of features,
    so comly best shapen of feture most faire
    Most cheerful of face, even as an owl
    most fresch of contenaunce even as an owle
10   **Is best and most favored over any other fowl.**
    is best and most favored of ony oder fowle
    Your manly face—shortly to declare—
    youre manly visage shortly to declare
    Your forehead, mouth, and nose so flat—
    your forehed mouth and nose so flatte
    In brief conclusion—are best likened to a hare
    in short conclusion best likened to an hare
    Out of all living creatures, except only a cat.
    of alle living thinges save only a catte
15   **I would say more if I knew what.**
    more wold i sey if i wist what
    That sweet face is very often cursed at,
    that swete visage full ofte is beshrewed
    When I think about a pimp so lewd.
    whan i remember of som bawd so lewd
    I ought to commend well the proportion of your body
    the proporcion of your body comende wele me aught
    From the shoulders down, back and front:
    fro the shuldre down behinde and beforn
20   **If all the painters in the land were sought together,**
    if alle the peintours in a land togeder were soght

**They couldn't portray anything worse though they'd all
   sworn [to do] it.**
a worse coude they not portrey thogh alle they had it sworn
Keep well your patience though I mock you.
kepe wele your pacience thogh i sende you a skorne
Your clothing hangs full gaily on you,
your garmentes upon you full gaily they hinge
As if it were an old goose [that] had a broken wing.
as it were an olde goose had a broke winge

25 **Your thighs misshapen, your shanks much worse.**
you thighes misgrowen youre shankes much worse
Whoever sees your knees so crooked.
whoso beholde youre knees so crooked
As if each of them asked Christ's curse on the other,
as ech of hem bad oder cristes curse
They splay so outward. Your hams are hook-shaped,
so go they outward youre hammes ben hooked
I never looked upon such a pair of gams!
such a peire chaumbes i never on looked

30 **You lift your heels so badly,**
so ungoodly youre heles ye lifte
And your feet are crooked, with evil luck.
and youre feet ben crooked with evil thrifte
Whoever might have the love of so sweet a person,
who might have the love of so swete a wight
She might be very happy that ever she was born.
she might be right glad that ever was she born
She who would once, in a dark night,
she that ones wold in a dark night

35 **Run for your love till she got pricked,**
renne for your love till she had caught a thorn
**I would wish her no more harm than to be hanged in the
   morning[—that is,]**
i wolde her no more harme but hanged on the morn
**She who has two good eyes and who chose for herself
   such a match**
that hath two good eyen and ichese here suche a make

Or once would lift up her hole for your sake!
or ones wold lift up here hole for youre sake
Your sweet love with bloody nails,
youre swete love with blody nailes
40   *Which feeds more lice than quails.*
whiche fedeth mo lice than quailes

Observing that medieval poets were far more inventive with insults than compliments, Jan Ziolkowski recognizes these five rhyme-royal stanzas as "the only ironic catalogue of a man's handsomeness found in Middle-English lyric poetry."[22] Addressing (in prose) the following verse-letter to a "trew love," who is truly as variable as "the weder cok" (l. 2), indicates that this entire lyric should be voiced with intense sarcasm.

The direct address to "you most froward" [unruly, unkind] (l. 4) can also be translated "you most perverse" or "deviant." Her ad hominem insults march *cap à pied* (face, shoulders, legs) like an angry *blazon*. All the animal similes are more insulting in Middle English than they seem in modernization. "Owle" (l. 9) is "a term of abuse and a type of ugliness"; "hare" (l. 13) can refer to a timid person; both "catte" (l. 14) and owl "of Hell" suggest the devil; "olde goose" (l. 24) still means "a fool."[23]

In her concluding stanza, the letter-writer slams her imagined replacement; may she be attracted to him "till that she had caught a thorn" (l. 35), which might mean "till she caught a skin-disease."[24] The final couplet is so angry that it defies explication. If its function is to close the letter with a "Sincerely yours," it provides a rather horrific self-image of the betrayed author. Her "blody nailes" (l. 39) anticipate getting her hands on his ugly face. But I think it more likely that she is continuing to insult "Youre [new] swete love" who breeds lice that cause a quail to lose its feathers and who has an eye disease.[25] If actually written by a male poet (as one can perhaps too readily assume about all Middle English lyrics), this "I" can be played as a repulsive shrew.

As if immediately in the return mail, "To you, dere herte, variant and mutable" provides a sarcastic thank-you note for the "lettre of derusion" (l. 7). After some deceptively florid prefatory comments, the spurned clerk fashions his bookish reply and challenges its recipient to "glose" (l. 16) its subtleties. He starts with bitter sarcasm, promptly descends into invective, and ends with a curse. Many words in this lyric seem deliberately difficult to decipher, as if intended to put his rival (if only fictively) woman-writer in her place.

> **To you, dear heart, fickle and changeable,**
> to you dere herte variant and mutable
> **Like Charybdis who is unstable.**
> like to carybdis which is unstable
> **O fresh flower, most pleasing of worth,**
> o fresch floure most plesant of prise
>   **Fragrant as the chrysanthemum to man's inspection,**
>   fragrant as federfoy to mannes inspeccion
> 5   **It seems to me by your behavior you are incredibly foolish,**
>   me semeth by youre contenaunce ye be wonder nice
>   **You, for meddling with any rhetorician.**
>   you for to medil with any retorucion
>   **To me, you have sent a letter of derision,**
>   to me ye have sent a lettre of derusion
>   **Composed all anew with many a curious clause.**
>   endighted full freshly with many corious iclause
>   **Wherefore I thank you as I find cause.**
>   wherfore i thanke you as i finde cause
> 10 **The English of Chaucer was not in your mind,**
> the inglisch of chaucere was not in youre mind
>   **Nor Cicero's terms with such great eloquence,**
>   ne tullius termes with so gret eloquence
>   **But you, so rude and spiteful by nature,**
>   but ye as uncurtes and crabbed of kinde
>   **Rolled them into a heap—as it seems by the sense.**
>   rolled hem on a hepe it semeth by the sentence
>   **And so I dare boldly without offense,**
>   and so dare i boldly withoute ony offence
> 15   **Answer your letter, as falls to the purpose;**
>   answere to your letter as falleth to the purpose
>   **And thus I begin—you may construe the meaning.**
>   and thus i beginne construe ye the glose
> **Christ of His goodness and of His great might**

crist of his goddnesse and of his gret might
> **Formed many a creature to walk on the ground.**
formed many a criator to walke on the ground
> **But whoever beholds you by day and by night**
but he that beholdeth you by day and by night
20   **Shall never have cause to be happy in heart,**
shall never have cause in hert to be jocound
> **Remembering your great head and round forehead,**
remembering your grete hede and your forhed round
> **With staring eyes, face large and huge,**
with staring eyen visage large and huge
> **And each of your boobs like a water-sack.**
and either of youre pappes like a waterbowge
Your pug nose with its wide nostrils [could],
youre camused nose with nosethrilles brode
25   **[As] a noble tool for the church**
unto the chirch a noble instrument
> **To snuff out candles burning before the cross**
to quenche tapers brenning afore the roode
> **Be dedicated best, upon my recommendation.**
is best apropred at mine avisament
> **Your lewd gazing, duplicitous in intent,**
your lewd looking doble of entent
> **With a courtly appearance entirely of a yellow hue**
with courtly loke all of saferon hew
30   **That will never fail—the color is so true!**
that never wol faile the colour is so trew
Your swollen lips, dead and greyish of color,
your babir lippes of colour ded and wan
> **With such a mouth similar to Jacob's brother,**
with suche mouth like to jacobes brother
> **And yellow teeth, nothing like the swan,**
and yelow tethe not lik to the swan
> **Spaced wide apart, as if each cursed the others,**
set wide asonder as eche cursed other
35   **In all the land, who could find such another**

in all a lond who coude finde suche another
[Who] of all features [is] so awful to see,
of alle fetures so ungoodly for to see
With breath as sweet as the elderberry?
with brethe as swete as is the elder tree
Your body is shaped all in proportion
youre body is formed all in proporcion
With hanging shoulders waving with every breeze,
with hanging shuldres waving with every winde

40   **Small at the waist as a wine barrel,**
small in the belly as a wine toune
With deviant feet and a crooked back behind.
with froward fete and crooked bak behinde
He who would always have you in mind
he that you wold have alway in minde
And who for your love would disturb our peace,
and for your love wold breke on oure reste
I'd want him to be locked up with Lucifer the deepest
   [in hell].
i wold he were locched with lucifer the depeste

45   **And, about your wardrobe, briefly to observe,**
and of youre atire shortly to devise
Your hair clips are colored like mudbugs[26]
your templers colured as the lowcray
With a saw-toothed hood, laid on like a pancake,
with dagged hood leid on pancake wise
Your padding and chest ornaments and all your foolish array—
your bolwerkes pectorelles and all your nice aray
Truly it seems to me you are a lovely girl.
treuly me semeth ye are a lovely may

50   **And, in particular, on holidays, when you caper and dance,**
and namely on haliday whan ye trip and daunce
Keeping your appearance like that of a wild goose.
as a wilde goos keping your contenaunce
Adieu, dear heart, for now I make an end
adew dere herte for now i make an ende
   Until such time that I have better space;

unto suche time that i have better space
I recommend scratchy skin and a head cold unto you
the pip and the pose to you i recomend
55 **And may God of His mercy grant you so much grace**
and god of his mercy graunte you so mikel grace
[That] in paradise eventually [when you are meant] to have a resting place,
in paradise ones to have a resting place
[You'll wait] **up by the shipyard, next to the Watergate,**
up by the navel fast by the water gate
To keep looking for passage when it comes late.
to loke after passage whan it cometh late
Your own love, trusty and faithful,
youre owne love trusty and trewe
60 *You have forsaken because of someone new.*
you have forsake cause of a newe

The letter's first, conventional and usually complimentary vocative "O fresh floure" (l. 3) is promptly subverted by comparing her odor to that of "federfoy" (l. 4, *febrifugia*, the "medieval aspirin"), a flower similar to the daisy of marguerite lyrics but with a bitter stink. Responding, in his own estimation (l. 6), as a skilled rhetorician, the lambasted cleric is amused that such a "nice" [simple] (l. 5) woman would presume to challenge him in the craft of Chaucer and Cicero. His insults exaggerate her physical deformities with Rabelaisian extravagance. Each of her "camused" (l. 22) nostrils could serve as a douter to snuff out the candles in church. "Dedicated" translates "apropred" (l. 27), which seems another example of his clerical jargon meaning "to acquire the right to the endowment and income of (a parish church)."[27] Her sardonically "courtly loke" is "saferon" (l. 29), indicating a choleric complexion; her gapped (so licentious) teeth are likewise yellow, indicating halitosis. She has "babir lippes" (l. 31) in a mouth like Esau's (l. 32) designed for cursing; this use of "babir" [swollen?] as an adjective escapes confident definition. "Baby" seems inappropriate; "babbling" or "lying" might do; "thick" could be a physical stereotype of the "Sarasin" (a rather inclusive name for the Other) and so a racial slur; or, the intended insult may target her genitalia.[28] Like "federfoy," the medicinal elderberry (l. 37) tends to stink, and these botanical references may hint at some meddling with witchcraft.

Ending as he began with Tartuffian piety (ll. 17, 55), the self-proclaimed superior poet writes a final rhyme-royal anti-blessing that is syntactically tortured and deeply obscure. He recommends "The pip and the pose" (l. 54) to her—that is, he wishes that she get a "head cold; catarrh" caused by an excessive build-up of mucus as well as a "disease of poultry in which a white scale forms around the tongue."[29] Then, when God "ones" [soon] (l. 56) prepares her resting place, he hopes she will miss the boat to Paradise while waiting on the dock "Up by the navel, fast by the water gate" (l. 57) with "water gate" perhaps referring to the entry to the Tower of London from the Thames, where goods were delivered (called "Traitor's Gate" since at least the mid-sixteenth century). Alternatively, the letter-writer may be wishing that his former "Charybdis" (l. 2) be left wading waist-deep with dank naughty bits.[30] The lyric's final couplet provides a sort of postscript in which he defends his own steadfastness against her prior accusations; he countercharges her, tit-for-tat, with infidelity—ending no doubt smugly confident that he has won their epistolary duel by at least three rhyme-royal stanzas.

"Somer is comen with love to toune" is commonly titled "The Thrush and the Nightingale" following an Anglo-Norman annotation in its primary textual witness: "Ci comence le cuntent par entre le mauuis et la russinole" [Here begins the *contek* between . . .]. The female nightingale, or "night-singer," is herself a type of thrush; the identification of the male "threstlecok" (ll. 18, 121) as "mauvis" may hint that his misogynist arguments will indeed be "malveis" ("mauvais")—that is, "bad" or "ill-advised." This relatively brief debate (though rather long lyric) consists of sixteen, twelve-line, tail-rhyme stanzas rhyming aabccbddbeeb. It starts as a reverdie celebrating the arrival of love with the return of the nightingale. Whether ornithologically accurate or not, nightingales supposedly returned to England on St. Valentine's Day. "Ic" (l. 7) rehearses the birds' overheard "strif" (ll. 7, 12). "I" promises that "ye mowen ihere" (l. 12) their debate verbatim, casting the reader in the role of eavesdropper as well. The thrush and the nightingale address each other throughout with familiar second-person singular pronouns, suggesting a prior albeit now strained intimacy, perhaps that of former lovers. She would "hereth" [praise] (l. 10) women; he would "shende" [disparage] (l. 11) them all. As such, their debate is an avian *querelle de la rose* writ small. Preceding their stanza-for-stanza *contek*, the first two stanzas betray an initial bias on the part of the presumably male reporter in favor of the thrush's criticisms (ll. 19–24).

With due courtesy, however, the poem lets the lady begin, apparently in reply to some precedent "blame" [rebuke] (l. 25). She will also have the final word.

    Late Spring has come with love to town,
    somer is comen with love to toune
        With blossoms and with birds' secret whispers.
        with blostme and with brides roune
        The hazelnut tree blossoms.
        the note of hasel springeth
        The dew darkens in the dale,
        the dewes darkneth in the dale
5   **For longing of the nightingale,**
        for longing of the nightegale
        These birds sing merrily.
        thes foweles murye singeth
        [Yet] I heard a debate between two—
        ic herde a strif bitweyes two
        One for happiness, the other for woe—
        that on of wele that other of wo
        Between the two together:
        bitwene two ifere
10   **One praises women in that they are gracious;**
        that on hereth wimmen that hoe beth hende
        The other would greatly shame them.
        that other hem wole with mighte shende
        That debate you may hear.
        that strif ye mowen ihere
    The Nightingale is one by name
    the nightingale is on by nome
        That would protect them [women] from shame;
        that wol shilden hem from shome
15   **She would clear them of harm.**
        of skathe hoe wole hem skere
        The Thrush would confine them all:
        the threstelcok hem kepeth ay
        He says, all night and also all day,

> he seith by nighte and eke by day
> **That women are fiends all together**
> that hy beth fendes ifere
> **Because they mislead every man**
> for hy biswiketh euchan mon
20 **Who most believes in them;**
> that mest bileveth hem upon
> **Though they be mild mannered,**
> they hy ben milde of chere
> **They are found to be false and fickle.**
> hoe beth fikele and fals to fonde
> **They cause woe in every land.**
> hoe wercheth wo in euchan londe
> **It would be better if they did not exist.**
> it were betere that hy nere
25 [Nightingale] **"It is a shame to blame a lady**
> it is shome to blame levedy
> **For they are noble of courtesy—**
> for hy beth hende of corteisy
> **I advise that you stop!**
> ich rede that thou lete
> **Never was there a breach so strongly**
> ne wes nevere bruche so strong
> **ruptured (with right nor with wrong)**
> ibroke with righte ne with wrong
30 **That one [of them] might not make [it] better.**
> that mon ne mighte bete
> **They gladden those who are angry,**
> hy gladieth hem that beth wrothe
> **Both the high and the low [born].**
> bothe the heye and the lowe
> **With joy they know how to greet them.**
> mid gome hy cunne hem grete
> **This world would be nothing if there were no women.**
> this world nere nout if wimmen nere
35 **She was made to be man's companion—**

CONTEK II: LOVE AND LOATHING · 237

     imaked hoe wes to mones fere
     There is nothing [else] so sweet."
     nis no thing all so swete
[Thrush] **"I may praise women not at all**
     i ne may wimmen herien nohut
     For they are sneaky and false of thought,
     for hy beth swikele and false of thohut
     As I understand,
     also ich am understonde
40   **[Though] they are fair and bright of hew;**
     hy beth feire and bright on hewe
     Their thinking is false and unfaithful,
     here thout is fals and untrewe
     For a very long time I have found them [so].
     ful yare ich have hem fonde
     Alexander the king warns about them
     alisaundre the king meneth of hem
     'There is no man in the world so crafty,
     in the world nes non so crafty mon
45   **Nor any so rich of land**
     ne non so riche of londe
     (I take witness of many and worthy [men]
     i take witnesse of monye and fele
     Who had been rich in the world's wealth)
     that riche weren of worldes wele
     [That] great was the ruin to them [caused by women].'"
     muche wes hem the shonde
 The nightingale, she was angry:
 the nightingale hoe wes wroth
50 [Nightingale] **"Fowl, it seems to me that you are despicable**
     fowel me thinketh thou art me loth
     Such tales to present.
     sweche tales for to showe
     Among a thousand ladies [thus] talked about,
     among a thousend levedies itolde
     I hold there is not one wicked

ther nis non wickede i holde
Where they sit in a row.
ther hy sitteth on rowe
They are meek and mild of heart.
hy beth of herte meke and milde
They know how to shield themselves from shame
hemself hy cunne from shome shilde
Within chamber walls,
withinne boures wowe
And the sweetest thing it is to wiggle in [the] arms
and swettoust thing in armes to wree
[Of] a man that holds them in bliss.
the mon that holdeth hem in glee
Fowl, why aren't you informed of this?"
fowel why ne art thou it iknowe

[Thrush] **"Noble Fowlesse, are you talkin' to me?**
gentil fowel seyst thou it me
I have been with them in the bedroom;
ich habbe with hem in boure ibe
I've had all my will.
i haved all mine wille
They will, for a little payback,
hy willeth for a litel mede
Do a sinful, hidden thing—
don a senful derne dede
Their soul to damn.
here soule for to spille
Fowl, you seem to be a liar.
fowel me thinketh thou art les
Although you are mild and soft spoken,
they thou be milde and softe of pes
You say whatever you wish.
thou seyst thine wille
I take to witness Adam
i take witnesse of adam
(Who was our first man)
that wes oure furste man

                That he found them wicked and evil."
                that fonde hem wicke and ille
[Nightingale] "**Cock, you are crazy!**
                threstelcok thou art wood
                Or else you are ignorant
                other thou const to litel good
75   **These women to shame.**
                this wimmen for the shende
                It is the sweetest flirtation
                it is the swetteste driwerie
                And the most in regards to courtesy that they know—
                and mest hoe cunnen of curteisie
                There is nothing else so noble.
                nis nothing all so hende
                The greatest joy that a man has here
                the mest murthe that mon haveth here
80   **Is when he is mated to his partner**
                whenne hoe is maked to his fere
                In arms to twine.
                in armes for to wende
                It is a shame to blame the lady.
                it is shome to blame levedy
                On their account, you shall depart sorry;
                for hem thou shalt gon sory
                Out of the land, I will send you."
                of londe ich wille thee sende
85 [Thrush] "**Nightingale, you are in the wrong.**
                nightingale thou havest wrong
                Would you send me out of this land
                wolt thou me senden of this lond
                Because I hold the right?
                for ich holde with the righte
                I take witness of Sir Gawain,
                i take witnesse of sire gawain
                To whom Jesus Christ gave might and main
                that jhesu crist gaf might and main
90   **And strength to fight;**

       and strengthe for to fighte
       As far and wide as he had traveled,
       so wide so he hevede igon
       He never found one [woman] true
       trewe ne founde he nevere non
       By day nor by night."
       by daye ne by nighte
[Nightingale] "**Fowl, on account of your false mouth,**
       fowel for thy false mouth
95   **Your 'wisdom' shall be widely known**
       thy sawe shall ben wide couth
       I strongly advise you to flee.
       i rede thee fle with mighte
       I [myself] have leave to be here,
       ich habbe leve to ben here
       In orchard and in arbor,
       in orchard and in erbere
       My songs to sing.
       mine songes for to singe
100   **I have never heard about any lady**
       herd i nevere by no levedy
       [Anything] but nobility and courtesy
       bote hendinesse and curteisy
       And joy that they did bring to me.
       and joye hy gunnen me bringe
       About much mirth they tell me.
       of muchele murthe hy telleth me
       Chum, I'm also telling you
       fere also i telle thee
105   **They live in longing.**
       hy livieth in longinge
       Fowl, you are sitting on a hazelwood branch.
       fowel thou sittest on hasel bou
       [As] you revile them, [so] may you have misery!
       thou lastest hem thou havest wou
       Your infamy shall spread widely."
       thy word shall wide springe

[Thrush]   "**It spreads widely, I well know—**
it springeth wide well ich wot
[**Go**] **tell him who doesn't know it.**
thou tell it him that it not
These sayings are not new.
this sawes ne beth nout newe
Chick, listen to my proverbs.
fowel herkne to my sawe
I will tell you about their law
ich wille thee telle of here lawe
[**Which**] **you don't acknowledge.**
thou ne kepest nout hem iknowe
Think about Constantine's queen
thenk on costantines quene
A spotted and green [**gown**] **pleased her very much;**
foul well hire semede fou and grene
Full sorely it caused her regret:
how sore it gon hire rewe
She fed a cripple in her bedroom,
hoe fedde a crupel in hire bour
And covered him with the bedspread . . .
and helede him with covertour
Look, whether women are true!"
loke whar wimmen ben trewe

[Nightingale]   "**Cock, you are wrong.**
threstelcok thou havest wrong
As I say in my song,
also i saye one my song
And as men widely know.
and that men witeth wide
They [**women**] **are brighter in the shade of a grove**
hy beth brightore under shawe
Than the day when it dawns
then the day whenne it dawe
In the *longue duree* **of summer.**
in longe someres tide
If you ever come into their domain,

come thou evere in here londe
They shall have you put in a strong prison,
hy shulen don thee in prisoun stronge
And there you will stay.
and ther thou shalt abide
130   **The lies you have made,**
the lesinges that thou havest maked
You will there forsake,
ther thou shalt hem forsake
And shame will befall you."
and shome thee shall bitide
[Thrush]   **"Nightingale, you say whatever you will.**
nightingale thou seyst thine wille
You say that women should kill me.
thou seyst that wimmen shulen me spille
135   **Damn whoever wishes so!**
datheit who it wolde
In Scripture it is found
in holy book it is ifounde
They bring many a man to ground
hy bringeth mony mon to grounde
Who were proud and bold.
that proude weren and bolde
Think of Sampson the strong—
thenk upon saunsum the stronge
140   **How much wrong his wife did him.**
how muchel his wif him dude to wronge
I know that she sold him.
ich wot that hoe him solde
It is the worst treasure trove
it is that worste hord of pris
That Jesus made in Paradise
that jhesu makede in parais
In a lock-box for to keep."
in tresour for to holde
145   **Then the Nightingale said,**

[Nightingale]   tho seyde the nightingale
"**Fowl, very handy is your story.**
fowel well redy is thy tale
[Now] listen to my wisdom—
herkne to my lore
It is a long-lasting flower,
it is flour that lasteth longe
And most praised in every land,
and mest iherd in every londe
150   **And lovely when dressed up.**
and lovelich under gore
In the world, there is no better doctor,
in the worlde nis non so goed leche
So mild of thought, so fair of speech,
so milde of thoute so feir of speche
To heal a man's sorrow and pain.
to hele monnes sore
Fowl, you will regret all your thinking;
fowel thou rewest all thy thohut
155   **You are doing evil which profits you not at all.**
thou dost evele ne geineth thee nohut
Don't do it anymore!"
ne do thou so namore

[Thrush]   **"Nightingale, you are stupid**
nightingale thou art unwis
To put so much value on them.
on hem to leyen so muchel pris
Your reward will be slim.
thy mede shall ben lene
160   **Among a hundred, there aren't five,**
among on hundret ne beth five
Neither of maidens nor of wives,
nouther of maidnes ne of wive
That keep themselves entirely chaste.
that holdeth hem all clene
Rather, they make woe in the land,

　　　　　　　that hy ne wercheth wo in londe
　　　　　　　Or bring men to disgrace—
　　　　　　　other bringeth men to shonde
165　　　　　　**And that is very evident.**
　　　　　　　and that is well iseene
　　　　　　　And, although we're sitting [here] in order to argue
　　　　　　　and they we sitten therfore to strive
　　　　　　　Regarding both maidens and wives,
　　　　　　　bothe of maidnes and of wive
　　　　　　　You're not saying a single truth."
　　　　　　　soth ne seyst thou ene
[Nightingale]　**"O Fowl, your mouth has dishonored you.**
　　　　　　　o fowel thy mouth thee haveth ishend
170　　　　　　**Through whom was all this world transformed?**
　　　　　　　thoru wham wes all this world iwend
　　　　　　　By a Maid meek and mild,
　　　　　　　of a maide meke and milde
　　　　　　　From whom sprang that Holy Child
　　　　　　　of hire sprong that holy bern
　　　　　　　That was born in Bethlehem
　　　　　　　that boren wes in bedlehem
　　　　　　　And [Who] tames all that is wild.
　　　　　　　and temeth all that is wilde
175　　　　　　**She knows nothing of sin nor of shame.**
　　　　　　　hoe ne weste of sunne ne of shame
　　　　　　　"Mary" was her proper name.
　　　　　　　marye wes hir righte name
　　　　　　　Christ protect her.
　　　　　　　crist hire ishilde
　　　　　　　Fowl, on account of your false speech,
　　　　　　　fowel for thy false sawe
　　　　　　　I forbid you [to remain] in this woody grove.
　　　　　　　forbed i thee this wode shawe
180　　　　　　**Go into the [open] field."**
　　　　　　　thou fare into the filde
[Thrush]　　　**"Nightingale, I was crazy**
　　　　　　　nightingale i wes wood

Or else I was ill-informed
other i couthe to litel good
To argue with you.
with thee for the strive
I say that I am overcome
i saye that ich am overcome
185   **On account of her who bore that Holy Son**
thoru hire that bar that holy sone
Who suffered five wounds.
that soffrede wundes five
I swear by His Holy Name
i swerie by his holy name
[That] I shall never speak [further] shame
ne shall i nevere seyen shame
About maidens nor about wives.
by maidnes ne by wive
190   **Out of this land I will betake myself**
out of this londe will i te
Nor will I take any reckoning as to where I fly.
ne rech i never weder i fle
Away I will banish myself."
away ich wille drive

In her opening argument, the nightingale affirms the sweet attractiveness of women, the joy they bring, the necessity of motherhood, and woman's creation as man's "fere" [companion]—the side-by-side equality of prelapsarian Eve "made" (l. 35) from Adam's rib. The nightingale does concede the possibility of a "breach" [transgression],[31] but nothing so severe that it cannot be corrected—by a woman. The thrush's riposte is that women's very attractiveness only camouflages their deceptiveness. He appeals to authority and the "witnesse" [testimony] (l. 46) of many conventional exempla that demonstrate that pretty women despoil rich and powerful men. A one-line narrative intrusion indicates the nightingale's "wroth" (l. 49) and thereby the following tone of voice to be impersonated by a reciter. Her loathing infuses her recurrent uses of the vocative "fowl" (ll. 50, 60, 67, 94, 146, 169, 178), which resonates in Middle English with both "fool" and "foul." To the contrary, all the tales that she has read are about good, meek, mild, and pleasant women who need no protective custody (ll. 56–57). Her reference "Ther hy sitteth on rowe" (l. 54) may actually be played while pointing to the ladies in her courtly audience.

The thrush usually addresses the nightingale as "Nightingale" (ll. 85, 133, 157, 181), suggesting his deference to her status or, at least, his polite manners. Nevertheless, his reply in stanza 6 is quite insulting—when he first calls her "fowel" albeit "gentil" (l. 61) and accuses her of being "les" [mendacious, faithless].[32] His two other uses of the epithet "fowel" (ll. 67, 112) are likewise performable as lapses into rudeness. The braggart's contempt is based upon his claim that he has penetrated many a bower at little expense, boasting about what he should be confessing as sin (ll. 64–66). He calls to witness Adam's (unmanly) blaming of Eve for humankind's fall.

The Nightingale's rebuttal of such ignorant insanity (ll. 73–74) is that women are the true experts in "curteisie"; they teach men the sweetest "driwerie" [courtly love][33] and most "murthe"—that is, "When hoe is maked to his fere" [When she is made his equal] (l. 80) as well as sexual partner. But the Thrush counters with the "witnesse" (l. 88) of Sir Gawain who—as if some sort of sexist Diogenes—searched everywhere for an honest woman and found none. More typically, Gawain is characterized as a notorious womanizer, the sort of knight common to pastourelles. Irate at his absurdity, the Nightingale preempts the Thrush's right to conclude this stanza after its ninth line.[34] She provides its last three lines by threatening to exile the Thrush for his slander, empowered as she is by her superior social standing in this *contek*'s avian court. In the next stanza, she grants herself "leave" (l. 97) to stay and sing.

Every word the Nightingale has heard about womankind is positive. Although she calls the Thrush "Fere" [companion] (l. 104; cf. alt. spelling of "fair"), no doubt she does so sarcastically to play off "Fowel" (l. 105). Her idiomatic insult (that he sits on a hazel bough) works both literally and metaphorically: he is standing on a thin branch, and he is "speaking nonsense."[35] She warns that his "word shall wide springe" [the scandalous folly of what he has said will be infamous] (l. 108).

The Thrush then simply co-opts her meaning of the word "word": "It springeth wide" [my wisdom is widely known] (l. 109). His next, obscure anecdote of Constantine's queen and a cripple seems a recollection of Fausta, the emperor's second wife, who was boiled to death for adultery with her stepson, Crispus. The expression "Foul [fully and fouly] well hire semed fou and grene" (l. 116) may anticipate the idiom "to give a green gown" (i.e., to stain clothing by having sex on the ground).[36] The gist of this anecdote about Constantine's "quene" [queen or whore] (l. 115) seems to be that even a sainted and imperial husband will be cuckolded.

For the first time, the Nightingale then addresses the Thrush as a cock (l. 121; cf. l. 18). The debate is no longer an argument, merely invective and contradiction. Fully outraged now, the Nightingale threatens that, should he ever dare to re-enter *Feminia*, they will imprison him. This threat may entail a somewhat ironic inversion of reality in that (before the canary) the Nightingale herself was a favorite songbird to cage, not the unfortunately named "turdidae."

In stanza 12, while accusing the Nightingale of speaking without restraint, the Thrush overstates her warning by objecting that she has threatened the death penalty (l. 134). He curses just before citing the Bible. The bribe accepted by unnamed Delilah is rather confusingly described as Christ's worst deposit in Heaven (ll. 142–4). The very obscurity of this reference and its tortured syntax may indicate that the role of the Thrush should be played with increasing desperation. After a one-line narrative intrusion (an opportunity for the reciter to do a double-take), the Nightingale can "wel redy" (l. 146) dismiss his nonsense.

Stanza 14 is the Thrush's last stand: he predicts that the Nightingale will receive little reward as an advocate of womankind's worth because, at most, 5 percent of women are chaste. So, in her final judgment of the Thrush, the Nightingale calls to witness Mary whose Son saved fallen nature and tamed all that is wild. She expels the Thrush, like Adam, from the *locus amoenus* of "this wode shawe" (l. 179) out into the fields. The Thrush immediately repents and accepts the rightness of his exile, vowing never to sin again.

The Thrush's largely unanticipated surrender may seem emotionally implausible at first blush. According to Thomas L. Reed, having reached an "argumentative deadlock" before invoking Mary, the poem ends with "a neat if somewhat miraculous conclusion. The work is, in short, cleverly mimetic of Mary's 'superlogical' role."[37] This debate's surprise ending may also be intended to mirror—that is, reverse—the sudden resolutions of many pastourelles in which a lower-class woman abruptly submits to a nobleman. Furthermore, the entire poem may be best played by a superior, if not literally noble, woman as the "Ic" who recites the Thrush's lines as well, but in a most mocking manner.

"Weping haveth min wonges wet," or "The Poet's Repentance," offers, at long last, what seems, at first, a former misogynist's apology.

    Weeping has soaked my cheeks.
    weping haveth min wonges wet
        Because of [my] wicked work and lack of intelligence,
        for wikked werk and wone of wit
        Unhappy I'll be till I have made amends for
        unblithe i be til i ha bet
        Offences committed—as the Bible commands—
        bruches broken ase bok bit
5   **Concerning the love of ladies (which I have forsaken),**
        of levedis love that i ha let
        That [love] fully does shine with a lovely light.
        that lemeth all with luevly lit
        Often I have put them in a song
        ofte in song i have hem set
        Where it is dishonorable to be set.
        that is unsemly ther it sit
        It [the song] survives and remains dishonorable
        it sit and semeth noght
10   **Wherever it is said in song.**
        ther it is seid in song
        Whatever I have written about them,
        that i have of hem wroght
        Certainly it is all wrong.
        iwis it is all wrong
    All wrongly I wrote about a woman [Eve]
    all wrong i wroghte for a wif
        Who caused woe for us everywhere in the world.
        that made us wo in world full wide
15   **She robbed us all of abundant wealth,**
        heo rafte us alle richesse rif
        Who had no need to saddle us so.
        that durfte us nout in reines ride
        A mighty one [Mary] stopped her harsh strife—
        a stithie stunte hire sturne strif

She, who is hidden in the heart of Heaven.
that is in heovene hert in hide
In her light, One lived
in hire light on ledeth lif
20 **And through her beautiful side He shone.**
and shon thourgh hire semly side
Through her side He shone
thourgh hire side he shon
As the sun does through glass.
ase sonne doth thourgh the glass
There has been not any wicked woman,
wommon nes wicked non
Since He was born.
sethe he ibore was
25 **There is no woman so wicked, that I know of,**
wicked nis non that i wot
Who dares wet her cheeks for profit.
that durste for werk hire wonges wete
They all live [free] from the least of vice
alle heo liven from last of lot
And all are as noble as a hawk in a hut;
and are all hende ase hawk in chete
Therefore, [while] on this earth, I grow sorry
forthy on molde i waxe mot
30 **That I have said sayings unsuitable.**
that i sawes have seid unsete
My fickle flesh, my false blood!
my fikel fleish my falsly blod
In a field, I'll fall at their feet;
on feld hem feole i falle to fete
To their feet, I'll fall often,
to fet i falle hem feole
For falsely, fifty times,
for falslek fiftyfolde
35 **Of all their infidelity, in slander,**
of alle untrewe on tele
As I formerly talked with [my] tongue.

with tonge ase i er tolde
Though tales out of tune are told in town,
thagh told beon tales untoun in toune
    Such news may happen, [but] I won't trust any of it at all
    such tiding mey tide i nul nout teme
    About bright brides with fair foreheads,
    of brudes bright with browes broune
40   **Before they gain bliss, these gay girls.**
    or blisse heo beyen this briddes breme
    In rude wartime, it would seem peace to whisper with them
    in rude were ro with hem roune
    So that one might embrace them as if he were home.
    that hem mighte henten ase him were heme
    There isn't a king, emperor, or tonsured clerk,
    nis king cayser ne clerk with croune
    These seemly attractive [women] to serve (who may seem shabby).
    this semly serven that mene may seme
45   **It would befit him [to be] on a mission**
    semen him may on sonde
    These attractive [ladies] so to serve,
    this semly serven so
    With both feet and hands,
    bothe with fet and honde
    For [she is the] one that has pushed us from woe
    for on that us warp from wo
Now woe in the world is gone away,
now wo in world is went away
50   **And well-being is come as we would wish,**
    and weole is come ase we wolde
    Through a mighty, modest maiden,
    thourgh a mighty methful may
    Who has hurled us from cold cares.
    that us hath cast from cares colde
    Forever I shall praise women,
    ever wimmen ich herie ay
    And ever in court support them
    and ever in hyrd with hem ich holde

55   **And, ever at need, I deny**
      and ever at neode i nickenay
      That I ever spoke [anything] that she did not want,
      that i ner nemnede that heo nolde
      Nor would nor will I [say anything],
      i nolde and nullit noght
      For nothing now—at need—
      for nothing now a nede
      Is true that I have written about them—
      soth is that i of hem ha wroght
60   **As Richard knew first to advise [me].**
      as richard erst con rede
  [Oh] Richard! Root of right reason [and of]
  richard rote of resoun right
      Reckoning of rhyme and song,
      rykening of rym and ron
      Over maidens meek you have the most might.
      of maidnes meke thou hast might
      On earth, I count you the merriest man.
      on molde i holde thee muryest mon
65   **By nature, as attractive as a knight,**
      cunde comely ase a knight
      Well-known cleric who knows the arts,
      clerk icud that craftes con
      In every kind of court your excellence is honored
      in uch an hyrd thin athel is hight
      And your good fortune is on [every] princely patron.
      and uch an athel thin hap is on
      Luck that nobleman has taken
      hap that hathel hath hent
70   **With courtliness in the hall.**
      with hendelec in halle
      May bliss be sent to him
      selthe be him sent
      In the land of all ladies.
      in londe of levedis alle

This lyric pretends to be a palinode repenting prior "wikked werk" (l. 3). Gayle Margherita, who provides Freudian readings of several Harley lyrics, finds "what makes 'The Poet's Repentance' such a fascinating poem is its seeming awareness of the poet's essentially negative speaking position, and of the problematic of negativity within courtly discourse in general."[38] The lyric's form is extremely complicated: six twelve-line stanzas (ababababcdcd) are linked to one another by concatenation. Furthermore, lines 8 and 9 of each stanza concatenate internally (between a final b- and initial c-rhyme). Sustained alliteration also pairs lines, and, in the manuscript, two lines of verse are presented as a single line of text.

Approximating *Kunstsprache* [art-speech], the semantics of this poem seem indecipherable at times, and its tone of performance, whether sham or sincere, is debatable. The current consensus seems to be that this palinode is too crafty to be sincere; its "playful duplicity" is often "audacious"[39]; furthermore, it follows a mock saint's tale in its manuscript.[40] In the first stanza, the poet confesses two sins: that he has been unfaithful to a lady's love (ll. 1–5) and that he has written many unseemly songs about women in general (ll. 6–9). Since these same lyrics apparently remain in circulation, the reputedly repentant poet may now be advertising to prospective patrons his repertoire as a poet-entertainer. "Bruches broken" (l. 4) is a bit confusing, probably meaning broken commandments for which one should make amends. However, "broken breaches" or "britches" (as in underpants) can imply "loss of virginity" or "adultery."[41] In addition to being a prolific poet, this "I" may be confessing—that is, bragging—about his former career as a cad and roué. My translation of "wroghte" (l. 11; cf. l. 58) renders the poet's "work" as a possible pun on "wrote," but "work" can also apply to committing sin.[42] By means of writing this poem, the penitent poet intends to offer satisfaction of the hand "ase bok bit" [as "a book" or *The Book* bids (l. 4), be it the Bible or a manual of sins or a handbook of versification].

The first four lines of stanza 2 repeat the commonplace slandering of Eve that the poet pretends to be renouncing—that is, that woman brought woe into the world. The idiom "in reines ride" (l. 16) may also suggest that Eve surmounted Adam sexually.[43] The antithetical conceit that light penetrating glass symbolizes the virginal impregnation of Mary at the Annunciation is also conventional; the claim that no woman has been wicked since her virgin birth is not. Furthermore, "A stithe stunt hire sturne strif" [A strong stop to her harsh enmity] (l. 17) sounds more appropriate to *Beowulf* than to a lyric of Marian devotion.

Stanza 3 is a prolonged (and so perhaps comically excessive) mea culpa with the poet falling prostrate before womankind to mortify his flesh with four consecutive lines of *f*-alliterations. However, the rhyme-required phrasing is again highly problematic. "Mot" (l. 29) can mean "I grow proud" as readily as "sorry."[44] For the sake of concatening "fet(e)," line 33 seems repetitve, but "To fet I falle hem often" can mean "To their feet I often fell them" as well.

Stanza 4 begins with a rejection of future gossip: "I nul nout teme" (l. 38). "Teme" does mean "to vouch, warrant," but a slightly more common usage of the verb was "to produce offspring, breed; also *fig.*; of a woman: conceive."[45] Another alliterative oddity occurs in the praise of "burdes ... with browes broune" (l. 39): "broune" could mean "shining" in reference to weapons, but in reference to the brows of women the adjective much more commonly denoted "dark, dull ... cheerless, frowning, gloomy."[46] After apologizing to womankind, this stanza then seeks pardon by praising "this" one in particular (l. 44) who drives away woe and deserves a quest. However, among the eleven possible definitions of "warp" [fling, expel] (l. 47), few if any have a positive connotation.[47]

Stanza 5 begins "Now" with rejoicing that all woe has been removed from the world because "a mighty, methful [tranquil] may" (l. 51); this sounds like a reprise of the curiously martial Blessed Virgin Mary. The meanings "cast" [throw] (l. 57)[48] are predominantly violent, and "hyrd" (l. 53) can suggest a combative as well as celestial retinue[49]—all in all, the idiom of *contek* rather than courtly love. But the poet seems to have made peace with at least one of "*This* semly" [worthy] (ll. 44, 46) Mary-like women. Rather than just recanting, the poet ultimately denies having badmouthed women, pleading innocence "ever at neode I nickenay" [ever at need I deny] (l. 54) as if he is under arrest.

The last line of stanza 5 introduces a character witness and an enigmatic context for interpreting this lyric's occasion: "As Richard erst can rede," which can be taken in a number of ways including "As Richard first was able to advise"[50] or, more simply, "As Richard first had the opportunity to read." The last stanza's extravagant praise of this knightly-clerk Richard, of course, begs the question as to who indeed this once famous "Richard" might have been—to which there is no convincing answer, so Thorlac Turville-Petre notes "*Sic transit gloria mundi.*"[51] Daniel J. Ransom finds the poet's concluding bow to Richard intended "to ironize, not lionize his rival."[52] However, it may be sufficient to assume that the poet and this "muryest mon" (l. 64) Richard were very close as well as very competitive friends. "Richard" might as readily be translated "Bro." The poet wishes him the best of luck and all happiness, that is "Selthe" (l. 71)—which has a strong sense of heavenly bliss—in the land of ladies. So, the formerly misogynist poet concludes his so-called repentance with what might well serve as a wedding toast performed by the best man—not to mention, he might be implying, the better poet.

Allegorically, marriage may symbolize the perfect harmony between God as Groom and humanity as His bride; yet marriage too often becomes the front line of strident *contek* between actual husbands and wives; yet, again, lovers as often enjoy the tit-for-tat exchange of clever jibes. The challenge for modern readers is to imagine a performance context in which such lyrics of loathing may be performed for fun. Everything depends on the performer's rapport with a target audience. When enacted among a homosocial company, or among friends (including lovers and wives), licensed loathing can alleviate frustrated desire. But when intended to wound the opposite sex (as Jankyn learns the hard way in the Wife of Bath's Prologue), such performed wittiness only exacerbates real resentment.

EIGHT

The Early Modern Machining of Verse

> There are many people who appreciate the expression of sincere emotion in verse, and there is a smaller number of people who can appreciate technical excellence.
>
> T. S. Eliot[1]

Most modern readers of lyric poetry, especially aspiring poets, who find themselves turning "others' leaves, to see if thence would flow / Some fresh and fruitful showers" (Sir Philip Sidney's *Astrophil and Stella*, Sonnet 1, 6–7), feel all but entirely entitled to ignore Middle English lyrics as stylistic and emotional exemplars. Although some modern critics, like H. A. Mason, rejected an oversimplified "contrast between the artlessness" of medieval lyrics "and art" of modern verse,[2] Ingrid Nelson acknowledges that "as [I. A.] Richards's theoretical work promoted the centrality of lyric poetry to English literature, he inaugurated a process of canon-making that increasingly neglected Middle English lyrics throughout the twentieth century."[3] Furthermore, whereas oral transmission of the ballads (i.e., actual performance) maintained their popularity, manuscript preservation of the lyrics largely did not. Worse still, the often-precarious textual records of Middle English lyrics do give an impression of their frequent failings as competent verse. The primary goal of this *Introduction to Middle English Lyrics* has been to revive the performed emotional viability of some representative lyrics, or, in T. S. Eliot's terms, to appreciate the "presence of this poetry" against an enduring disregard. This last chapter, however, addresses how and why Middle English lyrics first came to be considered formally incompetent—a false impression that may be best addressed, again in Eliot's terms, as "the pastness of the past."[4]

The anxiety of English poets regarding posterity's perception of their metrical competence predates the advent of print publication but became significantly intensified immediately thereafter. Anticipating the scrutiny of future readers as scanners of their verse, Geoffrey Chaucer (ca. 1340–1400), Thomas Hoccleve (ca. 1368–1450), Sir Thomas Wyatt (1503–1542), Henry Howard, Earl of Surrey (ca. 1516–1547), and William Shakespeare (1564–1616), represent over two centuries of lyric poets who all recognized an increasing pressure to transform the thing now called "lyric." The textual refashioning of lyrics by late medieval and early modern English poets had to satisfy new protocols for evaluating the poem-in-hand.[5] Indeed, C. S. Lewis once observed that "the grand function of the Drab Age poets was to build a firm metrical highway out of the late medieval swamp."[6] The fact that, ever since the free verse movement, rigid prosodic criteria no longer dominate our definition of "good poetry" allows an ongoing reassessment of the real success rather than supposed failure of Middle English lyrics as verse.

Our critical heritage that has so diminished the appeal of Middle English lyrics is largely the aftermath of self-promotion by Renaissance and subsequent poets. Joel Grossman considers in detail the emergence of "the long-standing notion of a rupture between medieval and Renaissance literary practice, the sense of a major epochal shift that potentially saw a 'rebirth' of Western culture and of perceptions of the self."[7] Grossman concludes "these received notions are themselves problematic, based on preconceived ideas of what 'Renaissance,' and indeed 'lyric,' actually entail."[8] The transformation of "lyric" from medieval performance script to modern text-in-hand was not a sudden rebirth, and the prosodic precision of a lyric was never asserted as an absolute criterion for assessing poetic competence. Nevertheless, once the rules of a "traditional" (i.e., classical) prosody were thought to apply to all English verse, whether narrative or lyric, whether stichic (line-by-line, like blank verse) or melic (stanzaic), whether silently read or recited, these metrical dictates supposedly legitimized a retrospective mis-assessment of the musicality of Middle English lyrics.

Strict rules of traditional prosody, modeled primarily on Horace and Virgil, posit the synonymity of a "syllable" with the "metrical unit" (to be scanned alternatively as long or short, as accented or unaccented). These ancient rules were not unknown to medieval poets.[9] And templates for predetermined measures (including, for example, the *formes fixes*) were to be preserved even in the absence of musical settings—that is, even after the etymology of *prosody* as "towards the song" has been forgotten. However, it was the recital or the singing of a Middle English lyric—not its transcription per se—that had to satisfy this audible perception of metrical competence.[10]

The poet and author of the first English essay on versification, George Gascoigne (1535–1577 CE), required regular English verse to preserve "natural" pronunciation as did "my master" Chaucer:

> there is none other foote vsed but one; wherby our Poemes may iustly be called Rithmes, and cannot by any right challenge the name of a Verse. But, since it is so, let vs take the forde as we finde it, and lette me set downe vnto you suche rules or precepts that euen in this playne foote of two syllables you wreste no woorde from his natural and vsuall sounde.

By "setting down unto you such rules," Gascoigne accepts that prosodic prescriptions precede composition that comes to be understood as the poet's final transcription. In building this firm textual highway over the gravel of Middle English manuscripts, however, there were several formal detours and potholes, among which were Thomas Hoccleve's intention to sustain decasyllabic lines; the initial efforts of English poets to import the Italian sonnet; and Shakespeare's representative expressions of Renaissance contempt for the formal and emotional conventions of medieval lyrics. These three seemingly unrelated phenomena—Hoccleve's prosodic anxiety, the regularization of the English sonnet, and Shakespeare's innovative conventionality—all indicate an increasing awareness that written records of the lyric needed to be reworked before presentation. The texts of lyrics came to be seen as things carefully *machined* on the page rather than as foul papers for performance. With print, any metrical misstep became as abhorrent as a typo. Copying his own poems in anticipation of their manuscript circulation, Thomas Hoccleve felt a comparable stress.

I. Hoccleve's Hand

Though unduly disrespected until relatively recently, Thomas Hoccleve (ca. 1368–1426) provides a late medieval example of a lyric poet anticipating that his writing would be viewed and its formal competence assessed as a thing on the page. Hoccleve's understanding of the decasyllabic line is generally considered to be an aesthetic mistake; even many medievalists have expressed a certain disdain for Hoccleve's crippled versification, but—in defense of this much maligned poet—he clearly worried that his lines would be scanned on the page (to the detriment of their subsequent recital).

As a professional scribe, Hoccleve carefully wrote his holographs to be seen by future readers; yet his verse sounds clumsy, especially in comparison to his exemplar, Geoffrey Chaucer. George Saintsbury, for example, ridiculed the "prosaic, hobbling, broken backed doggerel" of both Hoccleve and John Lydgate.[11] Jerome Mitchell identified this perception of Hoccleve's simple inability to properly accentuate his own lines as the single feature that "has most caused his reputation to fall into low repute."[12] Appreciation of Hoccleve as a confessional poet is currently on the rise, but more so because of "the very intimacy" indeed often "self-absorbed"[13] quality of his poetry, especially his *Series,* rather than on the basis of his experimentation as a self-deprecating yet didactic versifier.

In stanza 6 of his eight-stanza "Balade to Edward, Duke of York," Hoccleve candidly apologized to future readers for his text's "mis-metering." He modestly or honestly attributes the crudity of these lines to his own incompetence rather than to the instability of the English language or to the contamination of scribal (i.e., his own) transcription:

> If that I in my wrytynge foleye
> As I do ofte—I can it nat withseye—
> Meetrynge amis or speke unfittyngly,
> Or nat by just peys my sentences weye,
> 50 And nat to the ordre of endytyng [composition] obeye,
> And my colours [figures of speech] sette ofte sythe awry,
> With al myn herte wole I buxumly [happily]
> It to amende and to correcte him preye,
> For undir his correcioun stande Y.

Hoccleve's stanza should rhyme aabaabbab, but much of the rhyming is wrenched assonance that requires Hoccleve to disobey normal syntactic order. Hoccleve's shortcomings as a versifier may still be attributed to a "defaulte of tonge" (*Troilus and Criseyde,* V, 1793), but now in the sense that the writer was not primarily concerned with the actual vocalization (l. 48) of his lines.

Detailed analyses of Hoccleve's holographs have determined that he apparently counted syllables rather than feet. J. A. Burrow, for example, concludes, "It is clear ... that Hoccleve took pains to ensure that his lines were both constructed and spelled in such a way that their conformity to the syllabic 'rule of ten' would be apparent to readers of suitable competence."[14] There have been heroic efforts by well-intentioned apologists to regularize Hoccleve's lines into iambic pentameter. Jerome Mitchell, for example, proposes a quite plausible corrective recital of Hoccleve's "thwarted stress" by demonstrating that many allegedly defective lines "can be read in a *smooth* way as verses of cadence."[15]

If Hoccleve imagined his lines primarily as things to be seen rather than to be heard, however, his neglect of strict meter may be reassessed in terms of his anticipation of the ascendency of what is considered now normative "silent" reading. As Martin J. Duffell suggests, "In any account of the progress of the iambic pentameter, Hoccleve's metre must appear as a clear step backward from that of his masters." Duffel explains further that "there can be no doubt that Hoccleve's verse is predominantly iambic as well as decasyllabic," noting, however, that the poet gave "primacy to syllable count."[16] Perhaps the very notion of a "progress" from medieval to modern versification should be understood as a period of deliberate trial and error.

Hoccleve's main poetic achievement, though seldom recognized as a masterpiece, is his *Regiment of Princes*, which curiously preserves numerous vestigial, metaphorical, mostly insignificant, but perhaps also some genuine indications of anticipated public recital. There are many more signs, however, that Hoccleve expected his completed manuscript to be read as a book-in-hand. By my count, there are at least forty-two expressions of anticipated public recital, or of what Ruth Crosby termed "signs of oral delivery"—the implications of which remain hotly contested. The *Regiment* also presents extensive direct quotation of fictional speeches that may be excerpted and dramatically recited. There are some fifty-two additional expressions that dwell in the metaphorical limbo of the "talking book." Nevertheless, as many as forty-three statements by Hoccleve provide certain indications of the *Regiment*'s "textuality"—that is, of the author's assumption that he is creating a manuscript primarily intended to be circulated for solitary reading. Despite any fossils of orality, the presentation-copy of *Regiment* was meant to be appreciated as a handmade object to be handled by the reader. The *Regiment* makes some seventeen references to the "hands"—none to the "mouth" or to the "tongue." Hoccleve seems especially empathetic when describing his own subsistence income derived from "hand labor" (l. 4420).

Hoccleve also readily uses the verb "touch" to mean "deal with a topic" (ll. 5106, 5146) by means of either writing or speaking (l. 4748).

Not surprisingly, Hoccleve's conception of writing as handiwork—both the process and the product of chirography—frequently informs his imagery and poetic lexicon. One of the *Regiment's* most appealing (because so candidly autobiographical) passages is Hoccleve's extended description of the actual pain of writing itself (ll. 985–1008).[17] Hoccleve portrays writing primarily as the isolated labor of the author's mind, eye, and hand, but he here makes no mention of voice. Confessing and so excusing his own physical unsuitability to undertake more conventional works of manual labor, and thereby to alleviate his poverty, Hoccleve describes in remarkable detail the sheer physical effort of writing. The stooping it requires has ruined his back (ll. 985–7). But it remains unclear whether he is describing transcription or original composition—and, in terms of his own professional pain, both require equivalently hard hand-work.

In the first stanza of his complaint, Hoccleve addresses the common supposition of non-writers that writing is relatively easy work. It is in the second stanza that Hoccleve simultaneously affirms and laments the constraints that writing imposes on the scribe's mind, eye, and hand. This scribal trio must remain united in their effort to produce a text. In the third and fourth stanzas, Hoccleve emphasizes the harsh demands that writing imposes on the writer's "wittes." Other artisans can whistle while they work—that is, "Talken and make game and synge" (l. 1011)—but writing requires both solitary silence, "travallous stilnesse" (l. 1013), and the scribe's singular focus while staring at a blank page. It seems not improbable that Hoccleve thought reading his verse would require a similarly silent solitude that has since become the default meaning of "reading" itself, though public reading or "prelection"[18] long endured after printed publication became commonplace and remains not unheard of (especially when some guest poet is provided an honorarium).

In addition to the lone scribe's psychological anguish—not a small factor in Hoccleve's mental breakdown—handwriting causes corporal pain. In the fourth and fifth stanzas, Hoccleve laments that twenty-one years of writing have harmed every joint of his body, and especially his eyes. But the stomach also suffers because "stowpynge out of dreede / Annoyeth sore" (ll. 1019–20). Charles R. Blyth glosses "out of dreede" idiomatically as "doubtless," a reading that emphasizes stooping as the certain cause of

Hoccleve's ulcer, but the phrasing also indicates anxiety or the "dread" of writing as a cause of illness. What remains most absent from Hoccleve's self-consciousness regarding the process of writing (and presumably reading) is any sense of song.

The "Prologue" concludes with Hoccleve's anticipation of the task still at hand—the "hateful enditing" of piecemeal translation (ll. 2053–2056)—that is, his transcription of the following "Observanda." Hoccleve's self-consciousness regarding the process of writing generates several other references to the anticipated product as well—the material text. The *Regiment* intermittently invites the reader to consider a book's clasp (l. 1956), its joining (l. 3309), the circulation of a pamphlet (l. 2060), legal charters to be granted or denied (ll. 3142, 3159), testaments (ll. 4311, 4351–2), writs (i.e., injunctions l. 4096), and patents (l. 4789). These references to material texts seem the nuts and bolts of his own word-processing. But Hoccleve also envisions such book manufacture as creative, analogous to the workings of the Word. A divine charter of mercy has been written in Christ's blood (l. 3339). And God is three times identified as an *author*: of truth (l. 2393), of pity (l. 3025), and—in the final line of the poem—of peace (l. 5438); God-the-writer's "handiwork" (ll. 3340, 5421) is humanity. Hoccleve apparently had—as Chaucer did not—an unshakable confidence that his writing would endure in perpetuity (ll. 2369–2371) because the fixity of the page supersedes the ephemerality of spoken verse.

Hoccleve's dominant conception of the poem as a handcrafted thing helps to explain a number of other oddities about the *Regiment*. The composite design of the *Regiment* as a two-part text, for example, is largely a manufactured illusion, the sewing together of two discrete projects.[19] Furthermore, each half can be readily subdivided into roughly equivalent, smaller reading installments. All paratextual features that may be attributed to authorial control (including marginalia and illustrations) seem quite handy—that is, useful both for a sequential reading of the holograph in hand and for subsequent access to desired sections.

A similar use of visual design is the concluding lyric appended as a sort of envoi to Hoccleve's holograph (Huntington HM MS 111), which displays a rhyme pattern that can be truly appreciated only by studying the text-in-hand. Whereas the conclusion of the "Prologue," Hoccleve's twenty stanzas of "Words of the Compiler to the Prince" (ll. 2017–2156), had maintained the *Regiment*'s rhyme-royal pattern, these final "Verba compilatoris ad librum"

[Words of the compiler to the book] present three eight-line ("Monk's Tale") stanzas. Hoccleve's apostrophe is addressed "ad librum"—that is, to the book en route to any future reader rather than to the author's immediate patron.[20] Additionally, the rhyme scheme of these "Verba"—though visually far more complicated than Hoccleve's normative stanzaic patterns—sounds like a metrical mess:

	O litil book, who gaf thee hardynesse	A
	Thy wordes to pronounce in the presence	B
	Of kynges ympe and princes worthynesse,	A
	Syn thow al nakid art of eloquence?	B
5	And why approchist thow his excellence	B
	Unclothid sauf thy kirtil bare also?	C
	I am right seur his humble pacience	B
	Thee geveth hardynesse to do so.	C
	But o thyng woot I wel, go wher thow go,	C
10	I am so pryvee unto thy sentence,	B
	Thow haast and art and wilt been everemo	C
	To his hynesse of swich benevolence,	B
	Thogh thow nat do him due reverence	B
	In wordes, thy cheertee nat is the lesse.	A
15	And if lust be, to his magnificence	B
	Do by thy reed; his welthe it shal witnesse.	A
	Byseeche him of his gracious noblesse	A
	Thee holde excusid of thyn innocence	B
	Of endytynge, and with hertes meeknesse,	A
20	If anythyng thee passe of negligence,	B
	Byseeche him of mercy and indulgence,	B
	And that for thy good herte he be nat fo	C
	To thee that al seist of loves fervence;	B
	That knowith He Whom nothyng is hid fro.	C

The five audible couplets among these twenty-four lines (ll. 4–5, 8–9, 12–13, 16–17, 20–21) hopscotch through a maze of otherwise inconspicuous end rhymes. However, Hoccleve's use of the same three a-, b-, and c-rhymes in all three stanzas produces a sort of rhyme-mirroring, an overall design that needs to be discovered by studied viewing:

ABABBCBC CBCBBABA ABABBCBC.²¹

So, too, certain other prosodic features of Hoccleve's *Regiment* (now too readily criticized as mistakes) may also be reviewed as deliberate experiments with its visible construction. Hoccleve's occasional willingness to rhyme syllables that pair tense with lax vowels or that rhyme syllables that begin with alternatively voiced and unvoiced consonants sound like wrenched rhymes or, at best, near rhymes, but they look like quite exact "sight" rhymes.

Hoccleve (re)wrote each line's number of syllables till they reached a total of ten, planted a visually if not audibly apparent rhyme word in the final spot, and then moved his quill down one line and to the left margin. The only likely method by which Hoccleve could have achieved the ametrical regularity of this intended "rule of ten" would have been by finger counting. George Saintsbury recognized this probability and immediately renounced it as "the mere test of the fingers."²² I doubt that Hoccleve's contentment with such a raw count of ten syllables per line can be blamed on proto-Indo-European practice. He more probably thought his verse lines equivalent to rhythmic French decasyllables. But it is in terms of a hand-writer's self-consciousness that Hoccleve's innovation (not his presumed incompetence as a writer of English verse lines) may be re-evaluated. Perhaps, Hoccleve's very hands-on method of measuring the verse line was too innovative to be recognized as a quite logical formal plan—if not actually good.

As a paratextual indicator of the notion that Hoccleve understood each verse line to be primarily a unit of visually countable syllables, not an audible measure, the "Hoccleve Portrait" of Chaucer (BL Harley MS 4866 fol. 88) actually functions as an elaborate manicule or "little hand"; the finger-pointing gesture of Chaucer's image indicates Hoccleve's exactly ten-syllable line "Of his persone, I have heere his liknesse" (*Regiment of Princes*, 4995), which in turn refers the individual reader back to the portrait.²³

Hoccleve made what seems an intelligent mistake in the history of prosody—for the fifteenth century, at least. Yet, a twentieth-century experiment in versification curiously duplicates what may have been Hoccleve's formal intentions. What Martin J. Duffell perceives as Hoccleve's incompetence, he recognizes as Marianne Moore's deliberate innovation:

Moore and her imitators counted syllables anti-rhythmically ... But anti-rhythmic counting and the lack of these rhythmic props made

FIGURE 1. BL Harley 4866 (fol. 88r). Portrait of Chaucer in Thomas Hoccleve's *The Regiment of Princes* (1412). With permission of the British Library.

it impossible for Moore and her imitators to count their syllables by ear. As Gasparov notes, the syllabic regularity of Moore's verse is apparent only 'on closer scrutiny' (1996: 287), and scrutiny is essentially a visual operation designed to detect auditory events only after they have been transcribed. The most feasible method of producing such verse is to count the syllables on the fingers in the act of composition and check them on the page after it. The syllabism of these experimenters thus depended on counting by eye and fingers and not by ear in the time-honoured (and easiest) manner.[24]

Hoccleve's equivalent *dactylonomy* may be thought, therefore, a formal experiment well ahead of its time—subsequently thought a poetic failure by readers looking for Latinate regularity. With the increasing (but never total) hegemony of print publication, paratextual prompts—such as punctuation, indentation, interlinear spacing, line numbering, and so on—become standardized and so does the regulation of the verse line. And, in the sixteenth century, the modern word *lyric* becomes introduced to English prosody by George Puttenham with new formal expectations.

II. Machining the Lyric for Print Publication

As part of the mainstream of English lyricism—a mainstream in which Hoccleve did not swim—the sonnet, originating out of medieval Sicily, has proven to be, variously conceived, the single most enduring lyric form in English.[25] Its importation presents an interesting case study of how imitation of this "little song" was first rejected by Geoffrey Chaucer, and then subsequently adapted by two early modern poets for textual circulation (though composed perhaps initially for authorial or coterie recital), and then further machined for print publication.

The sonnets of Petrarch (1304–1374), which in Italy represented the culmination of the form's medieval precedents, subsequently gave birth to a poetic fad during the Tudor Renaissance. The sonnets of Sir Thomas Wyatt the Elder (1503–1542) and of Henry Howard, Earl of Surrey (1516–1547), may seem a total reboot of the English lyric in that "before Sir Thomas Wyatt no English poet acquired a substantial reputation for writing secular lyric poetry."[26] However, Geoffrey Chaucer (himself seldom given sufficient credit as a lyricist) was first to translate a sonnet composed by the laureate who "enlumyned al Ytaille of poetrie" (*Canterbury Tales,* IV, 33)—on his own English terms.

Chaucer rendered Petrarch's *Rima* 132 as three rhyme-royal stanzas that came to be commonly designated the "Cantus Troili" (I, 400–20) embedded in manuscripts of *Troilus and Criseyde:* "Its singularity (just this one *canzone*) thrusts the Italian renaissance into English medieval writing, but only to withdraw it again for well over another century."[27] Chaucer's cantus circulated independently as a stand-alone lyric as well.[28] Somewhat like Hamlet's "To be or not to be" soliloquy, Troilus's dramatic monologue is emotionally agitated, so metrically unstable. Also, like Hamlet's private reflection, Troilus's cantus presents a *sic et non disputatio* ("yes" v. "no" debate)—as such, a (frustrated) effort to rationalize intense passion in verse. Of course, by attributing the lyric to Troilus at a particular narrative moment, Chaucer's translation becomes a complete "re-mediation"[29] of the sonnet's autobiographical placement in Petrarch's songbook.

Print publication permits the modern reader to analyze what Chaucer's first audience and readers could never have appreciated—the details of his adaptation (see appendix A). Conventional points of comparison of English form-to-form translations and Petrarch's Tuscan verse include their respective diction, syntax, the scansion of each line and choice of rhyme schemes—all requiring scrutiny of the printed (so edited) texts. All such features of textual formatting—including the quality of typeface or transcription, margins, linear spacing, rubrication, illumination or any decoration of initials, punctuation, placement on the page, and so on—serve as visual prompts for an anticipated mode (or for multiple modes) of reading, be it for public recital or for solitary reading or for some combination of the two. One of the more easily overlooked features of Chaucer's transformation of the Italian sonnet into English rhyme royal is his substitution of a pentameter line for the Italian hendecasyllabic line—an equivalence that Wyatt and Surrey and most English sonneteers subsequently accept.[30] As a result of this "equivalence," the late medieval loss of final -e in English admits more masculine end rhymes (and so a final rising foot) whereas most Italian end rhymes are feminine (a falling foot).[31]

Although Chaucer's cantus maintains a line-for-line equivalence to the first three lines of *Rima* 132, his subsequent amplifications—which have aroused criticism of his translation's relative puffiness—seem sense-for-sense glosses of Petrarch's conceits. For example, Chaucer's seventh line "for always the more I drink, the more I thirst" preserves the paradox but not the pithiness of Petrarch's oxymoronic expression.[32] The sestet of *Rima* 132 has a somewhat exceptional rhyme scheme: cde dce. The rhyme words used to achieve this pattern are: "doglio/barca/governo carca/voglio/verno." To a Middle English poet's ear (or eye), the o-assonance of "voglio/verno" might seem sufficient to serve as a closing couplet. Chaucer's last two lines actually compress Petrarch's final tercet, and one may argue that his last two end rhymes achieve a more rhetorically emphatic closure—as will the final couplet of an English sonnet—achieving thereby "a splendidly eloquent version" of Petrarch's sonnet.[33]

Chaucer embeds this lyric in a narrative context that some readers perceive as ironizing the intensity of Petrarch's sincere intent. But, as a role to play, Troilus's internal monologue must first be received as a sincerely voiced cantus emotionally enacted by the fictional character himself: Troilus "Seyde yn his song ... As I shal sey; and whoso lyst it here / Lo next this vers may it fynden here" (*Troilus and Criseyde*, 397–399). Chaucer's transformation of the sonnet form into three rhyme-royal stanzas does not disrupt his narrative's melic pattern.[34] Indeed, rhyme royal may be considered Chaucer's formal equivalent for Boccaccio's ottava rima as well as for the French ballade. James Wimsatt has persuasively argued for the similarity of Chaucer's three-stanza "cantus" to the triple ballade, which (not unlike the sonnet) "may well be described as a chain with a logical progression."[35] The counterpoint to this observation is that, based on the evidence of his extant lyrics, Chaucer—who did dabble in terza rima—felt no need to adopt Petrarch's fourteen-line form. Furthermore, although the start of Chaucer's embedded lyric is marginally indicated as Troilus's "cantus" in many manuscripts, there is no clear prompt regarding its conclusion, and Chaucer's direct quotation of Troilus's extended complaint continues for two more stanzas.

It is important to recognize the extent to which immediate recognition of the fourteen-line sonnet has become a matter of textual formatting. Petrarch had composed his *Rime Sparse* between 1327 and 1368.[36] Chaucer, who traveled on diplomatic missions to Genoa and Florence in 1372–1373 and again to Milan in 1378, may or may not have had some chance of meeting an aged Petrarch in Florence, but more probably, as Martin M. Crow and Virginia E. Leland suggest, "Chaucer obtained manuscripts" of Dante and Boccaccio as well as Petrarch.[37] As K. P. Clarke emphasizes, "The point is that in Italy

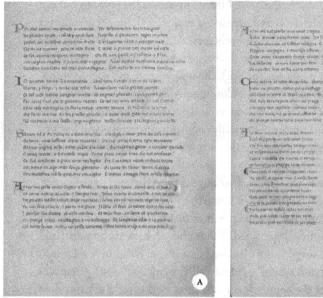

FIGURE 2. BAV Vat.lat.MS 3195 (Petrarch's autograph copy). *A, Rima* 132 "S'amor non è, che dunque è quel ch'io sento?" (fol. 30r). © 2023 Biblioteca Apostolica Vaticana. *B, Rima* 140 "Amor, che nel pensier mio vive et regna" (fol. 32r). © 2023 Biblioteca Apostolica Vaticana.

the authors who heavily influenced Chaucer were also supremely aware of the textuality of what they were doing, and this must be considered an important part of his literary encounter."[38] If so, it is highly likely that Chaucer saw Petrarch's sonnets transcribed as seven-line texts. This formatting was the norm for manuscript circulation of Petrarch's sonnets before the more conventional fourteen-line presentation (with indentation and line spacing of subsections) that prevailed in print.

Transcriptions of lyrics intended for recital tend to require substantially more rehearsal because they lack paratextual prompts that are now conventionally provided by edited, print publications to assist initial "sight" reading. For example, Petrarch's copy of *Rima* 140 provides only seven *puncti* at the endings of lines 4, 7, 8, 10, 11, 12, and 14. Lines 7 and 12, however, do not end in syntactic full stops and so these "points" seem intended primarily to prompt dramatic recital pauses. The manuscript's omission of a question mark at the end of line 13 presents a special intonation challenge for a first

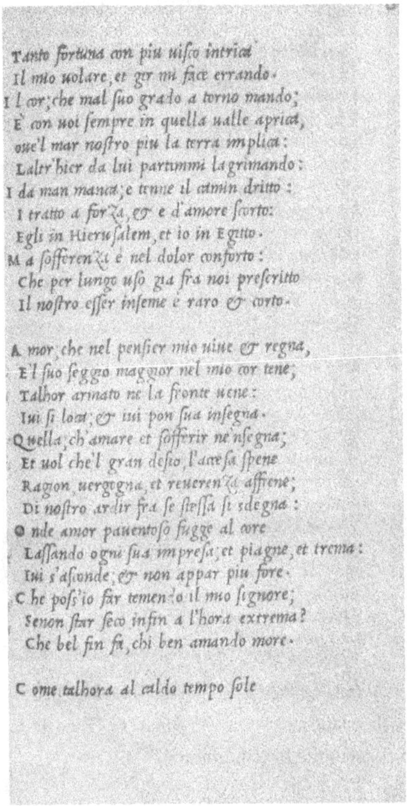

FIGURE 3. *Le cose volgari di Messer Francesco Petrarcha. The Rerum vulgarium fragmenta and Triumphi*, edited by Pietro Bembo. Printed by Aldus Manutius in Venice with a colophon dated July 1501. The John Rylands Library Collection: Aldine Collection Classmark: 20957. *Rima* 140 (p. 137). Copyright of the University of Manchester, used by permission and under Creative Commons license CC-BY-NC 4.0.

reading. To a certain extent, Petrarch's use of abbreviations also requires a reciter's practiced reading. Nevertheless, the remarkable neatness of Petrarch's hand indicates his desire to publish a readily readable text, even though his economical use of the page impedes immediate visual recognition of the sonnet's template as fourteen lines of verse.

It may only be a coincidence of lineation, but Chaucer may have actually thought of his rhyme-royal stanza as a textual "equivalent" of the seven-line formatting of the sonnet found in the earliest copies of Petrarch's sonnets. The fourteen end rhymes of *Rima* 140 (fol. 32r), for example, should properly be marked **abba abba cdc cdc**. However, if only the right margin's rhymes—that is, those of the seven even verse lines—are perceived to be *end* rhymes, then Petrarch's text appears to rhyme **babaa*** (i.e., "sdegna" serving as a proximate rhyme for "trema")**cc**. This seven-line pattern essentially

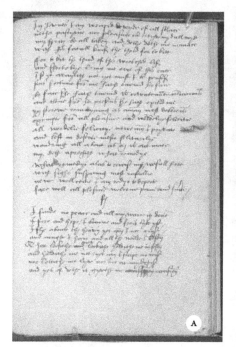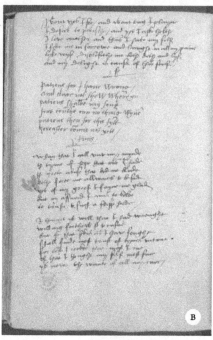

FIGURE 4. BL Add MS 1749 ("The Devonshire Manuscript"), Wyatt's "I find no peace and all my war is done" (fols. 82r & v)—a translation of Petrarch's *Rima* 134 "Pace non trovo e non ho da far guerra." With permission of the British Library.

matches the rhyme scheme of Chaucer's rhyme-royal stanza (ababbcc) (see appendix B). In any event, Chaucer apparently felt far more concerned about creating an equivalent audible and emotional rendition of *Rima* 132 than with reproducing a now normative fourteen-line format—as Wyatt and Surrey will do when translating *Rima* 140.

As there was a strong continuity of tropes and sentiments between Petrarch and the troubadours, so, too, there was a continuance of medieval verse forms and emotional poses well into the Tudor period. Sir Thomas Wyatt's "work does not represent a complete break with the past ... he is very close to the tradition of medieval lyric."[39] Indeed, Wyatt "uncomfortably straddles the arbitrarily but still generally applied dividing line between 'medieval' and 'Tudor' poetry."[40] Nevertheless, by the mid-sixteenth century, English poets imagined Petrarch or Horace to be the prosodic exemplars of English lyrics much more so than Chaucer. Surrey indeed celebrated dead Wyatt as "A hand, that taught what might be said in rhyme;/ That reft Chaucer the glory of his wit" ("Wyatt resteth here," ll. 13–14).[41] Surrey (whose presumption here may be excused by his sorrow) anticipates that Wyatt's verses will still be *said*, but he also, not unlike Hoccleve, conceives of poetic composition primarily in terms of the *hand*.

Two of the primary textual witnesses for Wyatt and Surrey's lyrics are the Devonshire manuscript (BL Add. MS 17492) and the Egerton manuscript (BL Egerton MS 2711). Circulation of the Devonshire manuscript, in particular, assumes a close synonymity of "reading" and "sharing" in that it was an initially blank book circulated among participatory contributors in the circle of Queen Anne Boleyn. The Egerton manuscript preserves Wyatt's lyrics transcribed by the poet himself who seems to have had no interest in seeing to the print publication of his lyrics, and "the early confinement of Wyatt's poems to manuscript copies underlines what seems to have been

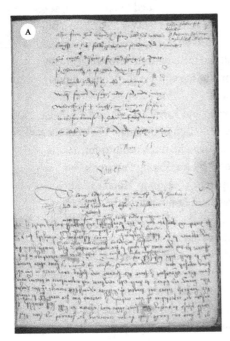 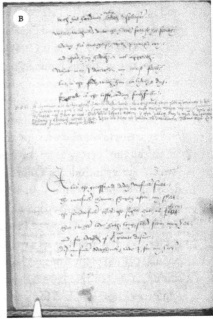

FIGURE 5. BL Egerton MS 2711, Wyatt's "The Longe love, that in my thought doeth harbar" (fols. 5v & 6r). With permission of the British Library.

the reluctance of early English printers to issue large-scale anthologies of English lyrics."[42] Though circulating as texts to be read, these poems remained revisable as well as recitable within an initial reception context of personal familiarity with the poet.

Every bit as much as Middle English lyrics, Wyatt's and Surrey's sonnets can be tagged as formally derivative and emotionally conventional. In terms of their anticipated performance, both Wyatt's and Surrey's lyrics continue to rely heavily on audible structure. And the two main manuscript witnesses for Wyatt's and Surrey's verse seem far less concerned with the exact scansion than *Tottel's Miscellany*, the first printed anthology of English poetry (1557 CE), will be.

Wyatt consistently strove to preserve the standard Italian octave (abbaabba). Petrarch had used a number of options for the sestet (cddcdd, cdecde, cdcdcd, cddcee, cddccd). Wyatt translated thirteen of Petrarch's sonnets that employed a cde cde pattern as the sestet (*Rima* 258, 169, 224, 102, 19, 49, 134, 189, 173, 57, 124, 21, 224) and four sonnets that used the somewhat more challenging terza rima–like pattern cdc dcd (*Rima* 82, 153, 269 and 140). Almost all of Petrarch's sonnets selected by Wyatt come to a full stop at the end of line 8, and then Wyatt preferred a cdd cee rhyme scheme for the sestet (see Appendix C). Wyatt thus also tends to favor what Surrey requires of the "English sonnet," a concluding couplet that conspicuously announces the entire lyric's completion.

When translating *Rima* 132, both Wyatt and Surrey (in contrast to Chaucer) take many liberties with Petrarch's diction and syntax. For example, Surrey seems to commit what my colleagues who teach form-to-form translation call the "heresy of improvement" by translating Petrarch's "bel" as "sweet." Surrey introduces a more apparent allusion to Horace's "dulce et decorum est pro [...] mori" [it is sweet and honorable to die ... for Love rather than for Rome].[43] Also unlike Chaucer, Wyatt and Surrey probably read early printed editions of Petrarch's sonnets rather than manuscript copies. Wyatt is thought to have used Alessandro Velutello's extremely popular edition of the *Canzoniere*, which is provided with extensive "espositione" (1525, reprinted twenty-six times within the century); this edition reinforces a now standard formatting found in the first Aldine printing of Pietro Bembo's edition (1501, the italic font of which supposedly imitates Petrarch's own handwriting).

In print, due to the spacing between the two quatrains and two tercets as well as that between the octave and sestet, Petrarch's sonnets are typically formatted as a four-part progression (rather than as a two-part or as a single fourteen-line construct). Visually, the 4/4/3/3 formatting of the Italian sonnet does not look so radically different from the 4/4/4/2 pattern of English sonnets.[44] Whereas Chaucer seems to have imagined his rendition of *Rima* 132 as a song-to-song translation, Wyatt committed himself to multiple attempts at a verse-line for verse-line equivalence. Surrey's English sonnets abandon the idea that English "equivalence" requires the duplication of Italian rhyme schemes in favor of a more highly elusive notion of analogous "total effect"; in so doing, Surrey initiated a formal tradition that all future English sonneteers reflect or revise.

Though Surrey's abab cdcd efef gg pattern proved most successful, Surrey also challenged himself to approximate more intertwined Italian rhyme schemes, as, for example in *Tottel* 2 and 10, which may be considered either examples of lyric "sprezzatura" or a somewhat retrograde celebration of "excessive" rhyming in English. Although Surrey's original poems have frequent echoes of Petrarch (as of Chaucer), only four of his sonnets in *Tottel's Miscellany* are translations of Petrarch's sonnets. The abab cdcd efef alternating rhymes of Surrey's three quatrains misrepresent the cohesive consonance of Petrarch's octaves in *Rima* 140 and 145. However, the pronounced audibility of the final couplet of the English sonnet is often thought to amplify the translation's concluding rhetorical punch.

Direct comparison of Wyatt's and Surrey's translations of Petrarch's *Rima* 140 provides an (often studied) opportunity to examine their respective formal choices. Petrarch's rhyme scheme was abbaabba cdccdc, which Wyatt replicates until the final tercet abba abba cdc cdd (*Tottel* 42) but which Surrey essentially ignored (*Tottel* 6). Both English poets preserve Petrarch's full stop at the end of line 4. Wyatt also duplicates full stops at the end of each tercet. Lines 11 and 14 of Surrey's sonnet conclude with a period as well, though the tercet pattern has been abandoned. Surrey adds one more period to end line 13, which helps to fortify the following final couplet.

It is noteworthy that the compilation of lyrics in *Tottel's Miscellany*, without being truly miscellaneous, obliterates the biographical progress of Petrarch's sonnets as sequenced in the *Canzoniere*.[45] Wyatt's phrasing often seems both syntactically and metrically "rougher" than Surrey's, perhaps because he struggled so valiantly to maintain the received octave/sestet template. For example, Wyatt's initial phrasing "long love that" seems to

Songes.

And saw in what estate I weary man was wrought,
By want of that they had at will, and I reiect at nought:
Lord how I gan in wrath vnwisely me demeane,
I cursed loue and him defied: I thought to turne the streame,
But when I well beheld he had me vnder awe,
I asked mercy for my fault, that so transgrest his lawe,
Thou blinded God (quod I) forgeue me this offence,
Vnwittingly I went about, to malice thy pretence.
Wherwith he gaue a becke, and thus me thought he swore,
Thy sorow ought suffice to purge thy fault, if it were more.
The vertue of which sound mine hert did so reuiue,
That I, me thought, was made as whole as any man aliue.
But here I may perceiue mine errour al and some,
For that I thought that so it was: yet was it still vndone,
And al that was no more but mine expressed minde,
That faine would haue some good reliefe, of Cupide wel assinde,
I turned home forth with and might perceiue it weil
That he agreued was right sore with me for my rebel.
My harmes haue euer since, encreased more and more,
And I remaine without his helpe, vndone for euermore
A mirror let me be vnto ye louers all:
Striue not with loue, for if ye do, it will ye thus befall.

Complaint of a louer rebuked.

LOue that liueth and raigneth in my thought,
That built his seat within my captiue brest,
Clad in the armes, wherin with me he fought,
Oft in my face he doth his banner rest,
She, that me thought to loue, and suffer paine,
My doutefull hope, and eke my hot desire.
With shamefast cloke to shadowes and restraine
Her smiling grace conuerteth straight to ire.
And cowerd loue then to the hert apace
Taketh his flight, whereas he lurkes and plaines
His purpose lost and dare not shewe his face,
For my lordes gilt thus faultlesse bide I paines,
Yet from my lorde shal not my foote remoue,
Swete is his deth, that takes his end by loue.

Com-

and Sonettes.

Complaint of the louer dysdained.

IF Ciprus, springes, whereas dame Uenus dwelt,
A well so hote, that whoso tasted the same,
Were he of stone as thawed yse shoulde melt,
And kindled finde his brest with sured flame,
whose moyst poyson dissolueth hath my harte
Thus creeping fire my colde limmes so oppresst,
That in the hart that harborde feruent lust,
Endlesse despeyre longer tradhome hath imprest,
In other so colde in frosen yse to founde.
Whose chilling venom of repugnant kinde
The feruent heat doth quenche of Cupides wounde,
And with the spot change infectes the minde:
wherof my hert hath talted, to my payne.
My seruice thus is growen into disdaine.

Description and praise of his loue Geraldine.

FRom Tuscane came my ladies worthy race:
Faire Florence was sometyme her auncient seate:
The Westerne yle, whose plesaunt shore doth face
Wilde Cambers clifs, did geue her liuely heate.
Fostred she was with milke of Irish brest
Her fire, an Erle: her dame, of princis blood,
From tender yeres, in Brittain she doth rest.
With kinges childe, where she tasteth costly food,
Honsdon did first present her to myne yient
Bright is her hewe, and Geraldine she hight,
Hampton me taught to wishe her first for mine:
And windsor, alas, doth chase those me from her sight,
Her beauty of kinde her vertues from aboue,
Happy is he, that can obtaine her loue.

The frailtie and hurtfulnes of beautie.

BRittle beautie that nature made so fraile,
Wherof the gift is small and short the season,

Flow

Songes

Of lingring doubtes such hope is sprong pardie,
That nought I finde displesaunt in my sight:
But when my glasse presented vnto me
The carelesse wound that bledeth day and night,
To thinke (alas) such hap should graunted be
Vnto a wretch that hat so oft ben shed,
For Britannia salte (alas) and now is ded.

Exhortacion to learne by others trouble.

MY ratclif, when thy rechelesse youth offendes
Receiue thy scourge by others chastisement
For such calling, when it workes none amendes
Then plages are sent without aduertisement:
Yet Salamon sayd, the wronges shal recure:
But wyat saide true, the skarrs doth aye endure.

The fansie of a waried louer.

THe fansy, which I haue reserued long,
That hath alway been enmy to myne ease,
Semed of late to rue vpon my wrong,
And bade me flye the cause of my misease
And I forth with did prease out of the throng,
That thought by flight my painfull heart to please
Some other way: til I sawe faith more strong,
And to my self I saide: alas, those dayes
In vaine wer spent, to runne the race so long:
And with that thought, I met my guyde, I gaine,
Out of the way wherin I wandred wrong,
Brought me amiddes the hilles in base Bullayn,
Where I am now, as restlesse to remain,
Against my will, full pleased with my pain.

SVRREY.

and Sonettes.

The louer for shamefastnesse hideth his desire within his faithfull heart.

THe long loue, that in my thought I harber,
And in my heart doth kepe his residence,
Into my face preaseth with bold pretence,
And there campeth, displaying his banner,
She that me learnes to loue, and to suffer,
And willes that my trust, and lustes negligence
Be reyned by reason, shame and reuerence,
With his hardinesse taketh displeasure,
Wherwith loue to the hartes forest he fleeth,
Leauing his enterprise with payne and crye,
And there him hideth and not appeareth.
What may I doe when my maister feareth,
But in the field with him to liue and dye,
For good is the life, ending faithfully.

The louer waxeth wiser, and will not die for affeccion.

YEt was I neuer of your loue agreued,
Nor neuer shall, while that my life doth last:
But of hating my self, that is past,
And teares continual sore hath me weried,
I will not yet in my graue be buried.
No, on my tombe poynt haue thou fixed fast
As cruell cause, that did my spirite soone hast,
From thunhappy bones by great sighes stirred,
Then if an heart of amorous faith and will
Content your minde without doen doing griefe:
Please it you so to this to doe reliefe,
Ye otherwyse you seke for to fulfill
Your wrath you cere and shal not as you wene,
And you pour self the cause therof haue bene.

C. iii.

The

require three accented syllables in a row. All of Wyatt's lines and all but two lines (7 and 8) of Surrey's translation in *Tottel's Miscellany* end in a comma or period or colon (*punctus flexus*) giving the impression that recital of these verses should be heavily end-stopped—a paratextual prompt to pause that good reciters today would try to ignore.

Alternating trochees and iambs throughout Surrey's pentameters avoid metronomic dullness and so may deserve more praise than Wyatt's rendition, but Surrey's translation sacrifices the dramatic tension of Wyatt's (and Petrarch's) concluding rhetorical question. Though surely more musical than Hoccleve's decasyllables, Wyatt's pentameters remain rather irregular in the Egerton manuscript (again as transcribed by Wyatt himself, not necessarily as to be recited). If "forest" and "fleeth" in line 9, for example, may be pronounced as one syllable each, then all fourteen lines of Wyatt's version of *Rima* 140 may be considered decasyllabic. To preempt possible mis-metering, however, *Tottel*'s editors "polished" (or machined) Wyatt's scansion. Line 5, for example, substitutes -s for -eth, making "learnes" monosyllabic before an inserted unaccented "to" as well as the comma for a phrasal rest:

E[gerton MS]   She that me learneth to love and suffer
T[ottel's Miscellany] She that me learns to love, and to suffer,

opposite page FIGURE 6. A, *Tottel* 6 "Complaint of a Lover Rebuked" (Surrey's "Love that liveth and reigneth in my thought"). *Songes and sonets written by the right honorable Lorde Henry Haward late Earle of Surrey, and others* (London: Apud Richardum Tottell, 1559). Short Title Catalog (2nd ed.) / 13863. With permission of the British Library. Image produced by ProQuest LLC as part of ProQuest® Early English Books Online (EEBO). www.proquest.com. Image published with permission of ProQuest LLC. Further reproduction is prohibited without permission. B, *Tottel* 42 "The Lover for shamefastnesse hideth his desire within his faithful heart" (Wyatt's "The longe love that in my thought I harbar"). *Songes and sonets written by the right honorable Lorde Henry Haward late Earle of Surrey, and others* (London: Apud Richardum Tottell, 1559). Short Title Catalog (2nd ed.) / 13863. With permission of the British Library. Image produced by ProQuest LLC as part of ProQuest® Early English Books Online (EEBO). www.proquest.com. Image published with permission of ProQuest LLC. Further reproduction is prohibited without permission.

Line 6 requires that "-es" in "willes" be read "-s" for a monosyllabic third-person verb ("wills") as must the possessive "lustes" ("lust's"); the print version also accommodates perception of a caesura and phrasal pause on first reading by providing a comma:

E And will that my trust and lust's negligence
T And willes that my trust, and lustes negligence

This same dialectical substitution of "-s" ("takes") for "-eth" in line 8 can be metrically accommodated by the pronunciation of final "-e" in "hardynesse" producing a perfectly iambic line:

E With his hardiness taketh displeasure.
T With his hardinesse takes displeasure.

Line 9's omission of "-al" in "wherewithall" allows "forest" to be disyllabic, again for the sake of ten clear syllables to pronounce:

E Wherewithal unto the heart's forest he fleeth
T Wherewith unto the heartes forest he fleeth.

In line 12, the *Miscellany* introduces a ":" (*punctus versus,* usually marking the end of a sentence) after "What may I doe," whereas editors now prefer a question mark at the end of line 13. Such modern and even early modern punctuation clearly anticipates the reader's need for directorial prompts when first viewing the text.

Paul A. Marquis observes that "as he acquires manuscript copies of the poems, the editor [of *Tottel's Miscellany*] sets about strengthening their prosodic line, with especial attention to the works of Surrey and Wyatt."[46] The quantity of a verse line's duration (originally an impression of audible measure) becomes translated into countable line length (a permanent feature to be scanned on the page). *Tottel's Miscellany* may thus be thought to have initiated a program of print publication that aided the reader by disciplining the lyric text, both prosodically and paratextually. Simply by expediting the increased circulation of early modern lyrics, print publication then diminished familiarity with Middle English lyrics. This prevailing means of reception, in turn, contributed to modern amnesia regarding the true quality of Middle English lyrics as poetically competent emotional performances. But early modern promotion of this incipient ignorance of Middle English lyrics was not entirely innocent.[47]

III. Negative Reviewing of the Middle English Lyric

Since "verse" no longer means "poem," it is difficult to concur with any facile disregard for Middle English lyrics on the basis of their apparent metrical incompetence alone. Yet, this illusion of formal crudity also fostered a blindness toward these lyrics' emotional integrity as well. Although many modern poets no longer care about rigid prosody per se, most do idolize the pose of a unique "voice" that Middle English lyrics seem to lack once printed on the page. T. S. Eliot described this modern expectation as "our tendency to insist, when we praise a poet, upon those aspects of his work in which he least resembles anyone else. In these aspects or parts of his work we pretend to find what is individual, what is the peculiar essence of the man."[48] George Gascoigne also and early articulated this post-medieval imperative to pursue poetic "invention":

> The first and most necessarie poynt that euer I founde meete to be considered in making of a delectable poeme is this, to grounde it upon some fine inuention. For it is not inough to roll in pleasant woordes, nor yet to thunder in Rym, Ram, Ruff by letter (quoth my master Chaucer), nor yet to abounde in apt vocables or epythetes, vnlesse the Inuention haue in it also *aliquid salis*. By this *aliquid salis* I meane some good and fine deuise, shewing the quicke capacitie of a writer.

The perceived uniqueness of the "I" of a modern poet largely usurps the role of a more universal "I" to be performed in Middle English lyrics. Although many modern lyrics do still welcome histrionic presentation, normative reading of the lyric has become more a matter of attending to the individual author's own recollection of "the spontaneous overflow of powerful emotions" (William Wordsworth's Preface to *Lyrical Ballads*, 1800). Interpreted only according to the same norms of reading, the "I" of too many Middle English lyrics comes to be viewed as lacking "invention."

William Shakespeare, whose name (rather than Surrey's) came to provide our alternative designation of the sonnet's "English" form, also provides intermittent but not insignificant indications of how the conventionality of former lyricists had fallen into utter contempt by the end of the sixteenth century. Shakespeare's sonnets first appeared in print in 1609, fifty-two years after *Tottel's Miscellany*, and his most familiar toying with—by then—clichéd Petrarchanisms, indebted themselves to the medieval *blazon* (shining eyes, blond hair, pale skin, etc.), is Sonnet 130, "My mistress' eyes are nothing like the sun." Yet, the versification of this monologic sonnet is nothing new. However, in *Romeo and Juliet*, Shakespeare both deploys and derides the already well-established conventionality of the English sonnet, writing both within and against the lyric tradition.

The sonnet-prologues to Acts I and II of *Romeo and Juliet* are quite workaday lyrics that serve merely as formally "heightened" plot expositions to be proclaimed by the chorus as a "we." The Prologue to Act I announces:

> Two households, both alike in dignity,
> In fair Verona, where we lay our scene,
> From ancient grudge break to new mutiny,
> Where civil blood makes civil hands unclean.
> 5   From forth the fatal loins of these two foes
> A pair of star-cross'd lovers take their life;
> Whose misadventured piteous overthrows
> Do with their death bury their parents' strife.
> The fearful passage of their death-mark'd love,
> 10 And the continuance of their parents' rage,
> Which, but their children's end, nought could remove,
> Is now the two hours' traffic of our stage;
> The which if you with patient ears attend,
> What here shall miss, our toil shall strive to mend.

The most famous excerpt from this sonnet is the (now clichéd) expression "star-cross'd lovers" (l. 6). Disclosing that Romeo and Juliet will have a "Death-mark'd love" (l. 9)—in addition to being a plot spoiler—requires the rather lifeless rhyme of "remove" (l. 11) with "love." The primary function of this utilitarian sonnet is to silence a not-yet attentive audience.[49]

The Prologue to Act II sounds far more invested in the "Now, now" of the play's emotions.

> Now old desire doth in his death-bed lie,
> And young affection gapes to be his heir;

>   That fair for which love groan'd for and would die,
>   With tender Juliet match'd, is now not fair.
> 5   Now Romeo is beloved and loves again,
>   Alike bewitched by the charm of looks,
>   But to his foe supposed he must complain,
>   And she steal love's sweet bait from fearful hooks:
>   Being held a foe, he may not have access
> 10 To breathe such vows as lovers use to swear;
>   And she as much in love, her means much less
>   To meet her new-beloved any where:
>   But passion lends them power, time means, to meet
>   Tempering extremities with extreme sweet.

Shakespeare's initial conceit is a rather morbid way of simply saying that Rosaline is out and Juliet is in, but the phrasing is conspicuously "witty" and, as such, answers an ever-increasing modern imperative to be innovative regarding "what oft was thought but ne're so well express'd" (Alexander Pope's "An Essay on Criticism," l. 297). Shakespeare's concluding wordplay of "extremities" and "extreme" (l. 14), and the fishing metaphor (l.8) that provides the rhyme of "hooks" for "looks" (l. 6), and the syntactic compression (asyndeton) of "passion ... power, time means" (l. 13), are all stylistic inventions that do please upon first hearing but that also reward rereading. However, the emotions to be enacted by Romeo and Juliet are quite conventional—very typical of Middle English lyrics about love and longing and loathing.

It is Mercutio who personifies a newest generation's contempt for poetic hackwork that merely repeats tired emotional commonplaces. Mercutio ridicules both Romeo's romantic clichés and pat rhymes. Asked by Benvolio to call his best friend, Mercutio expectorates blank verse:

>   Nay, I'll conjure too.
>   Romeo! humours! madman! passion! lover!
>   Appear thou in the likeness of a sigh:
>   Speak but one rhyme, and I am satisfied;
>   Cry but 'Ay me!' pronounce but 'love' and 'dove;'
>   Speak to my gossip Venus one fair word,
>   One nick-name for her purblind son and heir,

> Young Adam Cupid, he that shot so trim,
> When King Cophetua loved the beggar-maid!
> He heareth not, he stirreth not, he moveth not;
> The ape is dead, and I must conjure him.
> I conjure thee by Rosaline's bright eyes,
> By her high forehead and her scarlet lip,
> By her fine foot, straight leg and quivering thigh
> And the demesnes that there adjacent lie,[50]
> That in thy likeness thou appear to us! (II, i, 6–21)

This mock "conjuring" of Romeo performs a brilliant eruption of contempt for the familiar: for sighs, for "love/dove" rhymes, for blind Cupid, for shining eyes and ruby lips, and so on.

Original to the point of being incomprehensible, Mercutio then ridicules Romeo's erotic fantasies:

> If love be blind, love cannot hit the mark.
> Now will he sit under a medlar tree,
> And wish his mistress were that kind of fruit
> As maids call medlars, when they laugh alone.[51]
> Romeo, that she were, O, that she were
> An open *et caetera*, thou a poperin pear!
> Romeo, good night: I'll to my truckle-bed;
> This field-bed is too cold for me to sleep:
> Come, shall we go? (II, i, 33–41)

The inventiveness of this renunciation of Love sounds so modern, jaundiced—yet also quite medieval, choleric.

A little later, in highly alliterative prose, Mercutio verbally vomits his contempt for Romeo's carnal desire, his rhyming skills, and his hyperbolic infatuation:

> Without his roe, like a dried herring: flesh, flesh, how art thou fishified! Now is he for the numbers that Petrarch flowed in: Laura to his lady was but a kitchen-wench; marry, she had a better love to be-rhyme her; Dido a dowdy; Cleopatra a gipsy; Helen and Hero hildings and harlots; Thisbe a grey eye or so, but not to the purpose. Signior Romeo,

bon jour! there's a French salutation to your French slop. You gave us the counterfeit fairly last night. (II, iv, 38–48)

Yet Juliet proves to be a far better Muse than Rosaline had been. As if to demonstrate that the affective success of a conventional lyric form is almost entirely dependent upon sympathetic performance (actual or imagined), Shakespeare composed the dialogue sonnet of *Romeo and Juliet* (I, v, 93–106). Shakespeare has Romeo and Juliet alternatively speak the first two quatrains, then say alternate lines within the third quatrain, then exchange rhyme-joined lines within their final couplet, concluding with a first kiss.

> ROMEO If I profane with my unworthiest hand
> This holy shrine, the gentle fine is this:
> My lips, two blushing pilgrims, ready stand
> To smooth that rough touch with a tender kiss.
> JULIET Good pilgrim, you do wrong your hand too much,
> Which mannerly devotion shows in this;
> For saints have hands that pilgrims' hands do touch,
> And palm to palm is holy palmers' kiss.
> ROMEO Have not saints lips, and holy palmers too?
> JULIET Ay, pilgrim, lips that they must use in prayer.
> ROMEO O, then, dear saint, let lips do what hands do;
> They pray, grant thou, lest faith turn to despair.
> JULIET Saints do not move, though grant for prayers' sake.
> ROMEO Then move not, while my prayer's effect I take.

Having jointly completed the sonnet's abab cdcd efef gg scheme, their dialogue continues with alternating rhymes to perform the still most conventional speech act of love:

> Thus from my lips, by yours, my sin is purged.
> JULIET Then have my lips the sin that they have took.
> ROMEO Sin from thy lips? O trespass sweetly urged!
> Give me my sin again.
> JULIET You kiss by the book.

A cynic may find this all too clever or clichéd or adolescent, but it is the actors who make this lyric's emotion live again.

The modern reader of Middle English lyrics likewise needs to embody their emotions. This effort may be critically dismissed as a prolonged exercise in what W. K. Wimsatt termed the "affective fallacy." But then Wimsatt conceived of the "lyric" primarily as a "verbal icon" requiring expert analysis of the text as "a verbal sign which somehow shares the properties of, or resembles, the objects which it denotes."[52] Typically in an academic setting, such a palpable and mute lyric requires the reader to genuflect to the printed page because "lyric is the creation of print and critical mediation."[53] But Middle English lyrics were never meant to be perused while overlooking the ruins of some abbey. Middle English lyrics are communal because they are repeatable emotional acts rather than isolated, individuated, often idiosyncratic expressions of emotion.

An appreciation of most Middle English lyrics as performed impersonations augments comparable efforts to defend the merits of other popular, usually performance-intended verse from the default expectations of most twentieth-century, essentially elitist criticism. In his "Introduction" *to One Hundred Lyrics and a Poem,* for example, Neil Tennant, writing as a lyricist now publishing in print, recognizes the need for a reader's awareness of appropriate criteria for fully appreciating his (still performable) "lyrics," now so named as something other than the (studied) "poem": "In choosing what to put in this book and what to leave out, I have selected the lyrics that read best on the page but, in truth, that is not the normal habitat of a song lyric . . . these were written to be sung with music, not read as poetry."[54] From the start, publication of English lyrics in print mandated increased metrical precision, and splintered the (still sometimes fused) subgenres of popular and sophisticated poetry, and eventually freed the honorific designation of a "poem" from synonymity with pedestrian "verse." It is not the success of either classical prosody or the free verse movement that needs rethinking but a concurrent disregard for merely medieval or for merely popular poetry. From the start of the twentieth century, Harriet Monroe, founding editor of *Poetry Magazine,* fought blowback for publishing the sentimental versifying of Carl Sandburg and Joyce Kilmer rather than only the pensive likes of "Prufrock"—much to the chagrin of her foreign correspondent, Ezra Pound. Pound himself was apparently deeply embarrassed by the fact that he was a grand-nephew of Henry Wadsworth Longfellow, who, once upon a time, "pretty much invented poetry as a public idiom in the United States." but whose supposedly "limp examples of poetic conventionality" have become so habitually maligned by expert-readers. In Longfellow's defense, Christoph Irmscher reminds professional critics to "resist the arguments of those who find it hard not to scoff at ordinary readers."[55] Perhaps it should be no surprise, then, that the first scholarly study of Nobel Laureate Bob Dylan was performed by Betsy Bowden, a medievalist specializing in orality.[56]

Current research into the Middle English lyrics is profiting from multiple disciplinary perspectives, including investigations of compositional occasions, musical settings, the mise-en-page of each transcription, the means of circulation, and target audiences. Explication and commentary based upon this scholarship will enhance our historicized comprehension of the extant lyrics, which in turn can amplify our presentist enjoyment. Furthermore, the current popularity of "performance poetry" in what has been termed (perhaps a bit prematurely) our post-print milieu does invite, by analogy, reconsideration of the Middle English lyrics as extra-textual events. Stephanie Burt even suggests that "Contemporary poets, then—not all of them, but far more than a handful—come closer, more often, to the effects and to the conundrums posed by Middle English lyric, and by insular medieval verse practice, than most of the verse in English composed and circulated during the several hundred years in between."[57] Conventional—that is, textual—publication remains mandatory for the preservation and study of the Middle English lyrics, but such publication provides only the incipit for our resurrection of their emotive possibilities.

APPENDIX A

Petrarch's *Rima* 132 and Chaucer's "Cantus Troili" with Modern Translation

PETRARCH'S RIMA 132	CHAUCER'S "CANTUS TROILI"
[Modern English translation]	
S'amor non è, che dunque é què i' sénto?	If no loue is, O god, what fele I so?
[If it is not love, what then is it that I feel?]	
Ma s'ègli é amór, per Dio, che cósa, e quale?	And if loue is, what thing and which is he?
[But if it is love—by God!—what sort of thing is it?]	
Se buòna, ond' é 'l èffettó aspro e mortale?	If loue be good, from whennes cometh my woo?
[If good, from where is the effect bitter and deadly?]	
Se ria; ond' é sí dolce ògni tormènto?	If it be wikke, a wonder thynketh me,
[If bad, from where so sweet each torment?]	Whenne euery torment and aduersite
	That cometh of hym may to me sauory thinke,
	Ffor ay thurst I the more that ich it drynke.

S' a mia vóglia ardo; ónd' è 'l pianto e 'l lamènto!	And if that at myn owen lust I brenne,
[If at my free will I burn, from where is the crying and complaint?]	Ffrom whennes cometh may waillynge and my pleynte?
S' a mal mio grado'; il lamentar che vale?	If harme a-gree me, wherto pleyne I thenne?
[If in spite of myself, what good does complaining do?]	I noot, ne whi vn-wery that I feynte.
O viva mórte, o dilettòso male,	O quike deth, O swete harm so queynte,
[Oh living death! O delightful evil!]	
Còme puói tanto in mè, s'io nòl cónsénto?	How may of the in me swich quantite,
[How can you so control me, if I do not consent?]	But if that I consente that it be?
E s'io 'l cònsénto; a gran tórto mi dóglio.	And if that I consente, I wrongfully
[And if I do consent, I am wrong to complain.]	Compleyne, i-wis; . . .
Fra sè contrári vénti in frale barca	. . . thus possed to and fro,
[Between opposing winds, in a fragile boat,]	Al stereleess with-inne a boot am I
	Amydde the see, bitwixen wyndes two,
	That inne contrarie stonden euere mo.
	Allas, what is this wondre maladie?
Mi tróve in alto mar senza govérno.	
[I find myself in rough seas without a rudder.]	
Sí liéve di savèr, d'erròr si carca,	
[So light in understanding, so heavy in error,]	

Ch' i' medèsmo nòn só quèl ch' io mi vòglio;	
[That I myself don't know what I want.]	
E trémo a mézza state, ardéndo il vérno.	ffor hete of cold, for cold of hete, I dye.
[And I shiver in midsummer while burning in winter.]	

APPENDIX B

Petrarch's *Rima* 140

Amor che nel penser mio vive et regna [A]	e 'l suo seggio maggior nel mio cor tene	B
[Love that lives and rules in my thought	and holds his main throne in my heart]	
Talor armato ne la fronte vene [B]	ivi si loca et iui pon sua insegna.	A
[Sometimes comes armed onto my forehead	where he encamps and plants his banner]	
Quella ch'amare et sofferir ne 'segna [A]	e vol che 'l gran desio l'accesa spene	B
[She who teaches to love and endure	and wants that the great desire, the hot hope,]	
Ragion vergogna et reverenza affrene [B]	di nostro ardir fra se stessa si sdegna	A
[Reason, shame, and reverence control	scorns our ardor within herself]	
Onde Amor paventoso fugge alcore [C]	lasciando ogni sua impresa et piange et trema	D/A*
[So that fearful Love flees to the heart	leaving his entire enterprise and crying and trembling]	
Ivi s'asconde et non appar piu fore [C]	che poss'io far temendo il mio signore.	C
[Where he hides and does not appear outside	What can I do—my lord being so fearful—]	

Se non star seco infin a lora extrema [D]	che bel fin fa chi ben amando more.	C
[If not stay with him until the last hour	He who dies loving well makes such a good end.]	

APPENDIX C

A Comparison of Petrarch's and Wyatt's Corresponding Rhyme Schemes

Petrarch, *Rima* 140	AB,B;A.ABB,A.C,D;C.C,DC.
Wyatt, *Tottel* 42	A,B,B,A.A,BB,A.C,D,C.C,D,D.
Surrey, *Tottel* 6	A,B,A,B.C,D,C,D.EFE.F,G.G.
Petrarch, *Rima* 82	A,B;BA,ABBA.CD,C;DC;D.
Wyatt, *Tottel* 43	A,B:B,A.A,B,B.A,CD:D,CE.E.
Petrarch, *Rima* 258	AB,B,A,A,BBA.CD!EC,D,E.
Wyatt, *Tottel* 45	A,B,B,A.A,BBAC,D,D,C.EE.
Petrarch, *Rima* 169	AB,B,A;AB,BA.CD,E;CD,E.
Wyatt, *Tottel* 46	AB,B,A.B:B,A.A.CD:D.CE:E.
Petrarch, *Rima* 224	A,B,B,A,A,BB,A,C,DE,CD:E.
Wyatt, *Tottel* 49	A:B:B:A,A:B.BA,C,D:C:D:E,E.
Petrarch, *Rima* 102	AB,BA;AB,BA;CDC.D,CD.
Wyatt, *Tottel* 50	AB,BA.AB,B,A.CD,D.C:EE.
Petrarch, *Rima* 19	AB;B,A;AB,B,A.CDE;DC,E.
Wyatt, *Tottel* 52	A,B:B,A.A,B:B.A.C:D:D:C,E:E.
Petrarch, *Rima* 49	AB,BA;ABBA!CD,E!D,C!E.
Wyatt, *Tottel* 53	A,B,B,A.A,B,B,A.C.D:D.C,E.E.
Petrarch, *Rima* 134	A,B,A,B.A,B,A,B.C,D,E.C,D.E.
Wyatt, *Tottel* 54	A:B:B:A.A,B:B,A.C:D:D.C.E.E.

Petrarch, *Rima* 189	ABBA;AB;BA;CDE.C,DE.
Wyatt, *Tottel* 55	A,A,AA:A,A.AA.CD,D.C.E:E.
Petrarch, *Rima* 173	AB,BA;A,BB,A.C,D,E;C,D,E.
Wyatt, *Tottel* 56	A,B:B,A,A.BB,A.C:D:D:C:E,E.
Petrarch, *Rima* 57	A,B,B;A.A,B,BA,CD,E;DC.E.
Wyatt, *Tottel* 98	AB:BA.A,B:B:A.C.DD.C,E:E.
Petrarch, *Rima* 124	AB,BA.ABBA.C,D,E.CDE.
Wyatt, *Tottel* 99	AB:BA.AB:B.AC.D.D.C,E:E.
Petrarch, *Rima* 21	A,BBA;A,B;B,A.CD,E,D;C,E.
Wyatt, *Tottel* 100	A:B,B,A,A,B,B.A.C,D:D,C.E,E.
Petrarch, *Rima* 224	A,B,B,A,A,BB,A,C,DE,CD:E.
Wyatt, *Tottel* 102	AB:B:A,A:B,B:A:C,D,DC,E:E.
Petrarch, *Rima* 269	AB;BA.AB,B,A.C,D,CD,CD.
Wyatt, *Tottel* 106	A,B:B:A.A,B:B,A.C,D,C:D,E,E.
Petrarch, *Rima* 153	A,B;BA.AB;B,A.C,D,C.D;C,D.
Wyatt, *Tottel* 107	A,A.B,B.A.A,A.B:B.A,A:B,B,A.
Petrarch, *Rima* 310	AB,A,B;A,B,A,B.CDC;D,CD.
Surrey, *Tottel* 2	A,B:A:B:A,B:A:B:A:B:A:B:A,A.
Petrarch, *Rima* 164	AB,BA,AB:B,A.CD,E;C,D,E.
Surrey, *Tottel* 10	A:B:A:B:A:B,AB,A.B:AB.A,A.
Petrarch, *Rima* 145	A,B;B,A;A,G;B,A;C,D,C;D:C,D.
Surrey, *Tottel* 12	A,B:A:B.C:D:C:D.E:F:E:F,GG.

NOTES

ONE Introduction

1. There is no entry for *lyric* in the *Middle English Dictionary* [*MED*]. In reference to Latin composition, Matthew of Vendôme (ca. 1175) defined verse as "metrical discourse advancing in cadenced periods with the restraint that meter demands and made charming by a graceful marriage of words and by flowers of thought" (Galyon, *Matthew of Vendôme*, 27). John of Garland (ca. 1240) considered *lyricum* a subset of *historia* "about drinking and eating and feasting and love of the gods" (Lawler, *Parisiana Poetria*, 103).

2. Ballade (dance), rondel or rondeau (circle), and virelai (dance song) are the traditional French *formes fixes*. All three were readily and frequently set to music. Sometimes, other comparably musical forms (*chansons*) were also designated as *formes fixes*.

3. The *MED* identifies "lullai" as an interjection; according to the *Oxford English Dictionary* [*OED*], the first use of "lullaby" as a noun is in 1592.

4. Duncan, "Introduction," xvii. Rossell Hope Robbins estimated that, among all items indexed as verse, some 2,000 Middle English lyrics survive (*Secular Lyrics*, xvii). This seems a conservative estimate.

5. Burrow, *Medieval Writers and Their Work*, 54.

6. George Puttenham's use in *The Arte of English Poesie* (1589) is commonly cited as a first instance. However, Ardis Butterfield credits Colin Burrow with noting Edmund Spenser's 1579 reference to "that famous Lyrick poet Pindarus" in the *Glosse* to "October," the tenth eclogue of *The Shepheardes Calendar* ("Lyric Editing," 396 n. 51).

7. Boffey, "What to Call a Lyric?" 674.

8. Boffey and Edwards, *New Index of Middle English Verse* [NIMEV], xiii.

9. Paden, *Medieval Lyric*, 2. Anne L. Klinck provides an excellent and up-to-date study of the "decidedly problematic" genre, surveying both medieval stand-ins for the term and its use by modern medievalists (*Voices of Medieval English Lyric*, 4–26).

10. Butterfield, "Why Medieval Lyric?" 327.

11. Jeffrey, *Early English Lyric*, 1.

12. Christopher Cannon, extending Derek Pearsall's identification of *King Horn* as a "lyric romance," emphasizes the lyrical quality of this conventionally designated narrative poem as preserved in Harley MS 2253 "because Middle English romances are much more songlike than we customarily recognize" ("Lyric Romance," 91).

13. Child ballad 23.

14. Boklund-Lagopoulou, "'Judas,'" 30. "Drama" is another genre's name that apparently did not exist in Middle English; the *OED* cites its first common use in the seventeenth century (possibly 1521 at the earliest).

15. Boffey and Edwards, "Middle English Lyrics and Manuscripts," 1.

16. Such as British Library, Harley MS 2253; Bodleian Library MS. Eng. poet. a. 1; British Library Additional MS 22283; British Library Sloane Manuscript 2593; Cambridge, St. John's College MS S.54; and Oxford, Bodleian Library MS Douce 302.

17. Cambridge University Library MS Ff. 1. 6.

18. Oxford University, Balliol College MS 354.

19. Zumthor, *Essai de poétique médiévale*.

20. The version as presented in Maxwell S. Luria and Richard L. Hoffman's Norton Critical Edition of *Middle English Lyrics* is based upon Oxford University, Bodleian Library MS Douce 322, which provides as a title "Canticus amoris." Oxford University, Bodleian Library MS Ashmole 59 attributes its version of this "pytous lamentacoun" to John Lydgate and provides the context of its being a Marian visitation to some St. "Auncyoun" (ancient saint?).

21. J. Wimsatt, *Chaucer and the Poems of "Ch,"* 1.

22. Woolf, *English Religious Lyric*, 205.

23. Robbins, "Middle English Court Love Lyric," 208.

24. Nagy and Boquet, "Historical Emotions, Historians' Emotions."

25. Speirs, *Medieval English Poetry*, 47.

26. Named, respectively, after John Crowe Ransom's *The New Criticism* (1941) and I. A. Richards's *Practical Criticism* (1956).

27. Johnson, *Practicing Literary Theory*, 12–13.

28. Lerer, "Endurance of Formalism," 8. Helen Marshall and Peter Buchanan explore further efforts to negotiate "new formalism(s)" specifically in terms of chirographic (lit. "handwritten") preservation "grounded upon the unique historical circumstances as well as the specific forces of cultural and material production" ("New Formalism," 165). Marjorie Levinson, assessing the progress of New Formalism, observed, "Both kinds of new formalism [i.e., "activist" and "normative"] seek to reinstate close reading both at the curricular center of our discipline and as the opening move, preliminary to any kind of critical consideration" ("What Is New Formalism?," 560). However, Robert S. Lehman

challenges formal analysis as a guarantor of literary quality because of "the inability of formalism, both old and new, to answer the ontological question *what is literature?*" ("Formalism, Mere Form, and Judgment," 253).

29. Rosemary Greentree has provided a superbly annotated bibliography to help access many of the best close readings (*Middle English Lyric*).

30. Burrow, *Essays on Medieval Literature*, 1.

31. Jones, "Ihesus woundes so wide," 100. Susanna Fein (*Complete Harley*) has provided en face translations of all items (Latin, French, English, and macaronic) within Harley MS 2253, thereby also contextualizing them within their original mise-en-page.

32. Butterfield, "Why Medieval Lyric?" 334

33. Fein, "All Adam's Children," 221.

34. Stevens, "Medieval Music and Lyrics," 275.

35. Burrow, *Essays on Medieval Literature*, 23. Thomas Duncan has rather slyly remarked "an absence of authorial context . . . might hardly seem disadvantageous to readers approaching these poems from the standpoint of New Criticism" ("Introduction," xvi).

36. Salter, *Fourteenth-Century English Poetry*, 6.

37. Gray, "Songs and Lyrics," 86. Similarly, Jonathan Culler finds among other, historicized understandings of lyric that one "fundamental characteristic . . . is not the description and interpretation of a past event but the performance of an event in the lyric present, a time of enunciation" ("Lyric, History, and Genre," 887). So, too, Stephen Burt affirms the need to imagine lyric as a type of reincarnation: "Lyric, in the term's central, durable senses, tends or aspires to replace the live, mortal, present body of one person present in one place at one time . . . with something else . . . by means of a variety of forms and tropes, to a variety of emotive ends" ("What Is This Thing Called Lyric?" 439).

38. Cervone and Watson "Introduction," 5.

39. Woolf, *English Religious Lyric*, 6.

40. Kuczynski, "Textual and Affective Stability," 58.

41. Manning, *Wisdom and Number*, vii.

42. Duncan, "Middle English Lyrics," 37.

43. Davies, *Medieval English Lyrics*, 34.

44. Fussell, *Poetic Meter*, 81.

45. Johnson, "England, Poetry of II," 411b.

46. Cornelius, "Language and Meter," 112.

47. Wimsatt, *Chaucer and His French Contemporaries*, 44–45.

48. "Chaucer—as author, as 'laureate,' and as 'father' of English poetry—is a construction of his later fifteenth-century scribes, readers, and poetic imitators" (Lerer, *Chaucer and His Readers*, 3).

49. Butterfield, "Lyric Editing," 31.
50. Boffey and Edwards, "Middle English Lyrics and Manuscripts," 2.
51. Butterfield, "Lyric Editing," 31.
52. Osberg, "Alliterative Lyric," 42. For further detailed prosodic analysis, see, too, Osberg, "Alliterative Technique."
53. John Milton, "The Verse," prefatory note to *Paradise Lost* (1674).
54. Cornelius, "Language and Meter," 10.
55. Stevens, "'Music' of the Lyric," 127.
56. Wimsatt, "Chaucer and Deschamps," 142.
57. James I. Wimsatt explains that "in the *Art de dictier* Eustache Deschamps, Machaut's disciple and celebrant, refers to both the accompanying melody of a poem and the sound system of a poem's words as 'music.' The sounds of the words he designates 'natural music'" (*Chaucer and His French Contemporaries*, 5). Glending Olson explains "*musique naturele* is essentially the art of setting versified lyrics into various prescribed song forms" ("Deschamps' 'Art de Dictier,'" 720).
58. Stone, *Medieval English Verse*, 9.
59. With few exceptions, my modernizations are based upon the Norton Critical Edition of *Middle English Lyrics*, edited by Maxwell S. Luria and Richard L. Hoffman (soon to be re-edited by Ardis Butterfield).
60. Arn, "On Punctuating Medieval Literary Texts," 174. For a modern reader's use of print publication, however, Arn rightly defends the necessity of editing the largely unpunctuated manuscripts. For Thomas G. Duncan, "the ultimate goal in the editing of literary texts must be the restoration of artistic integrity" ("Editing Issues," 27).
61. See *The Legend of Good Women* (Prologue G, 86), where Chaucer has a rather obtuse Cupid claim that a naked or "pleyn" text has no need of further glossing.
62. Chickering, "Unpunctuating Chaucer," 107.

TWO Bringing the Middle English Lyric into Modern Play

1. A. A. MacDonald observes that "the spectacular artistry" of Middle Scots religious lyrics "renders them untypical of the medieval English vernacular lyric genre if considered as a whole" ("Lyrics in Middle Scots," 253).
2. McCann, "Blood and Chocolate," 48.
3. Manning, "Game and Earnest," 227–228.
4. Allen, "Grammar, Poetic Form," 199.
5. Addison, *The Spectator*, no. 70, May 21, 1711. In addition to his other accomplishments, Joseph Addison (1672–1719) was a superb classicist and author of Latin verse.

6. Stevens, "Medieval Music and Lyrics," 252.
7. Stevens, "Medieval Music and Lyrics," 160.
8. Burrow, *Essays on Medieval Literature*, 14.
9. Butterfield, "Poems without Form?" 195.
10. Butterfield, "Poems without Form?" 189.
11. Speirs, *Medieval English Poetry*, 63.
12. Robertson, "Historical Criticism," 26–27. One reason to think so is that the incipit of "Maiden in the mor lay" in the fourteenth-century Red Book of Ossory (Bishop's Palace, Kilkenny) seems to cue a suitable musical setting for a Latin contrafactum (alternative text) "Peperit virgo" ["The Virgin gave birth"; cf. Isaiah 7:14].
13. Donaldson, "Patristic Exegesis," 187; Spearing, *Textual Subjectivity*, 24.
14. Wenzel, *Preachers, Poets*, 210.
15. Speirs, *Medieval English Poetry*, 63–64.
16. Greene, "'Maid of the Moor,'" 506.
17. Harris, "'Maiden in the Mor Lay,'" 87.
18. Dronke, *The Medieval Lyric*, 195–196.
19. Waldron, "'Maiden in the Mor Lay,'" 217.
20. Duncan, "'Maid in the Moor,'" 161.
21. Stevens, "Medieval Music and Lyrics," 254.
22. Dronke, *Medieval Lyric*, 24.
23. Whitehead, "Middle English Religious Lyrics," 113.
24. McNamer, *Affective Meditation*, 12
25. Boquet and Nagy, *Medieval Sensibilities*, 109.
26. Olson, "Toward a Poetics," 231. See also Olson, *Literature as Recreation*.
27. Woolf, *English Religious Lyric*, 308. Rosemary Woolf differentiates the private reading of such "lyric proper" (385) from public song.
28. Klinck, *Voices of Medieval English Lyric*, 22.
29. Boffey, "Manuscripts of English Courtly Love Lyrics," 6.
30. Reddy, "Emotional Liberty," 269. See also Reddy, *Navigation of Feeling*.
31. Boquet and Nagy, *Medieval Sensibilities*, 123.
32. Woolf, *English Religious Lyric*, 164.
33. Greentree, "Lyric," 388.
34. Manning, *Wisdom and Number*, 35.
35. Allen, "Grammar, Poetic Form," 219.
36. Duncan, "Introduction," xxi.
37. Klinck, *Voices of Medieval English Lyric*, 45.
38. Lawton, *Voice in Later Medieval English Literature*, 63.
39. Murton, *Chaucer's Prayers*, 13–15.
40. Burrow, *Medieval Writers and Their Work*, 55.

41. Nelson, "Lyric Value," 148–9.

42. Rosenwein, *Generations of Feelings*, 9.

43. Kane, "Short Essay," 111. Instead of "courtly" vs. "popular," George Kane proposed four (in large part, chronologically sequential) subcategories of the Middle English secular lyric on the basis of style: plain, early decorated, polished (i.e., Chaucer), and aureate.

44. Stanbury, "Gender and Voice," 228.

45. Gibbs, "Cognitive Poetics," 160.

46. Rosenwein, *Generations of Feelings*, 3.

47. Rosenwein, *Generations of Feelings*, 6.

48. Burger and Crocker, *Medieval Affect*, 7.

49. Boquet and Nagy, *Medieval Sensibilities*, 143–144. The Cistercian division into "concupiscible" and "irascible" was established on a "foundation of attraction and rejection" (Boquet and Nagy, 152). The Order of Cistercians was founded in the early twelfth century to reform the Cluniac rule, which had itself been an early tenth-century reform of the sixth-century Benedictine monastic rule. Hymns attributed to St. Bernard of Clairvaux (1090–1153 CE), arguably the most highly influential early Cistercian, were translated into Middle English; as Dante's final guide in *The Divine Comedy*, St. Bernard sings a hymn to Mary (*Paradiso*, Canto 33, 1–39).

50. Copeland, *Emotion and the History of Rhetoric*, 1.

51. Stevens, "Music and Poetry," 65.

52. The personifications of emotions in the *Roman de la Rose* provide a checklist for the complex feelings caused by *fin'amor* [courtly love]—all of which are finally abjured by Lady Reason, who advises sexual abstinence instead (a rhetorically futile effort on her part).

53. Boquet and Nagy, *Medieval Sensibilities*, 137.

54. Copeland, *Emotion and the History of Rhetoric*, 7.

55. Boquet and Nagy, *Medieval Sensibilities*, 152.

56. Rosenfeld, *Ethics and Enjoyment*, 106.

THREE Playing Glad

1. The Latin tag *felix culpa* derives from the Easter Vigil Mass Proclamation, or *Exultet*, "O felix culpa quae talem et tantum meruit habere Redemptorem" [O happy or blessed fault that has earned such and so great a Redeemer].

2. Manning, *Wisdom and Number*, 7.

3. *MED* s.v. "bond" n. def. 1a.

4. *MED* s.v. "bond" cf. d2f. 3a.

5. *MED* s.v. "bond(e" n.(2) and adj.

6. The "Key" riddle, for example, reads "Wrætlic hongað bi weres þeoh / frean under sceate. Foran is þyrel / Bið stiþ ond heard" [A wondrous thing hangs beside a man's thigh / under a lord's lap-cloth / Perforated in front, it is stiff and hard]. Similarly, the expressions "ræseð mec on reodne" [she rubs me into redness] or "wæt bið þæt eage" [that eye is wet] in the "Onion" riddle may be interpreted innocently—or not.

7. Baird-Lange, "Symbolic Ambivalence," 5.

8. The female-focused equivalent of such foolery is "I have a hole aboue my knee" [I have a hole above my knee] composed in even more sing-songy tetrameter couplets. The sole textual witness for "I have a hole" itself suggests an innocent gloss ("sheath") in the margin.

9. *MED* s.v. "sel(e" n. def. 1a "bliss" and s.v. "sale" n.(2).

10. Scattergood, "Love Lyric," 54.

11. *MED* s.v. "somer."

12. Manning, "'Sumer Is Icumen In,'" item 2.

13. Reiss, *Art of the Middle English Lyric*, 11.

14. Roscow, "What Is 'Sumer Is Icumen In'?" 193.

15. Roscow, "What Is 'Sumer Is Icumen In'?" 190. Jeffrey Helterman ("Antagonistic Voices") also finds the lyric's apparent celebration of perpetual summer to be ironic and the cuckoo's song (not heard in summer) a reminder of cuckoldry.

16. Perspice Christicola que dignacio/ celicus agricola pro vitis vicio / Filio–non parcens exposuit mortis exicio / Qui captivos semivivos a supplicio / Vite donat et secum coronat in celi solio.

17. Jeffrey, *Early English Lyric*, 172.

18. Whitehead, "Middle English Religious Lyrics," 102.

19. *MED* s.v. "lust" n. defs. 1–4. The seventh deadly sin was normally identified as "Lussuria" (*MED* s.v. "luxuri(e" n.). Whereas "lust" lost its positive denotation, "luxury" lost its negative denotation of "lasciviousness" by the early eighteenth century, coming instead to mean "sumptuous, refined, exquisite, desirable" (see *OED* s.v. "luxury").

20. Fowler, *Bible in Middle English Literature*, 101.

21. Franklin, "'Fyngres heo hath feir to folde,'" 177.

22. *MED* s.v. "wo." for "woe" vs. s.v. "wouen" for "woo." Fr. Walter Ong explains such a pun gives "a *prima facie* startling appearance to an essentially drab fact" ("Wit and Mystery," 315). The drabness of religion occurs when the daily reiteration of incomprehensible mysteries becomes familiar, as, for example, when the crucifix becomes a necklace.

23. Flannery, "Tutivillus and the Policing of Speech," 250.

24. This hendecasyllabic line is seldom used in Modern English ver4e.

Furthermore, the counting of syllables in Middle English verse lines remains a rather iffy endeavor. I fear that a tendency of classical prosody to preserve an obscure, so seemingly expert terminology (like "hendecasyllabic" itself) has contributed to a general disinterest in detailed analysis of the phonology of verse. The Poetry Foundation provides handy access to many such terms www.poetryfoundation.org/. Nevertheless, during actual performance, the emotional impact of the sound effects of versification requires no further footnoting.

25. *MED* s.v. "craken" v. def. a. "To make a splitting or bursting sound; also, let a fart."

26. Hoppin, *Medieval Music*, 142.

27. Speirs, *Medieval English Poetry*, 83.

28. Fries, "'Other' Voice," 160.

29. Plummer, "Woman's Song," 150. John Plummer provides a list of nineteen comparable women's songs (pp. 151–152).

30. Crowther, "Middle English Lyric 'Joly Jankyn,'" 125.

31. Boquet and Nagy, *Medieval Sensibilities*, 173.

32. *MED* s.v. "daunger" n. def. 4a; cf. Jean de Meun's personification of *Dangiers*, i.e., the Rose's "self-dominion."

33. Originally, *blazon* was a heraldic term for the depiction of armorial bearings, transferred to designate a descriptive set piece surveying a woman's beauty, usually "cap à pied" [head-to-toe], with close attention to each physical detail.

34. Fein, "Lyrics of MS Harley 2253," 4175.

35. Gray, "Songs and Lyrics," 89.

36. Olson, "Toward a Poetics," 238.

37. Askins, "Brothers Orléans and Their Keepers," 27.

38. Arn, "Two Manuscripts, One Mind," 76. She adds, "The question of why he left the English manuscript behind in England cannot be answered conclusively, but it is more than likely that it represented a body of work that he had no intention of ever enlarging" ("Two Manuscripts, One Mind," 78).

39. Spearing, *Textual Subjectivity*, 231.

40. Chaucer, "Complaint of Venus," l. 80.

41. Edwards, *Ratio and Invention*, 68–69.

42. *MED* s.v. "ur(e" n.

43. *MED* s.v. "puissaunce" n. The merits of Charles's presumably non-native versecraft is presently undergoing substantial re-evaluation. Jeremy Smith concedes that "Charles—unlike some more accurate poets—allowed himself some leeway in rhyming . . . is no major criticism" ("Charles d'Orléans," 210–211). But Eric Weiskott rejects "immediately the most obvious explanation . . . that Charles was a language learner" ("Charles d'Orléans' English Metrical Phonology," 130); rather, "Charles's English aesthetic was not a Chaucerian aesthetic. Nor was it a

recognizably French aesthetic.... Charles in effect restarted poetic tradition" (137). Ad Putter affirms that "for every duff line there are a hundred that show his sensitivity to the sound world of English verse" ("English Poetry of a Frenchman," 155).

44. Perkins, "Musing on Mutability," 493.

45. Cf. *MED* s.v. "fain" adj. There is an unlikely but possibly cynical pun on "fein" n., meaning "pretense, deceit."

46. *MED* s.v. "baume" def. 5.

47. *MED* sv. "meten" v. def. 6a.

48. The DIMEV invites reference of "O excellent sovereign most seemly to see" to the thirty-four quatrains of "Excellent sovereign seemly to see" (N/IMEV 752 DIMEV 1238), an earlier farewell lyric attributed to "a Duke of York." Awareness of this earlier lyric, if that indeed may be assumed, blurs the distinction between the private reception and the coterie publication of such lyrics.

49. Gray, *Themes and Images*, 18.

50. The "Hail Mary" initially consisted of only the verses Luke 1:28 (Gabriel at the Annunciation) and Luke 1:42 (Elizabeth at the Visitation)—praise in anticipation of birth. The "Holy Mary"—petition in anticipation of death—seems a late fifteenth-century addition officially sanctioned in the mid-sixteenth century.

51. Manning, *Wisdom and Number*, 167.

52. Woolf, *English Religious Lyric*, 287.

53. Duffy, *Stripping of the Altars*, 256. Karen Saupe, *Middle English Marian Lyrics*, provides an excellent introduction to its eponymous topic.

54. Noting that the poem is accompanied by an illustration of a Carthusian monk praying to a representation of Mary with the baby Jesus, Karl Brunner categorized the poem as a "church-poem" (*Kirchenlieder*, in "Kirchenlieder").

55. Manning, *Wisdom and Number*, 160.

56. Raw, "'As Dew in Aprille,'" 413.

57. Manning, *Wisdom and Number*, 162.

58. Speirs, *Medieval English Poetry*, 69.

59. Stanbury, "Gender and Voice," 230.

60. The joyful praise voiced here for Mary balances the sympathy she inspires as Co-Crucified in lyrics of the "Stabat Mater" type.

61. Alan J. Fletcher reports that a scribe named "Selk included a reference to 'I syng a mayden' in a sermon that he compiled, in Latin, for the feast of the Assumption" ("Lyric in the Sermon," 208).

62. Manning, *Wisdom and Number*, 164.

63. Oliver, *Poems without Names*, 83.

64. Saetveit Miles, *Virgin Mary's Book*, 41.

65. Weber, *Theology and Poetry*, 57–58.

66. Reiss, *Art of the Middle English Lyric*, 161.

67. Steffes, "'As Dewe in Aprylle,'" 70. Steffes details the liturgical associations of the dew image.

68. Weber, *Theology and Poetry*, 59. Sarah Weber also notes that Isaiah 45:8 was the Introit for Feast of Annunciation and that Judges 6:34–40 was "used in the Prymer's antiphon for Prime."

69. The "M" stanza of Chaucer's "ABC," for example, states "the bush with flawmes rede / ... Was signe of thin [Mary's] unwemmed maidenhede" [The bush with red flames / ... was a sign of your unblemished maidenhead] (ll. 89–91).

70. Manning, "I Syng of a Myden." 12.

71. Wenzel, *Preachers, Poets*, 54.

72. *MED* s.vv. "drem" n. 1 and 2.

FOUR Playing Sad or Mad

1. Olson, *Literature as Recreation*, 151.

2. Perhaps an echo of the fifth-century abecedarius hymn "A solis ortus cardine."

3. James Ryman's 166 lyrics are preserved in Cambridge University L, MS Ee.1.12. The very comparable surviving poems of John Audelay (d. ca. 1426) are found in Bodleian MS Douce 302.

4. Having ridden five miles after the completion of "The Second Nun's Tale," apparently in "devout silence," the pilgrims meet a canon in flight and his yeoman at "Boughton under Blee" (*Canterbury Tales*, VIII, 556). From the hill, one can first see the towers of Canterbury cathedral.

5. Sisam, *Fourteenth Century Verse and Prose*, 169

6. Bennett, *Middle English Literature*, 391.

7. See *OED* s.v. "congeon," n. def. 1 "A dwarf, or congenitally deformed man," citing this poem as an example; also, more generally, a "simpleton."

8. Breeze, "Middle English *Cammede*," 150.

9. Turville-Petre, "Political Lyrics," 181.

10. Moore, *Secular Lyric in Middle English*, 78.

11. Copeland, *Emotion and the History of Rhetoric*, 327–328.

12. The scribal abbreviation for Latin "recipe" [take] survives as ℞ on pharmaceutical script.

13. Manning, *Wisdom and Number*, 145.

14. A comparable, though self-answering, riddle is "Hyt semes quite and is red": "It seems white and is red. / It is alive and seems dead. / It is one and seems two. / It is God's body and nothing else."

15. Kuczynski, "Theological Sophistication," 338.

16. Greene, "Meaning of the Corpus Christi Carol," 13.

17. Duffy, *Stripping of the Altars*, 35.

18. Manning, *Wisdom and Number*, 117.

19. *MED* sv. "beren" v. def. 1a. *vs.* sv. "boren" v. def. 1a.

20. *MED* sv. "pall" def. 3a.

21. It is tempting to translate "lithe" as "lies," but it denotes to "travel" perhaps specifically to "sail" (*MED* sv. "lithen" defs. 1–3), and the church is commonly imaged as a ship.

22. Starting in the thirteenth century, the Feast of Corpus Christi was to be celebrated on Thursday after the octave of Pentecost.

23. The enduring popularity of this lyric (or ballad, Child 2) was parodied as a cloying folk song in *National Lampoon's Animal House* (1978); its performance moves Bluto (John Belushi) to smash the singer's guitar and then feebly say "Sorry."

24. The Middle English word for "bark" has the figurative meaning of "the prepuce" (see *MED* s.v. "rind(e" n.(1) def. 4b), and "stone" can refer to "a testicle of a man or an animal" (see *MED* s.v. "ston" n., def. 14. *Anat.* a). Curiously, the *OED* cites no instance of the more familiar "coarse slang" significance of "bone" before 1654 (def. 11).

25. *MED* sv. "suster" n. def. 1a.

26. Such gifts are exchanged as signs of "love, affection between the sexes; also, courtly love," etc. (*MED* defs. 1a and b) sent to "a person one loves; beloved, paramour" (*MED* def. 2a).

27. *MED* s.v. "suster" n. def 3b (a); (c).

28. Claude Lecouteux reports that initially witches and sorcerers used a version of this phrasing to induce sleep and so resist torture, but that "during the sixteenth century, the doctor Richard Anglo provided a longer spell, intended to provide protection from thieves and to ensure the safety of livestock" (*Dictionary of Ancient Magic*, s.v. "Dismas," 109–110).

29. *MED* def. 2a.

30. Robbins, *Encyclopedia of Witchcraft and Demonology*, s.v. "Charms" p. 85b.

31. *MED* s.v. "wat" n.(2) "Also wat(t)e. Etymology of unknown origin; ?cp. Wat(te, shortened form of the proper name Walter." Apparently, the gender of the rabbit is difficult to determine.

32. "So howe"; *MED* s.v. "hou" interj. Def. 1(a) "in hunting cries borrowed from the French."

33. The "I" poet-witness identifies the "I" hare as "she." The hare is called "Watte" by a hunter (l. 45) and hostile housewife (l. 45); these may be default guesses recalling the grammatical gender of Old English "hara" as masculine (cf. Anglo-Norman "conin" and "rabotte")—comparable to calling an unfamiliar dog a "Good Boy."

34. The trope takes its name from an ascetic treatise, "De contemptu mundi," or "De Miseria Condicionis Humane" [On the Wretchedness of the Human Condition], that Pope Innocent III wrote in 1195 (i.e., before being made pope in 1198).

35. London, British Library Harley 2253, f. 59v.

36. Reiss, *Art of the Middle English Lyric*, 86.

37. Horace, *Odes*, Book I, xi, 7.

38. Fletcher, "Lyric in the Sermon," 204.

39. Fletcher, "Lyric in the Sermon," 205.

40. Manning, *Wisdom and Number*, viii.

41. Bodleian Library Digby 86), f. 163v–164 Bodleian Library Rawlinson G.18 (SC 14751), f. 105v; British Library Arundel 248, f. 154r.

42. Stevens, *Words and Music*, 386.

43. Chaucer's only (and more successful) use of this stanzaic form in a lyric is "La Prière de Nostre Dame" or the "A,B,C," thought by many to be Chaucer's earliest surviving lyric.

44. Addison, "Little Boxes," 134.

45. Funeral monuments, imagined or real, are not the only interpretive settings to consider when reading epigraphic verse. Adam Kumler, for example, reads vessels as "built spaces" for "Middle English short poems crafted and encountered beyond the confines of the manuscript page in the form of functional artifacts—vessels—that effectively made lyric part of their substance, their pragmatic purpose, and their social and political functioning" ("Lyric Vessels," 183).

FIVE *Compassioun* for the Passion (and Its Perversion)

1. Boquet and Nagy, *Medieval Sensibilities*, 180.

2. McNamer, *Affective Meditation*, 3.

3. Woolf, *English Religious Lyric*, 242.

4. Gray, *Themes and Images*, 139.

5. Robbins, "English Version of *St. Edmund's Speculum*," 249–250.

6. Salter, *Fourteenth-Century English Poetry*, 6.

7. Reiss, *Art of the Middle English Lyric*, 17.

8. Born Jacopo dei Benedetti (ca. 1230–1306), a Franciscan preacher-poet-fool who some thought mad and some thought saintly; Jacopone's dialogue poem "Donna de Paradiso" (*Laude* 92) is inherently dramatic; cf. "Stond wel moder vnder rode."

9. Whitehead, "Middle English Religious Lyrics," 117. The Descent from the Cross is also the focus of compassionate devotion for the sixth of the Seven Sorrows of Mary.

10. Cf. John of Grimestone's "Lullay, little child, rest thee a throwe," a thirty-two-line lullaby impersonating the Virgin; Grimestone borrows the refrain for his own carol/lullaby from "Lullay lullay lullay little child why weepest thou so sore." Grimestone's portable preaching book (National Library Scotland MS, Advocates 18. 7. 21 compiled in 1372) includes 246 items in verse, approximately half of which are adaptations from Latin originals.

11. Christian allegoresis interpreted God as the Groom of the Chosen People (Deuteronomy 14:2) to foreshadow Jesus in love with His *sponsa* as well, alternatively identified as the church, the elect individual, or all humanity.

12. *MED* def. 1a "A small tower."

13. *MED* def. 2a.

14. D'Arcy, "'Written in gold,'" 119.

15. Woolf, *English Religious Lyric*, 302.

16. Brewer, *English Gothic Literature*, 62.

17. Zimbalist, "Lyric Christ," 249.

18. Ingrid Nelson observes that "the music suggests that each set of three lines is a musical phrase, rendering the poem a set of long couplets with internal rhyme. Read in this way, the poem's strongest formal coherence is across the two voices, while the internal rhyme in each musical phrase asserts a porous sense of selfhood" ("Lyric Value," 152).

19. Whitehead, "Musical and Poetical Form," 239.

20. Line 50: "The time is come I shall to helle" anticipates the Harrowing of Hell by which Jesus freed Adam's faithful "kun" (l. 17) who died before His Resurrection.

21. Nelson, "Lyric Value," 150.

22. Murton, *Chaucer's Prayers*, 41. Murton's commentary refers specifically to Chaucer's attribution of an embedded lyric, the "Invocacio ad Mariam," to the anonymous Second Nun, who herself credits its composition to St. Bernard (*Canterbury Tales*, VIII, 30).

23. *MED* s.v. "pein(e" def. 1b vs. s.v. "pein(e" def. 2a.

24. *MED* s.v. "pin(e."

25. Cf. George Herebert's "Love III" or John Donne's "Holy Sonnet 14." There are also precedents for the *paraclausithyron* ("lament beside the shut door") in Greek and Latin elegies as well as in troubadour lyrics.

26. Kerby-Fulton, "Making the Early Middle Hiberno-English Lyric," 11.

27. Woolf, *English Religious Lyric*, 51, refers to the version preserved in London, Lambeth Palace Library MS 557 (f. 185v). The New Haven, Yale University, Beinecke Library, Takamiya Deposit (f. 84ra) version is almost identical.

28. *MED* s.v. "lok" n. def. 2a.

29. Baden-Daintree, "Voice and Response," 143.

30. Baden-Daintree, "Voice and Response," 143.

31. Galloway, "Theory of the Fourteenth-Century English Lyric," 317.

32. "Fere" can simply mean "companion"; however, "knitten in fere" denotes "unite in marriage" (*MED* s.v. "fere" n. def. 2a).

33. Stanbury, "Gender and Voice," 231.

34. Whitehead, "Middle English Religious Lyrics," 106.

35. *MED* s.v. "child" n. def. 1a.

36. Cervone, "Wondering through Middle English Lyric," 68.

37. A "Prayer for the Jews" (that is, "pro perfidis Judaeis") dates from before the eighth century and was likewise recited on Good Friday well into the twentieth century. "Perfides" may be translated simply as "without faith," but the epithet "perfidious" arouses intensely hostile emotions. Biblical inspiration for the scene of the *Improperia* (also dramatized by Corpus Christi pageants) includes Psalm 22 (cf. Matthew 27:46; Mark 15:34), Mark 15:29, Matthew 27:39, and Luke 24:35.

38. Herebert's twenty-three poems for the liturgical year (mostly verse translations) are preserved in his holograph British Library Add. MS 46919.

39. Woolf, *English Religious Lyric*, 40.

40. The DIMEV lists twenty-eight items under the subject heading "crucifixion" and seventeen under "cross, hours of."

41. Boquet and Nagy, *Medieval Sensibilities*, 232.

42. Whitehead, "Middle English Religious Lyrics," 113.

43. It remains a common exchange at the beginning of each Station of the Cross: Leader, "We adore Thee, O Christ, and bless Thee"; All, "Because by Thy holy cross Thou hast redeemed the world."

44. *MED* s.v. "coroune" n. def. 1a.

45. This line may play against the more common lyrical use of "gore" as in "lovelich under gore" [gown] (*MED* s.v. "gor(e" n. 2 def. 3a), intended to suggest the beautiful horror of Christ's crucifixion.

46. *MED* s.v. "stound(e" n. def. 3.

47. *MED* s.v. "stound(e" n. def. 1a.

48. Howes, "Adreynt in shennesse," 89.

49. The fact that "Mahoun" leads this dance of the seven deadly sins exemplifies the frequently demonized conflation of Islam with Judaism as generic "infidelity."

50. Crowther, "Bargain of Judas," 246.

51. Stouck, "Reading of the Middle English 'Judas,'" 196.

52. Crowther observes that Pilate, Judas, and his sister are "all three are traders in bodies" ("Bargain of Judas," 247)—a common anti-Semitic slur.

53. Schueler, "Middle English 'Judas,'" 842.

SIX Contek I

1. DeVun, *Shape of Sex*, 106.
2. Tison Pugh, focusing on three twelfth-century Latin poets, also explores how "many lyric genres of the Middle Ages . . . offer opportunities for queering authorial play through the contradictory conflation of private desires expressed in public discourse" (*Queering Medieval Genres*, 21).
3. McNamer, *Affective Meditation*, 169.
4. Each stanza's rhyming pattern is also unique: first, ababa*b (allowing the proximate rhyming of tense/lax vowels in "-lees" and "-nesse"; then, aaabb; finally, ababbcbc.
5. Perhaps "Farewell now my lady gay."
6. *MED* s.v. "ground" def. 1a.
7. *MED* s.v. "plesaunce" n. 1 def. 1a.
8. *MED* s.v. "plesaunce" n. 1 def. 2a.
9. *MED* s.v. "splen(e" def. 1d.
10. *MED* s.v. "chere" n. 1 def. 2a.
11. *MED* s.v. "lien" def. 1b, "With sexual implications."
12. *MED* s.v. "lenen" v.(3) def. 1a.
13. *MED* s.v. "presse" def. 4c, "critical situation."
14. *MED* s.v. "redres(se" n.
15. *MED* s.v. "braunch" def. 5.
16. *MED* s.v. "medlen" v. def. 1a for "mix"; def. 2a for "busy"; def. 4a for "sex."
17. *MED* s.v. "compaignie" n. def. 4.
18. Fein, *Complete Harley 2253*, vol. 2, 397.
19. "Annot and John" survives in BL MS Harley 2253 (fols. 63–63v). The amorous carol "Ichot a burde in boure bright" (NIMEV 1395 DIMEV 2325) provides a very proximate analogue (fols. 72va-73), but a more sober use of alliteration and a far more conventional expression of enthralled longing.
20. "Ichot a burde in boure bright" more simply says "solsecle of swetnesse" (st. 6).
21. Ransom, "'Annot and John,'" 140
22. Ransom, "'Annot and John,'" 128–129. See *MED* s.v. "queint(e" n., a clever thing or trick "with punning on cunte" def. 2.
23. *MED* sv. "derne" adj. def. 3. So, too, "þrustle" (l. 23, *Turdus philomelus*) and "nightegale" (l. 28) can but need not recall the hardly happy history of Philomela.
24. *MED* sv. "frith" n. def. 1a.
25. *MED* sv. "gome" n. 1 defs. 1–4.
26. *MED* sv. "man" n. def. 1a.
27. Fein, *Complete Harley 2253*, vol. 2, 123

28. Fein, *Complete Harley 2253*, vol. 2, 399 nn. 48–49.

29. Kathryn Gravdal reports that 18 percent of Old French pastourelles entail rape after the woman resists (*Ravishing Maidens*, 105).

30. Utley, *Crooked Rib*, 27.

31. Baechle et al., "Reassessing the *Pastourelle*," 23.

32. Harris, *Obscene Pedagogies*, 112. Carissa Harris adds that this lyric's "copying by a London cleric has intriguing implications due to the genre's emphasis on clerical predation, which is thwarted here because the aggressor chooses a higher-status target instead of a peasant maiden" (113).

33. Harris, "English and Scottish Pastourelles," 183.

34. Woolf, "Construction of 'In A Frith,'" 55.

35. Woolf, "Construction of 'In A Frith,'" 55–59.

36. *MED* s.v. "cloth" n. def. 3b "clothes of religion, garb of a priest, monk, etc."

37. Harris, *Obscene Pedagogies*, 111. The bracketing lyrics are "Most I ryden by Rybbesdale" (NIMEV 2207 DIMEV 3550) and "A wale white as whalles bone" (NIMEV 105 DIMEV 183).

38. Harris, *Obscene Pedagogies*, 112.

39. Harris, *Obscene Pedagogies*, 111.

40. Karl Reichl ("Popular Poetry and Courtly Lyric") suggests the French pastourelle "Au dous mois de mai joli" may have been its model.

41. See DIMEV items 807–869, NIMEV items 341–379 for lyrics beginning "As I"; all start with the recollection of a chance encounter.

42. Ingrid Nelson proposes an entirely different interpretation of the lyric's dramatic context, noting that "the poem does not indicate the gender of the first speaker, the rider. Two women discussing their travails in love is not without precedent in medieval literature . . . Reading both speakers as female suggests a different dynamic between the two, with the second, more experienced speaker warning the first away from the pleasure she rode out to seek" ("O my pleying," 5), a kind of reversal of the encouragement toward love we find in "Antigone's song" in Chaucer's *Troilus and Criseyde* ("Lyric Value," 154).

43. Alternatively, Patricia Abel ("Cleric, the Kitchie Boy") suggests imagining a man testing if his woman remained faithful during his long absence, a *contek* that helps explain how her indignation transforms into enthusiasm.

44. Nine eight-line stanzas rhyming XaXaXaXa. The off-rhyme lines approximate tetrameter; the rhyming lines, trimeter; if regularly iambic and reformatted as "fourteeners," the measure would be "common meter," which Samuel Johnson thought "the most soft and pleasing of our lyric measures" ("Life of Dryden," in *Lives of the Poets*).

45. The epithet "lemmon" (see *MED* s.v. "lemman") can have an extremely positive denotation—that is, "beloved person"—and can even be used in refer-

ence to Christ, Mary or a spouse. Yet, Chaucer's bitter (because cuckolded) Manciple rejects the "knavysh speche" (IX, 205) of referring to an adulteress as a "lemman." Chaucer's Parson particularly condemns *clerici* who take paramours: "And therfore han swiche preestes, and hir lemmanes eek that consenten to hir leccherie, the malisoun of al the court Christien, til they come to amendment" [And therefore such priests will have, and also their paramours as well who consent to their lechery, the curse of all the Christian court till they come to amendment] (*Canterbury Tales*, X, 903).

46. See *MED* s.v "bour" n. def. 2b "a lady's chambers." Mary is frequently envisioned reading a book in her bower when approached by the angel Gabriel at the Annunciation.

47. Though not itself listed in Bartlett Jere Whiting and Helen Wescott Whiting's *Proverbs, Sentences and Proverbial Phrases*, the aphorism "is betere on fote gon / Then wicked hors to ride" shares the pithiness of several "is better to ... than to ..." expressions (cf. especially items W558, W776, W92). The most familiar formula is St. Paul's "is better to marry than to burn" (1 Corinthians 7:9), which may be relevant here in a comically inappropriate way. A possible pun between "horse" and "whores" (cf. *MED* s.v. "ho(r(e" n.(2) def. 1a) is also not unthinkable.

48. Cf. "But soth is seyd, 'a fol can not be stille'" (Chaucer, *PF* 574—the sparrow-hawk's reproof of the cackling goose). Whiting, *Chaucer's Use of Proverbs*, 38.

49. *MED* s.v. "stille" adv. def. 1c for "quietly"; def. 3 for "meekly"; def. 4 for "secretly"; def. 5 for "continually."

50. *MED* s.v. "wonder" n.

SEVEN Contek II

1. Chaucer significantly toned down this categorical contempt: "Who shal trowe on any othes mo?" (*Troilus and Criseyde*, V, 1681).

2. This lyric was attributed to Chaucer by John Stowe in the mid-sixteenth century. Cf. Chaucer's "Fortune" or *"Balades de Visage sanz Peinture"* in which Lady Fortune defends the necessity of her constant inconstancy: "Right so mot I kythen my brotelnesse" [Right so must I acknowledge my mutability] (l. 63). The title "Against Woman Unconstant" provided for "Madame for your newfangleness" only reinforces a spurious logic common to such complaints "et crimine ab uno / disce omnis" [from the crime of one, learn about all] (*Aeneid* II, 65–66). Linne R. Mooney has discovered an interesting example of intertextual *contek*, a later lyric wherein "the writer revoices Chaucer's [first] stanza by reversing the gender in the first two lines" ("Late Fifteenth-Century Woman's Revision," 34).

3. Benson, *Riverside Chaucer*, 657 n. 7.

4. Kessel-Brown, "Emotional Landscape of the Forest," 229.

5. Fein, "Lyrics of MS Harley 2253," 4184, citing A. K. Moore, *Secular Lyric*, 53.

6. *MED* s.v. "manden."

7. "Breme" usually means "clear, loud; gay," see *MED* "brem(e" adj. def. 2b of sound, but can also suggest "cruel," even "savage," def. 3b (a) of animals.

8. *MED* s.v. "danken."

9. *MED* s.v. "wod(e" n. 3.

10. Manning, "Game and Earnest," 231.

11. Manning, "Game and Earnest," 233.

12. *MED* s.v. "knitten" v. def. 7 and def. 1a.

13. *MED* s.v. "cold" adj. def. 4.

14. *MED* s.v. "tikel" adj. def. 1b.

15. Other examples of which are John Donne's "Go and Catch a Falling Star" and the Fool's Prophecy in *King Lear* (III, ii, 82–97).

16. There is no entry for "rollion" in the *MED* or the *OED*; cf. "rullion," a fifteenth-century Scottish shoe.

17. O'Donoghue, "'Cuius Contrarium,'" 217.

18. DeVun, *Shape of Sex*, 110.

19. *MED* s.v. "cold" def. 4.

20. *MED* s.v. "grisle" n. and adj. More emphatically than Petrarch, "Chaucer's Envoy" at the conclusion of "The Clerk's Tale" screams that Griselda should not be taken as a role model.

21. Robbins, "Two Satirical Love Epistles," 416.

22. Ziolkowski, "Avatars of Ugliness," 13.

23. *MED* "oule" n. def. 2b, s.v. "hare" def. 1d, and s.v. "gos" def. 3.

24. *MED* s.v. "thorn" def. c. A less vulgar reading may be implied by analogy to Criseyde's fresh infatuation: "she hath now kaught a thorn, / She shal nat pulle it out this nexte wyke. / God sende mo swich thornes on to pike" (*Troilus and Criseyde*, II, 1272–1274).

25. *MED* s.v. "nail" n. def. 1d.

26. The meaning of "lowcray" is elusive. Maxwell S. Luria and Richard L. Hoffman suggest "striped cloth (?)" (*Middle English Lyrics*, 72). The two "templers," which are "a pair of ornamental bosses, often bejeweled, used to enclose hair coiled at the temple" (*MED* s.v. "templer" pl.), might also be envisioned as the color of a "locker" or a "latch" (*MED* s.v. "locre"). "Mudbug" for "low crayfish" (*MED* s.v. "crevise") provides the most insulting possibility.

27. *MED* s.v. "appropren" v. def. 1b.

28. *MED* s.v. "bobrelle" n. "The clitoris or the lips of the vulva."

29. *MED* s.v. "pose" n. and s.v. "pip(pe" n.

30. *MED* s.v. "navel(e" n. and s.v. "water-gate" n.(2) def. 1b) for medical sense;

cf. *OED* defs. 2b and 3 for later slang. Chaucer provides two possibly relevant references to a weir as a possible translation of this "watergate" (*MED wer(e* n. def. 1a "An obstruction or a barrier placed across a stream"): one refers to the gate of hell where the damned like dried-out fish are trapped (*Parlement of Foules*, 138); the other, in supposed praise of Venus, compares the randomness of falling in love to catching a fish (*Troilus and Criseyde*, III, 35).

31. *MED* s.v. "bruche" n. defs. 1 and 2.
32. *MED* s.v. "les(e" adj.
33. *MED* s.v. "druerie" n.
34. Lewis J. Owen ("Thrush and the Nightingale") defends assigning lines 94–96 to the Thrush rather than to the Nightingale in order to maintain their alternation of stanzaic speeches.
35. *MED* s.v. "hasel" n. def. 2b.
36. The *OED* provides no record of the slang idiom before 1586.
37. Reed, *Middle English Debate Poetry*, 208.
38. Margherita, *Romance of Origins*, 74.
39. Fein, "Lyrics of MS Harley 2253," 4176.
40. Fein, *Complete Harley*, vol. 2, 404.
41. *MED* s.v. "brech" n., and s.v. "bruche" n. def. 2b, and s.v. "spouse-brech(e" n.
42. *MED* s.v. "werken" v.(1) def. 12c and def. 3e.
43. *MED* s.v. "riden" v. def. 9.
44. *MED* s.v. "mode."
45. *MED* s.v. "temen" v. (1) def. 2a and def. 1a.
46. *MED* s.v. "broun" adj. def. 5. and defs. 1a and b.
47. *MED* s.v. "werpen" v.
48. *MED* s.v. "casten" v.
49. *MED* s.v. "hired" defs. 1a and 3a.
50. *MED* s.v. "reden" v. defs. 8a and b.
51. Turville-Petre, *Alliterative Poetry*, 23 nn. 61–72. E. G. Stanley ("Richard Hyrd (?)") has suggested that "hyrd" (l. 67) be considered part of a Richard's proper name, and Carter Revard ("Hurd in MS. Harley 2253") identified a contemporary tanner so named living in Ludlow.
52. Ransom, *Poets at Play*, 25.

EIGHT The Early Modern Machining of Verse

1. Eliot, "Tradition and the Individual Talent," 44.
2. Mason, *Humanism and Poetry*, 155.
3. Nelson, "Lyric Value," 136.
4. Nelson, "Lyric Value," 38.

5. In reference to the precedent evolution of medieval French versification, Steven Guthrie considers an analogous shift in prosodic expectations: "Another possibility, pure conjecture but worth mentioning is that manuscript circulation ... had an impact on the line that oral transmission alone would not have had ... Rhythmic experimentation increases perhaps because the access of poets to written verse increases" ("Meter and Performance," 81).

6. Lewis, *English Literature in the Sixteenth Century*, 237.

7. Grossman, "Dance of the Intellect," 262.

8. Grossman, "Dance of the Intellect," 271.

9. Geoffrey de Vinsauf (ca. 1210) contended that accentuation during a recital should be the same in verse or prose (Parr, *Geoffrey de Vinsauf's "Poetria Nova,"* 94–95).

10. Mutatis mutandis, regarding the debate as to whether or not Chaucer wrote true pentameters, James I. Wimsatt argues "it is reasonable to maintain ... that whatever conclusion one arrives at on the matter of stress, one can speak of Chaucer's having successfully created a version of the French natural music in English" (*Chaucer and His French Contemporaries*, 289).

11. George Saintsbury concedes only that "there are sometimes tolerable lines, the better being usually in Occleve" (*History of English Prosody*, vol. 1, 234).

12. Mitchell, *Thomas Hoccleve*, 97.

13. Sobecki, *Last Words*, 99.

14. Burrow, *Thomas Hoccleve's Complaint and Dialogue*, xxix.

15. Mitchell, *Thomas Hoccleve*, 109.

16. Duffell, *A New History of English Metre*, 100–102.

17. All citations of the poem are from Charles R. Blyth's edition of Thomas Hoccleve, *The Regiment of Princes*.

18. Joyce Coleman borrows the term "prelection" from "John of Salisbury, who borrowed it from Quintillian ... It is a slightly and hopefully permissible extension of meaning to include reading aloud within domestic and other settings as well" (*Public Reading and the Reading Public*, 35).

19. The position of Hoccleve's presentation portrait (BL MS Royal 17. D. vi, f. 40r) in the middle of the text encourages seeing the following "Observanda" as a discrete text.

20. Although an apostrophe to the book is quite conventional for such an envoi, Hoccleve's conceit of his book approaching the King "Unclothid sauf thy kirtil bare also" (5445) is not. Does Hoccleve imagine this "Bare tunic" to be a blank book cover (i.e., fly leaves without a leather cover)?

21. Chaucer had provided Hoccleve with some precedent rhyming extravagance in English with "To Rosemunde," "Womanly Noblesse," "Truth," "Gentilesse," "Lak of Stedfatnesse," "Against Woman Unconstant," and "Complaint to his

Purse," all of which use only three rhymes throughout three rhyme-royal stanzas. The overall rhyme schemes of these ballades all remain conspicuously audible, however. So, too, the six six-line stanzas of the "Lenvoy de Chaucer" at the end of "The Clerk's Tale" (*Canterbury Tales*, IV, 1177–1212), all rhyming ababcb (a sort of clipped tail-rhyme), anticipates Hoccleve's contrived rhyme play while remaining aurally perceptible.

22. Saintsbury, *History of English Prosody*, vol. 1, 233.

23. See Helen Barr's *Transporting Chaucer* for the further significance of Chaucer's portraits as manicules, again presupposing an individual reader's visual access to the lines being so indicated.

24. Duffell, *New History of English Metre*, 208.

25. The *Oxford English Dictionary* cites the proper title of *Tottel's Miscellany*—that is, *Songes and Sonnettes* (1557)—as the first use of the term *sonnet* in English; the OED notes, however, that Tottel's title may preserve a rare and obsolete usage of the word to denote only "a short poem or piece of verse; in early use esp. one of a lyrical and amatory character" (def. 2). Nevertheless, the definition of "sonnet" had become sufficiently fixed by 1575 that George Gascoigne's *Certain Notes of Instruction*—which serves as the OED's second earliest citation of "sonnet"—still functions as a clear description of the "English sonnet" (that is, three pentameter quatrains and a couplet). Gascoigne does, however, recollect the etymology of *sonetto* as "little song" and acknowledges the close association of the term *sonnet* with both the ballade and the rhyme-royal stanzaic patterns. Conversely, Peter Hyland has observed, "Rhyme royal echoes the structure of the sonnet" (*Introduction to Shakespeare's Poems*, 189).

26. Scattergood, "Love Lyric before Chaucer," 44.

27. Butterfield, "Medieval Lyric," 152.

28. It seems that the much-maligned editor John Urry was first to annotate that Troilus's song was based on Petrarch's sonnet in his 1721 edition.

29. Fulton, "Introduction," 5.

30. Analogously, blank verse comes to be considered the stichic equivalent in English of the quantitative (dactylic hexameter) line in Greek or Latin epic.

31. Only the final "maladië/dyë" (I, 419–20) couplet of Chaucer's translation of Petrarch's *Rima* 132 needs to be scanned as feminine rhyme.

32. Perhaps an echo of John 4:13–14, which would add a moralistic note of remorse to the erotic frustration.

33. Gray, "Songs and Lyrics," 97.

34. Chaucer's transformation of Petrarch's sonnet thus closely mirrors Boccaccio's three ottava *rima* stanzas given Troilo's equivalent complaint (*il Filostrato*, II, sts. 58–60).

35. Wimsatt, *Chaucer and His French Contemporaries*, 145.

36. Petrarch's project of revising and reordering the final autograph copy of the *Rerum vulgarium fragmenta* (BAV MS 3195) continued until his death in 1374. All quotations of Petrarch's sonnets follow Robert M. Durling's edition of *Rime Sparse,* and all quotations of Wyatt's and Surrey's sonnets follow Amanda Holton and Tom MacFaul's edition of *Tottel's Miscellany* (using the punctuation of the Q2 edition).

37. Benson, *Riverside Chaucer,* xixb.

38. Clarke, *Chaucer and Italian Textuality,* 4.

39. Gray, "Middle English Courtly Lyrics," 148. For example, "I am as I am and so I will be," a late amorous carol (ten quatrains, lacking refrain) was once plausibly attributed to Sir Thomas Wyatt.

40. Boffey, "Manuscripts of English Courtly Lyrics," 81.

41. Amanda Holton explains in far more detail how "in many respects . . . *Tottel's Miscellany* has very different interests from Chaucer, and both passively and actively takes issue with his work. In particular, it withstands his sympathetic engagement of women" (Holton, "Chaucer's Presence," 109).

42. Boffey, "Early Printers and English Lyrics," 25. Because of the Egerton manuscript's subsequent use as a commonplace book, the pages preserving Wyatt's lyrics often look like a hot mess. Such reuse of the manuscript's blank space suggests a certain disregard even for authorial copies of the poems after seemingly more definitive versions became available in print—a disregard that long extended to all manuscript records of Middle English lyrics as well.

43. *Odes* III. 2. 13. Cf. Wilfred Owen's bitterly sarcastic appropriation of Horace's full line that concludes "Dulce et decorum est."

44. The *OED* s.v. "Petrarchan" (adj. and n.), def. a cites no instances of this now commonly so labeled distinction between the Petrarchan (or Italian) 8/6 sonnet form and the English (or Shakespearian) 4/4/4/2 sonnet form prior to 1887.

45. Nevertheless, "as one progresses through *Songes and Sonettes* from the first to the last poem, the formal integrity of the anthology is manifest" (Marquis, "Printing History," 20).

46. Marquis, "Printing History," 15.

47. Cf. the prologue to *Pericles, Prince of Tyre* (thought to be a collaboration of Shakespeare and George Wilkins), spoken by a resurrected John Gower (the primary source of this play's plot) wherein the supposed superiority of early modern compositional skills is acknowledged: "If you, born in these later times, / When wit's more ripe, accept my rhymes" (I, Prol., 11–12).

48. Eliot, "Tradition and the Individual Talent," 37.

49. Cf. Hamlet's sarcasm in "Is this a prologue, or the posy of a ring?" (III, ii, 162).

50. Cf. Andrew Marvell's "thirty thousand to the rest" ("To His Coy Mistress," l. 16).

51. Cf. Chaucer's reference to "open-ers," the fruit of the medlar tree, in "The Reeve's Tale"—fruit that, like old men, "til we be roten, kan we nat be rype" (*Canterbury Tales*, I, 3871–3875).

52. Wimsatt, *Verbal Icon*, x.

53. Jackson, *Dickinson's Misery*, 8.

54. Tennant, "Introduction."

55. Irmscher, *Longfellow Redux*, 3, 17, and 71.

56. Bowden, *Performed Literature*.

57. Burt, "Response," 367.

WORKS CITED

Abel, Patricia. "The Cleric, the Kitchie Boy and the Returned Sailor." *Philological Quarterly* 44 (1965): 552–555.
Addison, Catherine. "Little Boxes: The Effects of the Stanza on Poetic Narrative." *Style* 37 (2003): 124–143.
Allen, Judson Boyce. "Grammar, Poetic Form, and the Lyric Ego: A Medieval *A Priori*." In *Studies in Medieval Culture*, vol. 16, edited by Lois Ebin, 199–226. Kalamazoo: Western Michigan University Press, Medieval Institute Publications, 1984.
Arn, Mary-Jo. "On Punctuating Medieval Literary Texts." *Text* 7 (1994): 161–174.
Arn, Mary-Jo. "Two Manuscripts, One Mind: Charles d'Orléans and the Production of Manuscripts in Two Languages (Paris, BN MS fr. 25458 and London, BL MS Harley 682)." In *Charles d'Orléans in England, 1415–1440*, edited by Mary-Jo Arn, 61–78. Cambridge: D. S. Brewer, 2000.
Askins, William. "The Brothers Orléans and Their Keepers." In *Charles d'Orléans in England, 1415–1440*, edited by Mary-Jo Arn, 27–46. Cambridge: D. S. Brewer, 2000.
Astell, Ann W. *Song of Songs in the Middle Ages*. Ithaca, NY: Cornell University Press, 1995.
Austin, J. L. *How to Do Things with Words*. Oxford: Clarendon Press, 1962.
Baden-Daintree, Anne. "Voice and Response: Lyric Rewriting of the Song of Songs." In *Middle English Lyrics: New Readings of Short Poems*, edited by Julia Boffey and Christiania Whitehead, 141–157. Woodbridge, UK: Boydell and Brewer, 2018.
Baechle, Sarah, and Carissa Harris with Elizaveta Strakhov. "Reassessing the Pastourelle Rape Culture, #MeToo, and the Literature of Survival." In *Rape Culture and Female Resistance in Late Medieval Literature*, edited by Sarah Baechle, Carissa M. Harris, and Elizaveta Strakhov, 17–28. University Park: Penn State University Press, 2022.
Baird-Lange, Lorrayne Y. "Symbolic Ambivalence in 'I have a gentil cok.'" *Fifteenth-Century Studies* 11 (1985): 1–5.
Barr, Helen. *Transporting Chaucer*. Manchester: Manchester University Press, 2014.

Bennett, J.A.W. *Middle English Literature*. Edited and completed by Douglas Gray. OHEL Vol. 1, Part 2. Oxford: Clarendon Press, 1986.

Best, Stephen, and Sharon Marcus. "Surface Reading: An Introduction." *Representations* 108 (2009): C–21.

Boffey, Julia. "Early Printers and English Lyrics: Sources, Selection and Presentation of Texts." *Papers of the Bibliographical Society of America* 85 (1991): 11–26.

Boffey, Julia. "The Manuscripts of English Courtly Love Lyrics in the Fifteenth Century." In *Manuscripts and Readers in Fifteenth-Century England: The Literary Implications of Manuscript Study*, edited by Derek Pearsall, 3–14. Cambridge: D. S. Brewer, 1983.

Boffey, Julia. *Manuscripts of English Courtly Love in the Later Middle Ages*. Woodbridge, UK: D. S. Brewer, 1985.

Boffey, Julia. "What to Call a Lyric? Middle English Lyrics and Their Manuscript Titles." *Revue Belge de Philologie et d'Histoire* 83 (2005): 671–683.

Boffey, Julia, and A.S.G. Edwards. "Middle English Lyrics and Manuscripts." In *A Companion to the Middle English Lyric*, edited by Thomas G. Duncan, 1–18. Cambridge: D. S. Brewer, 2005.

Boffey, Julia, and A.S.G. Edwards. *A New Index of Middle English Verse*. London: British Library, 2005.

Boklund-Lagopoulou, Karin. "'Judas': The First English Ballad?" *Medium Ævum* 62 (1993): 20–34.

Boquet, Damien, and Piroska Nagy. *Medieval Sensibilities: A History of Emotions in the Middle Ages*. Translated by Robert Shaw. Cambridge: Polity Press, 2018.

Bowden, Betsy. *Performed Literature: Words and Music by Bob Dylan*. Bloomington: Indiana University Press, 1982.

Breeze, Andrew. "Middle English *Cammede* 'Bow-Legged' in 'Swart Smekyd Smethes.'" *Notes and Queries* 239 (1994): 148–150.

Brewer, Derek. *English Gothic Literature*. New York: Schocken Books, 1983.

Brown, Carleton, and Rossell Hope Robbins. *The Index of Middle English Verse*. New York: Columbia University Press, 1943.

Brunner, Karl. "Kirchenlieder aus dem 15. Jahrhundert." *Anglia* 61 (1937): 138–151.

Burger, Glenn, and Holly Crocker, eds. *Medieval Affect, Feeling, and Emotion*. Cambridge: Cambridge University Press, 2019.

Burrow, J. A. *Essays on Medieval Literature*. Oxford: Clarendon Press, 1984.

Burrow, J. A., ed. *Thomas Hoccleve's Complaint and Dialogue*. Oxford: Oxford University Press for Early English Text Society, 1999.

Burrow, J. A. *Medieval Writers and Their Work: Middle English Literature and Its Background, 1100–1500*. Oxford: Oxford University Press, 1982.

Burt, Stephanie. "Response: *Hevy Hameres*." In *What Kind of a Thing Is a Middle*

English Lyric?, edited by Cristina Maria Cervone and Nicholas Watson, 355–369. Philadelphia: University of Pennsylvania Press, 2022.

Burt, Stephen. "What Is This Thing Called Lyric?" *Modern Philology* 113 (2016): 422–440.

Butterfield, Ardis. "Lyric Editing." In *What Kind of a Thing Is a Middle English Lyric?*, edited by Cristina Maria Cervone and Nicholas Watson, 30–60. Philadelphia: University of Pennsylvania Press, 2022.

Butterfield, Ardis. "Medieval Lyric: A Translatable or Untranslatable Zone?" *University of Toronto Quarterly* 8 (2019): 142–159.

Butterfield, Ardis. "Poems without Form? 'Maiden in the mor lay' Revisited." In *Readings in Medieval Textuality: Essays in Honour of A. C. Spearing*, edited by Cristina Maria Cervone and D. Vance Smith, 169–195. Woodbridge, UK: Boydell and Brewer, 2016.

Butterfield, Ardis. "Why Medieval Lyric?" *ELH* 82 (2015): 319–343.

Cannon, Christopher. "Lyric Romance." In *What Kind of a Thing Is a Middle English Lyric?*, edited by Cristina Maria Cervone and Nicholas Watson, 88–105. Philadelphia: University of Pennsylvania Press, 2022.

Cervone, Cristina Maria. "Wondering through Middle English Lyric." In *What Kind of a Thing Is a Middle English Lyric?*, edited by Cristina Maria Cervone and Nicholas Watson, 61–87. Philadelphia: University of Pennsylvania Press, 2022.

Cervone, Cristina Maria, and Nicholas Watson. "Introduction. Why stonde we? why go we no3t?" In *What Kind of a Thing Is a Middle English Lyric?*, edited by Cristina Maria Cervone and Nicholas Watson, 1–29. Philadelphia: University of Pennsylvania Press, 2022.

Chickering, Howell. "Unpunctuating Chaucer." *Chaucer Review* 25 (1990): 96–109.

Child, Francis James, ed. *The English and Scottish Popular Ballads*. 5 vols. Boston: Houghton, Mifflin, 1882–1898.

Clarke, Kenneth P. *Chaucer and Italian Textuality*. Oxford: Oxford University Press, 2011.

Coleman, Joyce. *Public Reading and the Reading Public in Late Medieval England and France*. Cambridge: Cambridge University Press, 1996.

Copeland, Rita. *Emotion and the History of Rhetoric in the Middle Ages*. Oxford: Oxford University Press, 2022.

Cornelius, Ian. "Language and Meter." In *What Kind of a Thing Is a Middle English Lyric?*, edited by Cristina Maria Cervone and Nicholas Watson, 106–134. Philadelphia: University of Pennsylvania Press, 2022.

Crowther, J.D.W. "The Bargain of Judas." *English Language Notes* 13 (1975–1976): 245–249.

Crowther, J.D.W. "The Middle English Lyric 'Joly Jankyn.'" *Annuale Mediaeval* 12 (1971): 123–125.

Culler, Jonathan. "Lyric, History, and Genre." *New Literary History* 40 (2009): 879–899.

D'Arcy, Anne Marie. "'Written in gold upon a purple stain': Mariological Rhetoric and the Material Culture of Aureate Diction." In *Middle English Lyrics: New Readings of Short Poems*, edited by Julia Boffey and Christiania Whitehead, 109–121. Woodbridge, UK: Boydell and Brewer, 2018.

Davies, R. T., ed. *Medieval English Lyrics: A Critical Anthology*. London: Faber and Faber, 1963.

DeVun, Leah. *The Shape of Sex: Nonbinary Gender from Genesis to the Renaissance*. New York: Columbia University Press, 2020.

Donaldson, E. Talbot. "Patristic Exegesis in the Criticism of Medieval Literature." In *Selected Papers from the English Institute, 1958–1959*, edited by Dorothy Bethurum, 170–188. New York: Columbia University Press, 1960. Rpt. in E. Talbot Donaldson. *Speaking of Chaucer*. London: Athlone, 1970.

Dronke, Peter. *The Medieval Lyric*. 3rd ed. Woodbridge, UK: Boydell and Brewer, 1996.

Dronke, Peter. "The Song of Songs and Medieval Love-Lyric." In *The Bible and Medieval Culture*, edited by W. Lourdaux and D. Verhelst, 209–236. Mediaevalia Lavaniensia Series 1, Studia 7. Leuven: Leuven University Press, 1984.

Duffell, Martin J. *A New History of English Metre*. Legenda MHRA Studies in Linguistics 5. Leeds: Legenda, 2008.

Duffy, Eamon. *The Stripping of the Altars: Traditional Religion in England 1400–1580*. 2nd ed. New Haven, CT: Yale University Press, 2005. First published in 1992.

Duncan, Thomas G. "Editing Issues in Middle English Lyrics." In *Middle English Lyrics: New Readings of Short Poems*, edited by Julia Boffey and Christiania Whitehead, 12–27. Woodbridge, UK: Boydell and Brewer, 2018.

Duncan, Thomas G. "Introduction." In *A Companion to the Middle English Lyric*, edited by Thomas G. Duncan, xiii–xxv. Cambridge: D. S. Brewer, 2005.

Duncan, Thomas G. "'The Maid in the Moor' and the Rawlinson Text." *Review of English Studies*, n.s. 47 [186] (1996): 151–162.

Duncan, Thomas G. "Middle English Lyrics: Metre and Editorial Practice." In *A Companion to the Middle English Lyric*, edited by Thomas G. Duncan, 19–38. Cambridge: D. S. Brewer, 2005.

Durling, Robert M., ed. *Petrarch's Lyric Poems: The Rime Sparse and Other Lyrics*. Cambridge, MA: Harvard University Press, 1976.

Edwards, Robert R. *Ratio and Invention: A Study of Medieval Lyric and Narrative*. Nashville, TN: Vanderbilt University Press, 1989.

Eliot, T. S. "Tradition and the Individual Talent" [1919]. In *Selected Prose of T. S. Eliot*, edited by Frank Kermode, 37–44. New York: Harcourt Brace Jovanovich/Farrar, Straus and Giroux, 1975.

Fein, Susanna. "All Adam's Children: The Early Middle English Lyric Sequence in Oxford, Jesus College, MS 29." In *Middle English Lyrics: New Readings of Short Poems*, edited by Julia Boffey and Christiania Whitehead, 213–226. Woodbridge, UK: Boydell and Brewer, 2018.

Fein, Susanna. *The Complete Harley 2253 Manuscript*. 3 vols. Kalamazoo: Western Michigan University Press, Medieval Institute Publications, 2014–2015.

Fein, Susanna. "The Lyrics of MS Harley 2253." In *A Manual of Writings in Middle English, 1050–1500*, vol. 11, edited by Peter G. Beidler, 4168–4206, 4311–4361. New Haven: Connecticut Academy of Arts and Sciences, 2005.

Flannery, Mary C. "Tutivillus and the Policing of Speech in Oxford, Bodleian Library, MS Douce 104." In *Middle English Lyrics: New Readings of Short Poems*, edited by Julia Boffey and Christiania Whitehead, 240–250. Woodbridge, UK: Boydell and Brewer, 2018.

Fletcher, Alan J. "The Lyric in the Sermon." In *A Companion to the Middle English Lyric*, edited by Thomas G. Duncan, 189–194. Cambridge: D. S. Brewer, 2005.

Fowler, David C. *The Bible in Middle English Literature*. Seattle: University of Washington Press, 1984.

Franklin, Michael J. "'Fyngres heo hath feir to folde': *Trothplight* in Some of the Lyrics of MS Harley 2253." *Medium Ævum* 55 (1986): 176–187.

Fries, Maureen. "The 'Other' Voice: Woman's Song, Its Satire and Its Transcendence in Late Medieval British Literature." In *Vox Feminae: Studies in Medieval Woman's Songs*, edited by John F. Plummer, 155–178. Kalamazoo: Western Michigan University Press, Medieval Institute Publications, 1981.

Fulton, Helen. "Introduction." In *Chaucer and Italian Culture*, edited by Helen Fulton, 1–15. Cardiff: University of Wales Press, 2021.

Fussell, Paul. *Poetic Meter and Poetic Form*. New York: Random House, 1965.

Galloway, Andrew. "Theory of the Fourteenth-Century English Lyric." In *In What Kind of a Thing Is a Middle English Lyric?*, edited by Cristina Maria Cervone and Nicholas Watson, 303–341. Philadelphia: University of Pennsylvania Press, 2022.

Galyon, Anthony E., trans. *Matthew of Vendôme's "The Art of Versification"* [*Ars versificatoria*]. Ames: Iowa State University Press, 1980.

Gasparov, M. L. *A History of European Versification*. Oxford: Clarendon, 1996.

Gibbs, Raymond W., Jr. "Cognitive Poetics of Middle English Lyric Poetry." In *What Kind of a Thing Is a Middle English Lyric?*, edited by Cristina Maria Cervone and Nicholas Watson, 159–181. Philadelphia: University of Pennsylvania Press, 2022.

Gillespie, Vincent. "Moral and Penitential Lyrics." In *A Companion to the Middle English Lyric*, edited by Thomas G. Duncan, 68–95. Cambridge: D. S. Brewer, 2005.

Gravdal, Kathryn. *Ravishing Maidens: Writing Rape in Medieval French Literature and Law*. Philadelphia: University of Pennsylvania Press, 1991.

Gray, Douglas. "Middle English Courtly Lyrics: Chaucer to Henry VIII." In *A Companion to the Middle English Lyric*, edited by Thomas G. Duncan, 120–149. Cambridge: D. S. Brewer, 2005.

Gray, Douglas. "Songs and Lyrics." In *Literature in Fourteenth-Century England, The J. A. W. Bennet Memorial Lectures, Perugia, 1981–1982*, edited by Piero Boitani and Anna Torti, 83–98. Tubingen: Gunter Narr Verlag; Cambridge: D. S. Brewer, 1983.

Gray, Douglas. *Themes and Images in the Medieval English Religious Lyric*. London: Routledge and K. Paul, 1972.

Greene, Richard Leighton. "'The Maid of the Moor' in the Red Book of Ossory." *Speculum* 27 (1952): 504–506.

Greene, Richard Leighton. "The Meaning of the Corpus Christi Carol." *Medium Ævum* 29 (1960): 10–21.

Greene, Richard Leighton. "A Middle English 'Timor Mortis' Poem." *Modern Language Review* 28 (1933): 234–238.

Greentree, Rosemary. "Lyric." In *A Companion to Medieval English Literature and Culture, C. 1350–C. 1500*, edited by Peter Brown, 387–405. Blackwell Companions to Literature and Culture Series. Malden, MA: Blackwell, 2007.

Greentree, Rosemary. *The Middle English Lyric and Short Poem*, Vol. 7 of *Annotated Bibliographies of Old and Middle English Literature*. Cambridge: D. S. Brewer, 2001.

Grossman, Joel. "'The Dance of the Intellect among Words': Wyatt's *In eternum* and Late Medieval Lyric Practice." In *Middle English Lyrics: New Readings of Short Poems*, edited by Julia Boffey and Christiania Whitehead, 262–272. Woodbridge, UK: Boydell and Brewer, 2018.

Guthrie, Steven R. "Meter and Performance in Machaut and Chaucer." In *The Union of Words and Music in Medieval Poetry*, edited by Rebecca A. Baltzer, Thomas Cable, and James I. Wimsatt, 72–100. Austin: University of Texas Press, 1991.

Harris, Carissa M. "English and Scottish Pastourelles and Rape Songs." In *Rape Culture and Female Resistance in Late Medieval Literature*, edited by Sarah Baechle, Carissa M. Harris, and Elizaveta Strakhov, 183–246. University Park: Penn State University Press, 2022.

Harris, Carissa M. *Obscene Pedagogies: Transgressive Talk and Sexual Education in Late Medieval Britain*. Ithaca, NY: Cornell University Press, 2018.

Harris, Joseph. "'Maiden in the Mor Lay' and the Medieval Magdalene Tradition." *Journal of Medieval and Renaissance Studies* 1 (1971): 59–87.
Heffernan, Thomas J. "Four Middle English Lyrics from the Thirteenth Century." *Medieval Studies* 43 (1981): 131–150.
Helterman, Jeffrey. "The Antagonistic Voices of 'Sumer is Icumen In.'" *Tennessee Studies in Literature* 18 (1973): 13–17.
Holton, Amanda. "Chaucer's Presence in *Songes and Sonettes*." In *Tottel's "Songes and Sonettes" in Context*, edited by Stephen Hamrick, 87–109. Farnham, UK: Ashgate, 2013.
Holton, Amanda, and Tom MacFaul, eds. *Tottel's Miscellany: Songs and Sonnets of Henry Howard, Earl of Surrey, Sir Thomas Wyatt and Others*. New York: Penguin Classics, 2011.
Hoppin, Richard H. *Medieval Music*. New York: Norton, 1978.
Howes, Hetta Elizabeth. "'Adreynt in shennesse': Blood, Shame and Contrition in 'Quis est iste qui uenit de Edom?'" In *Middle English Lyrics: New Readings of Short Poems*, edited by Julia Boffey and Christiania Whitehead, 87–98. Woodbridge, UK: Boydell and Brewer, 2018.
Hyland, Peter. *An Introduction to Shakespeare's Poems*. New York: Palgrave Macmillan, 2003.
Irmscher, Christoph. *Longfellow Redux*. Urbana: University of Illinois Press, 2006.
Jackson, Virginia. *Dickinson's Misery: A Theory of Lyric Reading*. Princeton, NJ: Princeton University Press, 205.
Jeffrey, David Lyle. *The Early English Lyric and Franciscan Spirituality*. Lincoln: University of Nebraska Press, 1975.
Johnson, Eleanor. "England, Poetry of II. Middle English, 1066–1500." In *Princeton Encyclopedia of Poetry and Poetics*, 4th ed., edited by Roland Greene et al., 411–414. Princeton, NJ: Princeton University Press, 2012.
Johnson, Eleanor. *Practicing Literary Theory*. Chicago: University of Chicago Press, 2013.
Johnson, Samuel. "Life of Dryden" from *Lives of the Poets*. 13 October 2009. Poetry Foundation. www.poetryfoundation.org/articles/69382/from-lives-of-the-poets
Jones, Natalie. "'Ihesus woundes so wide and the fons vitae': Text, Image and the Manuscript Context." In *Middle English Lyrics: New Readings of Short Poems*, edited by Julia Boffey and Christiania Whitehead, 99–108. Woodbridge, UK: Boydell and Brewer, 2018.
Kane, George. "A Short Essay on the Middle English Secular Lyric." *Neuphilologische Mitteilungen* 73 (1972): 110–121.
Kerby-Fulton, Kathryn. "Making the Early Middle Hiberno-English Lyric: Mysteries, Experiments, and Survivals before 1330." *Early Middle English* 2, no. 2 (2020): 1–26.

Kessel-Brown, Deidre. "The Emotional Landscape of the Forest in the Mediaeval Love Lament." *Medium Ævum* 59, no. 2 (1990): 228–245.

Klinck, Anne L. *The Voices of Medieval English Lyric: An Anthology of Poems, ca. 1150–1530.* Montreal: McGill-Queen's University Press, 2019.

Kuczynski, Michael P. "Theological Sophistication and the Middle English Religious Lyric: A Polemic." *Chaucer Review* 45 (2011): 321–339.

Kuczynski, Michael P. "Textual and Affective Stability in 'All Other Love Is Like the Moon.'" In *Middle English Lyrics: New Readings of Short Poems*, edited by Julia Boffey and Christiania Whitehead, 57–69. Woodbridge, UK: Boydell and Brewer, 2018.

Kumler, Adam. "Lyric Vessels." In *What Kind of a Thing Is a Middle English Lyric?*, edited by Cristina Maria Cervone and Nicholas Watson, 182–217. Philadelphia: University of Pennsylvania Press, 2022.

Landis, John, dir. *National Lampoon's Animal House.* Universal City, CA: Universal Pictures, 1978.

Lawler, Traugott, trans. and ed. *The Parisiana Poetria of John of Garland.* New Haven, CT: Yale University Press, 1974.

Lawton, David. *Voice in Later Medieval English Literature: Public Interiorities.* Oxford: Oxford University Press, 2017.

Lazikani, A. S. "Moving Lights: An Affective Reading of 'On leome is in þis world ilist' and Church Wall Paintings." In *Middle English Lyrics: New Readings of Short Poems*, edited by Julia Boffey and Christiania Whitehead, 31–44. Woodbridge, UK: Boydell and Brewer, 2018.

Lecouteux, Claude. *Dictionary of Ancient Magic Words and Spells from Abraxas to Zoar.* Translated by Jon E. Graham. Rochester: Inner Traditions, 2015. Published by Éditions Imago in 2014.

Lehman, Robert S. "Formalism, Mere Form, and Judgment." *New Literary History* 48 (2017): 245–263.

Lerer, Seth. *Chaucer and His Readers.* Princeton, NJ: Princeton University Press, 1993.

Lerer, Seth. "The Endurance of Formalism in Middle English Studies." *Literature Compass* 1 (2003): 1–15.

Levinson, Marjorie. "What Is New Formalism?" *PMLA* 122 (2007): 558–569.

Lewis, C. S. *English Literature in the Sixteenth Century, Excluding Drama.* Oxford: Clarendon Press, 1954.

Luria, Maxwell Sidney, and Richard L. Hoffman, eds. *Middle English Lyrics.* New York: Norton, 1974.

MacDonald, A. A. "Lyrics in Middle Scots." In *A Companion to the Middle English Lyric*, edited by Thomas G. Duncan, 242–261. Cambridge: D. S. Brewer, 2005.

Manning, Stephen. "Game and Earnest in the Middle English and Provençal Love Lyrics." *Comparative Literature* 18 (1966): 225–241.

Manning, Stephen. "I Syng of a Myden." *PMLA* 75 (1960): 8–12.

Manning, Stephen. "'Sumer Is Icumen In.'" *Explicator* 17 (1958): item 2.

Manning, Stephen. *Wisdom and Number: Toward a Critical Appraisal of the Middle English Religious Lyric*. Lincoln: University of Nebraska Press, 1962.

Margherita, Gayle. *The Romance of Origins: Language and Sexual Difference in Middle English Literature*. Philadelphia: University of Pennsylvania Press, 1994.

Marquis, Paul A. "Printing History and Editorial Design in the Elizabethan Version of Tottel's *Songes and Sonettes*." In *Tottel's "Songes and Sonettes" in Context*, edited by Stephen Hamrick, 13–36. Farnham, UK: Ashgate, 2013.

Marshall, Helen, and Peter Buchanan. "New Formalism and the Forms of Middle English Literary Texts." *Literature Compass* 8 (2011): 164–172.

Mason, H. A. *Humanism and Poetry in the Early Tudor Period: An Essay*. London: Routledge, 1959.

McCann, Daniel. "Blood and Chocolate: Affective Layering in 'Swete Ihesu, now wil I synge.'" In *Middle English Lyrics: New Readings of Short Poems*, edited by Julia Boffey and Christiania Whitehead, 45–56. Woodbridge, UK: Boydell and Brewer, 2018.

McNamer, Sarah. *Affective Meditation and the Invention of Medieval Compassion*. Philadelphia: University of Pennsylvania Press, 2010.

Mitchell, Jerome. *Thomas Hoccleve; a Study in Early Fifteenth-Century English Poetic*. Urbana: University of Illinois Press, 1968.

Mooney, Linne R., Daniel W. Mosser, and Elizabeth Solopova. The DIMEV: An Open Access, Digital Edition of the *Index of Middle English Verse*. Accessed 12 February 2025. www.dimev.net/

Mooney, Linne R. "A Late Fifteenth-Century Woman's Revision of Chaucer's 'Against Women Unconstant' and Other Poems by the Same Hand." *Chaucer Review* 34 (2000): 344–349.

Moore, Arthur Keister. *The Secular Lyric in Middle English*. Lexington: University of Kentucky Press, 1951.

Murton, Megan E. *Chaucer's Prayers: Writing Christian and Pagan Devotion*. Woodbridge, UK: D. S. Brewer, 2020.

Nagy, Piroska, and Damien Boquet. "Historical Emotions, Historians' Emotions" (translated by Greg Robinson). Hypotheses. Accessed 13 February 2025. https://emma.hypotheses.org/1213. Originally published as "Émotions historiques, émotions historiennes." *Écrire l'histoire* 2 (2008): 15–26.

Nelson, Ingrid. "Lyric Value." In *What Kind of a Thing Is a Middle English Lyric?*, edited by Cristina Maria Cervone and Nicholas Watson, 135–158. Philadelphia: University of Pennsylvania Press, 2022.

O'Donoghue, Bernard. "'*Cuius Contrarium*': Middle English Popular Lyrics." In *A Companion to the Middle English Lyric*, edited by Thomas G. Duncan, 210–226. Cambridge: D. S. Brewer, 2005.

Oliver, Raymond. *Poems without Names: The English Lyric, 1200–1500*. Berkeley: University of California Press, 1970.

Olson, Glending. "Deschamps' 'Art de Dictier' and Chaucer's Literary Environment." *Speculum* 48 (1973): 714–723.

Olson, Glending. *Literature as Recreation in the Later Middle Ages*. Ithaca, NY: Cornell University Press, 1982.

Olson, Glending. "Toward a Poetics of the Late Medieval Court Lyric." In *Vernacular Poetics in the Middle Ages*, edited by Lois Ebin, 227–48. Kalamazoo: Western Michigan University Press, Medieval Institute Publications, 1984.

Ong, Walter J. "Wit and Mystery: A Revaluation in Mediaeval Latin Hymnody." *Speculum* 22 (1947): 310–341.

Osberg, Richard H. "The Alliterative Lyric and Thirteenth-Century Devotional Prose." *Journal of English and Germanic Philology* 76 (1977): 40–54.

Osberg, Richard H. "Alliterative Technique in the Lyrics of MS Harley 2253." *Modern Philology* 82 (1984): 125–155.

Owen, Lewis J. "'The Thrush and the Nightingale': The Speaker in Lines 94–96." *English Language Notes* 7 (1969–1970): 1–6.

Paden, William D., ed. *Medieval Lyric: Genres in Historical Context*. Urbana: University of Illinois Press, 2000.

Parr, Roger P., trans. *Geoffrey de Vinsauf's "Poetria Nova: Documentum de modo et arte dictandi et versificandi."* Milwaukee, WI: Marquette University Press, 1968.

Perkins, Nicholas. "'Musing on Mutability,' A Poem in the Welles Anthology and Hoccleve's *The Regement of Princes*." *Review of English Studies* 50 (1999): 493–498.

Plummer, John F. "The Woman's Song in Middle English and Its European Backgrounds." In *Vox Feminae: Studies in Medieval Woman's Songs*, edited by John F. Plummer, 135–154. Kalamazoo: Western Michigan University Press, Medieval Institute Publications, 1981.

Pugh, Tison. *Queering Medieval Genres*. New York: Palgrave Macmillan, 2004.

Putter, Ad. "The English Poetry of a Frenchman: Stress and Idiomaticity in Charles d'Orléans." In *Charles d'Orléans' English Aesthetic: The Form, Poetics, and Style of Fortunes Stabilnes*, edited by R. D. Perry and Mary-Jo Arn, 145–168. Woodbridge, UK: Boydell and Brewer, 2020.

Ransom, Daniel J. "'Annot and John' and the Ploys of Parody." *Studies in Philology* 75 (1978): 121–141.

Ransom, Daniel J. *Poets at Play: Irony and Parody in the Harley Lyrics*. Norman, OK: Pilgrim Books, 1985.

Ransom, John Crowe. *The New Criticism*. Norfolk, CT: New Directions, 1941.
Raw, Barbara C. "'As Dew in Aprille.'" *Modern Language Review* 55 (1960): 411–414.
Reddy, William M. "Emotional Liberty: Politics and History in the Anthropology of Emotions." *Cultural Anthropology* 14 (1999): 256–288.
Reddy, William M. *The Navigation of Feeling: A Framework for the History of Emotions*. Cambridge: Cambridge University Press, 2001.
Reed, Thomas L. *Middle English Debate Poetry and the Aesthetics of Irresolution*. Columbia: University of Missouri Press, 1990.
Reichl, Karl. "Popular Poetry and Courtly Lyric: The Middle English Pastourelle." *REAL* 5 (1987): 33–61.
Reiss, Edmund. *The Art of the Middle English Lyric: Essays in Criticism*. Athens: University of Georgia Press, 1972.
Revard, Carter. "Hurd in MS. Harley 2253." *Notes and Queries* 224 (1979): 199–202.
Richards, I. A. *Practical Criticism*. London: R. and K. Paul, 1956.
Ringler, William A., Jr. *Bibliography and Index of English Verse in Manuscript, 1501–1558*. London: Mansell, 1992–1993.
Robbins, Harry Wolcott. "An English Version of *St. Edmund's Speculum*, Ascribed to Richard Rolle." *PMLA* 40 (1925): 240–225.
Robbins, Rossell Hope. *The Encyclopedia of Witchcraft and Demonology*. New York: Crown Publishers, 1959.
Robbins, Rossell Hope. "The Middle English Court Love Lyric." In *The Interpretation of Medieval Lyric Poetry*, edited by W.T.H. Jackson, 205–232. New York: Columbia University Press, 1980.
Robbins, Rossell Hope, ed. *Secular Lyrics of the XIVth and XVth Centuries*. Oxford: Clarendon Press, 1952.
Robbins, Rossell Hope. "Two Satirical Love Epistles." *Modern Language Review* 37 (1942): 415–421.
Robbins, Rossell Hope, and John L. Cutler. *A Supplement to the Index of Middle English Verse*. Lexington: University of Kentucky Press, 1965.
Robertson, D. W., Jr. "Historical Criticism." In *English Institute Essays 1950*, edited by A. S. Downer, 3–31. New York: Columbia University Press, 1951. Rpt. New York: AMS, 1965.
Roscow, G. H. "What Is 'Sumer Is Icumen In'?" *Review of English Studies* 198 (1999): 188–195.
Rosenfeld, Jessica. *Ethics and Enjoyment in Late Medieval Poetry: Love after Aristotle*. Cambridge: Cambridge University Press, 2011.
Rosenwein, Barbara H. *Generations of Feeling: A History of Emotions, 600–1700*. Cambridge: Cambridge University Press, 2016.
Saetveit Miles, Laura. *The Virgin Mary's Book at the Annunciation: Reading, Inter-

pretation, and Devotion in Medieval England. Woodbridge, UK: Boydell and Brewer, 2020.

Saintsbury, George. *A History of English Prosody from the Twelfth Century to the Present Day.* 2 vols. New York: Macmillan, 1906–1910.

Salter, Elizabeth. *Fourteenth-Century English Poetry: Contexts and Readings.* Oxford: Clarendon Press, 1983.

Saupe, Karen, ed. *Middle English Marian Lyrics.* Kalamazoo: Western Michigan University Press, Medieval Institute Publications, 1997.

Scattergood, John. "The Love Lyric before Chaucer." In *A Companion to the Middle English Lyric,* edited by Thomas G. Duncan, 39–67. Cambridge: D. S. Brewer, 2005.

Schueler, Donald G. "The Middle English 'Judas': An Interpretation." *PMLA* 91 (1976): 840–845.

Sisam, Kenneth. *Fourteenth Century Verse and Prose.* Oxford, 1921.

Smith, Jeremy. "Charles d'Orléans and His Finding of English." In *Charles d'Orléans' English Aesthetic: The Form, Poetics, and Style of Fortunes Stabilnes,* edited by R. D. Perry and Mary-Jo Arn, 189–220. Woodbridge, UK: Boydell and Brewer, 2020.

Sobecki, Sebastian. *Last Words: The Public Self and the Social Author in Late Medieval England.* Oxford: Oxford University Press, 2020.

Spearing, A. C. *Textual Subjectivity: The Encoding of Subjectivity in Medieval Narratives and Lyrics.* Oxford: Oxford University Press, 2005.

Speirs, John. *Medieval English Poetry: The Non-Chaucerian Tradition.* London: Faber and Faber, 1957.

Stanbury, Sarah. "Gender and Voice in Middle English Religious Lyrics." In *A Companion to the Middle English Lyric,* edited by Thomas G. Duncan, 227–241. Cambridge: D. S. Brewer, 2005.

Stanley, E. G. "Richard Hyrd (?), 'Rote of Resoun Ryht' in MS. Harley 2253." *Notes and Queries* 220 (1975): 155–157.

Steffes, Michael. "'As Dewe in Aprylle': 'I Syng of a Mayden' and the Liturgy." *Medium Ævum* 71 (2002): 66–73.

Stevens, John. "Medieval Music and Lyrics." In *The New Pelican Guide to English Literature, Part One: Chaucer and the Alliterative Tradition,* edited by Boris Ford, 248–276. Harmondsworth, UK: Penguin Books, 1982.

Stevens, John. *Music and Poetry in the Early Tudor Court.* New York: Cambridge University Press, 1979.

Stevens, John. "The 'Music' of the Lyric: Machaut, Deschamps, Chaucer." In *Medieval and Pseudo-Medieval Literature,* edited by Piero Boitano and Anna Torti, 109–129. Tubingen: Narr, 1984.

Stevens, John. *Words and Music in the Middle Ages: Song, Narrative, Dance and Drama, 1050–1350*. Cambridge: Cambridge University Press, 1986.
Stone, Brian. *Medieval English Verse*. London: Penguin Books, 1964.
Stouck, Mary-Ann. "A Reading of the Middle English 'Judas.'" *Journal of English and Germanic Philology* 80 (1981): 188–198.
Tennant, Neil. "Introduction." In *One Hundred Lyrics and a Poem: 1979–2016*. London: Faber & Faber, 2019.
Turville-Petre, Thorlac. *Alliterative Poetry of the Later Middle Ages: An Anthology*. Washington, DC: Catholic University of America Press, 1989.
Turville-Petre, Thorlac. "Political Lyrics." In *A Companion to the Middle English Lyric*, edited by Thomas G. Duncan, 171–188. Cambridge: D. S. Brewer, 2005.
Utley, Francis Lee. *The Crooked Rib: An Analytical Index to the Argument about Women in English and Scots Literature to the End of the Year 1568*. Columbus: Ohio State University Press, 1944.
Waldron, Ronald. "'Maiden in the Mor Lay' and the Religious Imagination." In *Langland, the Mystics and the Medieval English Religious Tradition: Essays in Honor of S. S. Hussey*, edited by Helen Philipps, 215–222. Cambridge: D. S. Brewer, 1990.
Weber, Sarah Appleton. *Theology and Poetry in the Middle English Lyric: A Study of Sacred History and Aesthetic Form*. Columbus: The Ohio State University Press, 1969.
Weiskott, Eric. "Charles d'Orléans' English Metrical Phonology." In *Charles d'Orléans' English Aesthetic: The Form, Poetics, and Style of Fortunes Stabilnes*, edited by R. D. Perry and Mary-Jo Arn, 122–144. Woodbridge, UK: Boydell and Brewer, 2020.
Wenzel, Siegfried. *Preachers, Poets, and the Early English Lyric*. Princeton, NJ: Princeton University Press, 1986.
Whitehead, Christiania. "Middle English Religious Lyrics." In *A Companion to the Middle English Lyric*, edited by Thomas G. Duncan, 96–119. Cambridge: D. S. Brewer, 2005.
Whitehead, Christiania. "Musical and Poetical Form in 'Stond wel, moder, under rode.'" In *Middle English Lyrics: New Readings of Short Poems*, edited by Julia Boffey and Christiania Whitehead, 227–239. Woodbridge, UK: Boydell and Brewer, 2018.
Whiting, Bartlett Jere, and Helen Wescott Whiting. *Proverbs, Sentences, and Proverbial Phrases: From English Writings Mainly before 1500*. Cambridge, MA: Harvard University Press, 1968.
Wimsatt, James I. "Chaucer and Deschamps' 'Natural Music.'" In *The Union of Words and Music in Medieval Poetry*, edited by Rebecca A. Baltzer, Thomas

Cable, and James I. Wimsatt, 132–150. Austin: University of Texas Press, 1991.

Wimsatt, James I. *Chaucer and His French Contemporaries: Natural Music in the Fourteenth Century.* Toronto: University of Toronto Press, 1991.

Wimsatt, James I. *Chaucer and the Poems Of "Ch."* Kalamazoo: Western Michigan University Press, Medieval Institute Publications, 2009.

Wimsatt, W. K. *The Verbal Icon: Studies in the Meaning of Poetry.* Lexington: University Press of Kentucky, 1954.

Woolf, Rosemary. "The Construction of 'In A Frith As Y Con Fare Fremede.'" *Medium Ævum* 38 (1969): 55–59.

Woolf, Rosemary. *The English Religious Lyric in the Middle Ages.* Oxford: Clarendon Press, 1968.

Zimbalist, Barbara. "The Lyric Christ." In *What Kind of a Thing Is a Middle English Lyric?*, edited by Cristina Maria Cervone and Nicholas Watson, 243–267. Philadelphia: University of Pennsylvania Press, 2022.

Ziolkowski, Jan. "Avatars of Ugliness in Medieval Literature." *Modern Language Review* 79 (1984): 1–20.

Zumthor, Paul. *Essai de poétique médiévale.* Paris: Éditions du Seuil, 1972.

INDEX

Abel, Patricia, 308n43
"Adam lay I-bounden bounden in a bond" (lyric), 38–40
Addison, Catherine, 120
Addison, Joseph, 18, 296n5
affective fallacy, 282–83
Agnus Dei, 55
"Alas alas vel evil have I sped" (lyric). See "Undo thy door my spouse dear"
"Alas departing is ground of woe" (lyric), 178–79
alcohol, last call for. See "Here I was and here I drank"
"Alyssoun." See "Bytuene Mersh and Aueril"
Allen, Judson Boyce, 18, 31
alliteration, 10, 13, 60, 66, 71, 89–91, 109, 116, 189, 192, 209, 216, 220, 252–53
Alliterative Revival, 12–14
"All this day Ich han sought" (lyric), 48–52
"All ye that pass by this holy place" (lyric), 124–25
"Als y me rode this endre dai" (lyric), 199–201
amans exclusus. See neglected lover, casting Jesus as
anger, playing. See unpleasant feelings (in Middle English feelings)
Annunciation, 74–76, 157, 252
anti-Semitism. See Jews
Arma Christi, recalling. See "Water and blood for thee I sweat"
Arn, Mary-Jo, 61
ars dictaminis (or *dictandi*), 185
"As I lay upon a night" (lyric), 72
"As I stood on a day me self under a tree" (lyric), 194
"As I went on Yule day in our procession" (lyric), 52–56

"At the time of matins Lord Thou were I-take" (lyric), 165–67
aubade, 1
Audelay, John, 4
audience, context, 4–6
Austin, J. L., 91
"Ave Maria," 145

Baird-Lange, Lorrayne Y., 41
"Balade to Edward, Duke of York" (Hoccleve), 258
Ball, John, 91–92
ballade, 1, 20, 64, 65–66, 120, 138, 201, 211, 267, 293n2, 313n21, 313n25
Bannytyne Manuscript, 4
Battle of Hastings, 6
"Behold me I pray thee with all thy whole reason" (lyric), 172
Bel Accueil. See "O excellent sovereigne, most semely to sene" (lyric)
Bembo, Pietro, 272
Best, Stephen, 7
Bibliography and Index of English Verse in Manuscript 1501–1558 (Ringler), xi
blazon, 57, 60, 62, 71, 186, 229, 278, 300n33
Blessed Virgin Mary, 15, 72–77, 126–31, 133–45, 217–18. See also Jesus Christ; Passion, compassion for/perversion of
BL Add MS, 270–71
BL Egerton MS, 271
BL Harley MS, 44, 61, 78, 198–99, 307n19
"blissful life a peaceable and a sweet, A" (lyric). See "Former Age, The"
"Blodles & bonles blodhad non bon" (lyric), 94–95
Blyth, Charles R., 260–61

Boccaccio, 211, 226, 267, 313n34
Boethius, 186
Boffey, Julia, 2, 25
Boklund-Lagopulou, Karin, 3
Bouquet, Damien, 23, 33
Bowden, Betsy, 283
Breeze, Andrew, 90
Brunner, Karl, 301n54
Buchanan, Peter, 294n28
Burger, Glenn, 33
Burrow, J. A., 8, 18–19, 258–59
Burt, Stephanie, 283
Burt, Stephen, 295n37
Butterfield, Ardis, 11, 19–21
"By a forest as I gan fare" (lyric), 102–7
"Bytuene Mersh and Aueril" (lyric), 57–60

Cannon, Christopher, 294n12
cantilena, 1
"Cantus Troili" (Chaucer), 285–87
Canzoniere, 272–73
"Care away, away, away." *See* "I am sorry for her sake"
carol, 1, 4, 11, 18–19, 21, 38, 44–48, 54–56, 83, 87–88, 94, 97, 199–200, 217–18, 220
cento, 5, 30
Cervone, Maria, 8
charm, 99–100, 101–2
Chase, Chevy, 18
Chaucer, Geoffrey, 3, 5, 11, 47–48, 92, 177, 195, 219, 226, 233, 256, 258; "Hoccleve Portrait" of, 263; sonnet translation, 265–67
Cinkante Ballades (Gower), 6
Clarke, K. P., 267–68
"Clerk's Tale" (Chaucer), 226
collage poem. *See* cento
Collins, Billy, 7
complaint (lyric type), 1, 15–16, 24, 36, 57, 59, 87–88, 91, 96, 102, 107, 133, 149, 158, 177, 182, 201, 207, 211
Commonplace Book (John of Grimestone), 149–50
complexion, term, 35–36
Consolation of Philosophy (Boethius), 186

contemptus mundi lyrics, 107, 109, 111
contrafactum. *See* "Perspice Christocola"
Copeland, Rita, 34, 36
Co-Redemptrix, 75, 144
Cornelius, Ian, 10, 13
"Corpus Christi Carol, The" (lyric), 5, 95–97
courtly love, 71, 201, 246, 253, 298n52
cradle songs. *See* lullaby
Crocker, Holly, 33
Crow, Martin M., 267
Crowther, J. D. W., 56, 173
"Cry of the Deer, The." *See* "Lorica [breastplate] of St Patrick"
Cuckoo-song. *See* "Sumer is icumen in"
Culler, Jonathan, 295n37
cynghanedd (bardic harmony). *See* "I wot a bird in a bower as beryl so bright"

dactylonomy, 265
debate, 117, 177, 194–95, 206–7, 209, 211, 234, 247, 266, 312n10
Depositio, picturing. *See* "Now goth sonne under wod"
DeVun, Leah, 177
dialogue lyric, 173
dialogue poem, 128, 211, 304n8
"Dies Irae" (lyric), 122
Digital Index of Middle English Verse (DIMEV), 24, 94, 179, 194
DIMEV. *See Digital Index of Middle English Verse*
ditty, 1, 40, 91
Donaldson, E. Talbot, 21
double croisée, 120
d'Orléans, Charles Duc, 3, 60–66, 300n43
Drab Age poets, 256
drinking songs. *See* "Here I was and here I drank"; "Tapster, fille another ale"
Dronke, Peter, 22
Duffell, Martin J., 259, 263
Duffy, Eamon, 96
Dunbar, Wiliam, 172
Duncan, Thomas G., 10, 22, 31
Dylan, Bob, 283

Earl of Surrey. *See* Surrey, Henry Howard, Earl of
Edwards, Robert R., 62
elegy, 125, 305n25
Eliot, T. S., 255, 277
emotives, 30
epistle, 53–54, 186, 226
epitaph. 124–25. *See also* "All ye that pass by this holy place"; "Here lieth under this marble stone"
"Erthe toc of erthe" (lyric), 108
Ethics (Aristotle), 36
Eucharist, meditation on, 94–95
eulogy, 74
Exeter Book Riddles, 40–41

"Farewell now my lady gay," 307n5
Fein, Susanna, 8
Findern Manuscript, 5
Fletcher, Alan J., 301n61
"Former Age, The" (Chaucer), 91–92
formes fixes, 11, 256, 293n2
Forty Hours' Devotion, 96
Fowler, David C., 48
Fries, Maureen, 55
Fussell, Paul, 10

Galloway, Andrew, 151
Gascoigne, George, 257
Gasparov, M. L., 265
gaudium (joy), 36, 83, 125, 178
gender, 126, 144–45, 163, 177–78
Gibbs, Raymond W., Jr., 33
"Go, hert, hurt with adversitee" (lyric), 178–79
God, 17, 21, 25–30, 39–40, 43–45, 50, 52–55, 62–70, 72–77, 81–83, 92–95, 100–111, 121–22, 131, 139, 152, 163, 172, 222, 254, 261. *See also* Blessed Virgin Mary; Jesus Christ
"God and saint Trinity / As I believe on thee" (lyric), 100
"God that all this mights may in heaven & earth thy will is oo" (lyric), 25–28, 30
Gower, John, 5, 6
"Gracious and gay on her light all my thought" (lyric), 181–82

Gravdal, Kathryn, 308n29
Gray, Douglas, 72
Great Condescension, 131–33
Greene, Richard E., 96
Greene, Richard L., 22
Greentree, Rosemary, 295n29
Grimestone, John, 4, 131, 149–50, 158, 158
Grossman, Joel, 256
Guillaume de Machaut, 3, 296n57

"Hail our patron and Lady of the earth" (lyric), 74
Harris, Carissa, 194, 198–99
Harris, Joseph, 22
"He bore him up he bore him down" (lyric). *See* "Corpus Christi Carol, The"
Helterman, Jeffrey, 299n15
Herebert, William, 4, 158, 170–72. *See also Improperia* [the *Reproaches*]
"Here I was and here I drank" (lyric), 42–43
"Here lieth under this marble stone" (lyric), 124–25
"Herod thou wicked foe whereof is thy dreading" (lyric), 172
"Hit wes upon a sereþorsday þat vre louerd aros" (lyric), 3
Hoccleve, Thomas, 5, 256–62
holograph, 258
Holton, Amanda, 314n36, 314n41
Holy Thursday. *See* "It wes upon a shere thorsday that our louerd arose"
"Honure, joy, helthe, and pleasuance" (lyric), 63–66
Hopkins, Gerard Manly, 10
Horace, 109, 256, 270, 272
Howard, Henry. Surrey, Henry Howard, Earl of
Howes, Hetta Elizabeth, 172
Hyland, Peter, 313n25
hymn, 1, 4, 25, 38, 54, 74, 77, 171, 298n49
"Hyt semes quite and is red" (lyric), 302n14

"I am as I am and so I will be" (lyric), 314n39
"I am as light as any roe" (lyric), 217–18
"I am sorry for her sake" (lyric), 23–25

"Icham of Irlaunde" (lyric), 18–19
"I conjure hem in the name of the Fader"
    (lyric), 100–102
"Iesu dulcis memoria." See "Swete Jesu, king
    of bliss"
"I have a gentil cok" (lyric), 40–41
"I have a hole aboue my knee" (lyric), 299n8
"I have a young sister far beyonden the sea"
    (lyric), 97–99
IMEV. See Index of Middle English Verse
Improperia [the Reproaches], 157–63
"In a frith as I con fare fremde" (lyric), 195–99
"In a tabernacle of a toure" (lyric), 133–39
"In every place ye may well see" (lyric), 222–23
Index of Middle English Verse (IMEV), 2, xi
"I ne have joy ne pleasance nor comfort"
    (lyric), 180–81
Irmscher, Christoph, 283
"I sing of a maiden" (lyric), 72–77
lyric "I" (speaker), 9, 29–33, 52–60, 74, 77–82,
    102, 114, 120–25, 128, 145–48, 151–52, 157,
    162–63, 189–199, 201, 210–11, 213–17, 229,
    234, 252, 277
"It wes upon a shere thorsday that our louerd
    arose" (lyric), 173–76
"I wot a bird in a bower as beryl so bright"
    (lyric): analysis of, 192–95; text of, 189–91

Jacopone da Todi, 128
Jesus Christ, 54, 74–75, 77–82, 88, 94–95, 97,
    107–52, 157–58, 163–76, 182–85, 239, 242
"Jesu that hast me dear I-bought" (lyric), 30–31
"Jesu that is most of might" (lyric): analysis
    of, 185–86; text of, 182–85
Jews, 152–78
John of Howden, 31
John of Garland, 293n1
Johnson, 308n44
"Jolly Jankyn." See "As I went on Yule day in
    our procession"
Jonson, Ben, 18
Judas, 3, 29, 157, 172–76

Kane, George, 32
"Keep well ten and flee from seven" (lyric), 2

Kessel-Brown, Deidre, 215
Kilmer, Joyce, 282
Klinck, Anne L., 25, 31
Kuczynski, Michael P., 95
Kumler, Adam, 304n45
Kunstsprache, 252

"law of God be to thee thy rest, The" (lyric),
    109–11
Lawton, David, 31
Lecouteux, Claude, 303
Ledrede, Richard de. See Richard de Ledrede
Lehman, Robert S., 294n28
Leland, Virginia E., 267
"Lenten is come with love to toune" (lyric),
    213–17
Lerer, Seth, 7
Levinson, Marjorie, 294n28
Lewis, C. S., 256
Life of Brian (film), 54
Longfellow, Henry Wadsworth, 282
"Lorica [breastplate] of St Patrick" (lyric), 102
"Love is soft, love is sweet, love is good sware"
    (lyric) 207–9
lullaby, 1, 96, 128, 131, 133, 293n3
"Lullay, lullay, litel child, why wepest thu so
    sore" (lyric), 131–33
Lydgate, John, 3, 5, 258
Lyrical Ballads (Wordsworth), 9

MacDonald, A. A., 296n1
Machaut, Guillaume de. See Guillaume de
    Machaut
MacNamer, Sarah, 23
"Madame for your newfangleness" (lyric),
    211–13
"Maiden in the mor lay" (lyric), 19–23
"Maiden mother mild / oeiz cel oreysoun"
    (lyric), 172
"Man, be war of thine wowing" (lyric),
    218–20
Manning, Stephen, 10, 18, 31, 44, 72, 74, 76–77,
    94–96, 111, 216–18
"man that should of truth tell, A" (lyric),
    92–94

manuscript, context, 4–6
Marcus, Sharon, 7
Margherita, Gayle, 252
Marquis, Paul A., 276
Marshall, Helen, 294n28
Mason, H. A., 255
Matthew of Vendôme, 293n1
McCartney, Paul, 18
McNamer, Sarah, 126
MED. See *Middle English Dictionary*
"Meeting in the Wood, The" (lyric). See "In a frith as I con fare fremde"
memento mori poems, 108–9
"Men rent me on rood" (lyric), 167–70
Middle English, 6, 10–14
Middle English Dictionary (MED), 75, 90, 100, 180, 188, 193, 216
Middle English lyrics: audience and manuscript context, 4–6; bringing into modern play, 17–37; contemplating death of Christ in, 126–78; early modern machining of verse, 255–84; emotional integrity of, 30–37; expressions of joy, 38–82; identifying, 1–4, 6; love and longing, 177–210; negative reviewing of, 277–83; overlooking, 6–10; to-do list, 14–16; unpleasant feelings in, 83–125
"Miller's Tale" (Chaucer), 206
MIlton, John, 13
misogyny, 36–37, 52, 220
Mitchell, Jerome, 258–59
Monroe, Harriet, 282
Monty Python, 54
Mooney, Linne R., 309n2
Moore, Arthur Keister, 216
Moore, Marianne, 263–66
"Mourning of the Hunted Hare, The." See "By a forest as I gan fare"
mouvance, 5
MS. Rawlinson C. 813 "Welles Anthology," 66. See also *various manuscripts*
Murton, Megan, 31
"My deth I love, my lif ich hate" (lyric), 201–7
"My folk now answer me" (lyric), 158–62
"My folk what habbe I do thee" (lyric), 158–62

"My ghostly father, I me confess" (lyric), 62–63

Nagy, Piroska, 23, 33
Nelson, Ingrid, 32, 145
New Criticism, 7, 32
New Formalism, 7
New Historicism, 7
New Index of Middle English Verse (NIMEV), 2, xi
Nicene Creed, 74
NIMEV. See *New Index of Middle English Verse*
"Now bairns birds bold and blithe" (lyric), 117–22
"Now goth sonne under wod" (lyric), 126–28
"Now is yole comen with gentil chere" (lyric), 46–48
"Now Springes the Spray." See "Als y me rode this endre dai"

OED. See *Oxford English Dictionary*
"O excellent sovereigne, most semely to sene" (lyric), 66–72
"Of all creatures women be best" (lyric), 222–26
"Off Februar the fyftene nycht" (lyric), 172
Oliver, Raymond, 75
"O mestress why" (lyric), 186–89
One Hundred Lyrics and a Poem (Tennant), 282
Olson, Glending, 296n57
Ong, Walter J., 299n22
Original Sin, 40, 91, 144, 156
Osberg, Richard H., 12
Owen, Lewis J., 311
Oxford English Dictionary (OED), 2
Oxford MS Bodleian, 78

Paden, William D., 3
Passion poems, 126–75
pastourelle, 16, 37, 194–95, 198–99, 209, 246–47
Peasants' Revolt, 91
"Perspice Christocola" (lyric), 45
Petrarch, 66, 180, 226. See also print publication; *Rima* 132; *Rima* 140

Philomena. See John of Howden
Plummer, John F., 55–56
Poetics (Aristotle), 83
poetry. *See various entries*
Poetry Magazine, 283
"Poet's Repentance, The." *See* "Weping haveth min wonges wet"
political protest, lyrics as, 91–94
Pound, Ezra, 282
Practical Criticism, 7
prayer, spell-casting *versus*, 101
print publication, 265–77
Pugh, Tison, 307n2
Puttenham, George, 265
Putter, Ad, 301n43

racial hatred. *See* Jews
Ransom, Daniel J., 192, 254
Reddy, W. M., 30
Reed, Thomas L., 247
Regiment of Princes (Hoccleve), 259–63
Reichl, Karl, 308n40
Reiss, Edmund, 109
Revard, Carter, 311n51
reverdie, 1, 38, 43–45, 57, 59, 145, 148, 213, 216, 234
Richard de Ledrede, 22
Richards, 255
riddle, 40–41, 94–95, 97, 99, 108, 299n6
Rima 132 (Petrarch), 285–87
Rima 140 (Petrarch), 289–89
Ringler, W. A., Jr., xi
Rising of 1381, 91
Robbins, Rossell Hope, 6, 101
Robertson, D. W., Jr., 21
Romeo and Juliet (Shakespeare), 278–81
rondeau, 1, 293, 293n2
rondel, 1, 22, 61–63, 293n2
Roos, RIchard, 5
Roscow, G. H., 44
Rosenfeld, Jessica, 36
Rosenwein, Barbara H., 32–33
rota, performing lyric as, 44. *See* "Sumer is icumen in"

Ryman, James, 4, 88–89

Saintsbury, George, 258
Salter, Elizabeth, 8
Sandburg, Carl, 282
Schueler, Donald G., 176
Second Coming, 91
Second Eucharistic Prayer, 76
serenade, 60, 72, 74, 128, 151, 206
"Serving Maid's Holiday, The." *See* "All this day Ich han sought"
Shakespeare, William, 256, 277–81
Sir Gawain and the Green Knight, 71
"Sluggy and slowe, in spetinge muiche" (lyric), 34–36
"smiling mouth, and laughing eyen gray, The" (lyric), 60–62
Smith, Jeremy, 300n43
"Somer is comen and winter gon" (lyric): analysis of, 156–57; text of, 152–56
"Somer is comen with love to toune" (lyric): analysis of, 245–47; text of, 234–45
Song of Songs, 127, 138–39
sonnet, 10, 123, 255, 265–69, 272–75, 277–78, 281, 292, 313n25, 314n44
Spear, John, 7
Spearing, A. C., 61
speculum conscientiae, 116
Speculum Ecclesiae (Edmund of Canterbury), 126, 172
Speirs, John, 22
sprezzatura, 273
"Spring." *See* "Lenten is come with love to toune"
St. Edmund of Canterbury, 126
St. John's Eve. *See* "Maiden in the mor"
"Stabat Mater," 128
Stanbury, Sarah, 74
Stevens, John, 13–14, 34
Steves, Michael, 76
"Stond wel moder vnder rode" (lyric), 140–45
Stone, Brian, 14
Stouck, Mary-Ann, 175
"Sumer is icumen in" (lyric), 43–45

Surrey, Henry Howard, Earl of, 256, 265–66, 270–73, 275–77
"Swart smoked smiths smattered with smoke" (lyric), 89–91
"Swete Jesu, king of bliss" (lyric), 77–82

tail-rhyme stanza, 59, 234
Tanakh, 158
"Tapster, fille another ale" (lyric), 41–42
Tennant, Neil, 282
"Thenc man of mi harde stundes" (lyric), 167–70
Theodulph of Orléans. See "Weal herying and worship be to Christ that dear us bought"
Theotokos, 75
Theresa of Avila, 82
"This maiden hight Mary she was full mild" (lyric), 128–31
"Thrush and the Nightingale, The." See "Somer is comen with love to toune"
"Thus I complain my grevous hevynesse" (lyric), 178
Todi, Jacopone da. See Jacopone da Todi
Tottel's Miscellany, 272–73, 275–76, 278, 313n25
"To you, dere herte, variant and mutable" (lyric), 229–34
translatibility, question of, 32–33
Tribe of Ben, 18
Troilus and Criseyde (Chaucer), 266–67
Turville-Petre, Thorlac, 254

"Undo thy dore, my spuse dere" (lyric), 149–52
"Unto you most forward this letter I write" (lyric), 226–29

Velutello, Alessandro, 272
virelai, 1, 293n2
Virgil, 256

Waldron, Ronald, 22
"Water and blood for thee I sweat" (lyric), 163–65
Watson, Nicholas, 8
"Weal herying and worship be to Christ that dear us bought" (lyric), 170–72
Weber, Sarah Appleton, 75
Wenzel, Siegfried, 21, 77
"Weping haveth min wonges wet" (lyric), 248–54
"Whan netilles in winter bere roses rede" (lyric), 220–22
"When Adam delved and Eve did span" (lyric), 91–92
"When earth hath earth I-won with woe." See "Erthe toc of erthe"
"When I see blossoms spring" (lyric), 145–48
"When the turuf is thy tour" (lyric), 108–9
Whitehead, Christiania, 23
"Wife of Bath's Tale" (Chaucer), 219–20
Wimsatt, James, 267
Wimsatt, W. K., 282
"Winter wakeneth all my care" (lyric), 122–23
"With pacience thou has us fed" (lyric), 83–89
Woolf, Rosemary, 9, 31, 72, 127, 139, 148, 158–62, 195–99
Wordsworth, William, 31
"Worldes bliss ne last no throwe" (lyric), 115–17
Wyatt, Sir Thomas, 256, 265, 270

"Yesterday" (McCartney), 18

Ziolkowski, Jan, 229
Zumthor, Paul, 5

WILLIAM A. QUINN is a Distinguished Professor in the Department of English at the University of Arkansas. He is author of *Chaucer's Rehersynges: The Performability of the Legend of Good Women* and *Olde Clerkis Speche: Chaucer's Troilus and Criseyde and the Implications of Authorial Recital.*

New Perspectives on Medieval Literature: Authors and Traditions
EDITED BY R. BARTON PALMER AND TISON PUGH

An Introduction to Christine de Pizan, by Nadia Margolis
(2011; first paperback edition, 2012)

An Introduction to the "Gawain" Poet, by John M. Bowers
(2012; first paperback edition, 2013)

An Introduction to British Arthurian Narrative, by Susan Aronstein
(2012; first paperback edition, 2014)

An Introduction to Geoffrey Chaucer, by Tison Pugh
(2013; first paperback edition, 2014)

An Introduction to the Chansons de Geste, by Catherine M. Jones
(2014; first paperback edition, 2015)

An Introduction to "Piers Plowman," by Michael Calabrese
(2016; first paperback edition, 2017)

An Introduction to the Sagas of Icelanders, by Carl Phelpstead
(2020; first paperback edition, 2024)

*An Introduction to Literary Debate in Late Medieval France:
From "Le Roman de la Rose" to "La Belle Dame sans Mercy,"*
by Joan E. McRae (2024)

An Introduction to Jean Bodel, by Lynn T. Ramey (2024)

An Introduction to Middle English Lyrics, by William A. Quinn (2025)

www.ingramcontent.com/pod-product-compliance
Lightning Source LLC
Chambersburg PA
CBHW022235170925
32783CB00002B/11